HISTORY OF GERMANY

HERMANN PINNOW

HISTORY OF GERMANY

PEOPLE AND STATE THROUGH A THOUSAND YEARS

Translated from the German

by

MABEL RICHMOND BRAILSFORD

NEW YORK

THE MACMILLAN COMPANY

*The German original, "Deutsche Geschichte," was published
in Berlin in 1929*

FIRST PUBLISHED IN ENGLISH 1933

CONTENTS

INTRODUCTION

THE GERMANI

THE EMPIRE OF THE FRANKS

FIRST BOOK

THE EMPIRE OF THE KAISERS
900–1200

SECOND BOOK

THE TOWNSFOLK
1200–1500

vii

29949

Contents

INTRODUCTION

THE GERMANI
THE EMPIRE OF THE FRANKS

INTRODUCTION

MORE than ten years have passed since the German people, of their own will, set up a new system of government. The student of German history will find in its first recorded events a parallel to this revolution; while the liberation of the Eastern Franks from Carolingian rule offers a similar departure from the traditional form of government.

In the year 911 the German tribes elected a Frankish duke to be their king. After his early death their choice fell upon the Saxon duke Henry, who was successful in compelling the homage of the remaining tribes. These events revealed the will of the scattered German peoples to form one corporate whole; they laid the foundation of the German State, and may be regarded as the beginning of German history.

Both these elections were dependent upon the mutual agreement of two tribes. Their spokesmen were the lords temporal and spiritual. The acclamation of the chosen king by the crowd gathered there, was the only vestige remaining of the right enjoyed by the Ancient Germani to share in his election.

On the other hand, the delegates to the National Assembly at Weimar were elected by the whole German nation— neither class nor sex affecting the value of their vote. The first German king failed to accomplish his most immediate task—the union of the German tribes. But a united empire was the birthright of the members of the Weimar Assembly. Their work offered an illustration of the whole weight of the influence wielded by a modern state, when they attempted to realize the will of the German people—'to build up their empire anew on a foundation of liberty and justice, to serve the cause of peace at home and abroad, and to further the progress of the community.'

This contrast between the two governments is the result of a thousand years of history, and it is the German people themselves who have brought it about. The State is the expression of the common will. Economic, social, and intellectual changes affect the State, and the political situation in its turn reacts upon these developments. To describe the interplay between people and government is one of the most difficult tasks of the historian. Formerly it was

Introduction

his habit to set political events so much in the foreground, that development on other lines was mentioned only as an appendix to 'true' history. Older readers will be familiar with this type of narrative. During the last decades historians have taken pains to give a truer estimate of the importance of economic and social changes: even the 'economic' view of history attempts to trace all historic events to the changes in economic life. In the following attempt to describe the growth of the German nation and its government during the past thousand years, the historian begins with an account of the daily life and work of the people, and leads up, through the alterations in social structure and intellectual changes, to the formation of the State. This method of approach seems better adapted than the earlier attitude to measure the forces which determine collective development, and to foster the political sense no less than the historical.

THE GERMANI

We speak of the German race and the German people. We are conscious of a racial character which distinguishes us as Germans, and is so deeply rooted that it is discernible through all superadded characteristics. As a rule it is less clearly understood that the racial character has features which are not original but acquired. As a matter of fact the race itself has been subjected to the shaping of history. Climate and soil, economic changes and social structure, political events and outside influences—these all help to mould the national character. Such influences are as liable to strengthen its peculiarities as to weaken them, and it is undeniable that the nations of the present day are more easily distinguishable from each other than were their predecessors.

The consciousness of a common racial character was not one of the decisive factors in the resolution of the German tribes to found a political union. They shared their inheritance of blood and of language with other branches of the West Germanic family—the Western Franks in Gaul and the Anglo-Saxons in Britain. It is true that these distinguishing racial features of all the German tribes had been profoundly affected by the introduction of foreign

4

The Germani

elements: but the tribes remaining in Germany had not endured changes of such a kind as might strengthen any existing consciousness of homogeneity. The farther the Germani spread towards the south from their homes by the North Sea and the Baltic, the more varied were the elements which they absorbed—Celts, Slavs, and the members of a prehistoric race. At a later date also, the structure of the German nation was profoundly affected by the introduction of foreign blood, so that none of the great European peoples to-day can show a stronger admixture. If none but the 'pure-blooded' can be reckoned as true Germans, then at least two-thirds of the German people must pass for a lower order of natives, and it is doubtful whether the worthiest will be found amongst the elect. A thousand years ago our forefathers were sharply divided in speech from the Slavs in the east. In the west, the area in which the German tongue was spoken was restricted by the adoption of the Romance language, an offshoot of the Latin, by the Western Franks, who were the masters of Gaul. But at that date there were no hard and fast boundaries, and great variations in speech had already arisen amongst the German tribes. The High German permutation of consonants which set in in the seventh century A.D. changed the language of the Southern Germans, the Alemanni, Bavarians, and Franks, and extended as far as the Lombards in Italy. The Low Germans continued to speak in the old way, with 'pund, eten, and ik,' and began to employ the same article for masculine and feminine nouns. Their language remained akin to the Anglo-Saxon, out of which the English language was developed, and the resemblance between the two would be still greater to-day had not Anglo-Saxon itself developed along its own lines.

The Saxons were first united to the other German tribes by Charlemagne—but military and political events had already built up the nucleus of the German States. The limits within which the German tribes were to develop had been fixed by the wars between the West Germans and the Romans. Later, all the tribes living on German soil were forced by the Frankish conquerors to become subjects of their state. When Franconia fell to pieces, the inhabitants of Germany preserved their political homogeneity and set up one of the tribal dukes as their leader. These events were milestones along the road followed by

5

the West German tribes on their way to become the German nation.

When the Germani came into touch with the Romans they had already subdued the Celtic population of Middle Germany. At that time cattle-rearing played the chief rôle in their domestic economy. Their agriculture was still so undeveloped that they were obliged from time to time to remove to new fields. A growing population was a continual incentive to the acquisition of new soil. Thus the Germani were accustomed to wandering. Wood, pasture and ploughed land belonged not to the individual but to the community of the district—and the government was adapted to the alternations of war and peace. It consisted of an assembly of free men. They met under arms and ordered the affairs of the village, the district, and the tribe by general decree. They divided the fields, gave laws, and chose a leader for the army. Although certain families enjoyed special consideration, there was neither a priesthood nor a nobility with definite privileges.

The Germani had no difficulty in dealing with the Celts on the far side of the Rhine. German tribes established themselves west of the Lower Rhine, the Cymbrians and Teutons overran South Germany and Gaul, before they were conquered by the Roman armies, a century previous to the beginning of our era. A generation later the leader of the Swabian army, Ariovistus, made himself ruler of Middle Gaul. But to insure the safety of Italy the Romans interfered in the wars between Germans and Celts. In 58 B.C. Caesar slew the Swabian king and subdued Gaul.

The legions governed the conquered peoples from behind the Rhine frontier, and kept the German onslaught at bay. Under the reign of Augustus, the Celtic territories south of the Danube were also incorporated in the empire. The frontier now ran out at an obtuse angle along the Rhine and the Danube. The Romans would have found it an easier task to defend the empire if their dominion had been extended as far as the Elbe. Already they believed themselves to be within sight of this goal, when Arminius, as a Roman author relates, brought the empire, which had made no halt on the shores of the ocean, to rest on the banks of the Rhine. When towards the end of the first century the idea of a shortening of the Rhine-Danube boundary became in a modest degree an actual fact, the

6

The Germani

Limes, the Roman 'boundary-way,' extended from the Rhine near the Lahn estuary as far as the Danube, which it touched at Regensburg.

The Rhine frontier stood for about 400 years. It made it possible for Roman culture to penetrate Gaul, and prevented the formation of a West German settlement between the Elbe and the Atlantic Ocean. It is true that the left bank of the Rhine was colonized by Germani, German tribes occupied Gaul and the banks of the Danube, Germani manned the legions and rose to the highest offices. But almost all became Romanized, including the tribes which thronged into Gaul after the fall of the Rhine frontier. The Germani on the right of the Rhine were affected even more strongly by their forced settlement within their own boundaries than by the Roman influence. The land was more carefully cultivated and came under individual ownership. Distinctions began to be made in property and rank, high-born masters cultivated their lands by means of serfs and bondmen. Their command of the soil arose from the fact that a great portion of the newly won land had fallen to their share. In many cases the partition of land amongst the tribes may still have been decided by the sword. But as wars became less frequent, the remnants of different tribes which had been scattered during the Roman invasions were reunited. Members of different tribes became close neighbours, as the area of cultivated land was extended. In the second and third centuries, when the Germani, driven by land-hunger, spread over the Danube and Rhine boundaries, portions of the various tribes were welded together into communities. The history of the German peoples had begun.

The Alemanni pushed forward from the Middle Elbe to the Upper Rhine. About the year 250 they held all the district between the Limes and the Rhine—they advanced into the Vosges, into Switzerland, even into Italy. Some energetic Roman emperors offered a stubborn resistance and threw them back repeatedly over the Rhine: Trèves was the centre of the war of defence, the imperial residence and one of the most important cities of the empire. The defence was broken about 400. At that time the Burgundians, a people from east Germany, became the neighbours of the Alemanni on the Middle Rhine: their capital was Worms.

7

Introduction

The Saxon border was extended to the south and west about the year 300, after the migration of the Lombards from the lower Elbe: in the neighbourhood of Wesel their new territories reached almost to the Rhine. The marches of the North Sea coast remained in the possession of the Frisians. Franks and Alemanni owned the land east of Saxony, and the Thuringians the territory lying between the Elbe, the lower Main, and the Danube. The provinces of the Danube were not occupied till the sixth century. Their conquerors were the Marcomanni, the former inhabitants of Bohemia, the land of the Boyers, who had taken the name of Bavarians.

All these tribes were sooner or later subdued by the Franks. Even their tribal groups were composed of differing nationalities. It was only by degrees that the three great families became clearly distinguishable—the Salii (Sea-Franks), the Ripuarians (Franks from the banks of the Rhine), and Chatti. The Salii first crossed the Rhine, in the middle of the third century, at the same period during which the territory between the Boundary-way and the Rhine was lost to the Alemanni. In the course of the fifth century they extended their occupation as far as the Somme. Meantime the Franks from the banks of the Rhine occupied the country of the Ubii near Cologne, and the Chatti the valley of the Moselle. Their advance was checked before the mountain pass which opens upon the Paris basin, and by the Eifel and Jura Mountains: in the south beyond Spire, a halt was called by the Alemanni to their victorious march.

The Roman resistance to the Franks became noticeably weaker about the year 400. The Roman Empire had been penetrated at other points by Germani from the east, and in the year 410 Alaric, the King of the Visigoths, conquered the capital of Italy. The East Germani never made the transition to a settled life: they remained nomads, building up a powerful kingdom by their prowess as warriors. Goths, Burgundians, and Vandals are the heroes of the peoples' migration: their deeds are celebrated in saga: but their kingdoms collapsed—their nation melted away, together with those which they had vanquished. The West Germani on the other hand endured, because they took permanent root in the soil, and with all their expansion never broke loose from their mother country. Only the Rhineland kingdom of the Burgundians, who were of East Germanic descent, collapsed before the assault of the Huns. In the year 451, upon the Catalaunian fields of Gaul, West and East Germani united together under Roman leadership against their invasion; but many Germans fought also on the side of the Huns. It was not alone in this battle that the Frankish peoples were found in the service of Rome— during the course of their expansion diplomatic agreements played a more important rôle than military decisions. What they strove for originally was not dominion but land. It was only by degrees that the Salian dukes won their way to a throne. The change when it came produced a corresponding change in the character of the Frankish advance: royal campaigns of aggression succeeded the forays of a people in search of land.

THE EMPIRE OF THE FRANKS

In the year 486 the last vestiges of Roman rule in Gaul were wiped out by Clovis, a king of the race of the Merovingians, who had not yet passed his twentieth year. Ten years later he conquered the Alemanni—the only tribe which was still capable of threatening the empire of the Franks. In a final campaign he seized the land of the West Goths as far as the Garonne. The remaining Frankish princes he removed by murder. Uniting wide tracts of German and Roman territory under a strong Government, he founded the Empire of the Franks. He left four sons to divide his inheritance. As a rule they and their successors presented a united front to foreign enemies. Sharing the fate of the Romanized Germans in Gaul, of the Burgundians and of other fractions of the Visigoths, the Thuringians were overthrown and the Bavarians brought into dependence. A generation after Clovis's death, the Frankish dominion extended from the Atlantic Ocean to the Saale and the Bohemian forest, from the Mediterranean to the Zuydersee. The Frankish Empire had become the chief power in the West, on a par with the Eastern Roman Empire, which from its seat in Byzantium bore sway over the east and south.

Profound changes in the structure of state and nation resulted from the extension of Frankish rule. By right of conquest, public property passed into the hands of the

9

king, together with all the land left ownerless by the flight
of its possessors: he received in addition the revenue from
the taxes and tolls of the conquered country. His means to
power had increased: his subjects in Gaul had been trained,
as vassals of Rome, to submit to imperial absolutism:
under these circumstances kingly authority was able to
dispense with the people's support and establish itself on
the model of the Caesars. The royal ban—i.e. the right to
command and to forbid, with power to punish—corresponded to a prerogative of the Roman consuls and
emperors. The king's peace took the place of the people's
peace. Among the court officials the cupbearer, the lord-
high-steward, and the marshal were survivals from the
Germanic retinue: the titles of the treasurer and director of
the Court Chancery point to Roman origin: the first was
called Chamberlain (Camerarius) and the second Referen-
darius. The count who governed the district, summoned
the army, and presided over the people's court of justice,
combined Roman with Germanic authority. Side by side
with the old popular nobility there sprang up a nobility
who owed their title to services rendered, and their estates
to the royal gifts of land. Important rights were granted
to nobles and churchmen which included a limited jurisdiction within the area of their estates. On the other hand,
the status of freeman was steadily losing in importance.
To escape the burdens of military service, and to dispense
with the assistance of the people's courts of justice, many
put themselves voluntarily under the protection of a feudal
lord and paid taxes to him./The people's court of law was
overshadowed by the royal court of law: the yearly assembly
of the whole people, which had formerly borne the responsibility of political decisions, degenerated into a military
review. In intellectual life the acceptance of Christianity
brought about a change fraught with important consequences. When Clovis accepted baptism after his victory
over the Alemanni, Christianity was already the ruling
faith in Gaul. He was, however, the first Germanic prince
to enter the Catholic community. His treaty with the
Gallic bishops, who acknowledged the supremacy of the
Bishop of Rome, was of assistance to him in his wars: for
the other German tribes against whom he fought had
accepted the teaching of Arius, which was damned by the
Church. But it was a long time before Christianity gained

The Empire of the Franks

a hold upon the hearts of the people. During the sixth and seventh centuries, when the old ideas of religion and morality were eradicated, the country relapsed into barbarism.

At that time the king had no other way of rewarding services in peace or war but by gifts of land. But as soon as the aristocracy became possessed of land and political rights, they showed themselves to be the enemies of kingly authority and of political unity, and remained throughout the Middle Ages their most dangerous opponents. The efforts of the nobility to gain independence were helped forward by dissensions in the royal family. In accordance with Germanic rights of succession, the kings divided the empire. Even among Clovis's immediate descendants the succession gave rise to bitter quarrels, which continued to the end of the Merovingian rule. In the three divisions of the empire, which were gradually formed, officers of the royal court, the mayors of the palace, seized the power in their own hands. Towards the end of the seventh century Pipin was mayor of the palace in Austrasia—a name which covered the eastern portion of the empire, including the territory of the German tribes. Pipin conquered the mayor of the palace of the Western Franks, and thus became uncrowned king over the whole empire. His son, Charles Martel, in his turn had a hard struggle with the nobles. In order to have an army at his command, he gave away royal and ecclesiastical property to the lords who fought at his side: they took the oath of allegiance as his vassals, and in their turn enfeoffed others who followed in their train as knights. Thus the feudal system took the form which it was destined to preserve. In 732, Charles with his army of knights drove back at Tours and Poitiers the Arabs who had broken in from Spain.

The deliverance of the West from the threatening danger of Islam was of world-wide importance in history. When the pope was hard pressed in Rome by the Emperor of the Eastern Roman Empire and by the Lombards, he sought, albeit in vain, for support from the conqueror. Yet Charles's son, Pipin, whose education in the cloister had given him a refinement foreign to his rough father, recognized the advantages of an alliance with the leading spiritual power in the West. With his support Boniface became the 'Apostle of the Germans.'

Introduction

Beginning his missionary labours in Friesland, he preached Christianity in Hesse, Thuringia, and Bavaria. He founded new bishoprics in Bavaria and elsewhere, set the Frankish Church on a firm foundation, and brought the bishops into close connection with the pope. It was with his consent that Pipin deposed the Merovingian king in 751. Then his Franks raised him upon his shield, proclaiming him after the old custom: the diadem and the anointing oil were the gift of the pope. In his turn the Frankish king defended the pope against the attacks of the Lombards and enlarged the area of the papal dominion: the Papal State grew out of Pipin's gift. The Middle Ages were heralded by the alliance between Church and State.

Charlemagne stands on the threshold of the history of the Middle Ages. He founded that world empire in which Emperor and Pope were the two ruling powers. By unceasing labour, unchecked by discouragement, he incorporated the independent Germanic tribes into the Frankish State: the Lombards in Italy, the insubordinate Bavarians, and finally, after thirty years of conflict, the Saxons. When all these tribes had been united, a German State could be formed which was strong enough to repel the advancing flood of Slavs, and to win back as far as the Vistula the territory abandoned by the Eastern Germanic tribes at the time of the migration. Charles himself played a part in this struggle. He set up a line of marches along the frontier territories of the wide empire, which promised additional security to the inhabitants by their fortresses and by the increased powers given to the counts of the marches (*Markgrafen*). The marches were most numerous in the east. They extended from the Eyder, which was protected against the Danes by a fortified camp, the Danewerk of later times, as far as the Danube. After the victory over the Awars, Lower Austria was gradually colonized by Bavarian peasants, while in the Alpine districts the Germanic immigration assumed larger proportions.

Charles's empire had the same significance in western Europe which the Byzantine Empire held in the east. In Rome, where the memory of the departed world empire had never been wholly extinguished, on Christmas Day of the year 800, the supreme ruler of the Church, calling itself the Catholic, that is, the Universal, set the imperial crown upon the head of the King of the Franks. We must

The Empire of the Franks

suppose that Charlemagne had been aware of this intention:
yet afterwards he spoke with ill humour about the proceedings before the altar at St. Peter's. He was accustomed
to bend the Church to his private views and resolves: but
now the pope had acted upon his own initiative. Perhaps
also he foresaw dangers in the future—hereafter the Church
might be able to boast of having founded the Western Empire.

The union of the peoples of central Europe under one
leader was of short duration: but throughout the Middle
Ages it remained the ideal form of the political State.
Unity in thought and feeling, which is the distinguishing
mark of the Middle Ages, was also directly encouraged by
Charlemagne as he strove to regulate the life of his empire
as a homogeneous whole. Where the separate authority of
the dukedoms still functioned in the provinces, he abolished
it. The division of the empire into counties upon one
pattern made it possible, in spite of many shortcomings,
to govern them from a uniform standpoint, an end which
was not again attained until the absolute monarchy instituted a government by aid of functionaries. A further
resemblance may be traced in the fact that the ruler
exercised great legislative powers. Taking into consideration
the great number and diversity of tribal rights, one realizes
that it would have been vain to attempt to create a homogeneous system of law: but Charlemagne made no secret
of his endeavour to equalize them. The highest court of law
worked for the same end.

The king did not adhere in his judgments to the traditional forms of Germanic law. But his endeavours after
right and justice were remembered with gratitude by the
German people. He lives on in French saga as the imperial
warrior; but the Germans honoured him for centuries, as
the wise law-giver and the upright judge. Charlemagne
openly sought to crown his labours by directing the spiritual
life of his people. The medals which he struck about the
beginning of the century declared the 'Christian Religion'
to be the fruit of his government, and under religion he
included the Christian sciences and education. He was
justly proud of the qualities which he had inherited. But,
like all the leading men of his time, he believed the
acquisition of a higher culture to be possible only when
one had access to the intellectual treasures of antiquity,
which could be communicated by the Church alone.

Introduction

In these matters Charles acted with the same energy which distinguished his work as a statesman and warrior. We can trace his endeavours in the founding of monasteries and monastery schools, in his advice to the monks to write Latin 'like educated people,' in his request to the priests to preach so that the people could understand, and in the beginnings of lay education, in connection, of course, with the Church. And they were not without fruit. During his reign and in the following period there was a marked increase in the scientific, educational, and artistic activities of many German monasteries. A bishop of Metz superintended the building of the minster at Aix: this building, the first made of stone on German soil, was the symbol of a dominion which united the greatest part of the western territory under the Sign of the Cross.

Of the many songs which kept alive the memory of the heroic age of the Migration, the *Song of Hildebrand* was the only one written down in the monastery at Fulda. Yet a Christian poetry in the German tongue was beginning to spring up side by side with the Germanic epic. Even before the middle of the ninth century a Saxon poet, probably with the help of a priest, had written the history of Jesus and his disciples: a few decades later the monk Otfried von Weissenburg composed his Book of the Gospels —the Saxon poet writes in a popular style, employing the old Germanic alliterative measure in which the most important words of every line are made to correspond through the strong accentuation of the first syllable. Otfried writes like a learned man, and employs the end rhyme, which had been first used in late Latin verse. But he too is filled with an admiring love for his people: he undertakes his task in order that the Franks, bold, mighty in war like the Romans and Greeks, and zealous in God's service, should be able to sing in their own tongue the praises of their Creator.

In western Franconia and in Italy, where the traditions of Roman culture were still active, intellectual life attained a higher development than in Germany. Even in economic respects Germany was at that time far behind her neighbours. Nevertheless a great advance had been made in husbandry. Cultivation on the three-field system, originating in the Romanized West, had become general, and has remained almost unchanged for nearly

The Empire of the Franks

a thousand years as the accepted method of German agriculture.

In cases where the soil, in spite of more systematic cultivation, did not produce enough for the needs of his growing family, the peasant was able to increase his holding by turning the surrounding forest into arable land. This he did throughout a long period, with the consent and the help of his neighbours. He had therefore no lack of soil to grow his food, and learned self-reliance through this exertion of independence. Even when the peasant sacrificed his freedom by putting himself under the protection of a feudal lord, his capacity for work was so great that his master would be satisfied with a minimum of service and tribute. The ruthless exploitation which became common at a later date under a capitalistic régime, at a time when land was scarce, was impossible in Germany for centuries after this period. Yet even in Charlemagne's time, the number of those who renounced their freedom was on the increase. His world policy hastened the process of social reconstruction by rendering the burden of military service insupportable to many. Charlemagne recognized this danger and tried to check it; but the measures which he took—the lessening of the obligation which compelled the freeman to assist at the people's courts of justice, and the lightening of military service for the poorer freemen—could not hinder its development. The fall of the freemen corresponded with the rise of the propertied nobles, who already showed a rapid numerical increase. When no more conquests were being made, and the stream of royal gifts threatened to run dry, the close connection of the nobility with the Crown was loosened, and Charlemagne's immediate successors became involved in a sharp struggle with their powerful vassals.

As in the time of the Merovingians, the independence of the nobles was fostered by the quarrels of succession in the royal family. As a matter of principle the Church was on the side of imperial unity. Yet its attitude towards the imperial Government soon underwent a change. Under Charlemagne, State and Church formed a unity ruled over by the emperor: he presided over the assembly of the Frankish bishops, who without help from the pope, themselves decided upon questions of doctrine. But a few years after his death a similar assembly declared that spiritual

15

Introduction

authority took precedence of temporal. Pope Nicholas I worked with the object of removing the bishops from the royal jurisdiction and detaching them from the State. By this means the influence of the princes of the Church upon the conduct of temporal matters became more and more restricted.

In the year 843, Charlemagne's grandsons divided the empire into three parts at the Treaty of Verdun. The central empire on the Rhine, including Burgundy and Italy, fell to Lothar, the eldest, who retained the imperial crown: West Franconia to Charles, and East Franconia to Lewis. He was given the nickname of 'the German'—in the eighth century the speech of the Eastern Franks was already known as the 'German,' i.e. the popular, language, in distinction to the Romance language of West Franconia, and the Latin. Later, the northern district of the central empire—Lorraine—was divided between East and West Franconia: Burgundy and Italy were independent. From the year 880 Eastern Franconia extended as far as the Scheldt; it embraced all the German-speaking territories, together with a strip of land on the Maas, where the Romanic population preponderated.

These boundaries stood with but slight alteration until the year 1648. In the meantime, East and West Franconia were again united under Carolingian rule. But differences, not of speech alone, became increasingly apparent. In France, money early began to play a part in domestic economy. Germany dealt in natural products: the Western empire fell apart into a number of almost independent vassal lordships. In Germany, hereditary dukedoms developed in Franconia, Swabia, and Lorraine on the lines of the constitution of counties; amongst the Saxons and Bavarians they were set up in the course of the wars of defence against the Normans, Slavs, and Hungarians.

Under the last of the Carolingians, the hereditary dukedoms took their own course: in the end the Duke of Lorraine actually attached himself to France. Only the bishops stood for the idea of political unity. When the House of Charlemagne became extinct in 911 on the death of Louis the Child, Archbishop Hatto of Mayence, a relative of the Frankish dukes, agreed with the Saxons on the question of a successor. Saxons and Franks stood in fairly close relationship to each other. At an assembly in Forchheim

The Empire of the Franks

they elected Conrad, the Duke of Franconia to be their king. But neither in his possessions, his ducal authority, nor his ecclesiastical backing did he find the support necessary to defend his claim to the kingdom. Before his death he himself designated the powerful duke Henry of Saxony as his successor. When the Franks and Saxons assembled once more, this time at Fritzlar, it was upon him that their choice fell.

The Saxon race had accepted the leadership of the German people. Henceforth German and Frankish history each followed its own road.

FIRST BOOK

THE EMPIRE OF THE KAISERS

900–1200

FIRST PART

GERMANY'S UNITY AND SUPREMACY

THE family group of the Franks had been dissolved: the sons had grown up and struck out their own paths. But each took with him an heirloom from the home of their common childhood. Germany owed to Franconia the principle of unity in nation and government: the German tribes were caught up into the current of the ideas promulgated by Church and Empire, which now embraced the whole world. Thus they came to envisage the path of their further development: to the Germans, as to other peoples, was given the task of forming themselves into a nation.

But as soon as the German kings had taken the first steps in this direction, they adopted, as their own personal task, the idea of dominion over the West, reshaping it as they did so upon a new basis. This dual aim lies at the root of the richness and the glory, and also of the shortcoming and the fatality, of our national history.

At that time Germany, even more than the other parts of the former Carolingian Empire, was an exclusively agricultural country. There were indeed other industries, and other important sources of revenue gradually made their appearance under the Saxon emperors, but in the beginning their profit was negligible.

At an even later period than the Saxon, a learned man divided the population into priests, farmers, and soldiers. There were no townsmen. It is difficult for us in these days to imagine how exclusively the manner of life and thought, social position and political influence were determined by the ownership or cultivation of the soil.

In later capitalist times, the effort to attain a sheltered life and worldly honour took a thousand different forms. At that time in small and great alike it was expressed in the desire for 'more land!'

Arable land was almost entirely in the hands of private owners: but there was still a sufficiency of woodland, capable of being converted into arable, within the boundary of the community, and in the virgin forest. Existing fields were enlarged by cultivation, and new farm buildings erected, sometimes beside the village green, sometimes standing solitary at a distance from their neighbours—and new villages founded. The place-names ending in *rode* (rooting up), *ried* (marsh), *schlag* (filling), *metz, hau* (hewing), *schwand, brand* (burning), *hagen* (fence), tell of the years of toil which were the lot of the individual, no less than of the community.

The unequal struggle with the forces of the forest was not everywhere carried on with the same energy. But in the thirteenth century the soil which nourished the German people had been extended and made fruitful to its extreme natural limits, and the goal had been reached for which they had striven for many hundred years.

As a rule the peasant could only become possessed of his piece of land by hard labour. But other methods were employed by the lords of the soil. According to a reckoning made about fifty years earlier, 41 royal palaces and large estates and 730 smaller crownlands were gifted by Otto I only, to ecclesiastical lords. The number would have been still higher if the reckoning had been made nowadays. One valuation gives the average size of the ecclesiastical crownlands as from 9,000 to 18,000 rods, and an extent of from 30,000 to 60,000 as 'no very rare exception.'

A comparison with modern conditions can only be made with regard to the extent of the great estates—not to their composition and manner of working. At that time the landlord's property consisted of a number of medium-sized, smaller, and very small portions, which lay scattered within different and sometimes widely separated boundaries, and surrounded by fields belonging to peasants and other landed proprietors. Because of this scattered position there was no other method of cultivation possible than that of the smallholder. The three-field system was almost universally employed.

On the fields of the village community, oats, rye, millet, and more rarely wheat, were cultivated, and in the gardens peas and beans, vegetables and fruit of various kinds. Everyone kept fowls and one or more pigs, and the majority a few sheep. Oxen and cows were used as beasts of burden, and more rarely horses. The methods of this peasant labour may be known from these indications. Its produce was handed by the tributary tenant to the steward, who was to be found in almost every village.

In addition, the lord of the manor possessed large lands

adjacent to his own manor and the socage-farm. He cultivated them himself, or had them cultivated; and this style of husbandry gives their distinctive character to the economic methods of the tenth and eleventh centuries. It is evident from this that the extent to which these conditions obtained has been overestimated; to-day we incline to believe that such methods were only employed over about one-sixth of the property of the lord of the manor. But there was an authority behind this economic arrangement which made it far superior to the peasants' husbandry. The lord of the manor had various means of cultivation at his disposal, and he had above all many varieties of labour, his own menials, who lived as a rule in the manor itself, and peasants, who were under obligation to serve him with their own labour, and that of their teams. He would not only set the individual a definite and invariable task, but was able to command them all when important works were to be carried out, such as clearing a forest or draining a marsh.

Hence the private husbandry of the lord of the manor was better able than the peasants' smallholding to satisfy more refined demands. Wheat, peas and beans, vegetables, flax, hemp, plants for dyeing such as woad and saffron, began to take up a larger proportion of the area under cultivation, vinery and horse-breeding were at first carried on almost exclusively upon the estate, while at a somewhat later period the keeping of sheep passed gradually into the same hands. Also in the matter of clearing and occupying new country the lord of the manor had facilities at his disposal far superior to those of the peasants.

The peasant daily witnessed and carried out these labours, housing his lord's cattle in his own stall throughout the winter, carrying his grain to the mill, and to the bakehouse on his lord's estate, and his hops to his lord's brewery. In this way he came to understand the working of a superior household: something of what he learnt must have been useful to him in his own more humble sphere. When the system of husbandry under the lord of the manor collapsed in the twelfth and thirteenth centuries, the peasant farmer was able to take its place with his own labour.

One must admit that it is not easy to prove this sequence of cause and effect. The connection is much more easily understood between the industries carried on in the manorial household, and the urban handicrafts which later came to perfection. But as we estimate the size of the manorial household on a much smaller scale than was formerly done: so we are no longer inclined to postulate a highly developed handicraft within the manorial activities. There were certainly handicraft workers, both men and women, belonging to the estate. There is no doubt that the peasants were obliged to furnish not only bread, beer, complete garments and cloths of linen and wool, tools, weapons, and pots, but also grain, malt, woven fabrics, wool, skins of animals, and even iron. All these had to be worked up. Yet the craftsman on the estate could boast only a modest skill. Sombart draws a comparison unflattering to both between the mediaeval craftsman and the workman upon a modern estate—and in the first beginning, country craftsmen who were freemen inclined to work for the towns.

In the development of trade the estate played a much more important rôle. Primarily its products were, of course, employed in meeting the needs of the manorial household. These must have been considerable, particularly in the monasteries. In the tenth century the larger monasteries such as Fulda and Prüm in the Eifel had a population of nearly two hundred monks: that is to say, translated into the language of national economics, they formed some of the great centres of consumption of that period. But the property produced more than it could possibly make use of.

The most lordly train of serving-men could not consume the 9,694 cheeses which were rendered every year to the Count of Falkenstein: the heads of the Cathedral of Trient had over 14,000 to dispose of. What was the monastery of Heisterbach to do with 'the rivers of wine and mountains of salt with which its farms supplied it from time immemorial?' The lord of the manor was obliged to sell: 'what once answered to his needs, had now grown to be superfluous.' The peasant too, who had to render a tribute in money, was obliged to sell, to obtain it. The proceeds of the industry of the manorial farm, and the taxes paid by the peasants fell to the lord of the manor, and enabled him to purchase the satisfaction of his more refined demands. This development acted as an incentive to the interchange of goods and money, and made business more brisk in the markets. This was the chief reason for the great increase of markets in the course of the tenth century. During the time of the Carolingians only six markets are mentioned throughout the entire German territory: in the sixty-six years of the Ottos we find thirty-one places in Saxony and Friesland alone, which are expressly mentioned as market towns.

The freeman on his hide of land could no longer vie in importance with the lord of the soil and of the markets upon it. As soon as the lord of the soil had once made good his footing within the confines of the village, he tried by every possible means to restrict the rights of revenue belonging to the community within their own borders and to acquire them for himself: in this aim, which extended also to forest and lake land, he was frequently successful.

The members of the community themselves stubbed up the forest, widened their fields, and established new farms. As they did so, they loosened the ties which bound the community together. Attacked from within and from without, the community of the village could no longer afford effective protection to the individual. Tribal support had long ceased to be operative. Every disaster fell with double weight upon the individual: whether it was the failure of crops, the death of cattle, military service, war-taxes, or the exaction of a legal penalty. Men dreaded even a summons before the court of justice: the complaint of the corruption of the judges sounds like an unbroken cry through these centuries. In most cases the judge was—the lord of the manor. In the end there was no alternative even for the proud man, but to renounce his freedom, and in so doing to transfer his property, to the lord of the manor.

This happened so frequently, and under such varying circumstances, as to give rise to many different formulas of transference. One man might be in the just possession of inherited land, with the certain prospect of leaving it to his child and his children's children: with others the right of disposal was doubtful. The one had few, and the other had many, tasks and services to perform: here the tenant need scarcely be conscious of the loss of his freedom, there his position was not far removed from that of the serf—moreover, there were many freemen in various districts of Germany who conveyed only a portion of their property to the lord of the manor, and succeeded in preserving their freedom. Only by degrees were these differences so far adjusted that the tenants were able to form one class—that of the peasants. Yet within the space of the tenth and eleventh centuries it became evident that the serfs as a whole were approximating, legally and socially, to the more fortunately situated tenants; while the tenants who were more highly placed, the stewards and soldiers of the lord of the manor, were being assimilated into the ranks of the masters. Hence the loss of freedom gradually ceased to imply a loss of importance. In the peasant class, which was formed in the twelfth century by the union of the small tenants with the free peasants, there was a powerful feeling of class-consciousness, an earnest endeavour to order the affairs of the village after their own judgment.

It is therefore evident that the seignorial right did not weigh so heavily upon economic and social life as was formerly believed. But the system made it extremely difficult for the German people to grow into a nation.

Even before the princely power had interposed between the people and the sole authority of the king, the seignorial right cut off from all participation in questions affecting the life of the nation those tenants and those freemen who were in any way dependent upon the master—that is to say, the overwhelming majority of the German people. Under the Merovingians and Carolingians the great class of freemen had already little by little lost their political rights. They were no longer allowed to act as the representatives of political authority in the community: as lawgivers and judges, or as soldiers. The development of the seignorial right marked the last stage of this evolution.

The lord of the manor ordered the economic life of his tenants, and became by degrees the ruling power throughout the community. Social standing was decided by relationship to him, he exercised public authority as lord paramount under the king, and was able to make his power felt, even by those freemen who were not dependent upon him. Where the lord of the manor ruled, his subjects lost the feeling that there was still a higher authority, the whole body of the people.

But the king was in constant need of new officers and soldiers, and only by grants of land was it possible for him to hire them. It was nothing less than his duty to further the growth of the seignorial prerogative. Feudal tenure had occasionally been granted under the Carolingians, to enable the holder to perform some service or fill some office. Even before Germany broke away from the United Empire, the larger tenures were in fact almost invariably hereditary. This had as a natural consequence the hereditary transmission of offices. At the time of the Saxon kings the hereditary transmission of the important offices which were held by a count was formally recognized. These involved administration, jurisdiction, and the command of levies, and already the lords of the manor who held hereditary public offices were acquiring more extensive prerogatives.

Even under the Saxon emperors, many were allowed to strike medals, to levy taxes, and to hold markets, and the development went on without a break under the succeeding rulers. States arose within the State: their gain was the king's loss.

At the same time the great lords of the manor were nominally vassals of the king, bound by oath to obey him as the supreme liege lord. This connection very often failed, however, exactly in that particular for which it had first been devised, as an obligation to military service. It was seldom possible for the king to punish with effect. Behind the one refractory vassal stood his negligent and wilful fellows. The difficulty of maintaining the army had the effect of making it comparatively small: in one battle there were seldom more than from two to three thousand knights engaged. As soon as a fair number of troops had assembled, their leader must make haste to get to grips with the enemy. The prospect of booty acted as a spur to valour: the ranks grew thin when a decision was long delayed. With such armies it was possible to repel an invasion, and to venture on more ambitious enterprises such as the Italian campaigns and the Crusades, which aroused an answering enthusiasm in the great mass of vassals; but the feudal levies could not, under all circumstances; be a reliable weapon always ready to the king's hand. This was true of other cases, in which compulsion can be employed by a modern Government. Universal taxation was unknown. It is true that revenues of the most varied kind and of considerable value flowed into the king's coffers: the merchant must pay toll on road, river, and market: since the time of Otto I the miner had been extracting silver from the mines of Saxony: the Master of the Mint looked for profit in the coining; great men gave presents and paid money to gain an office or a privilege: conquered peoples brought tribute. Yet the king fell more than once into financial difficulties: the Ottos frequently executed deeds of mortgage, and we learn that Henry III was even reduced to pledging his crown. The imperial laws did not run throughout the country and were subject to interruption: when in the thirteenth century efforts were made to bring order into the legislative confusion, it was significant that they were not of the king's making.

In all these matters the mediaeval state cannot be compared with the modern. Its inherent unlikeness arises in part from its different economic basis. When there is no money in circulation, the vassal is indispensable. When the king has no fixed residence, his documents must fall into confusion: he must spend a disproportionate amount of time on the road—Charlemagne has been credited with 12,000 miles in the saddle—and he is not on the spot when he is needed. But unlike their descendants of a later date, the men of that time would never have allowed the State to regulate their existence, from rising in the morning to going to bed at night. Their conception of the aim of the State was quite other: the king must maintain peace and good government and defend the Church. The rest was a matter for the Church itself. Care for national well-being, the common weal, social equalization, high national aims—it was only by degrees that such things were introduced into the conception of the task of government.

The foundation of the king's authority sufficed to meet all demands which were made upon it. He was, and remained, up till the height of the Middle Ages, the greatest landed proprietor within his empire, notwithstanding the gifts of property which he was constantly bestowing. The Saxon emperors invariably made good their losses by the confiscation of a devolving fief or by new conquests in the East, and later rulers found other expedients. The palaces of the kings on the northern slope of the Harz Mountains were the centres of such exemplary husbandry, that the Saxons and the first Salian Franks preferred to let them enjoy a longer occupation.

Germany's Unity and Supremacy

Moreover, the idea of kingly government was firmly rooted in the heart of the nation. They wished to be led by a king: in him they saw the fulfilment of their desire for peace and good government, and the representative of God upon earth. Time and again this popular sentiment proved a source of strength to the throne. For the very reason that the conditions of legal authority were not clearly defined, it was possible for commanding personalities to manipulate it after their own will and pleasure. The extraordinary importance of personality in these early centuries becomes evident when we begin to follow the course of political history.

In the electoral assembly at Fritzlar, the Franks and Saxons set up the Saxon duke Henry to be their king. Thus the honour of leadership fell to the Saxon tribe, which little more than a century earlier, and last of all the tribes, had been forced, after the most embittered resistance, into the Frankish Empire.

The kingdom of the Franks had meant the leadership of the West, and a share in world-wide ideals. Now the pendulum was swinging in the opposite direction, to the side of North-Eastern ascendancy, and of development on the lines of the separate tribes.

An election on the part of Saxons and Franks laid too narrow a basis for the new power. With an unerring eye for possibilities, Henry I succeeded in a few years in gaining the recognition of the other dukes. The Swabian and Bavarian dukes became parties to a bargain. The king made them extensive concessions in the matter of Church property. To arm themselves for the war against the Hungarians, these dukes had bestowed a great part of the property of the monasteries upon their vassals: according to a later reckoning only 114 estates out of 11,860 were left to the monks of Tegernsee. Lorraine was under the rule of the French king (p. 16), but as the king was more and more hard pressed by his vassals, the Duke of Lorraine also in 925 submitted to Henry's supremacy. The rise of the German Empire can with justice be reckoned from that day. It is true that its founder had to be content with formal recognition from the heads of the tribes. When the Franks fought with Henry against the Lorraines, and later the Bavarians supported him in the war with Bohemia, it was because these two tribes found the enemy an uncomfortable neighbour. For the rest, Henry had to rely upon his Saxons.

Even the terrible menace of the Hungarian invasions produced no common system of defence. Henry purchased for Saxony a nine years' truce, built strongholds, formed a troop of horse, exercised them in successful campaigns against the Slavs, and conquered the Hungarians—without securing lasting peace for Saxony from her wild guests. Nevertheless a permanent gain had been won. The Saxons themselves now possessed fortresses and horsemen. As a military power they no longer stood below the other tribes: seeds had been sown from which municipal life could be developed. Henceforth the energy of the war against the Slavs was no longer dissipated in aimless expeditions, led by the border nobility in search of booty; it had become the business of the king and the whole tribe. Their greater exertions produced corresponding results: the inclusion of Brandenburg in the land of the Heveller; the founding of Meissen among the Slav tribe of Daleminces, the subjection of the Elbe Slavs as far as the Baltic shores: and the formation of a German territory between the Eyder and the Schlei.

As Duke of Saxony, Henry had known fighting: he had composed the tribal wars between the Danes on the one hand and the Saxons and Slavs on the other, and secured and broadened the boundaries of Saxony. In addition, by his prowess and self-restraint he had stablished and settled the German throne. The dukes agreed without demur to his son Otto's succession.

'In Aix assembled the dukes, the leading counts, and the most honoured of the other nobles, in the colonnade which abuts the Cathedral of Charlemagne.' They placed the new ruler upon the throne which had there been set up and did him homage. The solemn procession made its way to the church. The Archbishop of Mayence called upon the people joyfully to salute the chosen king, and with words of consecration he handed him the sword and sword-belt, mantle and clasps, sceptre and staff. The Archbishop of Cologne took part in the ceremony: King Otto was anointed with the holy oil and crowned with the golden diadem. All the tribes were represented by their head-men, and the dukes performed their office at the coronation feast.

Germany's Unity and Supremacy

Whereas the new king's father had declined the assistance of the Church at his enthronement, it played the chief part in his own. Charlemagne's imperial building formed a frame for the brilliant proceedings. The scene presented an epitome of the father's life-work—and held out to the son the possibility of yet more to be accomplished. Henry had had to fight for the acknowledgment of his royal power: Otto was able to make that royal power effective against the opposing powers of the dukes, and to found a united empire. He too had a hard battle to fight. But this full-blooded man was never so happy as in battle: his energy was so great as to be almost an embarrassment to him, often breaking out in uncouth actions, and even disturbing his sleep. But in battle it could have free play; his friends called him the Lion.

It was not long before friction arose with the Frankish duke Eberhard. Otto did not possess his father's gift of sparing the susceptibilities of others. Tribe began to rise against tribe: the Saxons on the one hand believed themselves to be the first people in the world; on the other the ill-will borne by the Franks to their obtrusive neighbours was nourished by the remembrance of their own former leadership. And in the kings' family itself there was disaffection towards the royal head: Otto's elder brother, Thankmar, the fruit of a former marriage of Henry I, which had been dissolved, joined with a younger brother Henry in a league with Eberhard. In the castle of Eresburg, at the altar of the private chapel, a Saxon warrior stabbed his lord's elder brother. Then the conflict spread into Lorraine: Giselbert, Duke of Lorraine, who was the king's brother-in-law, with the French king and the Archbishop of Mayence, took sides with the rebels. Otto was reduced to extremities. Then the Duke of Swabia brought men to his support: the Dukes of Franconia and Lorraine met their death, the one in battle and the other by drowning in the act of flight—Otto recognized that he had been saved 'as by a miracle of God.' Henry was pardoned, only to set on foot another conspiracy by which the king was to be murdered and himself raised to the throne. When the attempt miscarried, he threw himself at last at his brother's feet. Otto's forgiveness was always as prompt as his anger, and often turned to his own hurt. But in this case his self-restraint was rewarded: hence-

31

forth as Duke of Bavaria his younger brother stood faithfully at his side. The king kept Franconia for himself and gave Lorraine to Conrad the Red, to whom he married his only daughter. He gave Swabia, which was also left without a master, to his son Liudolf. All five dukedoms were thus in the hands of the royal family.

His throne being thus secure, it was possible for the king to resume the war in the east on a larger scale. During the years of internal confusion, the Slavs to the north-east of the Elbe had attempted to shake off the rule of Germany. They were vanquished by degrees by Hermann Billung. Still more toilsome were the wars on the Spree and the Havel. It is true that Margrave Gero vanquished his enemies repeatedly on the battlefield, and did not disdain to employ cunning and murder: but in the end Otto himself had to hasten to his assistance. German rule was extended as far as the Oder. The Slavs paid tribute to the king, the Church, and the German lords of the manor: and the first German peasant settlers made their home amongst them. The bishoprics of Magdeburg, Havelburg, and Brandenburg undertook the work of their conversion. In Schleswig, somewhat later, three German bishoprics were also established, and the King of the Danes was baptized.

Henry I had rested only ten years in the grave. In that short space of time his son had brought his work to a conclusion far surpassing any plans which his father had made, and each achievement was an incitement to fresh effort.

The task of the national settlement of Germany was preparing the way, almost imperceptibly, for extra-national and imperial aims.

The French king had tried to make use of the unrest in Germany to win back Lorraine. When this failed, an understanding was arrived at between the two rulers, and from that time Otto considered it his duty to support the throne in France. He took the field in person against the powerful vassals of the French king, and pressed forward as far as Paris and Rouen. He summoned the Church to the aid of the threatened kingdom and sent the levies of Lorraine to fight on the battlefields of France. Otto's wars in France brought him into touch with the chaos in Burgundy: the King of Burgundy also became his dependent.

Germany's Unity and Supremacy

Before this time, the breaking up of the kingdoms of the Lombards in northern Italy had tempted the dukes of Southern Germany to a raid across the Alps. With the Dukedom of Frioli, Henry of Bavaria conquered the east; Liudolf of Swabia fought against Milan. The Margrave Berengar, who aspired to the throne of Milan, still held out against the king. Hoping to improve his prospects, he seized the person of Adelaide, widow of the last king. This gave Otto the pretext for invasion. As Adelaide's deliverer he crossed the Alps, meeting with no resistance. In Pavia he celebrated his coronation as King of the Lombards and his marriage with Adelaide—the imperial crown seemed to be within his reach. But the Pope rejected Otto's solicitation: Liudolf deserted the army, and new troubles were brewing in Germany. Otto returned from Italy with the title of King of the Lombards.

It must have seemed to him that all his work was to be begun anew. Once more he had to struggle for the stability of his throne, once again to fight with an enemy from the east—and to make another attempt upon the imperial crown. But every recurring task was undertaken with undiminished vigour, and carried out with deeper insight, and as it were upon a higher plane.

Liudolf felt himself slighted by the way in which Otto had arranged matters in Upper Italy, while, on the other hand, Conrad the Duke of Lorraine had drawn Otto's disfavour upon himself.

These two came to an agreement. Once again the Arch-bishop of Mayence made common cause with the aggrieved parties, and when the insurrection broke out, the discontented vassals in Bavaria and Saxony saw that their hour had come. This time Otto had still fewer resources at command than during the first struggle with his kins-men. The fact that, in spite of his own distress, he put his kingly duty before all other, saved him the crown. At that time, the districts of south and west Germany were once more overrun by the Hungarians. The insurgents tried to make terms with them. Otto led an army into Bavaria against the robbers.

This brave attitude produced a fortunate turn in his affairs—the rebels lost their adherents and their dukedoms.

In the following year, Otto was able to lead an army of all the German tribes against Hungary. Even Bohemia was represented, while the guilty Duke Conrad contributed a number of horsemen from Lorraine. In 955 a battle was fought near Augsburg, which was being besieged by the Hungarians and bravely defended by Bishop Ulrich.

Like Henry I, Otto rode against the enemy under the victorious banner of St. Michael. The success which he gained was even greater. After a fluctuating battle, in which Duke Conrad atoned for his faults by his death, the Hungarians turned and fled, and few of the fugitives escaped. Now at last an end was made of the Hungarian peril. The Hungarians gradually settled down on the land, and were won to Christianity by missionaries from Passau: German peasants emigrated in great numbers to the sparsely inhabited districts along the banks of the Danube, beyond the forests between Bavaria and Bohemia. In the course of another century, the whole of Austria, together with the greater part of Carinthia and Styria, were won by their labour for the German Empire.

But now came the task of setting the empire in order anew. Within a few years the dukedoms of Lorraine, Swabia, and Bavaria, together with the three Rhineland sees, were left vacant through the death of their occupants. But Otto did not abolish the ducal office. He made over the dukedoms of south Germany to the noble families which were settled there. The governorship of Lorraine, with the Archbishopric of Cologne, was given to Otto's brother Brun, who was distinguished both as a statesman and a man of learning, Mayence to a son, and Trèves to a cousin, of the king. Other high Church dignities fell to relatives and close friends. Henceforth the ecclesiastical power was to render that support to the king which the temporal power, even in the hand of blood-relations, had never rendered. The Church dignitaries were called upon to act as a counterpoise to the ambition of the temporal princes.

To this end Otto gave them equal rights and an equal share in landed property with the temporal powers, and before long more than the half of German soil was in their hands. The gain to the Church was self-evident: but the State also reaped an advantage. It gained men who had been trained in the government of large territories. High forms of service in the interests of humanity and morality were no longer considered the special prerogative of the sovereign: they were included in the settled round of governmental duties. The unity of the State was fostered by the passing of ducal rights into the hands of men from whom there was nothing to fear in the matter of hereditary succession. But all these advantages would become problematic, or even menacing, in the event of a quarrel between the temporal sovereign and the head of the lords spiritual.

Otto seems to have foreseen this sequence of events, otherwise he would not have been able so quickly and decidedly to take his further steps. Conditions in Italy were favourable to his plans. Ten years had passed since Rome had refused the king his coronation: now another, and, it must be confessed, still less worthy, pope summoned him to his help against Berengarius. He was soon overthrown: his kingdom now for the first time came actually under German rule. In the year 962 Otto with his queen received the imperial crown from the hands of the pope. The United Germano-Roman peoples had formed the basis of Charlemagne's empire; from the time of Otto I the imperial crown was worn by the German king.

Germany's ascent had been steep and laborious. Let us pass it in review. Some modern judges see in Otto's Italian policy and in his coronation as emperor—both fall under the same head—'the most brilliant political action which to this day has blessed the German nation.' For others these events were, and are, the source of all the ill which came upon the German people in later times. This view is supported by the fact that for centuries German blood was poured out like water upon the Italian battlefields; while the effort to achieve their distant aims made the emperors incapable of fulfilling their immediate tasks—those of uniting the German people into one nation and of obtaining room for their expansion in the East.

Italy was at that time the corridor for the lucrative trade which connected the East with France. When the German king brought the north of Italy under his rule he added rich sources of taxation to the kingdom and gained for the German people immediate access to one of the highways of world traffic. But northern Italy could only be held if the local bishops remained loyal. Economic considerations already played their part in the politics of Rome.

The Empire of the Kaisers

The king was further urged along this path by the anxiety to establish his dominion over the temporal powers. The Pope of Rome was at the same time the spiritual head of the German bishops, into whose hands Otto had committed the most important offices of his empire. Sanctified tradition pointed the same road. Patronage of the Church had lent glory and honour to the Frankish dynasty. The imperial crown was the most honourable constituent in that Carolingian inheritance which Otto felt himself called upon to restore and administrate. His contemporaries, whom Latin culture inclined to such ways of thinking—and such cultured men alone were at that time considered capable of holding political opinions—looked upon the period of the old Roman Empire as the Golden Age of Mankind. In the empire of Charlemagne they saw a revival of this happy time, and in a third empire the only salvation from the unrest, misery, and peril of the present. Its chosen instruments could only be Germany, the most powerful State of that era, only her king Otto, heir of the Franks, their leader against the heathen Slavs and Hungarians, the king of the Lombards, the strong man who was able to control France and Burgundy. The Holy Roman Empire of the German nation, as it later came to be called, was a federation of Central Europe in the form which was then practicable. It was the outcome of motives which were alike ideal and practical—both inherited and of recent growth. Imperial policy and the public will created it and kept it alive for two hundred and fifty years. The founder of this empire was, after Charlemagne, the only ruler of all Germany to whom contemporaries and posterity alike have given the name of Great.

If the policy of Rome had been an obstacle to the immediate solution of the great national questions, it contributed indirectly to this solution, in ways which should not be underestimated. When the German king of Saxon race turned to Italy, he became an advocate of relations which had long existed between south-west Germany and the country on the far side of the Alps. His foreign policy was put at the service of a tribe which was not Saxon—and expanded into a national policy. This necessarily had an effect upon the development of national consciousness, and in the end gave stimulus and support to the German advance across the Elbe. Until Otto's time only tribal names were employed. The word _German_ signified the language alone: under Otto it was first used for country and people.

The great work was not accomplished in one effort. Otto had still to face long years of struggle: his impetuous humour carried him again beyond what was necessary and useful. The pope repented his treaty with the Lion: he was ignominiously and not undeservedly deposed. The Romans were made to swear that they would never choose a pope without the consent of the emperor and his son. When they rebelled, the offenders were made to feel the power of the sword. In the struggle for southern Italy the Byzantine world-power proved its superiority. The war ended in an amicable arrangement: the Byzantine Court acknowledged Otto's imperial rank and agreed to the marriage of a Greek princess with the son of the emperor. In Rome the wedding 'was celebrated with brilliant festivities amid the rejoicing of all Italy and Germany.'

The mother of Otto I sprang from the Saxon nobility: both his wives had been of royal blood: now his son was united to a princess of the empire.

When Otto came home across the Alps after the ceremony, he was to witness only one more German spring. The road to Saxony passed through St. Gall, where his newly married son took possession of the most beautiful books in the library of the monastery.

Magdeburg had been raised by Otto to an archbishopric. The city on the Elbe, which had grown up around one of Charlemagne's fortresses, was to outvie all the cities of the empire. There was still much to be done. But the Kaiser's work was over. He held his last parliament in Quedlinburg. With the host of German nobles came the Duke of Bohemia, and the son of the Duke of Poland, also ambassadors from Denmark, Hungary, Bulgaria, Russia, Rome, southern Italy, Byzantium, and Africa. The Saxon palace was the focus of a whole world-empire.

In Otto II, the Saxon blood of his father mingled with the Roman blood of his mother Adelaide. He was brilliantly gifted and had had an excellent education: his wife was Theophano, a highly educated Greek princess. But he had an abundance of sound Saxon virility. He was the right man to carry on his father's succession, if time had been granted him to cultivate it.

When new difficulties arose with the dukedom of Bavaria and Lorraine, he did what even Otto I had never dared, and divided them. At that time, Carinthia and Frioli were separated from Bavaria, and the western dukedom split up into Upper and Lower Lorraine. The French king, who in sympathy with the chaos in Lorraine had made a demonstration as far as Aix, was paid by Otto in the same coin. He invaded France. Before Paris, he assembled the priests who accompanied the army upon Montmartre, and announced to the people in the city: 'I am going to have such a Hallelujah sung to celebrate my victory as you have never before heard,' whereupon the priests exerted all the power of their lungs. So Otto took his revenge upon the French for the eagles upon the palace of Aix, which they had turned round to face westwards.

With a feeling of satisfaction he began his march into Italy. Here too his imperial authority must be established. This led to a conflict with Greeks and Saracens. The German armies pressed on through Apulia and Calabria, but south of Cotrona the emperor suffered a reverse. He spurred his horse into the shallow water near the shore and boarded a Greek ship. As soon as it cast anchor before the headquarters which he had left behind, he jumped into the sea, and reached land in safety. He prepared a new expedition at Verona. German and Italian nobles sent a contingent of troops, and elected his son to succeed him. The emperor pressed forward, and died in Rome, not yet thirty years old.

Otto III had passed his third year. His next male relative, Henry the 'Quarrelsome' of Bavaria, aimed at the throne. Parties were divided; at first the high Church dignitaries were found in opposite camps. But Archbishop Willegis of Mayence, who had been raised by his own abilities from a humble position, worked so tirelessly to increase the king's following, that the Bavarian was obliged to resign his claim. Otto I's league with the bishops still further held good. The child's mother and grandmother, who acted as regents, found wise and resolute advisers in the princes of the Church, of Mayence and Worms.

His inheritance was indeed appreciably diminished in the west and east. France, where the House of Capet had come into power, withdrew entirely from German influence. The Slavs had risen on the other side of the Elbe, in the same years in which Otto II suffered defeat in Italy. The Saxon counts had not expected that the oppressed people, on whom they had laid burden upon burden, would be able to break their fetters. All the country was lost on the western bank of the Elbe. Here a great task was awaiting Otto, when at the age of fifteen he succeeded to the government. But the son of a Greek mother despised the 'Saxon roughness.' His training by Bishop Bernwart of Hildesheim and others had led him to turn away from the world of action. He was attracted towards Rome. There he found the men who appealed to his nature. One of these, Bishop Adalbert of Prague, preached the transitoriness of this world, and was the apostle of the ascetic ideal—those twin obsessions which, in the last years of the tenth century, drove many into the forest and the desert. There, expecting the end of the world, they tried to placate an avenging Deity by mortification of the flesh. Another who influenced the young emperor was Gerbert, the Archbishop of Rheims, a preacher able, as if by magic, to evoke the old world-conquering Rome before the eyes of his pious listeners. The emperor's mind was befogged alike with dreams of empire and of escape from this evil world. He mingled with the penitents in the caves at the foot of the Aventine. He raised Gerbert to the papal chair, and intoxicated himself with the idea of ruling the world with his help from his Roman palace: a second Constantine, with a second Sylvester. *Renovatio Imperii Romani*—the renewal of the Roman Empire—was proclaimed by the inscription on the imperial seal. While Sylvester II united Hungary closely with the papal see, Otto set up the Archbishopric of Gnesen over the grave of his friend Adalbert, who had there found a martyr's death. It was a heavy blow for German rule in the east: for it delivered the Polish Church from dependence upon the Archbishopric of Magdeburg.

But national considerations had no place in Otto's dream of world-empire. His last act on German soil was to visit the tomb of Charlemagne. The end came swiftly in Italy.

Southern Italy revolted from German rule, the Romans joined the insurrection. Death overtook the emperor while he was preparing for war. The sword of German knights cleared the way home for his corpse.

Once again Willegis of Mayence assured the succession to the Saxon house. With Henry II, the grandson of Otto I's brother Henry, a man of action came once more to the throne.

Otto III's neglect of Germany had wounded her self-esteem. It was remembered against him that instead of keeping faith with 'the land of desire and joy,' he had preferred intercourse with Italy the 'harlot.' A king was needed who would care for Germany: and Henry cared for her, sparing no pains to this end.

During the last years of Otto III, Boleslav the Bold had founded a kingdom of Great Poland, which included Poland, Moravia, Silesia, Lusatia, and Bohemia. At first, Henry was obliged to let him do as he pleased. Then war began, which was to last through a decade and a half. Bohemia came again under the sovereignty of the empire; but Lusatia remained in Polish hands. In the west, Henry succeeded so far as to secure the union of Lorraine with the empire. By three pilgrimages to Rome, he restored at last the domination which Otto I had exercised in Italy. Thus he fulfilled the promise which was inscribed upon his seal. *Renovatio Regni Francorum*—the Restoration of the Empire of the Franks. His life work laid the foundations of the future.

It is most remarkable that Henry should have gone down to posterity, not as the warrior that he was, but as 'the Saint.' It is at least open to question whether he was distinguished above other rulers for his piety. Moreover, he was not at all indulgent to the claims of the Church, but rather disposed as he thought best of bishops' sees and Church property, about which he declared 'to whom much is given, from them much may be taken.' Yet when some decades later the wave of ecclesiasticism in Germany rose to a great height, his portrait took shape as that of a ruler who had travelled through the world as a penitent, and had been taken up into heaven as a saint. Legends grew up around the generous founder of the Bishopric of Bamberg—the sick and childless monarch —the promoter of the new way of thought—and obscured his true likeness.

The Saxon dynasty expired with the death of Henry II.

Germany's Unity and Supremacy

The nobles of the empire assembled on both banks of the Rhine between Worms and Mayence. It seems certain that only the two descendants of the Ottos on the female side were considered for election; both were grandsons of Conrad the Red and the daughter of Otto I; both were named Conrad. The Archbishop of Mayence, who had to give the first vote, nominated the elder of the cousins. His vote was decisive. With Conrad II begins the race of Frankish or Salian emperors. Under Henry II the empire's centre of gravity still lay in the north-east: in his time the Saxon monasteries reached their highest development. Under the Salian Franks, the Rhine territories became the focus of the empire. Like his predecessor, Conrad II never over-reached himself: fortune favoured him. The former exhausted his strength in laying a firm foundation, upon which his successors were able to build. The area ruled over by the German king was continually enlarged, till in the middle of the century it attained its greatest dimensions.

Conrad found no great difficulty in reducing eastern affairs to order. The ruler of Poland was obliged to resign his claim to Lusatia, renounce the name of king, and acknowledge the supremacy of the empire. In the north, the powerful King Canute of Denmark and England was won over, though at a heavy price, to be a friend and the father-in-law of the king's son Henry. The territory of Schleswig came into Danish possession. In Italy also, the king made a league with the stronger powers: in the north with the lay-princes, in the south with the Normans. In this way he was able to concentrate his forces for more important ends. The childless King of Burgundy had already nominated Henry's predecessor to be his heir. Conrad demanded that the title should descend to himself, and carried his point against all opposition. His stepson, Duke Ernest of Swabia, who broke faith with the king and kept it with his friend, fell on the battlefield in conflict with Swabian vassals, to live again in altered guise in saga and folksong. The Burgundian nobles were forced by the power of arms to do homage at Geneva to the new king. Thus a wealthy country was won, and a bulwark against French influence in the south-west.

With Germany's ascendancy in Switzerland, the way to Italy was assured across Mont Cenis and the Great St. Bernard.

The Empire of the Kaisers

If the acquisition of Burgundy can only be compared with the gains of Otto I in Italy, Conrad's domestic policy makes him akin to the greatest of his predecessors. In the spiritual lords, Otto had created a counterpoise to the dukes' passion for self-aggrandizement. Yet since that time the lords spiritual and temporal had made common cause at many decisive moments. All the expedients of the Crown had not been effective beyond their own day: it was left to Conrad to devise a novel plan rich in possibilities for the future. He acknowledged the right of heritage in small feudal tenures, where it had not yet been established as in the case of the larger. By assuring them of their means of subsistence, he attached the great mass of bound vassals to the king's party. Royalty took root in the same ground, which nourished the power of the great vassals. Thus the foundations of their power were shaken and the power of the throne was enhanced.

By a similar train of thought the king was led into direct relations with the rising citizen class. Former rulers had repeatedly parted with their market rights to the great landowners, particularly the clerical. Conrad showed himself less generous. He too fostered the development of town life; but he retained the town settlements as far as possible in his own hands. He had pointed the way to popular monarchy; a widely different path was struck out by his successor.

Conrad's life was written in a fresh and intelligent style by his Court chaplain Wipo. But the other clerical historians have grudged a halo to this monarch who, in addition to his close-fistedness, adhered to the old way of filling the bishops' thrones, not by election, but royal nomination. Yet stones have a voice: the commanding walls of his family monastery at Limburg on the Hardt and the mighty pile of the imperial cathedral at Spire may speak his fame when the chroniclers are forgotten.

'Charlemagne's stirrups hang at Conrad's saddle,' said his admiring contemporaries. At twenty-two years of age, Henry mounted the charger; it stood waiting for him, saddled and bridled. For the first time in German history there was nowhere any revolt against the succession. When the young king turned the charger to the east, it bore him to brilliant victories.

The Polish Empire quickly collapsed after the death of

its founder. The Duke of Bohemia tried to profit by this fact, to set up an independent empire of the Slavs with its centre in Prague. Henry forced him again to acknowledge his supremacy, and henceforth Bohemia remained true to the empire. Friendly relations continued with Poland. When the King of Hungary, who had been exiled by one of his foes, appealed to Henry, he interfered in this case also, and conquered the enemy. The two rulers entered Stuhlweissenberg with a great train. The people prayed that Bavarian law might run in the country: their king took the oath of allegiance. German emigrants settled in greater numbers in the transferred territory between March and Leitha. The empire had reached its farthest limits—the German king's authority extended from the Rhône to the Carpathians, from the Eyder to the country south of Rome. Henry's appearance on the stage of Italian politics was no less impressive. Three aspirants were disputing the papal throne. At the synods of Sutri and Rome, Henry had all three set aside, and in the year 1046 obtained the election of Suidger of Bamberg to the papal see: from his hand he received the imperial crown. When Suidger died in the same year, Henry sent the Romans a second German pope, and in the following years a third and fourth. Only once in all the previous centuries had a German, under Otto III, attained the papal dignity. Did the emperor elect these Germans in order that they might use their influence for him in every part of the world, in Italy, France, Scandinavia, Poland, and Hungary? Such a calculation would be in keeping with Henry's love of power, and might count as part of 'a political system which was as simple as it was effective.' But there is much to be said against this view. Firstly, the system did not prove to be effective: even the first of the German popes, who was granted a longer exercise of his office, did not use it in any sense as a tool in the hand of the emperor. Henry cannot have been so blind as to overlook this possibility. Neither was his nature so simple as this view presupposes. Other impulses struggled for mastery with the demon of the love of power.

Between the ninth and tenth centuries, a wave of new spiritual life flowed over the south and west of Europe, taking the form of a strict ecclesiasticism. From the strength of the movement, one may deduce the misery of the

The Empire of the Kaisers

millions, whose names are never mentioned by the historians in their chronicles of the wars and feuds of those in authority. Too long these men had been the victims of robbery and bloodshed at the hands of their rulers, both great and small, and had been pillaged without pity by the barbaric nations which overran their lands. Even into the religious haunts of peace the wild spirit of the age had forced its way. The French nobility, in particular, who were curbed by no powerful kingly authority, seized the property of the monasteries, while within the walls untamed passions were snapping the bonds of discipline. The longing for peace, for purity of inward and outward life, for spiritual illumination, became an overmastering desire. The will to a new life took its rise in the cloisters. In the Burgundian monastery of Cluny, leading abbots devised a severer cloister discipline. This included the renunciation of all personal property; unbroken silence at certain hours, and all day and night on feast days; they were enjoined to eat no meat, to perform humiliating penances, and the most strict obedience. The vices of a lawless age must be rooted out. Other monasteries joined in: a monks' Church, immediately subject to the pope, opposed the secular Church. Before long it, too, was seized by the reforming spirit. A storm broke out against the marriage of priests, which had become general, in spite of the veto of Church and emperor: the universal custom of paying dues by means of the transfer of Church offices was condemned as 'simony,' or 'usury.' Even the laity felt the influence of the new movement: small and great were united in a vow to keep the peace. We find a pronouncement like this: If a peasant has injured another peasant or a knight, the injured party must let fourteen days elapse; within that time compensation may be offered. He who fails to offer it must be pursued even to death by the whole community. Then a common bond was formed: on those days of the week on which Christ suffered, from the Wednesday evening to Monday morning, peace must reign over the whole land, and a breach of 'the Peace of God' fall under the ban of the Church.

The reforms of Cluny could be immediately carried out only in the extreme west of Germany, and first in Lorraine. The German nobility, from which sprang a large proportion of the monks, were repelled by this demand for the extinction of the *ego*. The bishops could not take kindly to the institution of the 'Peace of God,' and expressed the opinion that 'In the Empire the Emperor was an adequate guardian of the interests of peace.' In his later years Henry II was won over to the Reform: thereupon the bishops waived their obedience, and war was only prevented by the death of the king.

A quarter of a century had passed since then. The idea of Reform had taken root even in the interior of Germany, and found an ardent advocate in Henry III. The unheard-of austerity of its demands awoke an answering chord in the monarch: his ecclesiastical education, the influence of his wife Agnes, who was a native of southern France, furthered its development. He submitted to humiliating penances; favoured the reformed monasteries; set up the 'Peace of God' after his own fashion: he even gave up all claim to the tribute which, since time immemorial, the bishops had rendered to the king when they took over their office. He met with stupidity and resistance. But the hostile world must be compelled to follow the path which he was treading. With this end in view, he set out for Italy.

Scarcely had he arrived there, when one of the synods which he had appointed launched a sentence of excommunication and deprivation of office against those bishops who had been guilty of simony: a few weeks later followed the appointment of the new pope. Although Suidger was not openly friendly to Reform, his elevation seemed of great moment to its advocates.

And in the year following the emperor set a convinced Reformer upon the papal chair, who worked with all his might and quite openly to free the Church from dependence upon the Crown. Under his pontificate, the papal decrees were no longer dated, as had always been the custom, from the year of the emperor's accession. These popes were not obliged to serve as the political tools of an imperial world-government. Rather they were to be bound to the Crown, that they might renew the world from the standpoint of the Church, in the name of those ideals of which Henry was the self-constituted champion.

The plan can be explained only by an exaggerated feeling of domination. Lay and clerical authority, Church and State, whose relationship had been clearly defined by

Otto, were inextricably intermingled. The haughty monarch ignored the forces which were struggling for expression in the inarticulate mass of the people; the vainglorious king shunned the path which might have led him to a popular government. Thus a great inheritance was quickly squandered. Already the supports which Otto I had devised for the throne were beginning to totter: one clerical dignitary refused to yield the king the oath of allegiance: another disputed his right to summon a bishop before him. Lay princes took part in revolt after revolt. Even the acquisitions in the east of the empire were now lost. When Henry III came to the throne he had no need to raise a finger to create peace: in his last years he was no longer master of the growing unrest, and on the far side of the Alps the pope was sharpening the weapons which he himself had put into his hands. When the Church was once strong enough to oppose the throne, the German emperors lost that unconditional control of the bishops which had been the strongest bulwark of their authority.

The Papacy and the empire had been raised on the foundations of the Roman world-empire. Under Frankish rule, the German tribes had been admitted to share in the ancient inheritance of learning which enriched the south and west of Europe. They had remained true sons of the Church: the German kings had given a new form to the conception of world-empire, and exacted for the German people the respect of other nations. But such favours and achievements were paid for by a fatal slackening of the national development. Almost at the same period in which the empire was founded, the ancient learning as it had been handed down by the Church was victorious in the intellectual field. But the developments which were antagonistic in the political world could here be mutually helpful, and after a few centuries the waters which had risen in the far country were flowing together with the native stream to form one mighty river.

Anything which has come down to us from Carolingian literature has its source in the world of Christian thought and feeling, and was composed either by priests or under their direct influence. This is the principal source, even towards the end of the Carolingian period. Here and there a priest may introduce a German word amongst the Latin. Travelling scholars of a later, more stirring, century could handle these mongrel forms with wit and flight of fancy, but there is nothing of these to be found in the oldest poem in this style which has come down from the time of the Ottos.

Here a learned versifier discourses 'de quodam duce / theme hêron Heinrîche / qui cum dignitate / thero Beiaro rîche bewarode' (about a duke, the Lord Henry, who worthily governed the Bavarian Empire). But already another poet is employing more fluent strains in which to address his beloved: 'Suavissima nunna / coro mîner minna / resonant odis nunc silvae / nun singant vogele in walde' ('Sweetest nun, make proof of my love: the woods resound with songs—now the birds sing in the forest'). Finally we find a few German rhymes in the Latin grammar of some valiant schoolman: He writes, remarkably enough:

Der heber gât in lîtun	tregit sper in sîtun
Sîn bald ellin	ne lâzet in vellin.
imo sint fûoze	fûodermâze
imo sint burste	ebenhô forste
unde zene sîne	zwelifelnige

(The boar goes to the hillside with the spear in his flanks— he is so bold and strong that he cannot fall. His feet are like a cart-load, his bristles tall as forest trees: and his teeth twelve ells in length.)

There are a few more couplets in this style: they are the solitary pure-German verses which have come down to us from a century and a half.

But there is no doubt that the old epic poetry lived on, and continued to flourish among the people: this we know from the historical works of the period. They sang of the heroes and their deeds in warfare, of Henry and his son Otto, of the rough Gero and of Bishop Ulrich, who defended Augsburg with such great courage against the onslaught of the Hungarians. Stillness brooded over the listeners when the singer took up the tale of Liudolf, the insurgent; they laughed aloud in their relief when the song turned to the comical Kuno Kurzbold, Count of Niederlahngau, who slew the lion, but ran away from women and apples. Those who worked in such material had inherited the laws of their composition from the singers of the migration of the German tribes. But in educated circles German song was no longer in high repute. Its singers were lost in the gay crowd of minstrels, who were well rewarded—and despised.

47

The Empire of the Kaisers

It was the monk who at that time and for long after was the leading figure in literary creation. It is true that many monasteries had suffered severely under the incursions of Hungary: in Bavaria they had been almost wiped out. But many famous schools, such as Fulda, carried on their teaching undisturbed. In other districts the monks returned when the tempest had passed, and resumed their studies and their teaching with fresh zeal—this was the case in St. Gall and in Reichenau, whose monasteries were still the pride of Swabia. In the judgment of professional men, the men of the tenth century who were able to write could compare favourably in theological knowledge and classical erudition with the authors of the Carolingian period. It is true that they were fewer in number and their horizon was more limited. The majority of the imperial annals of the Carolingian period end as chronicles of the cloister. But these monks themselves were sons of their tribe and of their century. What had been sung from old time among the people, found an echo in the silent cell and clamoured for utterance: tidings of the deeds of the great, no less than the newest ballads of the minstrels, found their way across the monastery walls.

While the first Saxon king still sat upon the throne, Gerald, the tutor in the school at St. Gall, set the task of composing a German epic in Latin hexameters. This was the origin of Ekkehard's famous poem of Walter and Hildegunde. Posterity has to thank the tutor, and pay the scholar his meed of admiration. His Latin, indeed, is not very brilliant, although it is strongly reminiscent of Virgil. It was not approved at the time, and was touched up in the following century. But his work is not without fluency and play of imagination. The events unfold themselves without haste and without wearisome delay: we are shown the flight from the court of the Hun king, the struggle at the Wasgenstein, and the feast of reconciliation. He depicts men and their humours with a few strokes. The rough jesting speech made by the mutilated after the battle has justly become famous.

No other German poem breathes such iron defiance in the face of destiny: though they are forced into the artificial mould of a learned language, the wild passions of that primitive time are beating in the veins of the monkish scholar. But in significant passages Christianity vindicates

Germany's Unity and Supremacy

its humanizing work. When night falls after the first day of battle Walter throws himself upon the earth

And speaks, to the eastward turning,
Holding his naked sword in his hand, the words which follow:
'O thou Creator of all, who rulest the world which thou madest,
Nothing without thy command, nothing without thy knowledge
Can happen—I give thee thanks, that thou from the knavish weapons
Of yonder enemy's host and from shame, hast kindly preserved me.
Gracious God, I beseech thee here, with a contrite spirit
Thou who art minded to blot out transgression, but not the transgressor.
Let me meet my companions at last within thy heavenly kingdom.'

It may have been a few years later—perhaps at the beginning of the reign of Otto I—that a monk in a monastery in Lorraine set himself to narrate 'the Flight of a Captive in a Parable.' A calf runs away from the stall, is taken prisoner by the wolf, and after suffering terrible alarm is set free by the fox's cunning. This most ancient of mediaeval animal poems strikes us as didactic and pedestrian: it cannot be compared either with Ekkehard or with the later German animal fables. Yet it proves that the worlds within and without the monastery walls were not by any means so completely sundered as we are prepared to believe.

It is true that the author worked upon a Latin model, which in turn goes back to Aesop. But we know that animal sagas were current at that time among the German people, growing out of the intimate familiarity of the Germani with nature and fed by the inventions of travelled minstrels. It was thus the common heritage of the people that the monk set forth as the fruit of his own experience. He worked from a foreign model, yet his writing was in the closest relation to popular views and the conditions of the time. The ravenous wolf sings monkish songs: the calf draws his attention to the fact that King Henry has ordained universal peace. His contemporaries would certainly find a number of similar allusions in the poem. At this distance of time they escape us.

The voice of the new age echoes most clearly from the

cloisters of Saxony. In the border territories, many monasteries had gone up in flames during the Hungarian invasions, but in the centre of the country Korvey, Herford, and Gandersheim remained inviolate. Year after year the Court took up its abode in the Saxon palaces. Henry I and Otto I are not to be compared with Charlemagne: the father had no intellectual interests and even the son had no vital connection with literature and art. Yet he surrounded himself with men of standing; he summoned learned men from abroad to the German schools, and made the younger members of his family attend the Saxon cloister schools. In his youth, the emperor's brother, the restless Brun, was given an unusually broad classical education.

But more than by any literary stimulus the monks were inspired by the knowledge that the bond of common descent united them with the ruling house. Widukind of Korvey sings the fame of the Saxon race, Otto's deeds are celebrated by Roswitha of Gandersheim. The Saxon monk does not indeed write in classical Latin, and his horizon is bounded by the frontiers of Saxony. The other German tribes are either stupid or cowardly or vacillating, or all three together. The Saxons are the first nation in the world, their kings may be compared to Augustus: Otto's dominion stretches as far as Asia and Africa. But the love of tribe and home, which breathes from every line, reconciles the reader to such overstatements, even to his grossly exaggerated praise of the members of the royal family. No other work of these centuries can compare in these respects with Widukind's *History of the Saxons*. Roswitha is much more cultured and can write fluently. But what she relates of Otto's battles and victories produces a somewhat thin and colourless effect. Some of the dramas are more lively, which she wrote for her companions in the nunnery, to supersede the shameless Terence. They won for the authoress, though not entirely with justice, the title of 'the first German poetess.'

Roswitha's attempt remained without a successor. Yet the German drama of a later period grew out of the religious poetry of this century. When St. Gall reached its prime towards the end of the ninth century, a monk wrote variations upon the text of the Gospel for the Church Psalmody. At Easter the choir of angels chanted: 'Whom seek ye in

the grave, ye followers of Christ?' The three Maries replied:
'Jesus of Nazareth, who is crucified, ye citizens of the
heavenly kingdom.' And again the angels: 'He is not there,
He is risen, as He foretold you: go hence, and publish
abroad that He has risen from the grave.' From these
humble seeds, drama, opera, and oratorio developed in the
course of centuries.

The free song-forms set to the air of the *Hallelujah* by
a monk of St. Gall during this period proved much more
easily manageable. Rhythm, verse length, and form of
strophe changed with the flow of the melody. This could
be adapted to matter of the most varied kind. And in
the course of the same tenth century men who were versed
in Latin—either monks or wandering scholars—employed
themselves in translating into Latin the jesting tales of
the minstrels. The new matter which at that time was
making its way into Germany from the East, and developing into an extensive literature of entertainment, found
friends even amongst those who had gone through the
discipline of the monastery schools. So here we meet with
the charming 'lying' fairy tales: the king's daughter is
given to him who can so tell lies as to force the king to
call him a liar. A Swabian tells a tale of a hare which
he had caught: it carried under its tail a document which
declared that the king was descended from a serving-man.
The king can no longer contain himself: 'Thou liest and
the document lies.' So the Swabian gets his daughter.

At the time of the first king of the Salian Franks, a
German author succeeded in composing a genuine min-
strel's epic, the *Rudlieb*, in the Latin tongue. Young
Rudlieb says farewell to his mother, wins favour and
honour at the Court of a strange king, and on his way
home must put to the proof twelve rules of conduct which
his royal friend has given him as a farewell gift. Fragments
are still extant which tell of the hero's efforts to win a
bride and treasure. Old Germanic sagas and matter borrowed from abroad are woven into a picture of daily life,
which was now presented for the first time in such extent
and diversity to German hearers. Scenes from far and
near are depicted with the same vivid perception: the
battles of kings and their reconciliation-doings at the
Courts the great, the daily life of the peasants, their
homes, their betrothal and marriage-customs, men and

beasts, dream and reality. The poet is remarkably successful in his portrayal of varied and stirring scenes. One must not look to him for delicate character-drawing: still less for originality of invention. Many motives which here make their appearance for the first time recur in the later romances of chivalry: Rudlieb is led, like Parsival, by Good Instruction: like Tristan, he is an excellent hunter and player upon the harp. Later writers, of course, have not borrowed from Rudlieb: like him they drew upon a mass of tradition which is now lost. But it is not the less remarkable that this Bavarian monk (the poem was composed in the cloister of Tegernsee) has so intimate a knowledge of traditional sources that he is able to make free use of them. He does not, indeed, take great pains to press the material at his disposal into the foreign mould. In many passages German turns of expression peer out from under the loose cloak of Latin speech, so that one is tempted to seize and hold them:

> dic, sodes, illi nunc de me corde fideli
> tantum liebes, veniat quantum modo loubes,
> et volucrum wunna quot sint, tot dic sibi minna
> graminis et florum quantum sit, dic et honorum,

(She says: wish him from me, with my heart's love,
As many good things as there are leaves upon the tree,
As much love as there are birds in the air,
As much honour as there are blades of grass.)

Rudlieb was composed at latest ten years after the death of that bold schoolmaster of St. Gall who composed the only verses written in pure German during this period. In order to supersede the ugly word-for-word translations which were then current, he turned the Latin writers into fluent German, thus composing the first theological books in the German language. He gave foreign words a German form, and did not even shrink from the attempt to replace with German the Latin definitions of philosophical expressions. There is an integral connection between his scientific labours and the poetical works of his time. The subjects which moved and delighted the people had fought step by step for their right to a place in the poetry of the Latin scholars. At last the moment came when the foreign cloak was rent away · the poets dared once more to write German as they spoke it.

Germany's Unity and Supremacy

The creative impulse can work by the means of spacial art more immediately than through language. At this period, the will to create found its suitable expression not in poetry, but in works of stone and colour. St. Michael in Hildesheim, or the wall paintings at Reichenau, are more perfect manifestations of the German spirit than the Song of Ekkehard.

Music and architecture are farthest removed from the imitation of the actual. German masters have excelled in both arts. The language of painting and sculpture, which other peoples employed to such happy effect, was still foreign to the German spirit: the meaning of things was still infinitely more essential to it than their material appearance. In stone it first discovered the material for creation on a grand scale—a means of revealing the secret of the divine and the human.

Once the Saxon emperors had begun to build, churches sprang out of the ground on every hand. Side by side with the emperors, the princes of the Church whom they had raised to so great honour, worked as zealous master builders. They were the leading spirits at the height of the Middle Ages: the Gothic cathedrals were for the most part built by the citizens. The shifting of the centre of authority, occasioned by the change in the ruling houses, is mirrored in the history of their building. Otto I raised his dukedom of Saxony to be the leading country in Germany. He built the Cathedral of Magdeburg. In the first half of the eleventh century, Saxon ecclesiastical architecture attained its perfection. Hildesheim, Quedlinburg, Halberstadt, and Goslar must be mentioned before all others. Otto's brother Brun gave the impetus to great building activity on the lower Rhine: the churches of St. Pantaleon, St. Andrew, and the Holy Apostles were erected in Cologne. The foundation of the Bishopric of Bamberg by Henry II aroused the territories of central Germany to great activity.

In the years before and after A.D. 1000, cathedrals were also built in rapid succession along the Rhine from north to south: Mayence, Worms, and Strasburg. Spire at first lagged behind. Finally, Conrad II, the first of the Salian Franks, founded the cathedral there, which surpassed all the churches of Germany in its magnificent dimensions. For while the Salian Franks were in the ascendant, the middle Rhine became the centre of civilization.

The Empire of the Kaisers

Architecture was foreign to the Germani: the words which deal with it in the German language are borrowed from the Latin. For a long time the Germans worked the stone as though it were wood. All the forms of decoration which had been evolved in wooden buildings, plaited work, figures of animals and men intertwined, decorated the stone capitals of the pillars in all the varied forms dear to the Germani. The architect took the ecclesiastical buildings on Roman soil as the pattern, both for the laying-out of his ground-plan and for its superstructure. The Palace Chapel which Charlemagne built in Aix consisted of an eight-sided centre room, over-arched by a cupola and surrounded by a sixteen-sided covered way. But such central buildings never became acclimatized in Germany. The future belonged to the elongated building of which the Roman basilica was the pattern. A central nave was divided by rows of pillars from the two narrower aisles, and rose high above them; small windows broke the wall-space beyond the rows of pillars. The altar stood in the apse, which formed the semicircular termination of the central aisle, generally in the east of the building. In early Christian times it was already customary to introduce a transept between the apse and the nave, extending on each side beyond the central building; this was the origin of the cruciform shape. On these principles German artists developed 'Romanesque' ecclesiastical architecture. The tower, which on Roman soil still stood apart from the main building, was incorporated by them into the main structure. The intersection, i.e. the square formed by the crossing of the transept and the nave, determined the entire arrangement of space. On the far side of the transept, the nave was continued as an intersected square, so that the apse widened into the choir: the area of the choir was raised by heightening the roof of the crypt, or place of burial.

St. Michael in Hildesheim is one of the most remarkable buildings, 'the first perfect production,' of the Romanesque style in Germany. Bishop Bernward built the church at the beginning of the eleventh century. He was a connoisseur in architecture and sculpture, in painting, brass-founding, and the art of the goldsmith. His mind had been expanded by the holding of high office, and by journeys to Rome and Byzantium: he was distinguished as a collector and as a patron. If he did not superintend the building in a technical sense, yet his unerring taste may be detected in details no less than in the whole. Transept and east choir are repeated in the west, the cruciform shape becomes a double cross, movement is answered by counter-movement. There is a rhythmical interchange of pillars and piers of red and white, the colours of love and innocence. Not by a superficial glance, but by a patient pacing of the interior, can men of the present day hope to unlock the secret of this style of building. The men of the period drew fresh springs of life from these well-proportioned spaces, and it is very difficult for us to feel as they felt. The meaning of the exterior is far more easily to be understood by the men of our day. The ponderous masonry, whose massiveness is rather emphasized than concealed, the flat roof—the painting dates from the thirteenth century—the powerful central tower, the slender turrets at the transepts, all these help us to realize the aspiration of that time, bound to earth, yet eager to rise.

The cathedral at Spire was built later than the time of Conrad II. Son and grandson carried on and completed the work, in which Salian Franks and later rulers of the 'empire' found a sepulchre. The original plan was altered during the long course of construction. When the empire collapsed, the peace of the dead was broken by Louis XIV's soldiers, and the eastern part of the building fell into ruin. But the ground-plan remained unchanged in spite of all deviations, destruction, and restoration. And this ground-plan is an amazing one, bearing witness to an extraordinary breadth of conception and command of space. The cathedral was not intended for a place of assembly for the community: the entire population of Spire would not have sufficed to fill it. Its most immediate secular purpose was entirely obscured by the desire to give expression to the search after God. The spirit which conceived the proportions of the ground-plan speaks no less eloquently in the design of the crypt, which dates from the time of the founder.

In all the churches of this period one must take into consideration the fact that the effect of space was enhanced by painting. The picture, as we understand it to-day, did not exist. Like the architect, the artist worked over great spaces. His creations broke up and covered the great wall-spaces, pillars and shafts, arches and ceilings. Thus painting was subject to the exigencies of space and architecture. Little has come down to us from these early times. That which remains shows that the painters also employed foreign material to create new matter, in the same monumental spirit which inspired the architects, and, as in their works, the urge to infinity is expressed, now with restraint and now with passion. The end of the tenth century was to bring the Last Judgment upon the empire. In the centre the Judge of the world is throned in a Glory, with open arms, showing the marks of his wounds: on his right Mary lifts her hand in supplication. In the middle distance stands the band of Apostles, below the dead are rising from their graves. Winged angels fly above the Judgment Seat proclaiming the day of retribution.

Here and there the artists treated of secular subjects: thus Henry I had his victory over the Hungarians depicted in a wall-painting in the palace at Merseburg. The illumination of manuscripts was more strongly influenced by tradition, which was at the disposal of favoured monasteries in the shape of numerous examples from early Christian times. From this, the fact comes to light that certain centres clearly excelled in the practice of this art: about A.D. 1000, the Reichenau and St. Maximin at Trèves, and under Henry II, St. Emmeram at Regensburg. The work produced by these centres was taken by friendly and neighbouring monasteries, by those who had a right to it and by those who had none. It was the pride of every monastery and every church to possess beautifullly decorated manuscripts. As early as the ninth century the monastery of Reichenau had eighty-seven mass books, many of which were certainly decorated with pictures. The most valuable possession of the Library of St. Emmeram, which in A.D. 980 again contained over five hundred works, was the *Golden Manuscript*, an imperial gift from the end of the ninth century.

Equally widespread was the endeavour to obtain a treasure of costly metalwork. Archbishop Brun's collection, which was certainly got together under peculiarly favourable circumstances, included gold and silver vessels, beakers, basins, candlesticks, censers, and one silver horseman. Many of the pieces, of course, were of foreign, and particularly of Byzantine, origin, which might be more correctly described

Germany's Unity and Supremacy

as from Asia Minor; they had a powerful influence upon native production. It was expressly stated of Bishop Bernward: 'that he took specially gifted youths with him to the Court or on long journeys, and urged them to practise everything which appealed to them as most worthy in every art.'

The sacred crown of the empire was an important work, which was probably made in Germany for Conrad II. Four out of the eight gold plates of the circlet show the portrait of Christ, and of three of Conrad's ancestors, in enamelled work. The portrait of Christ bears the inscription: 'Per me reges regnant,' 'through me kings reign.'

The motto of imperial majesty was to become before long the battle-cry of Germany.

RISE OF THE PAPACY

THE history of the Saxon and Salian emperors tells of various battles on the frontiers of the empire.

But at that period, and for long afterwards, the German people were spared the necessity of turning their weapons against an equal foe. This good fortune lasted till the beginning of modern times. But at the height of the Middle Ages, the German throne was forced to pit itself against the great world-power of the Papacy. The result of this conflict was more serious than any in which other European nations were involved during those centuries. Though their wars might not always achieve victory, yet they strengthened the national consciousness, and worked in the end for the cause of unity. The German kings were warring against a power which fought with spiritual as well as carnal weapons, and was firmly entrenched in the hearts of the whole Western world. This conflict brought civil war to the German people, strengthened the powers of disunion, and shook the throne to its foundations.

Scarcely eighteen months separated the hour in which the young King Henry IV, blessed by the Pope, saw the enemy in Germany at his feet, from that in which he took his penitential journey to Canossa. But a generation earlier, the powers which brought about this sudden change of fortune had gained an influence at the imperial Court, and must have been at work for a long time in the heart of the nation. Otherwise it would be impossible to explain how the earnest monks who were preaching in those days were able so quickly to gain an influence over such wide circles of the population. At the beginning of the eleventh century, the western parts of Germany had been seized and penetrated at the first attempt by the monks of Cluny. Yet in the sequel only few monasteries were won over. The man had not yet arisen who was to interpret to the blunter German nature the reform which had been first felt and devised by Roman intelligences. That task was reserved for Abbot William, the scion of a noble Bavarian house, who became the head of the Monastery of Hirschau in the Black Forest twenty years after the death of Henry III.

Rise of the Papacy

His fiery eloquence, together with his simple faith in God, which placed Providence high above all human wisdom, gained him ascendancy over men's minds.

Very soon the life of the monastery in the grassy valley of the Nagold was regulated to the smallest detail. When the monk rose for his nightly prayers, he was made to sit while he put on his undergarments, and cover his legs before he threw off his blanket. He must arrange the bed in such a way that the pillow should be invisible under the blanket. When he lay down at night, he sat on the stool which stood beside the bed while he took off his shoes: he sat on the couch, raised both feet at once and spread the blanket over himself, before he was allowed to remove his undergarments. If he had a communication to make during the time of silence, he was obliged to employ certain signs, whose enumeration fills fifteen pages of a quarto volume. If, in speaking with the abbot, the monk noticed that he was annoyed with him, he must fling himself at once upon the ground. Thus the day was ordered by rule, in all matters both small and great, and every movement of the individual will suppressed as it arose. No knowledge was more important than the knowledge of obedience.

The Bavarian aristocrat imposed this duty upon his fellow monks even more strictly than was the case in Cluny. All must enrol themselves unconditionally in the ranks of God's army and fight his battles by unceasing prayer.

From of old, the Benedictines had drawn most of their equipment from the writers of ancient times. William of Hirschau and other leaders were not personally averse to classical studies. But it was inevitable that their disciples should scent danger, even destruction, in preoccupation with the works of the heathen. The following advice was given to the man who wished to mention an ancient secular book in the language of signs understood by the men of Hirschau:

'First make the universal sign for a book: then touch your ear with your finger, as a dog does when he scratches himself with his foot: for an unbeliever can without injustice be compared to such an animal.' Where this was the prevalent opinion, the classics in the monastery libraries were apt to find their way into the fire.

All the more fervently did the monks turn their thoughts to architecture. This, too, had its roots far back in heathendom: but the Christian spirit had long since transformed its language into the loftiest expression of divine worship. Abbot William built a church in Hirschau, with which no other abbey of the Romanesque period in Germany can compare in size. It was the rule for monks and laymen to be strictly separated even at service time. Laymen were accommodated in the nave, the choir was reserved for the monks. A lofty barrier of stone, with the reading desk, shut off the nave from the monks' church. The superior importance of the choir was expressed by the greater elaboration of the ground-plan: the side aisles were continued beyond the transept and closed with their own apse. All the churches built by the men of Hirschau adhere strictly to this pattern: there was no room in the new architecture for the diversity of creation which is a distinguishing mark of the old. Paulinzella is far behind the Hirschau model in the matter of dimensions. But what a noble effect is produced by its simple lines! The heaviness of the earlier period has vanished from its construction: it soars upwards freed from the trammels of earth; Romanesque architecture has reached its maturity.

Paintings, gilded sculptures, coloured windows, and many-coloured carpets beautified the interior. On feast days processions passed up the nave, with banners and pictures, crosses and reliquaries, veiled in a cloud of incense. On such occasions the monastery coffers yielded up their treasures. Silken vestments embroidered in gold and embellished with jewels, a gilded candlestick with the four evangelists above whom stood the cherubim, six ewers, to which the artist had given the shape of lions and serpents—these were some of the treasures possessed by the monastery of Zwiefalten.

As time went on, an equally powerful effect was produced by the inexhaustible hospitality of the monks, their care for the sick and poor, and the strictness of their discipline. It was customary for the monk who had lost his temper in the presence of laymen to stand barefooted at the church door on the following feast day, with uncovered head, that all might recognize him: a serving-man stood beside him to explain to all present the cause for which he was doing penance.

Before long the new order had become dominant in the whole of Swabia, and spread from thence to Central Germany, Bavaria, and Austria. At William's death more than a hundred monasteries had been won over to the Hirschau Reform. But far beyond the monastery walls spread the example of these monks whose life was made up, not of service, but of imitation, of their Lord. They carried the light, towards which thousands were striving out of the darkness and misery of this world. High and low thronged to the monastery gates to share in their blessedness. They were content to serve the monks and nuns as unlettered men, as lay brothers and sisters—to do their household tasks: in the kitchen, in the hospital, at the monastery gate—to work as masons, or farm labourers. There was nothing extraordinary in the fact of a nobleman herding swine, or the son of a count lighting the fire under the oven. Before long there were many monasteries which contained twice as many 'bearded' men as monks. Often it was impossible to house all those who served within the monastery walls: in that case they lived in adjoining buildings under one master according to special rules. Even in the villages, for the first time on German soil, men and women were banded together in brotherhoods and sister-hoods, under spiritual oversight, almost in the manner of the monasteries.

Wherever this people's movement made headway, all attacks from opponents were powerless to check it. Of these there was no lack. The Benedictine monks, who lived in the old fashion, the secular priests and particularly the married men amongst them, found themselves exposed to the people's contempt. They brought accusations against the reformers, that their rules were full of superstition, that in their zeal for the dogmas of men they forgot the command-ments of God, that their blind submission to the authority of the abbot and the pope were not according to Scripture. Bishops, who were actually attracted to the new thought, turned against the monasteries which, as the movement increased in strength, were escaping from beneath their control. But even the opponents of the new thought reaped the advantage of the growing piety of the people.

For a long time the Church, through its ownership of land, had been economically most closely connected with the bulk of the population. As landed proprietor it exercised an extensive overlordship, and was able in ever-increasing numbers to bring the cases which could in any way be interpreted as a breach of ecclesiastical law before its own legal courts rather than before those of the secular arm. In the end the religious movement gave the Church a power over men's minds which it had never before attained in Germany.

Now, once again, the religious poets sought and found the way to the hearts of the people. For a century and a half clerical scholars had been writing exclusively in the Latin tongue, whether their theme was the Christmas Gospel or the newest romance of the minstrels. Now we meet again with compositions in the German language, clumsy for the most part in form, but arresting through their depth of feeling. Under the Carolingians, religious poets had already told in the German tongue of the mercy of God towards sinners. They wrote out of their own conviction of salvation: through their words rang the joy of the message which was for all nations, and could now be heard by the German people in their own tongue.

A totally different note is sounded by the Swabian poet, who was apparently the first who dared to be a pioneer in German composition. In his presentment, consciousness of sin overcomes the certainty of salvation: the joyful evangel of new life is drowned by the sombre warning: the wages of sin is death. 'Remember death'—*memento mori*—is the basic thought of the composition. 'Foolish is that man who finds a fair tree on his journey, and takes his rest beneath it. Sleep overcomes him, so that he forgets whither he should go. Then, when he leaps to his feet, how sorely does he repent! Ye are all like to this man: ye must go hence. But the tree is the world in which all are tarrying. Evil world, how dost thou deceive us! Thou hast gained the mastery over us, therefore we are deceived!' The cares and troubles of this earthly life are also the theme of the poem written by a dignitary of Bamberg Cathedral: but the light of the cross sheds its comforting rays above the darkness of the world. 'Blessed be the Cross, the best of all Trees.' It is the Mast, the world is the Sea, the Lord is the Sail and the Steersman, good works are the Cordage, which direct the ship towards home; the kingdom of heaven is the Homeland, where we would fain be. The poem was written by command of the bishop, when the clergy of the cathedral began their communal life according to the revised regulations of the monastery. But it is more than occasional verse: when in 1064 the bishop set out for the

Rise of the Papacy

Holy Land, whence he was never to return, the Crusaders knew no other song which could better express their feelings.

Pilgrimages to the Holy Land were frequent in these decades. But Pope Gregory VII was the first to conceive the idea which summoned Western Christendom to a common journey. He was the man capable of uniting in one mighty stream all the sources of religious emotion which had sprung up here and there, and directing it as he would.

It was not from the papal throne that the call to free itself from the world went forth to the Church. The Reformers of Cluny were the first to declare war against simony and the marriage of priests. But their proposals were accepted by bishops and popes, of whom the most zealous was Leo IX, one of the German pontiffs appointed by Henry III. Three times in the six years of his pontificate he crossed the Alps: he spent some time in France and Germany—on the Rhine, in Lorraine, Franconia, Saxony, Bavaria—and summoned many synods. In this way he hoped to bind the bishops more firmly to Rome, and to inspire them with his own desire to fight for the freedom of the Church. When he accepted office, he took the young priest Hildebrand back to Rome with him. Hildebrand had spent more than a year in Germany as attendant to one of the popes deposed by Henry III, and afterwards some months in Cluny. Under the succeeding popes he became more and more the guiding spirit of Roman policy. The measures taken by the popes were made to serve the ends which he pursued. In the first place he established a new order of papal election. It decreed that the popes must be chosen from the cardinals, the highest rank of ecclesiastics, thus excluding the influence of the Roman nobility no less than that of the emperor. An epistle 'To All Men' announced the new order to Western Christendom. At the same time Hildebrand declared war in another field, no less significant for the relations between pope and emperor.

It was not only against 'simony'—the payment of dues on the acceptance of a religious office—that the Papacy had set its face. Rather it was exerting itself to exclude all lay participation in the bestowal of ecclesiastical offices—the so-called lay-investiture. If this point were carried, the German Crown would lose the right of filling the bishops' thrones.

The Empire of the Kaisers

Only a king who was subject to Church government could agree to this proposal: only a pope who aimed at setting the Church above all worldly authority could raise such a demand. This, and no other, was Hildebrand's object. The men of Cluny demanded the freedom of the Church: it was with the hope of divorcing the religious from the secular that they desired the abolition of simony and of the marriage of priests. But for Hildebrand, the separation of religious and secular authority was no more possible than the separation of soul and body. In his conception, the Church was set over the secular power by the same law which makes the soul master of the body. The Church must command, if it is to be free. The idea could not be carried out without a revolution in the accepted order, nor without a bloody struggle. Hildebrand knew this: but for him there could be no hesitation. He was indifferent to mankind, to their joys and sorrows. Only one idea had weight with him, and this idea he called Righteousness. To his God he prayed: 'Lord, take me from the earth, if thou wilt not use me for the welfare of Mother Church.' In his epistles the word of Jeremiah constantly recurs: 'The prophecy, cursed be the man who restrains his sword from blood, shall not be fulfilled in my case.'

He found allies for the fight. The Normans in southern Italy and Sicily held their land as vassals of the pope, and swore to support the Church of Rome with all their might, in every place and against all men. In northern Italy the Papacy gained support from the common people, to whom it appealed against the authority of the revolting bishops.

Popular opinion made such a step possible in Germany. After the war began, this possibility was successfully utilized by the Papacy. Everything depended upon the attitude of the German Government towards the demands of the papal chair. Hildebrand's conduct makes it probable that up to the last moment he was not clear on this point. This might well be the case: for changing influences at the Court gave rise to contradictory measures.

After the death of Henry III, his widow Agnes of Poitou acted as regent for the heir to the throne. In earlier times women had reigned in Germany, and the empire had not been ill-governed in consequence. But the Empress Agnes, a quiet, very religiously-minded woman, had not a strong hand, and she lacked highly placed advisers who would have made the affairs of the empire their own. In former crises, the bishops who were faithful to the king had stepped into the breach. Now the great dignitaries vacillated between loyalty to the empire and a leaning towards the new demands of the Church. Still less could the secular princes be depended upon: the regency offered them a welcome opportunity of recovering what they had lost, and of gaining new acquisitions.

Lords spiritual and temporal sought their own advantage, each man fighting sometimes for his own hand, sometimes in alliance with one or other of his neighbours. New men of humbler origin gained influence at Court: for the first time, vassals who were bound by their birth to socage service, obtained a share in the government. Imperial questions were decided by personal considerations. Rudolf of Rheinfelden, a young man of Burgundian origin obtained the position of a duke in Swabia and became the king's brother-in-law. A rumour was spread by the disappointed aspirants to the dukedom that the Burgundian had abducted the emperor's daughter from the care of her guardian, and had won his position by this bold stroke. Bavaria was given to the Saxon, Otto of Nordheim, Carinthia to a man who belonged to the noble family of Zähring. Such government by favouritism may have driven the lords spiritual and temporal to unite in a *coup d'état*. When the empress with her twelve-year-old son was staying at Kaiserswerth, the boy was enticed on to a ship and carried to Cologne. The mother seems to have made no attempt to recover him: she waited only till her son had been pronounced of age, and then sought peace in an Italian convent.

The business of the empire, and the education of young Henry, were now in the hands of Archbishop Anno of Cologne. But, as he took no steps to gain the boy's confidence, so he cared more for the affairs of his archbishopric and the promotion of his relatives than for the defence of the imperial rights. When he came to power, the empire was obliged to choose sides in the quarrel of the two popes. At a convocation of the bishops of Lombardy, where German bishops had also taken part, one of these had been raised to the Papacy in accordance with the new form of election, the other in defiance of it. In spite of her strict religious opinions the empress, after some hesitation, had declared for the second. Her convictions, however, were not strong enough to lead her to support him with an army.

Now the question had come up for final decision. Anno sent his nephew to Rome, where the choice fell upon the first pope whom Hildebrand had elected. The empire had given its consent to the encroachment upon the emperor's rights.

No later than the following year, Anno was forced to share his authority with Archbishop Adalbert of Bremen. He too was an ambitious man. Many years earlier he might have become pope, but had declined the honour. His great desire was to raise his own Bremen to the status of a northern Rome, and as a matter of fact it was during his period of office that the Archbishopric reached the highest point of its history. He was animated, cheerful, and fond of display, different in every respect from the reserved and taciturn Anno. It was no wonder that he won the lonely heart of the royal boy. When Henry was declared to be of age, he trusted himself wholly to the counsel of the Archbishop of Bremen. But this aroused the jealousy of the other princes: led by Anno, they threatened the king with the loss of his throne, unless he would remove Adalbert. Henry was obliged to submit. The empire did not gain by this measure. The bond-vassals now obtained a decisive preponderance at the Court. Under their influence the monarch, who was now grown up, tried to re-establish the power of the throne. The object was justifiable: but the means were so ill-chosen that the cleavage between the king and the nobles grew wider, and the ground was made ready for the papal pretensions.

Occasionally, under the leadership of Anno, and more frequently under that of Adalbert, the Government had conferred wealthy monasteries upon bishops and other great men. This created bad blood amongst the monks, who had become aware of their own importance: they were joined by powerful supporters, and in cases of open rebellion the Government did not always come off victorious. Moreover, the king was blamed for taking money from the bishops whom he elected: though this had been the recognized custom as late as the reign of Conrad II, it now met with embittered resistance. The injured parties made their way to Rome: the pope had become the umpire, where once the king's word had been law. He summoned

66

before his judgment seat the two most distinguished representatives of the German Church, the Archbishop of Cologne—the same Anno who had once had to decide the question of his recognition—and the Archbishop of Mayence: both were compelled to swear amendment.

When Henry resolved to fill the archbishop's throne at Milan against the will of the pope, the latter came for the first time into direct conflict with the emperor: he excommunicated his leading counsellors. This took place shortly before the death of the pope; when Hildebrand as Gregory VII became head of the Church, Henry acknowledged him, although his elevation to the Papacy had not in any respect followed the provisions of the new order. Henry gave way also in the matter of Milan. Once again the empire had acknowledged defeat.

Gregory believed that he could take a further step. No less than six bishops of the Archbishopric of Mayence were summoned to answer in Rome to the charge of simony. One bishop alone made his appearance. The quarrel rose to such a height that the Archbishop of Trèves, in the name of the lords spiritual of Germany, lodged a protest against the manner in which Gregory was handling the affairs of the Church.

At that time, as another German archbishop had indignantly written, the pope regarded the bishops as stewards of his property, and ordered them about as he liked. Why did not Henry take advantage of this temper?

The king dared not bring the matter to a decision by arms, because he himself was now in sore straits. He had been attempting to secure firm support in Saxony for his authority. The plan was a good one, so good that it has been correctly judged to be a legacy from the far-sighted statesman Adalbert of Bremen. In the low-lying country of Thuringia, where there were still some remains of royal property, and more which had been abandoned during the last decades, the king hoped to form a *congeries* of castles and royal estates, which would make him lord over the territory between Eisenach and Goslar, and would give him a firm grip of that important corridor. But in this undertaking he had to reckon with the mistrust of the princes, and the difficulties raised by those who were most nearly concerned.

The noblemen objected to the revival of antiquated royal

rights over their possessions, and the poor men to the burdens laid upon them in farming and building. The plan could only succeed if it were carried out with caution. But caution did not come into the calculations of the young ruler. All too long he had been forced to submit to the yoke of princely tutors and advisers: now he intended to be king and to make his power felt. His friends, who came from the ranks of the Swabian bond vassals, certainly did nothing to modify this determination. They lorded it in the new castles, gave judgment in the Swabian fashion, and made no attempt to adapt themselves to the native character of the population. Already the sensitive pride of the Saxons had been wounded: the king was holding the heir of the dukedom captive on account of the share he had taken in a revolt of Otto of Nordheim, and did not set him at liberty on the death of the old duke. When the nobles summoned the tribe to defend their rights, the great majority of the peasants answered the call. The Saxons assaulted the Harzburg. In the dead of night Henry escaped with a few companions. Guided by a huntsman, they journeyed for three days by secret pathways through the forests, without food or shelter, till at last they reached the Frankish territory.

The princes did not lift a hand to help the king. They rejoiced over his defeat: to some, even, the moment seemed favourable to shake off his yoke. In this situation Henry learnt of the elevation of Gregory VII to the papal chair. Now he reaped the benefit of the melancholy experiences of his suppressed childhood. For the moment he bowed to superior force, meaning, when better days came, to take up the struggle anew. In his humble letter to the pope, he gave the first proof of that statesmanship which at a later period was to extricate him from the most difficult positions. And soon his luck turned. The citizens of Worms had driven out their bishop, and given the signal for similar revolts in Cologne and Trèves. The episcopal cities had begun their fight for freedom—the middle classes were beginning to play their part in German history—and their first movement of independence turned in favour of that united power which was to make head against the princes. When Henry appeared at the Rhine, the men of Worms received him with acclamation and came to his help. His league with the cities had a salutary effect upon the lords spiritual, and when the king took the field once more against the Saxons they became parties to a treaty. It is true that Henry was obliged to consent to the destruction of the castles, but the unbridled licence shown by his enemies soon placed complete victory within his grasp. The desecration of the tombs of the Harzburg, including those of the king's kinsmen, constrained the princes to make common cause with him. In 1075 the Saxons were beaten and forced to unconditional surrender.

After this success, Henry could think of taking part in the controversy with the Papacy. The bitter feeling which the pope's actions had aroused amongst the bishops seemed to ensure him their alliance. The next steps taken by Gregory were calculated to strengthen the bond. While the war with the Saxons was drawing to a close, at the Lenten synod of the year 1075 the pope removed four German bishops from their office. At the same synod he pronounced the excommunication of five of the king's counsellors, and, for the first time, a general veto upon investiture.

It must be admitted that these measures were not in the first place directed against the king, but against the German princes of the Church. Gregory did not communicate to the king his decree against lay investiture. On the contrary, he offered to negotiate with him, and even expressed his congratulations upon the victory over the Saxons. On Henry's side, when he learnt of the veto on investiture, relations with the pope were not broken off. But he continued to nominate the bishops in Italy, showing that he looked for no result from negotiations. It would be unjust to blame him for this attitude. For Germany, modifications in form could make no change in the fundamental significance of the veto on investiture. If Gregory was of a different opinion, it was owing to the fact that he was not thoroughly conversant with German conditions. For more than a hundred years, the German kings had to a great extent disposed of secular property and secular rights of ownership to the spiritual lords. The fact that they possessed this power of disposal was one of the chief bulwarks of the throne. At a later date, a way was found out of the difficulty by making a distinction between investiture in the episcopal office and the disposal of Church property. But no one had yet thought of this distinction. For this reason war was inevitable.

The Empire of the Kaisers

But it was still doubtful who would take the decisive step. Henry was considering a march into Italy. The undertaking was not without prospects of success, for at the moment the pope was involved in difficulties in northern and southern Italy. But the decision was not taken. The king may have been deterred by the still unsettled conditions in Germany. Then Gregory struck the first blow.

In a letter which he wrote to Henry, in December 1075, he reproached him for his nomination of the Italian bishops and his intercourse with the excommunicated councillors, and warned him to be obedient to the command of God. Not a word was written on the subject of the investiture of the bishops in Germany. The verbal message given to the messenger was the less unequivocal: On account of his 'crimes'—that is to say, of his way of life—Henry must not only be excommunicated but deposed. This left no room for doubt as to what lay before the king, and now one event followed on the heels of another.

No later than January of the following year, a synod at Worms, in which twenty-four German bishops took part together with the king, decided that Gregory was no longer pope and could no longer reckon upon their obedience. This decision met with general approval, and it was probably at that time that Henry addressed the letter to the pope which contains the well-known words: 'Henry, king by God's appointment, and not by reason of unrighteous usurpation: to Hildebrand, who is no more to be called pope, but a monk full of deceit. . . . I, Henry, king by the Grace of God, together with all our bishops, we say to thee: come down, come down!' Scarcely a month later, a synod in the Church of the Lateran decided upon Henry's sentence, which was couched by the pope in the solemn form of a prayer to the Prince of the Apostles: 'Holy Peter . . . hearken to me, thy servant. . . . By virtue of thy power I take from King Henry, who in unspeakable presumption has risen up against thy Church, the command of the whole empire of the Germans and of Italy: release all Christians from the oath which they have sworn to him, and forbid anyone to serve him as their king. And because he has scorned to obey like a Christian, in thy stead I declare him to be excommunicated.'

Opinions may differ as to the apportionment of right and

Rise of the Papacy

wrong between king and pope. But it was no longer a question of who had right, but of who had might on his side. And the might was on the side of Gregory. Even if he had violated the form which was usual and valid in the Church, he was and remained pope, in spite of all declarations of bishops and king. Where he was, there was the Church. His auxiliary troops were formed from the monks who lived according to the revived rules, and the common people who at that very time were thronging to the German monasteries. Would the bishops take sides against them? The young king, who had with much ado escaped destruction in the Saxon war, was likely to prove a broken reed in the event of a popular rising. Neither could he be safely counted upon as a defence against Rome, for it was barely a year since, having felt his need of them, he had first approached the German bishops. Such considerations may have led many of the bishops to make their peace with the pope. The secular princes had still less inducement to declare for the king: to the majority, his difficulties offered a welcome opportunity of reaping their own advantage. Their defection set in no later than the summer of 1076. Already steps were being taken to elect a new king. But this does not seem to have been Gregory's wish: he desired to defeat Henry rather than to depose him. When at the Diet of Princes at Tribur the king promised the papal ambassador satisfaction and obedience, it seemed possible that an understanding might be arrived at with the pope.

But this prospect did not meet with the approval of the princes. With the object of preventing the lifting of the ban, they invited Gregory to consult with them and come to a decision respecting the king. If the nobility were to unite with the Papacy against Henry, he would be lost. Therefore at the last moment, in piercing winter cold, he took the road across the Alps.

He was accompanied by his consort, Bertha of Susa, and their little son of two years old, followers and serving-men, with a considerable number of councillors. His wife's mother, the widow of the Count of Savoy, gave them assistance in crossing the Alps, though not without adequate compensation. The pope was already on his way to Germany. Disquieted by the news of Henry's approach, he turned back and was received into the Castle of Canossa. He was

The Empire of the Kaisers

safe in the home of Matilda, Countess of Tuscany, who was devoted to his cause.

The partisanship of the times has made it difficult to judge of the further course of events. The following picture, with more or less variation, has been presented by later research. The king spent three days in the village at the foot of the castle, engaged in pious exercises: from time to time he climbed the hill, dressed as a penitent, and showed himself several times at the gate. Meanwhile negotiations were going on in which the countess and the Abbot of Cluny, Henry's godfather, who was also in the castle, acted as mediators. The king took upon himself to make his peace with the German princes within a certain time, according as Gregory should counsel or decide: and to ensure the pope a safe conduct into Germany. This the princes of the realm, who were present, promised upon oath. On the same day the castle gate was opened, Henry fell at Gregory's feet; both king and pope burst into tears. Then Gregory broke silence: he received the king and the other excommunicated persons back into Church fellowship, and gave them the sacrament.

Contemporary writers differ widely in their estimate of these events. One of the pope's adherents regards them as Henry's 'unprecedented humiliation': one of the most faithful of Henry's followers maintains that he received 'blessing in place of cursing.' Henry certainly humbled himself before the pope: not as a Christian before the Head of Christendom—for the fulfilment of the command of the Church neither could nor can imply humiliation—but as a king: he acknowledged the pope as arbitrator in matters which concerned the internal policy of Germany. But he gained various advantages by this humiliation. He was freed from excommunication; Gregory treated him once more as the King of Germany; it was no longer possible for the princes to appeal to the pope in their conflicts with him. Gain and loss were most closely intermingled, but afterwards Henry succeeded in balancing the loss by frustrating the establishment of the papal court of arbitration. This achievement ought to be placed in the foreground in any judgment upon Canossa. In itself it represents neither victory nor defeat: rather it represents the result which the king was able to draw from it.

The wisdom of Henry's action in turning to Gregory, in

order to avert the imminent alliance of nobles and pope, quickly became evident. There was nothing to hope from the princes. They elected a rival king in Rudolf of Rheinfelden, who had been Henry's brother-in-law. It is true that the number of bishops who took part in the election was not large, thus already showing one good result of the pilgrimage to Canossa. Henry drew his most reliable support from the upper and middle Rhine, and the south-east of the empire. In addition to the nobles, citizens and peasants flocked to his banner. The coronation of the rival king at Mayence immediately produced a revolt of the citizens, attended by much bloodshed: in the following year a crowd of peasants fought for him at the Neckar. Their common antagonism to the princes drew the king and the lower ranks of the people together. The war lasted nearly three years, while Gregory still hesitated to give his decision: he wished to wait for the moment when, as the arbitrator recognized by both sides, he could put an end to the conflict between the kings. Herein lay the weakness of his position. Henry made use of it in a masterly way, and kept the pope waiting till his chance was lost. For the longer the war lasted, the greater was the number of bishops who attached themselves to Henry. The old alliance between the throne and the lords spiritual was so firmly grounded in existing conditions, that its power began once more to be felt. In spite of occasional checks, Henry's authority was continually on the increase.

A witness to the growing power of the king is the transformation—almost, one might say, the rebuilding—of the cathedral at Spire. The foundation-stone of the cathedral had been laid about half a century earlier; now it was resolved to finish the interior with a vaulted roof. This decision may have been arrived at originally on practical grounds. The frequency of church fires, of which the records of that day inform us, must have suggested the idea of replacing the wooden roof by one of stone. At the same time this indicated a great artistic advance: for the first time, there was no break in the material unity of wall and roof. The upward spring of pillar and arch, no longer broken by horizontal rafters, could continue to soar unchecked in the curving lines of the roof. The ground-plan, the main body, and the individual details of the early Christian basilica had long since been transformed under German inspiration: a new building had been produced by this transformation—the Romanesque cathedral. The vaulted roof indicated the last step in the achievement of an independent style. Technical difficulties did not act as a deterrent; from ancient times single portions of the Romanesque churches—the burial places, the apsidal end of the choir—had been covered with a vaulted roof. The accomplishment of that final unity of artistic creation was due, not to the accumulation of technical experience, but to the extreme exertion of every faculty, which was apparent in the war between pope and emperor. The fact that a vaulted roof was in process of construction at Cluny, the stronghold of papal authority in the West, may have contributed to this result: the vaulting of the imperial cathedral would show the world that the supporters of the imperial dignity had no mind to yield place to the Papacy. This may also have been the reason why the king took that active interest in details such as the size of the windows, to which his faithful biographer calls special attention.

'This building is worthy of praise and admiration above all the works of ancient kings. What adornment in gold, silver, precious stones, and silken vestments the king has bestowed in addition upon this cathedral can scarcely be believed by those who have not seen them.' The most precious article in the treasure was the golden altar, a gift from the Emperor of Byzantium.

When Gregory could no longer shut his eyes to the fact that the time was past for papal arbitration, he came out openly on the side of Rudolf. Once more he launched a ban of excommunication against Henry, and announced to the people of Rome that if Henry did not repent, he would shortly die. But it fell out otherwise than the pope expected. On this occasion the excommunication produced only a negligible effect in Germany, and six months after Gregory's prophecy Rudolf was fatally wounded in battle against Henry. Gregory's action had no other result than to make the king resolve to do what he had neglected at the beginning of his conflict with the pope: he had a rival pope elected— the highly respected Archbishop Wibert of Ravenna—and marched with an army across the Alps.

In northern Italy, the adherents of the two parties encountered each other. Countess Matilda was not able alone to check the passage of the German army. Gregory's most powerful vassal, the Norman duke Robert Guiscard, was preoccupied with his own affairs. Henry arrived before Rome. But his army was not large. Again and again they attempted to storm the city: again and again the oppressive heat forced them to retire. At last in the third summer, at noon on a hot day, a squire, who was picking up arrows under the walls, discovered an unguarded spot: on his signal the nearest soldiers hastened up with ladders. So the city of Leo, on the right of the Tiber, fell into the king's hands: in the following year the gates on the left side opened to him. Wibert's election was confirmed by a synod: from his hand Henry and his consort received the imperial crown. Gregory held out in the Engelsburg, and Robert Guiscard was drawing near for his deliverance. The emperor set out for the north. Treachery opened the gates to the Normans, and they spread such terror with fire and sword that Gregory, who had summoned them, could not remain in their company. He died in the following year at the Norman Court at Salerno, summing up his life in these bitter words: 'I have loved righteousness and hated iniquity: therefore I die in exile.'

But Henry's life was opening out before him. At that time he was only thirty-five years of age. At last he succeeded in coming to an understanding with the Saxons, his bitterest enemies. This success forced the new rival king, who had been elected by some of the princes, to flee into Lorraine, where he died soon afterwards. Only in a few places did the war still linger on. Henry employed such moderation in reducing the confusion to order that even the majority of the bishops, who did not acknowledge Wibert as pope, submitted to the royal authority. But the strife still continued over church matters, and was now beginning to affect the heart of the nation. Bitterness increased with the number of controversial writings. A monk of the period, with Gregorian sympathies, wrote that the pope alone has a right to obedience. He who insists upon unconditional obedience towards any other man is a godless person and a blasphemer. Royal authority rests upon a covenant with the people: if the king governs ill, then he breaks that covenant, and the people are set free from their obligations. The arguments written in monasteries and bishops' palaces in support of both parties, were carried by monks and lay brethren into the houses of peasants and citizens, and into all places where people were gathered together on court days and market days. Women at their spinning-wheels, craftsmen in their workshops, quarrelled over the rival claims of emperor and pope. Again and again, stormy scenes were enacted in the churches while the priests were performing their office. Monks with whom the peasants were disputing the possession of a field were attacked by the armed mob, threatened, and roughly used.

The civil war in Germany could only be ended by peace between pope and emperor. But Urban II was as little disposed to concession as Henry himself. At first, indeed, it seemed doubtful whether he would be able to maintain his position against the emperor's rival pope.

Then Countess Matilda of Tuscany, who was forty-three years of age, took upon herself to strengthen the anti-imperial party by contracting a mock marriage with the seventeen-year-old son of Duke Welf of Bavaria. Access to Italy was jeopardized by the alliance of Henry's enemies in south Germany and central Italy.

Once more the emperor believed that he would be able, by a march over the Alps, to scatter his enemies before they were able to unite. But he did not know his opponent. Urban II cherished the same objects as Gregory: but he knew how to adapt the choice of means to the circumstances in which he was placed. Thus the success fell to him, for which the other had striven in vain.

The old allies of the Papacy, the cities of Lombardy and the Normans, came once more to his aid. He was able to win over the emperor's son, and his second wife, the daughter of a Russian grand-duke. Henry's son was crowned King of Italy, and swore fealty to the pope: his wife launched the most shameless accusations against her husband. This put new weapons into the pope's hands. The German throne had no longer a part to play in Italy: it was no longer a world-power. The time was ripe for putting an idea into practice which had already occurred to Gregory VII: through a great enterprise to make the papal leadership visible to the eyes of the whole world.

In 1095, at the Synod of Piacenza, Urban II renewed the sentence of excommunication against Wibert, the emperor, and their adherents, and preached a pilgrimage to the Holy Land. The summons was then carried into Burgundy and France. While the Papacy was raised to a triumphant height by the religious enthusiasm of the common people, the emperor seemed to have vanished out of sight and out of mind in some obscure valley. Only when the unnatural connection of Countess Matilda with the son of Welf was broken off, was he able to escape across the Alps out of the Veronese territory, where an asylum had been offered him.

It was with empty hands that he turned home again after seven long years. But events now began to work out more favourably than could have been expected; Germany was weary of strife. The emperor persuaded the princes to elect his second son Henry to be king, in place of the rebellious Conrad. Wibert's death made it easier to adjust the subjects of dispute. The great Church problems were not solved, but shelved. Henry had fought long enough for his imperial rights, now he assumed his kingly duties. His last years were filled with work in the cause of peace: the cause which was dearest of all to the common people was now nearest to the heart of the king. In 1103, at a diet in Mayence, universal peace throughout the empire was proclaimed for the first time. Peace in the country—for certain districts—had been known before: Henry himself at an earlier date had ordained a Peace of God over the whole empire, which under pain of Church penance forbade all private warfare during seasons of festival, and also between Wednesday evening and Monday morning. But the new peace of the empire, as he conceived it, was universal, and within the space of the four years during which it was valid, it knew no restrictions either of place or of time. Its penalties did not discriminate between free man or thrall.

'No man,' so the order ran, 'shall force his way into the house of another, or set it on fire. No one shall attack another with intent to rob him. He who offends shall lose eye or hand: he who defends the offender shall suffer the same punishment.' The work of peace encountered great obstacles, and would have required a longer time to overcome them. The assistance of the princes would have been necessary to make the peace effective, for the empire possessed no adequate organization. Still greater obstacles arose from the fact that the peace threatened at one stroke to rob an important class of its means of livelihood—the knights by whom the castles were manned, who were members of the lesser nobility

Their opposition destroyed what would have been a

blessing to the people at large. In Henry, the emperor's son, they found a man who made their cause his own. He may have viewed with concern his father's vain effort at reconciliation with the pope, which left the latter free at any time to ally himself again with the princes. He may have been afraid that the discontented nobles would throw difficulties in the emperor's path, and utilize a new war with the Papacy to effect his downfall. To ensure his own succession to the crown, he placed himself at the head of the malcontents. This was the hardest stroke of all for the emperor: a conflict with his own son, who was pulling down what he had built up with ceaseless care. Can one blame him for his hesitation, or for his offer to negotiate? It only fanned the embers of rebellion into a flame: the eastern territory was lost to the empire: the Rhine was to be the place of decision.

There the son professed himself willing to be reconciled, with such appearance of truth that the father dismissed his army, while the younger Henry undertook to win over the princes, who were assembled in Mayence, to the same peaceful course.

When the drawbridge of the neighbouring castle of Böckelheim was drawn up behind the emperor, he became his son's prisoner. In the palace of Ingelheim, he was compelled to read before him and the papal ambassadors a confession of sins which he had never committed, and to resign the throne. He escaped to Cologne, where the citizens came to his help: he found support among the nobles of Lorraine. His son's assaults were beaten back. There the emperor died, at the age of fifty-six. The pope's ambassadors refused him burial in consecrated ground: it was not until five years later that the corpse was solemnly interred in the cathedral at Spire. In the ceaseless battles, with which Henry's life was filled, he had won his way out of youthful impetuosity into prudence and strength, and through all changes had held fast to what he believed to be right.

For fifty years, if one reckons the years of the regency, the personality of Henry IV stood as the focus of the history of the empire: fifty years after his enforced abdication Frederick Barbarossa was crowned emperor. The half-century which divides the two monarchs witnessed the reign of three emperors from three different houses: Henry V, the last of the Salians; Lothar of Supplinburg, from the tribe of the Saxons; and Conrad III, the first of the House of Staufen. No emperor came even approximately near to reigning as long as the penultimate Salian and the second Hohenstaufen, and none has had the same influence upon the evolution of Germany. German history has followed the lines which were already clearly laid down under Henry IV: the preponderance of the Church and the growing strength of princely authority determine the course of this half-century. A brief survey will be sufficient. More vital for the future of Germany are the underground currents which were bearing her towards the secular glory of Barbarossa's empire.

Henry V was constrained by his own past to allow the princes greater influence in the affairs of the empire. It seemed natural to him, and was not contested by the lords spiritual, that he should also take part in the election of the bishops, and retain their investiture, with their secular rights, in his own hand. Where the bond-vassals were concerned, they never forgot that he had led them into battle against Henry IV. Thus he was able to cross the Alps at the head of a larger army of knights than any German ruler before him. The pope with whom he had to do made matters easy for him, and Henry profited to the full by his ignorance of German affairs.

The agreement between pope and emperor was read aloud in St. Peter's: the emperor would waive his right to the investiture of bishops, the pope would advise them to waive their right to Church property. Then came what Henry must have foreseen: a storm of indignation swept away the agreement. This was seized upon by the emperor as an excuse to hold the pope prisoner till he would give permission for investiture to be resumed in the old fashion, and promise to officiate at the coronation of the emperor. But the difficult problem was not to be solved by chicanery and violence. The opposition, which had first arisen in Italy and Burgundy, was steadily gaining ground in Germany: moreover, Henry was involved in increasing difficulties with the lords temporal. In the end the idea was victorious, that temporal and spiritual should share the right of the investiture of bishops: that to the Church must be rendered the things that were the Church's, and to the empire the things that were the empire's. On this foundation the Concordat of Worms came into being in 1122. It enacted that bishops should be chosen from the cathedral chapter, or the priests of the cathedral, in the presence of the king or of his representative. The one chosen should receive from the king his rights as a temporal ruler, and a sceptre in sign thereof, and from the pope his religious authority, with a ring and staff.

The great war had ended in a compromise. The Papacy had gained the point that the bishops should no longer be appointed at the caprice of the German kings, but the kings had retained the important right of participation in their election.

Henry V was the last scion of the Salian royal house. If his wishes had been followed, the princes would have elected his nephew, Frederick of Hohenstaufen, to succeed him. Under Henry IV, Frederick's father had attained to ducal power in Swabia: the son had increased the great possessions of the Staufen family on the upper Rhine and in Franconia. But the papal party were afraid that in his dealings with the Church he would follow in the footsteps of the last of the Salians. Their opposition was successful, for the other princes envisaged a limitation of independence at the hands of that powerful candidate.

For the first time in German history the right of descent was set aside at the king's election. The crown was bestowed upon Lothar of Supplinburg, a man whose sympathy with the Church could be relied upon. He could look back upon a long and successful life. As Duke of Saxony he had fought victoriously against the Slavs, and had given the county of Holstein to the noble family of Schauenburg, and the Markgravate of Meissen to that of Wettin: in 1134 he bestowed the Nordmark—the northern district—upon Albert the Bear, who came of the race of the Ascanien. With Lothar are thus connected the beginnings of German colonization east of the Elbe, which in later years was to attain such great importance. As king he could rely upon the papal party among the princes. With the help of his son-in-law, Henry the Proud, a duke of Bavaria belonging to the family of the Welfs, he also succeeded after a long struggle in forcing the Staufen to give up the claim to the imperial property which they advanced as heirs of the Salians. But his close connection with the Church compelled him to yield to the demands of the Papacy. He resigned his right of participation in the election of bishops, and accepted the possessions of the Countess Matilda of Tuscany from the pope, in feudal tenure, for which he agreed to pay him tribute.

How this action was viewed from the papal side is shown by a picture painted after Lothar's death for the Lateran. It shows the emperor as vassal, kneeling with clasped hands before the pope; the inscription reads:

The king becomes the pope's vassal, from him he receives the crown.

Lothar had nominated Henry the Proud as his successor. But seeing that Henry united under one government Bavaria, the inheritance which came to him from his father, with the dukedom of Saxony, and extensive possessions in Swabia and Italy, he would have been an unwelcome master to the German princes, and to the pope a dangerous neighbour. For this reason the Staufen now attained the end for which they had striven in vain at the time of Henry V's death. Conrad, the brother of Frederick of Hohenstaufen, was elected king. According to a contemporary, Conrad III was 'without doubt a brave warrior, and, as befits a king, of manly and noble disposition. But some evil fate hung over him, so that the empire began to totter.' Like his predecessor with the Staufen, he had to wrestle with the powerful Welfs: and other sources of disorder also claimed his time and labour. In the midst of these conflicts he heard Bernard of Clairvaux preach the Crusade from the pulpit of the cathedral in Spire. He was so impressed that he took the cross, which was more than the pope himself had expected.

The second Crusade, which led the king as far as the walls of Damascus, was without result. The king returned home a sick man, and died in a few years.

The throne lay in the dust, overthrown by the alliance between the princes and the pope.

THIRD PART

THE EVOLUTION OF THE POWER OF THE PEOPLE

BUT the next reign was to witness a revival of kingly authority.

Frederick I, the Red Beard, followed Conrad III. He ushered in the period which a romantically minded posterity has chosen to regard as the epitome of the glory of empire. It is true that for long years this empire was disputed, and after his death was as if it had never been. Yet there is a glory inseparable from the four decades of his reign, which casts into shadow all other periods of our empire's history. It is the glory attendant on all true and deep experience, both of individuals and of nations. This great experience came to the masses of Barbarossa's subjects, when for the first time they began to find their way out of darkness into light, under the guidance of a ruler in whom more classes than ever before could find the embodiment of their own ideals.

In the first centuries of the empire, under the Saxon and Salian emperors, the masses were largely dependent upon the feudal lord in economic, in social, and even in judicial matters. In the twelfth century a change began to come over this situation. The multitudes of nameless serfs fought their way out of dependence into some degree of freedom of action: the rabble of feudal tenants was formed into a community and became the peasant class. Hence arose the conditions which were with some variations to endure into the nineteenth century. Not till that date did the masses of the German peasantry win complete personal freedom, the right of independent property: only then could the peasant class begin to develop into what it is to-day. What happened in the twelfth and thirteenth centuries, therefore, was one of the most important transformations which our nation has experienced. Like other great changes in the national structure it cannot be traced to one or many groups of causes; it was not accomplished with tumult and shouting. Lines of development of the most varied nature converge for the making of the destined product—the new creation arrives unheralded. Who will decide, how free-will and necessity are interwoven? The

The Power of the People

peasants cannot be said to have acted with violence, for the object which they strove for was not denied. The feudal lords scarcely troubled themselves to defend the system on which their privileged position was founded: for that which had once been a power had lost its meaning and importance.

The king had been forced to grant land to the nobles because he was in need of functionaries and soldiers; feudal tenure had become hereditary property. The lords had to go through the same experience. They too needed increasing numbers of servants of the most varied kinds, and could only recompense them sufficiently by gifts of land: their tenure also became hereditary and was permanently withdrawn from the control of the giver. The more the feudal system developed, the more the foundations on which it rested were undermined. About the year 1150 'It was a scandal,' complains an abbot of the once-wealthy monastery of Fulda—'Laymen occupied all the fee-farms of the foundation. They gave and withheld what they pleased. When a layman had occupied a farm for some time, he kept the best fields for himself and his son inherited them by feudal right, so that more hides of land were lost than retained out of such a property.—There was yet another, still more insupportable wrong. The princes of the different territories took in fee what they pleased of the estates of the neighbouring monasteries, for no one said them nay. But the poorer sort broke into the woodlands belonging to Saint Boniface and tilled the land for themselves. The abbot resisted these evils with all his power, and succeeded in recovering some portion of all the estates, more of one and less of another.'

But such success was of short duration. The feudal lords were obliged to acknowledge that the mere possession of land no longer counted as a sound basis of authority. Therefore they were the more determined to stabilize and increase the revenues from their landed property. For a long time they had derived a great part of their income from the tributary tenants. Little by little the overlords reduced the area under their own management, and gave away to the peasants good portions of the land which had once been cultivated from the manor. In return the peasants agreed to a fixed tribute, or frequently to a payment in money. The manor still stood, but it was no longer the

83

centre of great agricultural activity. The authority of the feudal lord had been exchanged for property, yielding rent. By this means the overlord was relieved from the anxiety of managing his estate, and was free to devote himself to political and military enterprises. These were likely to produce larger revenues, and were more adapted to the changing times. More and more, as agricultural work sank in general estimation, deeds of chivalry alone seemed to be worthy of effort.

Those tenants who were ambitious of improving their condition took advantage of this development. Tributary tenants succeeded in having their copyhold made heritable; all who could, tried to obtain as copyhold fief a plot of land which had hitherto been under cultivation by the feudal lord. When the rendering of tribute was changed into the payment of a fixed sum of money, every class of peasant reaped the advantage. They had no need to fear any considerable raising of the rent, and the gradually increasing yield of the fields accrued to the peasants themselves. The services which the feudal lord was still able to demand were only unwillingly and grudgingly rendered. 'If a man had to serve the monastery for fourteen days, he served for barely eight, and he who had eight days' service to render, worked at most for three days or for none at all.' So by degrees the tenants won a greater right of disposal over their own labour. Similarity of employment became the criterion of social position, and the old distinction gradually disappeared between the descendants of freemen and thralls.

All who owed tribute to the manor formed a feudal community. All were subject to the law of the manor, which consisted of a collection of traditional rights and customs: all work in house and field was carried on as the community ordained: all celebrated their festivals in common, and helped each other in time of need. Thus the feudal community was a fellowship of law and labour; it regulated social and moral relations.

In the course of the twelfth and thirteenth centuries almost all the ground suitable for cultivation was brought under the plough. About 1250 the area of cultivated land, in distinction to forest, between the Rhine and the Elbe was practically as large as it is now. The forest was preserved as it then stood: its chief product was valuable

The Power of the People

timber. At that period, also, there arose so many village settlements, that at the present day their total number is not essentially greater. In any comparison between then and now, one must take into consideration the fact that many villages were wiped off the face of the earth by wars and pestilence, while others developed into towns. Through the labour of its peasants Germany became a fruitful and blooming country: the plain of the upper and middle Rhine was known as 'The Garden of Germania.'

In other walks of life also, community of work was being recognized as a growing force. The same century which saw the rise of the peasant class, witnessed the formation of the middle class and the flowering of chivalry. The 'burgher' or citizen took his name from the 'burg'—or fortified settlement. The name is old, and was attached to those who bore it, at a time when it stood for something quite new and strange in the world of the early Middle Ages. The 'burg' had a place within the framework of feudal economy: here lived the lords of the manor, with their serving-men, both free and bond. The burgher was distinct from them all, in so far as his existence was not unconditionally dependent upon the possession of land or the will of a landowner. It is true that the citizens of the Middle Ages practised cattle-rearing and agriculture, more or less extensively: even cities such as Lübeck, which we are accustomed to regard as purely mercantile, possessed much pastoral land. In the Middle Ages, pigs and cows were common sights in the streets of the largest cities.

But the citizen was even then something other than a peasant, adept at manual labour and practising a trade; the city was something other than a great village. Cities could only arise where, as in the case of bishops' seats, there was greater demand, and a supply sufficient to meet it by barter. These conditions were present in bishops' seats, which were often to be found in the south and west in former Roman cities (Augsburg, Cologne, Mayence, Trèves), or in the neighbourhood of monasteries (Essen, Hersfeld) or royal palaces (Frankfort on the Main, Mühlhausen, Nuremberg), or the castles of counts or knights.

Here the peasants, artisans, and merchants assembled on regular market days. This was well-pleasing to the lord of the manor, for most agreeable profits accrued from market, toll, and coining rights, as well as from the court

85

of justice and the town-watch. All these rights were in the king's gift. A cross, which was set up on the market-place, sometimes with a sword, a hat, or a glove hung upon it, was the sign of the King's Peace, and threatened the disturber with severe punishment. In the north-east particularly, a stone giant—Roland—stood, from the four-teenth century, as a sign of the city's jurisdiction. Market days followed each other at ever shorter intervals. Artisans and merchants, who could count upon considerable gains, built a little wooden house beside their market stall, and took up their abode there. This origin is clearly to be seen in the houses on the market-place of Münster in Westphalia. Thus a new settlement was formed at the gates of the old: in the latter the lord of the manor resided with his people —the *Familia*—in the former the 'citizens,' who lived by trade and commerce. In time the new settlement was also fortified. In many market towns, the two dwelling-places stood for a long time side by side, arousing violent con-troversy between the lord of the manor, who wished to hold fast by his own rights, and the new settlers, who intended to manage their affairs in their own way. The various revolts of the citizens of the Rhineland against their bishops had their origin in these disputes (p. 68). At last settlements of this kind also developed into one urban community: on every hand the new proved itself stronger than the old.

Many of the new settlers were freemen: a strong con-sciousness of brotherhood united them all, founded upon the similarity of their position, their needs, and their aims. The lord of the manor was forced for good or ill to come into contact with them. There were economic questions which could only be settled by agreement with the citizens' representatives: moreover, if new immigrants were not to be discouraged, it was necessary to treat them with con-sideration. Now and again the king or prince of the country interfered in favour of the citizens. Henry IV and Henry V freed the inhabitants of Worms and Spire from paying taxes to the royal custom-houses, and from burdensome obligations towards their feudal lord. Conrad of Zähringen ensured to the citizens of Freiburg in Breisgau this right amongst others to elect their own bailiff (*Vogt*) and priest, and to superintend their own market through market inspectors. Such privileges reacted in time upon the less

The Power of the People

fortunate cities. Ready money was to prove itself the town-dweller's best ally; an income in cash became of special value at a time when the ownership of land had lost its former significance as a basis of authority. Under these circumstances the urban community was able to attain to an increasing measure of self-determination.

City air brought liberty—every man living in the city received his freedom after a year and a day, if the feudal lord did not establish his claim upon him. No citizen could be constrained to armed service, except in defence of the city. The same law applied to all—a municipal law, which was suited to the special economic circumstances of the citizens. In judicial matters all were subject to the representative of the feudal lord, who was as a rule elected by themselves: in matters of administration to the municipal council. But it was not long before the municipal council exercised the entire function of government, judicial and administrative. As a general rule, the feudal lord was able to demand a small tribute only, for the plots of land which were acquired by the citizens: only those citizens acquired municipal rights who possessed a piece of land within the city.

Personal freedom, legal equality, universal military service, and a common interest in meeting the costs of expenditure—especially those entailed by the defence of the city—these were the foundations of the municipal system. Amidst the disintegration of the feudal state, the germs of a new body politic were coming to life in the cities.

The countryman was strongly attracted by these freer conditions of life. From the eleventh to the thirteenth century there was a steady increase in the population of Germany, which was most apparent in the years between 1100 and 1200. Already the east absorbed a proportion of the surplus, but it was not until the thirteenth century that the colonization of east Germany began in earnest. Up to that date the cities were the chief goal of all for whom life on their native soil was too circumscribed, its compulsory service and tribute too oppressive. Specially rapid was the growth of those town settlements which were founded in the midst of a fruitful countryside—at the river fords, or at the junction of important trade routes. As late as the seventeenth century, the citizens of Worms were able to boast that its market was attended by peasants

The Empire of the Kaisers

from a hundred villages. How great was the importance of the trading centre is proved by a summary of the development of the cities of east Germany. We learn from this source that out of the three hundred cities which are known to have been founded in that territory, only approximately thirty grew beyond the confines of a small agricultural town. In certain cases, moreover, the utilization of natural resources and special traditions affecting the artisans favoured the development of a city. There were salt cities such as Lüneburg and Halle, mining cities such as Goslar and Freiberg: Nuremberg was already known for its hardware—toys from Nuremberg, linen from Constance, swords and helmets from Cologne, armour from Innsbruck, sword-blades from Passau, were all highly esteemed. Special fame attached to the green and dark blue cloth of Flanders, reddish cloth from Swabia, and the self-coloured cloth made of coarse wool from Regensburg.

By the year 1200 certain cities, such as Cologne and Brunswick, had already covered the area whose dimensions were not to be exceeded till the nineteenth century: the same is true of Erfurt. The sacred city of Cologne surpassed all others. In the year 1180 its citizens began to fix a new line of ramparts and moat: the area of the fortified city was greater than that of the two cities next in size—Strasburg and Augsburg—taken together. For nearly 700 years the area of the city remained essentially unaltered; not till the fortifications were demolished could it find space for new development.

But a considerable time was yet to elapse before the cities became a power in political life. In the beginning, the whole energy of the citizens was expended upon earning a living, and shaping the life of the growing city. The typical child of his age was he who only awaited his lord's command to take shield and sword down from the wall, and leap upon his charger. Such men were required by kings and princes in ever-growing numbers.

From the beginning of the struggle over investiture, down to the middle of the twelfth century, Germany was filled with war. Frederick I created peace, but he built many new castles to make his possessions secure. In those days there was a popular saying about one of his ancestors: 'Duke Frederick always has a new castle to draw at his horse's tail.' Frederick I was not far behind him: the

The Power of the People

majority of the castles, whose ruins overlook the valleys from the heights of the Swabian mountains, were built in his time. Many of the princes imitated the emperor. The number of free-born knights was not adequate: they were soon outnumbered by the bond vassals. The profession of chivalry produced the same effect as the calling followed by peasants and citizens: community consciousness sprang from identity of occupation, bridging over inequality of birth. Free and bond were blended into one knightly class. The knight was differentiated by his military service from peasants and citizens, who lived by the work of their hands. His privileged position was protected by a special system of law. A peculiar and highly developed notion of honour, together with a refinement of customs, united in a lofty fellowship all who belonged to the profession of chivalry. Knighthood represented the leading class in the social structure.

The profession brought a growing influence to bear upon the shaping of life in all fields of secular activity. The right of birth was now balanced by the right which was founded upon achievement, thus loosening the rigidity of the national structure. Before that time it had been almost impossible for an able man to rise, except in the priestly class: a career was now gradually thrown open to those also who lived in the world. It was not given to everyone to grasp the good fortune which beckoned him. Once upon a time an Italian city was being besieged by Frederick I on a march towards Rome: in advance of the rest a stable-boy rushed to the hill on which the fort was built. With a little axe, such as these men used to carry at their saddle-bow, he cut himself steps in the rock and climbed upwards, paying no heed to the innumerable missiles which were hurled upon him from above. An armed knight met him at the battered gate of the city. Although the stable-boy carried neither shield nor sword, nor any weapon save his axe, he overthrew the knight and came off unhurt. The emperor sent for him and would have dubbed him knight upon the spot. But he replied, he was a plain man and preferred to remain in his own class: with this he returned to the horses under his care. There were others, however, whose actions had distinguished them from their fellows, who were able to adapt themselves to the new situation.

The magic charm of hope threw its glamour over the

lives of the people and lent wings to their days. What had once been a barren wish now seemed to be attainable. Property, honour, and power beckoned more imperiously. The age became more worldly—labour more joyous. Pride in one's calling was openly professed, and first by the knights. Wolfram von Eschenbach, who as few others have done discerned the reality through the gay world of appearance, proclaims his pride in his calling: 'Schildes ambet ist min art' ('My very life is in my profession of arms'). A poet of the thirteenth century makes an old peasant extol the value of his labour:

> Now let us drive the spade and share;
> For certes, many a lady fair
> Is fairer for the crops we grew:
> Many a king is monarch too,
> Because our harvests brought him gain—
> The proud man boasts himself in vain:
> His pride and boasting could not stand
> Unless the peasants tilled the land.

It is not till a later date that the work of the townsmen gets its meed of praise. Yet the scanty records which we possess prove that the property of certain cities could even then compare with that of the great feudal lords. About the middle of the eleventh century, when the Archbishop of Mayence journeyed to the Holy Land, he was accompanied by a great number of wealthy citizens, a fact which aroused much remark at the time. A few decades later, a citizen of Mayence sent to a community of monks eleven wagon-loads of wine, and through his gift made it possible to found a new monastery. Such citizen foundations were of frequent occurrence in the Rhineland towns.

Men were now able to use their calling as a path to advancement. The barriers which separated one calling from another had not yet become insurmountable. When a man saw a better prospect of advancement along a new path, he could adopt it without great difficulty. A wealthy steward might be granted a knight's fief, build a castle beside his farm, and ally himself with the nobility. There was then no strict division between artisan and shopkeeper, tradesman and wholesale merchant: the man who made the goods himself offered them for sale, and often carried them to foreign markets. If he were an enterprising

The Power of the People

man, he might easily come to devote himself entirely to trade, as being more profitable, and gradually rise to the respected position of the wholesale dealer. The growth of economic and social opportunity forced men to become more versatile: their growing familiarity with foreign customs and points of view worked in the same direction.

Many thousands of German knights and squires, secular priests, and monks travelled with the Hohenstaufen into Italy and the East. Even at an earlier date travelling students had not been rare: but it was not until the twelfth century that the figure of the wandering scholar was evolved, idling his way through the world, and singing his own verses in praise of wine, women, and song. Many of the more ambitious attended the high schools of France, where the new scholastic philosophy was coming to maturity. Rainald of Dassel, Frederick the First's Chancellor, Otto of Freising, the emperor's uncle, Vizelin, the apostle of eastern Holstein, and many others who came to eminence, spent years of their youth in France. His journeys took the German merchant ever farther afield in foreign parts. Merchants from the Rhineland visited the fairs in Champagne. Frisians sailed as far as Iceland and Greenland; as early as the twelfth century the Baltic towns dominated the trade of many places in Scandinavia. Under Henry VI captains from Bremen and Lübeck sailed at times as far as the Levant. Tradesmen of southern Germany kept up regular communication with the Italian ports. Citizens of Regensburg had relations with the countries on the Danube and with Constantinople. Artisans and minstrels also undertook long journeys: we find German masons in France and Italy, German miners in Hungary, and, somewhat later, in Serbia.

Peasants who had settled in the new eastern territory returned to the old home in the hope of persuading others to emigrate. News of strange men and manners penetrated Germany through innumerable channels, working a revolution in life and thought. The horizon expanded immeasurably and the heart swelled with the consciousness of being a citizen of this great world. Only once again, at the end of the eighteenth century, did the Germans relive this experience.

Their contact with the Eastern world was particularly fruitful. Relations with Byzantium were newly established

The Empire of the Kaisers

under the Saxon emperors (p. 37): they can be clearly traced in the development of art (p. 56). In the twelfth century, the capital of the Eastern Roman Empire acquired additional importance as a meeting-place for the Crusaders, and as a most important market for goods. Even before the Crusades, the Mohammedan Levant exercised a powerful influence upon the south and west of Europe; the Germans were its debtors in many ways, chiefly through their utilization of the high scientific attainments of the Arabs. These gifted people had adopted much of the precious culture of the late period of the Syrian and Egyptian Empires—of the Jews, Indians, and Persians. Arabian scholars translated the writings of the Greek philosophers, mathematicians, naturalists, and physicians into their own language: the taste of Arabian artists was formed upon the edifices which were the legacy of the Romans, and they in their turn erected magnificent buildings, with rounded arches, slender towers, and cupolas. In Spain, in particular, the Moorish universities imparted the wisdom of the Arabs to Occidental students. Christian scholars there increased their knowledge of astronomy and mathematics, though the method of reckoning with 'Arabian' figures and with letters (Algebra) was adopted later. They translated the works of Greek physicians from Arabic into Latin, they became acquainted with new remedies and new treatment of disease, and studied their application under Jewish physicians. Hartmann von Aue makes his *Poor Henry* seek a cure first in Montpellier and then under the wise master in Salerno: both were centres of Arabian science.

New connections were formed through the Crusades, which soon made themselves felt in daily life, at least in the upper classes of society. In foreign parts, the Crusaders had become acquainted with many things which seemed to them desirable. The Italian ports were monopolizing the trade with the Levantine coast towns: goods from Italy were sent to Germany, to be conveyed to the northern and eastern countries of Europe. Germany was beginning to be involved in world-trade, which had formerly ignored her. Goods now reached the German merchant at second-hand, which had formerly come to him through three or four intermediaries: food and luxuries such as rice, sugar, spices, rare clothing materials, cotton, damask (from

The Power of the People

Damascus), muslin (from Mosul), silk and velvet, works of art, such as carpets woven in many colours, embroideries, ivory carvings, objects in gold and enamel, and many others. New habits were introduced with these objects: the women learned to use powder and scent, the men to wear a beard: rich clothing began to be appreciated: dwelling and sleeping rooms were provided with softly upholstered furniture. Fortifications and military equipment of all kinds were further developed after the Arabic model: the magnificent castles of the Levantine princes aroused the German nobles to emulation. Even their attitude of mind was affected by the same influence. Many a man who had left his home burning with fierce fanaticism, was unable to shut his eyes to the superiority of Arabic civilization. He learnt to respect the religious opinions of his enemy, and came back a more tolerant man than he had set out. The Crusaders were affected no less powerfully by the experiences which they underwent in common, than by these foreign influences. Knights from all countries of the world began to feel themselves members of a homogeneous brotherhood—advanced nations became tutors to the backward. The opportunity was eagerly seized by the Germans, always desirous of learning. Even at that period, it was customary in better society to interlard the native speech with French words: the German poetry of chivalry contains marvellous examples of such forms of greeting and courtesy. The communal life of the Crusades also sharpened their insight into the peculiarities and failings of other nationalities and the merits of their own. Violent altercations, frequently ending in blows, were of common occurrence amongst the knights of the different nations. Yet in the end, the massing together of so many types of virile manhood was calculated to strengthen the leaning to secular ideals, as the ill success of the later Crusades must have undermined their confidence in the papal leadership. The horizon was expanding; men were becoming more conscious of their common humanity. This too was one of the effects of the Crusades, and not by any means the least important.

But the time was still far distant when men would dare to take their own conscience as the law of their being. The Church was, and remained, the director of man's conscious life. The outward and visible signs of attachment to the Church were daily increasing: the worship of the saints and their relics became more and more widespread—(there were churches which possessed over five hundred relics)—and pilgrimages became more frequent. Side by side with this went an eager striving to penetrate more deeply into the mysteries of the faith—to bring life more into line with doctrine. To this desire one may attribute the rise and spread of new religious communities. About the year 1100 the orders of the Cistercians and Premonstratensians were founded in France, the second by the German Norbert, who was later to become Archbishop of Magdeburg. Both orders were founded upon the common principle of strict discipline, to be maintained by means of a close union of the monasteries, and yearly conferences between the leaders.

Similar ideals were active outside the orders—in many collegiate churches, the canons lived like monks.

Yet the new orders themselves offered an example of the active piety which was striking out new paths. Their starting point was detachment from the *ego*, and they aimed at exerting a more powerful influence upon the world outside the monastery. The 'Grey Brothers' of the Cistercian Order devoted themselves particularly to work on the land. While all around them the property of the feudal lord was being let out to tenants, they cultivated their domains themselves, with the help of many lay brothers. Their work as husbandmen is inseparably bound up with the colonization of eastern Germany: they showed themselves particularly adept at making swampy districts habitable. The Premonstratensians took up with peculiar zeal the task of preaching and the cure of souls. Both orders set a higher ideal before them than that of the Benedictines. They broke with the monkish tradition, which set the cultivation of one's own *ego* as the central point of the religious life. But the novice who renounced the world to enter a new order was inspired by the duty of working for the world outside the monastery walls. At one time the monks had sought renown in the pursuit of religious learning and in teaching and educating their scholars. Now their ambition was seeking a new outlet. But even the Benedictines no longer took the lead in learned activities. In France new methods of learning and instruction had been evolved: but it was very rarely that a manuscript dealing with these

The Power of the People

subjects found its way into the library of a German monastery. In this respect Germany lagged behind her neighbours.

Yet a rich reward awaited the efforts of the religious, who were increasingly anxious to abandon their isolation and to help in solving those questions which were agitating the lay world. In former centuries the monks had already recorded the events of their time: during the struggle over the investiture many of the controversial writings issued from monasteries. With the coming of peace, they resumed their task of recording the history of the empire, the bishopric and the monastery, and the lives of prominent men. But here and there the religious historian seems to follow the course of the world's history with new sympathy and a less hampered judgment: it may even happen that he no longer addresses himself exclusively to religious readers.

This is true in both respects of the work of Bishop Otto of Freising, who wrote about the year 1150. He came of the race of the Babenbergs. The emperor Frederick I was his nephew. In his youth he entered the Cistercian Order: he gives enthusiastic praise to the monkish profession, which renounces all earthly good. But his keen sympathy with monkish renunciation does not dim his clear vision of practical things: he looks upon the material possessions of the monastery as the gift of God. What God has designed will come to pass. Right and wrong, success and failure, work together to a higher unity; every growing thing creates its own opposite, till in the end the ever-renewed antithesis finds its point of agreement.

It was from this point of view that Otto wrote his work *On the Two Kingdoms*. To him, as to Augustine and his many imitators, the course of history represents the conflict between the Kingdom of God and the kingdom of this world: but the idea gains unwonted life and warmth under his treatment. When he describes how the good must suffer and the great must be brought low, he grips the reader with the force of a personal experience: his view of the eternal triumph of the Reign of God is the fruit of his own hope and full of sweet consolation. In order to elucidate the thoughts in his first book by applying them to current events, he wrote a second entitled *The Deeds of Frederick*. Even if its intention does not vouch for the truth of the whole picture, Otto's work marks a turning-point in the

95

The Empire of the Kaisers

historical writing of the Middle Ages. It draws upon material of unique range and fullness, and claims not only scholars, but the outside world for its readers.

While Otto was working at his books, simpler authors had been making their appeal in German to a wide public. About the year 1100 the Life of Archbishop Anno of Cologne was written, and about 1150 a rhymed *Chronicle of the Emperors*. In both cases the authors were priests: both take a wide sweep, and both enrich their subject with a store of theological learning. But they have also in common the habit of addressing themselves to the laity, in the manner of travelling minstrels: the writer of the *Chronicle of the Emperors* occasionally employs a style to which the knights must have listened with pleasure.

In addition to the few scattered works on historical subjects, those books dealing with religion in which the priests addressed themselves in the German language to the 'man in the street' became ever more numerous. They ranged from stories out of the Old and New Testaments, legends and narratives of pilgrimages in the other world, to songs in praise of the Virgin, a comment on the Lord's Prayer, and bitter censure of unworthy priests. For a time the Christmas and Easter miracle plays still clung to the Latin tongue, but their scope was gradually enlarged and German songs were introduced. The Easter hymn 'Christ is risen': the Whitsuntide hymn 'Now pray we the Holy Ghost'—go back to the time of Barbarossa. The revolt of the stricter-minded against such secularization drove the miracle play at times out of the church, and made it at home in more secular places. The work of these clerical poets is not to be compared with the secular writing of the period. Yet their achievement was of supreme importance. By introducing an abundance of fresh thought and sensation to the people at large, they brought a contribution of imperishable value to the mind of the community.

Other arts which stood at the service of God, now felt the same urge to communicate their riches. The language of form became more eloquent, the sublime took on more gentle features. This change was owing in particular to the efforts of the monks. For architecture, which still held the first place amongst the arts, was in the twelfth century no longer encouraged, as in former times, by the bishops, and only in isolated cases by the emperors: worldly ambition now occupied the chief place in their thoughts. The joy which the princes and lords took in building was now not seldom seen in the planning of spacious dwellings: one may mention the imperial palace of Henry III in Goslar in the eleventh century; in the twelfth, Henry the Lion's castle at Brunswick, and the palace of Frederick I at Gelnhausen. But such edifices were not yet as numerous as the cathedrals, while abbey churches were still being built in great numbers.

The vaulted building, which was the last great achievement of Romanesque architecture, was more and more generally adopted: first on the Lower Rhine and in Westphalia, and by the second half of the century, in south Germany also. Saxony, which still held the first place in the eleventh century, gave the lead to the Rhineland provinces. The 'Lion's tracks' may still be traced in Saxon architecture: Henry had the church of St. Blasius built in connection with his ducal castle in Brunswick, and founded the cathedrals in Lübeck and Ratzeburg. Local diversities are obvious. There is an infinite difference between the Westphalian style of architecture, which is the embodiment of permanence, and the rich maturity of the Rhenish building. Yet certain common features are more or less evident in these structures: the Rhenish churches abound in towers, which range from slender turrets to the massive tower above the intersection of the nave. The outer wall is divided perpendicularly by arcades (*Lisenen*) connected under the principal cornice by a frieze of rounded arches: the entrance is elaborated into a doorway with pilasters or pillars. The richest detail is found in the great Rhenish cathedrals which were completed in the last decades of the twelfth century. In addition to the detail just mentioned, the mass of the wall in the west choir of the cathedral at Worms is broken up by blind niches on the ground floor, great rosettes in the centre storey, and graceful inter-columniation underneath the spring of the roof ('dwarf-galleries'). A wealth of individual forms is subordinated to the ruling conception: liberty in unity is the peculiar mark of the chief period of Romanesque architecture.

Architecture found a sister art in sculpture. Forms of decoration which in earlier times were painted upon portions of the building were now carved by the stonemason

out of the material of the structure itself. Figures of men
and animals began to sport on the capitals of the pillars
and above the doors. Their prevalence in the churches of
southern Germany may perhaps be accounted for by the
greater share taken in the work by travelling journeymen
from Lombardy. Sculptors now ventured to carve the image
of the Crucified and the figures of dead saints as reliefs, or
to represent them as independent figures. The representation of the Descent from the Cross upon the so-called
'extern stones' in the forest of Teutoburg, is over fifteen
feet high. Dating from the year 1115, it is still timid in
expression, but defined with extraordinary clearness: it
is the oldest example of German sculpture of large size
whose date can be fixed with certainty. Other representations of the Crucified were gradually set up in the
majority of the churches: from the roof of the centre aisle,
suspended above the entrance to the choir, the image of
the sublime sufferer dominated the interior. The oldest
works of this kind which have come down to us, carved
in wood or moulded in brass, date from the eleventh and
twelfth centuries.

The greatest advance had been made in the art of brass-
founding, and it was increasingly put to secular uses.
Since the beginning of the eleventh century, when the
Fall and Salvation of Man had been portrayed on the
gates of Hildesheimer Cathedral, the art of brassfounding
had become indigenous in Saxony. From the brass on the
tomb of Rudolph of Swabia, which was executed soon
after 1080, there is a steady improvement in execution,
till the magnificent bronze lions were produced, which
Henry, Duke of Saxony set up in 1166 before his castle in
Brunswick. It is true that such an animal had never been
seen by the sculptor: a small Byzantine vessel made in
the shape of a lion may have served him as a model. But
he has really represented the king of beasts.

The goldsmiths alone could bear comparison with the
brassfounders. An ingenious and clear plan of construction
is as evident in the great candelabra which Frederick I
presented to the Minster at Aix, as in the Shrine of the
Three Kings at Cologne.

Painting did not keep pace with the working of metal:
the change in the style of building limited the scope of
the wall-painter, while the art of the illuminator suffered

The Power of the People

by the alienation of the new orders from learning. Here and there, it is true, beautiful prayer-books were still produced in the old style by expert monks. Yet the pen drawings which have come down to us are more remarkable, as the instinctive outlet of that great need for expression, which was typical of this period. Some hundreds of these drawings adorned the 'Pleasure Garden' (now unfortunately destroyed) of the abbess Herrand of Landsberg in Alsace. What an observant eye this woman possessed, how freshly she could render what she saw! And—what unrestrained *joie de vivre* lives in her little pictures!

But the decisive factor lay in this, that secular poets began to sing of the sweet and bitter of life in the world, not as part of their stock in trade, but as the expression of their own deeper and wider experience. By right of his property and calling, his education and training, the knight was free to develop his own personality: he was most strongly influenced by the changing times, and became the representative of the new poetry.

The natural man, untrammelled by the religious point of view, delighted to open his heart to the pleasures of nature. During the 'Spring-time of the Minnesingers' the song of birds, the rippling of brooks, the beauty of flowers, the passing of Summer, play and dance on the heath, courage of men and beauty of women, the joys and pains of love, all unite in a lofty song, which breathes from every line the love of nature.

It is a song, such as the world had not listened to since the far-off days of antiquity. Unknown men and women in the early period, and, at the beginning of the thirteenth century, the bearers of famous names, alike sing of nature and love: narrative poets vie with masters of lyric song. The Song of the Nibelungs gives warning that 'Sorrow at last may be, even for the youngest, the wages of Love'; but it tells also how the bright sun is mirrored in the weapons of heroes. Wolfram von Eschenbach, who can enter into a woman's feelings better than any other of his time, is no less able to describe the magic of the woodland solitude and the awe of the falling night.

The newly discovered note of a sentiment common to all mankind, blends with the full tone of Christian piety. The first duty of the day is to go to church: before the battle the knight makes his prayer to God. After the

The Empire of the Kaisers

victory he thanks the Lord: His name is named in greeting and farewell, in request and thanks. Battle for the Faith, defence of the Church and its servants, is laid as a duty upon the novice when he is dubbed knight. When Walther von der Vogelweide grows old, he unites a melancholy review of his past life with a flaming summons to the Crusade:

> Bethink you, knights, bethink you: / it is not yours to fail
> Ye wear the shining helmet / and trusty coat of mail:
> The strong shield to defend you / the consecrated sword.
> To conquer in this battle / would I were meet, O Lord!

Upon this foundation of feeling for religion and for all mankind grew the virtues, to which the knight laid claim for himself and his peers, as members of the order of chivalry. The first is knightly courage, which is proved in armed service. It summons the knight, not only to fight bravely in his Lord's battles, but also to seek adventure and conquest, possessions and honour in foreign countries. By training and by ceaseless practice, he must set himself to develop and maintain dexterity in the use of weapons and a warlike mind. From the profession of arms sprang also the knightly ideal of honour. In addition to the Teutonic virtues of courage, faithfulness, and generosity, it includes a number of social obligations, the defence of the weak, the sparing of a conquered foe, while it made at least one moral demand upon its followers—constancy— the firm will which cannot be shaken. These were cultivated in common with the knightly virtues, which were included in the comprehensive idea of discipline: a noble bearing, becoming gestures, rich clothing and all kinds of social accomplishments, such as knowledge of hunting usages, proficiency in dancing and playing the harp. But discipline requires an inner culture—an avoidance of the too much and the too little in feeling, demeanour, and speech. Its fairest flower was that noble *Moderation*, which corresponds perhaps in some degree with the Greek ideal of virtue, and the modern idea of balance.

Such a man, the 'pattern of worldly honour,' is painted by Hartmann von Aue at the beginning of his *Poor Henry*.

> He was a flower of youth:
> He was a mirror of joy:
> Always true and constant as a diamond,
> He wore the crown of discipline.

The Power of the People

He was the refuge of the oppressed;
A shield to his vassals—
He was generous in right measure:
He knew neither superfluity nor want.
He carried lightly the heavy burden
Of lordship and knightly service.
He was the channel of good counsel,
And sang right well of love.

The essential feature, the service of women, is indeed only indicated in this description. To place his weapon, his honour, his discipline, at the service of the adored lady, is for all poets the crown of knightly living.

When one remembers that the lady in the case was usually married, one begins to question what it was in real life which corresponded to the poetical picture of the service of women. However that may be, it is certain that in addition to the respect shown in Germanic times to the lady of the house, woman gave the tone to social life. From that time a society without women was unthinkable.

There was certainly a great gulf between the ideal picture painted by the poets, and the reality in which the knights passed their lives. Outward polish was very often found in company with inward roughness, and even with unbridled licence. In the same way, the great majority of the knights found no difficulty in reconciling worldliness and religion.

Such a combination indeed matched the conditions of their life. It was the younger sons of the nobility who filled the monasteries. A castle chaplain would often give the knightly youth instruction in reading, less frequently in writing, and also, but rarely, in other branches of learning. In many monasteries there were monks who were well able to describe the life of chivalry both by word and pencil. On the other hand, the artistic skill of the monks was once more in demand with the princes and knights. Richly woven carpets, beautifully painted prayer-books, carving and working in gold, point, if not to an origin in the cloister, at least to a monkish adviser.

But the lion and the lamb did not always lie down peaceably together: and the chivalrous ideal contained much that was difficult to assimilate. How could the glory of the life of chivalry be reconciled with the demands of Christian humility, the search for warlike adventure with the peace which was commanded by the Church: the service of women with loyalty to the marriage vow? It was inevitable that these contradictions should produce a sense of strain.

Yet inward tension is one of the conditions of the development of personal character. Outstanding personalities came to light amongst the Court poets, through their struggle to reconcile the discrepancies in the knightly ideal.

Gottfried von Strassburg is well aware that the devil makes a mock of men: but he allows the passion of love to triumph over shame and ruin. Walther von der Vogelweide wrestles again and again with the question: 'How man three things may gain, which ever will remain?' The three things are worldly good, knightly honour, and the grace of God. Hartmann von Aue lets his *Poor Henry* find health when he conquers the hot desires which demand a virgin's sacrifice for their satisfaction. 'Faith' is the name given by the poet to this self-conquest. It is 'Constant Faith' also which shows the way to the *Parsival* of Wolfram von Eschenbach. The Grail is vouchsafed only to the perfect: but perfection is impossible without Faith—Faith towards God, towards women, and towards one's own aspirations.

> Who never, by his body's guilt,
> Has turned his soul from God aside—
> And who, let good or ill betide,
> Has earned men's honour and their praise—
> Well has he ordered all his days.

The *joie de vivre*, springing from the unconscious self, was ennobled by earnest moral effort. The worthy man who, a century earlier, would almost inevitably have retired from the world behind the walls of a monastery, now played his part in the battle of life, winning honour and respect. The period which witnessed such a revolution was certainly one of the greatest ever granted to the German people.

The old confines had become too narrow for the wave of new vigour which was overflowing the traditional boundaries of economic, social, and religious life. Not again, until the nineteenth century, was the need of expansion so universally felt, as at that period amongst the western and southern peoples of Europe. But to no nation were such favourable opportunities for expansion offered as to the Germans. From the Baltic to the Adriatic Seas, wide territories stretched before the German homesteads. Being

The Power of the People

thinly populated by Slavs and Magyars, they did not produce a fraction of the yield which would have been extracted from them by a dense population employing the methods of a more advanced civilization. Charlemagne and the Saxon emperors had failed in their attempts to win back by the sword the former Germanic possessions on the far side of the Elbe. The gradual penetration of German settlers had a more lasting effect. Lower Austria, Styria, and Carinthia were won for Germany: the Magyar wedge thrust between north and south Slavonia was strengthened by German immigration.

Not before the middle of the twelfth century did the stream of German settlers begin to flow into the Slav territory east of the Elbe. At this time the subjugation of the border countries by German rule offered a new home to all, who by reason of the growth of the population were unable any longer to find work, or to obtain land, for themselves.

The emperor Lothar initiated the movement, to which he was attracted through his Saxon dukedom. His work was carried on by the border-land princes in Holstein: by the counts of Schauenburg, in Mecklenburg; by Lothar's nephew Henry the Lion, in the Mark of Brandenburg; by the Ascanien; and on the middle Elbe by the race of Wettin.

Conquest and settlement went hand in hand: but the superiority of the German weapons was not the decisive factor. On their own initiative, the princely houses in Mecklenburg and Pomerania, which still stood after their subjection to Henry's supreme authority, lent their assistance to the German settlement. The independent nobles from the frontier territories—the piasts of Silesia and the rulers of Bohemia and Hungary—acted in the same way. Even if the German settler was far less amenable to taxation than the Slav peasant, there were advantages connected with him which far outweighed this drawback. His iron ploughshare, which turned over the sods, was far better adapted to the cultivation of a stiff and fruitful soil than the light wooden hook-shaped plough of the Slavs, which only loosened the earth's surface. By his energy and untiring industry, the immigrant was differentiated, greatly to his advantage, from the native, whose initiative had been killed by oppressive vassalage. If the foreign nobles had only understood the advantages of the German working methods, they would have thanked God for the newcomers, like Wizlaw of Rügen, who looked back with horror to the former times: 'God forbid, that the country should ever sink back to its former state, that the Slavs should drive away the German settlers, and begin themselves to cultivate the land again!'

Almost the whole of northern and central Germany took part in the immigration. Southern Germans settled more particularly in the Baltic Provinces and in Brandenburg—the name of the 'Fläming' chain of hills is reminiscent of the settlement of the natives of Flanders, who were most numerously represented there—Germans of the centre in Lusatia, Silesia, and Bohemia; the Saxons who colonized Transylvania came from the farthest west and from the central Moselle.

In the territories under German rule, colonization generally began with the building of castles. After this, the princes and feudal lords sent messengers into the surrounding country to invite the settlers. Each peasant received a relatively large hide of land as his own property, which he could leave to his heirs, divide or sell: he was free to emigrate, and, as a rule, was not required to pay tribute for three years, or for as long as fifteen years, in cases where he had to bring the woodland under cultivation.

The leader of the band of settlers, who was frequently a man of knightly family, was granted many hides of land and the position of hereditary mayor, with the right to judge the less important cases, and not seldom also with a licence to sell drink.

The first cities in the eastern colony were founded in the twelfth century, in addition to very numerous free village communities. Yet the great majority of the city foundations on the far side of the Elbe belong to a later period. On the other hand, the activities of the Church, even at that early time, were of the highest importance. They not only introduced Christianity and a higher code of morals, but they were also responsible to a great extent for the spread of cultivation and the growth of a German spirit. Most prominent in this work of civilization were the Cistercian monasteries, which lay for the most part farthest to the east (Doberan, Chorin, Lenin, Oliva, Leubus), and those of the Premonstratensians. Before long the monks were able to people with German settlers the great uncultivated regions, ceded to them by the German and Slav nobles, and to utilize their natural resources: in the course of a few generations, deserts were transformed into flourishing fields, while important villages and prosperous towns had sprung up on every side.

Thus all classes in Germany had won back their old homes, and by their common labour cleared an ample space for future generations to live in. It was the greatest German achievement of the Middle Ages.

FOURTH PART

THE GLORY OF THE EMPIRE

BUT the paths struck out by the imperial house of Hohenstaufen were altogether alien to this development, and led far afield towards Italy and Asia. All their enterprises after untold sacrifice came to nothing.

While life in Germany was growing ever richer and more fruitful, her rulers were meeting disaster on the far side of the Alps, and bringing ruin upon themselves and the throne. But it was only at a comparatively late period that their subjects ceased to support this imperial policy. With singular unanimity they honoured Frederick Barbarossa as their ideal leader. He initiated this foreign policy, and for a long period they gave him ungrudging support in his Italian campaigns, and followed him in such numbers to the East that this expedition came to be known as the 'German Crusade.'

Frederick's popularity can only be compared with that which was enjoyed by the so-called 'great' rulers of Germany—Charlemagne and Otto the Great. He shared with them the gifts which are indispensable to a great prince: a sharp eye for facts; a high ideal of sovereignty; a vehement and tenacious will. But it was only on rare occasions that the hard kernel of his nature came to light. His sense of reality did not dull his imagination; he concealed all angry emotion under 'his customary smile'; he had the art of gaining his opponents by adroit speech and winning the vanquished by gentleness. His well-balanced character fulfilled the difficult demands of 'Moderation' which were made upon the chivalry of his time; this fact explains the powerful influence of his personality upon his contemporaries.

In great measure also his political ambitions were suited to the needs and desires of the majority of the German people. The four decades of his reign meant a time of repose for the whole of Germany, to which for long years she had been a stranger. The very circumstances of his election impelled Frederick to reconcile the warring elements in his empire. His first care must be to put an end to the war between the Staufen and the Welfs. Conrad III had

The Glory of the Empire

nominated his nephew to the princes as his successor, thus passing over his own son, who was not yet of age. Without the consent of the powerful Welfs, the election would scarcely have been possible. Frederick punctually fulfilled the engagements which he had entered into, and also furthered the understanding—albeit with difficulty and at the cost of considerable sacrifices. In the year following Frederick's election, Welf, the uncle of Henry the Lion, was granted feudal rights in central Italy, and a little later the dignity of Duke of Bavaria was given to the Lion himself, in addition to the dukedom of Saxony. While in one direction his desire for expansion was greatly hampered by the creation of an independent dukedom of Austria, he was left a free hand to establish his authority in Saxony and to expand in the east: he even acquired the right of installing the Saxon bishops. He commanded in his wide empire, if not by his own right, yet by the absolute power which he wielded and his boast, that 'no king and no archbishop had anything to say in his territories,' was literally borne out by the facts.

In other matters also Frederick supported the pretensions of the princes, whose power had been steadily increasing. Yet what he gave away with one hand, he took back with the other. Above all, he endeavoured to renew the alliance between the throne and the bishops, which had been broken at the time of the investiture dispute. In this he was successful. Cleverly making use of the possibilities which were offered to the king by the Concordat of Worms, he was able to fill the bishops' thrones with men who were inclined to support the Crown. There was no lack of such men. The high tide of the religious movement had begun to ebb; the taste for secular activity was growing amongst the higher ranks of the clergy, inclining them to place themselves at the king's disposal.

Not a few of the bishops proved themselves Frederick's faithful and able helpers in counsel and in battle. Of these the most prominent was Rainald of Dassel. Raised to be Chancellor of the Empire and Archbishop of Cologne, during a whole decade he shaped the course of imperial politics. Once again, as in the days of the Saxon emperors, the alliance between the king and the bishops acted as a counterpoise to the power of the secular princes and as an assurance of peace in Germany. As Frederick in this case had recourse to the tried system of his predecessors, so he adopted the methods employed by the princes of his time to strengthen their authority. By purchase and exchange he increased the possessions of the House of Staufen in Swabia and Alsace, in the Palatine and in Franconia, and extended them towards the north-east as far as the territory of Meissen. He also strengthened his own authority by building castles, which he garrisoned with his bond vassals, and tried to reform the administration by replacing the vassals by functionaries. Through his marriage with Beatrice of Burgundy, he gained northern Burgundy, Savoy, and Provence, and opened up new possibilities of increasing his possessions. In the course of a few years he succeeded, without an appeal to arms, in adding to the resources of the Crown; in forming a new and close alliance between himself and the leading classes of the population; and in winning that universal popularity which is the reward of the peacemaker and the defender of the right.

When one realizes the state of affairs after the investiture dispute and the wars of the Welfs, when the royal authority had collapsed under Frederick's predecessors, one is tempted to wish that he had pursued the objects of the first years of his reign till the end of his life, and that the path of his Italian policy had never been struck out. Yet this wish ought not to influence one's judgment upon Frederick's later undertakings. If he had refused to allow the pretensions of the powerful princes, his successes could never have been attained: but as a result of his compliance the north and almost all the east of the empire were removed from under his immediate command. This was an evil inheritance for a successor who was not gifted with Frederick's art of managing men. At a critical moment he himself was to discover the drawbacks of this dual government. He succeeded in overthrowing Henry the Lion; but he was not able to prevent the fall of the one from raising a multitude of other nobles to a position of power, and thus providing for the future a scarcely less formidable menace to the royal authority.

It is open to doubt, therefore, whether the path which Frederick took under the pressure of circumstances could have led to the permanent establishment of a centralized government. The fact that he followed it for so long a time

The Glory of the Empire

can only be explained by his Italian plans. In Italy he hoped to be richly compensated for all the limitations of the royal authority to which he and his predecessors had had to submit at the hands of the princes. He intended to make immediate use of all that he hoped to acquire there, for the strengthening of his position in Germany. A peace policy in Germany and aggression in Italy were dependent upon each other. Frederick could be content with little here, because yonder he hoped for greater gain: he could devote himself to the objects which beckoned him on the far side of the Alps, because in Germany he had attained to greatness. In his Italian plans, therefore, one can as little detect a false step which could and should have been avoided, as the revival of any policy followed by former emperors.

It is true that Frederick appeared at first in the old rôle of protector of the pope. Long before he had been elected king, the Romans had overthrown the papal government in their city; under the leadership of Arnold of Brescia, who summoned them to fight against the secularization of the Church, they had maintained their independence. An invasion of the Normans was threatening from the south. Frederick promised to help the pope against all his foes. He roughly dismissed an embassy of Romans who brought him the offer of a Roman coronation, and received the imperial crown from the hands of the pope in St. Peter's. The Romans tried to force their way over the Tiber and almost succeeded in interrupting the ceremony. Arnold had already fallen into Frederick's hands and had been executed. But this was no help to the pope. In his disappointment he turned to the Normans and made an alliance with them. Secret enmity took the place of co-operation.

In the diet at Besançon, the tension gave way in a stormy encounter between the hotheads of either side, Chancellor Rainald and Cardinal Roland. Two years afterwards, when the latter was raised to the papal chair by a majority of the cardinals, Frederick decided for the man who had been chosen by the minority. He was acting strictly within the letter of the law, which traditionally employed the emperor as the protector of the Church: he was supported by both princes and people. But his motives were quite distinct from the attitude of former emperors towards the Italian question. Otto I strove for the mastery of Italy, in order to keep the pope dependent upon himself. Frederick I fought against Alexander III, because he wished to gain Italy.

The struggle for Italy was already in progress before Alexander III was raised to the Papacy. During his first march upon Rome, Frederick had become acquainted with the possibilities which beckoned him on the other side of the Alps. There he had found wide territories estranged from the empire, including the cities of Lombardy, which were flourishing to an unprecedented degree. If the paramount rights of the empire could be reasserted, the cities might be induced to furnish such considerable sums as could not be demanded from Germany.

In this also Frederick showed that he was a man of his time, and able to appreciate the value of ready money. Wherever possible, he replaced vassals by functionaries, and took hired professional soldiers into his service. The final goal of his Italian plans was the throwing open of modern resources in order to strengthen his imperial authority. In principle, no doubt existed of the sovereign rights of the empire, and the fact that just at that time the antique Roman Code was again in the ascendant in the Italian schools of law, stood the emperor in good stead: for according to Roman law the property of the State cannot be lost through lapse of time. Another opportunity was offered to the emperor, when the cities of northern Italy sought his help against Milan, their too powerful neighbour. The German princes were willing to support the undertaking; the knights were tempted by the prospect of honour and gain.

Frederick set out with a great army on his second Roman campaign. Proud Milan was obliged to submit. A diet held on the fields of Roncaglia formulated the imperial rights, learned men from the School of Law at Bologna lending their assistance to the deputies from the cities. But a hard and bitter conflict had yet to be waged before these resolutions could be carried into effect. Success was with the imperial arms: in 1162, after a long siege, Milan was compelled to surrender, and was demolished: the inhabitants were forced to take refuge in four open villages. This cruel vengeance was a triumph for those who had been oppressed by Milan; the fact that Frederick entertained the like feelings, both before and after the contest, is a blot upon his memory, and was to bring its own revenge.

The destruction of the leading city roused Frederick's remaining enemies to an extreme effort; they were no longer disputing the measure of their freedom, but fighting for their right to live the life which they had won for themselves with infinite labour.

The Papacy was their ally: for the fulfilment of Frederick's plans would have meant the end of papal independence also. Frederick could not stand against the united efforts of his opponents.

It is true that a fourth Roman campaign was once more brilliantly successful. Rome was taken, and the emperor was crowned once again in St. Peter's, this time by the hand of his rival pope. But immediately afterwards disaster overtook the German army; a frightful epidemic, to which thousands fell victim, compelled them to a retreat which was almost a flight. Seven years later Frederick appealed once more to a decision by arms. But the princes no longer supported him as in former times. At a critical moment, the emperor made what seems to have been a personal appeal for help to Henry the Lion, who refused his request. When Frederick attempted to bring reinforcements to the troops which were besieging Pavia, he suffered his first defeat in the open field near Legnano in 1176. He was obliged to have recourse to negotiation. Here he was more successful. For the Papacy also had been greatly weakened by the struggle, and Alexander III was ready to make terms. As Frederick abandoned the rival pope, it was open to Alexander to claim that he had upheld the independence of the Papacy through a twenty years' struggle. This fact decided him. He was willing to meet the emperor in the matter of the appointment of the German bishops, and—what was more important to Frederick—in the matter of the imperial property in Italy.

On this basis the Peace of Venice was concluded in 1177.

Outwardly it meant a complete victory for the Papacy. But this did not trouble Frederick, for he had gained almost all that he valued. Equally happy was the conclusion of his negotiations with the Lombards. In the course of a six years' truce, their position in regard to the emperor had become worse rather than better. They still preserved governmental rights within their own city, but only by

The Empire of the Kaisers

special arrangement outside the city boundaries. They obtained this privilege from the emperor at the cost of resigning a number of sovereign rights, and parting with considerable sums of money.

Even before this time the emperor had put an end in Germany to the dual authority, whose dangers had become only too apparent in the hour of need. With great caution, not as accuser, but as judge, he took measures against the Lion. Henry, whom a contemporary calls 'the haughtiest of mankind,' had made many enemies by the ruthless way in which he sought to extend his frontiers. Again and again Frederick had refused to give ear to their complaints; now he listened to them, and made certain of their support in the coming struggle. Repeated summonses to the Imperial Court of Justice remained without effect. Henry became an outlaw, lost his fief and finally his own estates, all this being accomplished under the strictest adherence to the forms of law. His resistance was broken by a great imperial army led by Frederick himself. He had to thank the emperor for the fact that his family estate round Brunswick and Lüneburg was given back to him. Saxony and Bavaria, the last of the tribal dukedoms, were parcelled out. Part of Saxony fell to the son of Albert the Bear, and West-phalia to the Archbishop of Cologne. Styria was separated from Bavaria, and became an independent dukedom, the remainder was given to Otto von Wittelsbach.

Frederick had fought his last campaign. The year after the conclusion of peace with the Lombards, he summoned the chivalry of Germany around him at Mayence, to cele-brate the attainment of his eldest sons to the rank of knighthood. The knights streamed thither in tens of thousands, many from countries outside Germany, together with an innumerable multitude of the common people. Frederick, now a vigorous man of sixty, himself took part in the tournaments. All that distinguishes this period from others, its buoyant energy, its delight in knightly glory, the close bond between the nation and their imperial leader, the fruitful marriage between international and national sentiment—all this could be witnessed in the most striking fashion during those Whitsun days at Mayence. Neither before nor since has such a festival been celebrated in Germany, and never has the emperor been so close to his people.

The Glory of the Empire

Two years later he held another great festival on the far side of the Alps, to celebrate the betrothal of his son Henry with the heiress of the Norman Empire. Milan, with which the emperor had made a treaty, acted as host on this occasion. These events are closely connected, and indicate the last stage in Frederick's Italian policy: the endeavour to insure his permanent rule in central Italy by the annexation of Sicily. The natural opposition of the Papacy led to new battles on Italian soil, and also to complications with the lords spiritual in Germany. But his anxiety for a new Crusade—Jerusalem had been conquered by Saladin— before long forced the pope to compliance. The victory remained with Frederick, and his successor was able to maintain the situation as he had left it. Afterwards came the sudden revulsion. The reason is clear to us who come after; the gain of Sicily meant the encircling of the papal territory—a situation which must be resisted by the pope with the last ounce of strength. The imperial lust for power had overstepped its natural boundaries. Frederick must have thought otherwise. He had reached the goal which he had pursued for three decades, undeterred by the heaviest rebuffs: the mastery of Italy as the basis of his imperial power.

There was only one prize which he could seek yet more ardently: to fight as the leader of Western Christendom for the liberation of the Holy Sepulchre. In earlier Crusades the direction had been undertaken by the Papacy, and the accomplishment, as a rule, by the Western nations. Now the pope was thrust on one side, and Western chivalry was prevented from bearing a part in this new enterprise by a war between England and France. The third Crusade was 'The German Crusade.' When Frederick announced his resolve on the day of 'Christ's Diet' at Mayence, his summons met with a joyful response. The chivalry of Germany had stood aside during the first Crusade, and the memory of the unlucky second campaign was inseparably connected with the names of their emperor. Now they were able at last to take an honourable share in the common task of the Christian peoples. The emperor led his army almost to the Promised Land. Then Fate called him away. 'God acted according to his inscrutable decree, justly no doubt, but not mercifully.' So wrote a monkish contemporary. But we know that Frederick fell at the height of his success, being spared the knowledge of the failure of his enterprise, which even he would scarcely have been able to avert.

The first events in the reign of Henry VI showed how completely his father's power had been dependent upon his personality. Henry the Lion returned from his English exile, and dared once more to take up arms. The king was obliged to be content with a composition. He received the imperial crown in Rome; but his attempt to take possession of his wife's Norman inheritance ended in failure. This failure reacted upon Germany. A great number of princes from Saxony and the Lower Rhine allied themselves with the Lion, to overthrow the emperor. Behind the league stood the English king, Richard the Lion-heart, the ruler of the Sicilian kingdom, and the pope. An extraordinary stroke of luck came to the help of the emperor, who was thus threatened, and he was wise enough to make the most of fortune's favour. On his return journey from the East, Richard fell into the hands of the Austrian duke, and was handed over to Henry, who forced him to render the oath of allegiance, to pay a great ransom, and to induce the revolting princes to lay down their arms. Peace was now assured in Germany. The emperor employed the English gold in raising a powerful army of knights, and preparing a new expedition against Sicily. In Palermo, during the same year of Richard's release, Henry was crowned King of the Norman Kingdom. German vassals ruled as Government officials over the imperial domains in Italy and Sicily. But this was only intended for a beginning. France and Spain also, and even the Eastern Roman Empire, were to acknowledge Henry's supremacy: a new Crusade was to bring the East within the circle of his dominion; his Norman kingdom was to be the bridge uniting the East and West into one world-empire. Every where the first steps were being taken towards the carrying out of this tremendous plan, when the emperor was struck down by a fever in the flower of his youth. The dream of world-supremacy collapsed at his death, and with it what the Saxon emperors had achieved, the Salians had maintained, and Frederick Barbarossa had waked into new life —the unity of the German people and their importance as a world power.

Now for the first time, a dual election took place in

The Glory of the Empire

Germany. The supporters of the Staufen set up Philip, Barbarossa's second son, to be Henry's successor; the princes of the lower Rhineland chose the Welf, Otto IV, the son of Henry the Lion. This dissension was encouraged by Pope Innocent III, for it ensured the establishment of his own authority. Papal supremacy succeeded to imperial. First, the Staufen, and after his early death, the Welf was excommunicated. Frederick II, the son of Henry VI, who held his Norman kingdom as a vassal of the pope, owed his succession to papal support. Otto's throne relied upon English backing; and the French victory over the English troops at Bouvines in 1214 was the decisive factor in his fall, and smoothed the way for the 'Priests' King.' For the first time a war between foreign nations affected the succession to the German throne. Frederick II himself became a menace to the pope by his aggressions in Italy. Empire and Papacy entered upon their third great struggle in which Frederick and his son, Conrad IV, both fell victims. By order of the French prince, to whom the pope had made over the Norman Empire, the last of the Hohenstaufen ended his young life upon the scaffold.

Frederick II, the last representative of the glories of the imperial throne, lived on in the mind of the German people. For centuries, in their longing for the restoration of the empire, they clung to the hope of its return. The fall of that proud race will never cease to arouse the profoundest human sympathy. But none of the later rulers took a leading part in shaping the course of German development. What was needful for her future was acquired without their help—even, it may be, in their despite.

SECOND BOOK

THE TOWNSFOLK
1200–1500

PREFACE TO THE SECOND BOOK

THE tragic fall of the House of Staufen meant the end of the Western Empire as it had hitherto been understood. Nations, in the modern sense of the word, began to be formed, and began more and more to influence the course of history. The States of Western Europe—France, England, and the Kingdom of Spain—attained the most powerful development; but in the East also, in Hungary and in Poland, which was united with Lithuania in 1386 to form one kingdom, the feeling of nationality was growing in strength. In 1397, the three Scandinavian States united under the leadership of Denmark. Germany and Italy, the two pillars of the empire, developed on opposite lines. The central government split up into a multitude of separate governments, and the political connection between the two peoples was broken off.

The result of the enfeeblement of the imperial government was the rapid loss of Germany's pre-eminence among the nations: her national life still suffers from the effects of the disintegration which had now set in. Any chronicler of the History of the Empire would fain pass quickly over the details of this collapse. The main outlines are lost: the threads are hopelessly entangled.

But the three centuries which followed the climax of the imperial power cannot be summarized by a historian of the German people as collapse and disintegration. For it was at this very time that the townsfolk won their way to economic and intellectual standing, and began, though not with permanent success, to play their part in national life. By their advent they popularized intellectual and public life, and spiritualized the world of business, being the first to gain recognition for the part which it played in public morals. The citizen filled the gap which had yawned for centuries between the small governing upper class and the mass of the agricultural population ruled by them. The chasm was bridged over, the nation could now form one corporate body, whose energies rose from lowest to highest, and reacted from the higher upon the lower classes. No period, therefore, has been more important in the evolution of the community than the centuries between 1200 and 1500, which from the other standpoint have been

The Townsfolk

frequently characterized as the 'Transition Period' between the Middle Ages and modern times, or even as the 'Period of Disintegration.' A new creation was being built up out of a thousand atoms—pregnant with life, though its form was as yet undetermined.

FIRST PART

CITIES AND PRINCIPALITIES

THE rise of the middle class had already begun in the twelfth century. The powers which were then developed were also active in other classes of the population at that period, and till far into the next century, especially amongst the peasantry.

When the feudal manor of the old German provinces was converted into an estate yielding rent, the former vassals became in increasing numbers the tenants of the landlord. They owed him tribute and service, and were still bound to him legally and politically. But in general the obligations were not oppressive, the compulsory service, for example, was limited to ten or twelve days in the year. And time was on the side of the peasants. The population was growing, the land which was fit for cultivation was becoming barely sufficient for their needs. As the area of settlement grew more restricted, the ground underwent a remarkable rise in value, while the taxes remained essentially the same: the peasant reaped the benefit of this situation. The towns were spreading on all sides and their demand for the necessities of life was proportionately increasing. The rapidly growing output of silver resulted in a rise in price: this meant for the peasants a regular market and a good profit. There were expedients to hand when the need for land became pressing. In the course of the thirteenth century, the remaining portion of the soil of old Germany, suitable for cultivation, was, as we have seen, brought under the plough. When no more land could be made arable, younger sons sought their fortune in the town, or migrated to the east.

Also in the matter of legal status, the peasants gained in independence. Many freemen put themselves under the jurisdiction of a feudal lord, in order to enjoy the advantage of his protection: they paid a small tax, but their liberty remained unimpaired. The position of these men of better family, and of the former bondsmen, was then equalized, as had happened in the ninth and tenth centuries, in the case of the serfs and the freemen, who put themselves under the protection of a lord of the manor. When his sovereign rights were increased, others became subjects of the feudal lord. A relationship of vassalage was set up, which almost ignored the old divisions; the serfdom of the earlier time was changed.

But gain which comes to a man without any corresponding labour on his part will do him little good. If we may believe the chronicles, insubordination and an evil upstart spirit gained ground among the peasants. We hear of their gluttony and drunkenness, of feasting in the church, of wild dances in the churchyard. In Austria a number of 'dung-hill cocks' proved so refractory, that the nobles removed from the neighbourhood. It was equally vexatious when the peasant set himself, in defiance of prohibition and of ridicule, to ape the knight, with a long sword, striped hose, elaborately quilted doublet and embroidered cap sewn with tinkling bells, even going so far as to copy his bearing and manner of speech. The Bavarian knight, Neidhart von Reuental, poured the keenest ridicule upon them. But he aimed at the applause of his fellows, who were sated with love poetry and craving for strong meat: his ridicule is a cover for the envy of the knight, who has hard work to make both ends meet, while the peasant has enough and to spare. Neidhart, however, was exaggerating, and other writers with him. The peasantry remained sound at heart, and continued till well into the fifteenth century to work for a greater measure of self-determination.

While the peasantry were working their way upwards, chivalry remained, for a little while, at its height. Everyone connected with it found work and gain on the far side of the Alps during the wars of the Staufen. The knights born in serfdom—the bond vassals—proved indispensable in the service of the princes, and sometimes also at the king's court.

The opening years of the thirteenth century are memorable for the work of the great poets, who gave a literary form to the ideals of chivalry. The religious orders of knighthood entered Germany and acquired a peculiar national character. The order of Teutonic knights admitted men of German descent only, while the Knights of St. John and the Templars knew no such limitation. During the same period, Walther von der Vogelweide, with his political poems, fought on the king's side against the abuses of the Church—he was the first political poet to write in German.

Cities and Principalities

Men also belonging to the knightly class opened up a new and wide field for the use of the German tongue. They began by composing their legal documents in German. About 1230 appeared the first great law-book in the German language: the *Mirror of the Saxons*. Eike von Repkow, who composed the work originally in Latin, translated it at the request of his lord into the mother tongue. This law-book was followed by the first German Imperial Code, the *Acts relating to Public Peace*, published in Mayence in the year 1235. Two decades later, German won its way into the city charters, and towards the end of the century it triumphed in the royal Court of Chancery.

By that time, chivalry was already fighting for its life. Ideals were the first to wither. Ulrich von Lichtenstein made a pilgrimage through the country 'in the service of women'; some very beautiful songs and a few outspoken jests were the outcome of this journey. The popular dance songs of Neidhart von Reuental have life and swing: but they are addressed no longer to the lady, but to the peasant girl. The delicate exotic flower of chivalry was withering away. The adored lady was turning again into the *Hausfrau*—instead of wandering knights, the poet could depict the feudal lords whose talk was of the cowshed, and the prices of corn and wine. Soon anxieties became more pressing. The rents from landed property did not rise with rising prices. Unless a man could retrench, he fell into debt: if he had many children, the inevitable impoverish- of his race stared him in the face. The extinction of the Staufen dynasty put an end to warlike employment in the emperor's service. At the beginning of the fourteenth century, the armies of chivalry in the service of the princes met their first defeat in battle against Swiss and north German foot soldiers. Misfortunes crowded in on all sides. Many yielded to the temptation to keep their heads above water by robbing and plundering; from the middle of the thirteenth century the robber barons had become the dreaded scourge of peasants and citizens. Others sought an honourable living as mercenaries in foreign service, or in the service of their sovereign as councillors, stewards, or governors of his castle. The sun of chivalry was setting, the day of the *bourgeois* was about to break.

Germany had become a wealthy country through the labour of her peasants. Wealth gave rise to new demands.

The Townsfolk

Even in earlier centuries the peasant had not always been content with the produce of his own land. Gradually it became the rule for him to purchase at least a part of his clothing and his household stuff. In addition to finer articles, there was an increasing demand for articles of general utility. Moreover, the growing employment of ready money had an inspiriting effect upon trade and commerce. The richest silver mines in the world were found within the empire, and it was in the thirteenth century that their working first reached high-water mark. The old mines were situated in the Harz Mountains and the Black Forest, in Styria and the Tyrol, and to these were now added new workings in the Erzgebirge near Meissen, in Bohemia and Moravia: gold was produced in Silesia, and in greater quantities in Hungary.

Town life in Germany grew out of these beginnings: the importance of the citizen class resulted from the evolution of trade and commerce, in the fifteenth century. The interval was noteworthy for the systematic improvement in the conditions of life, both outward and inward, and it marked the beginning of the wealth, independence, and intellectual culture of the middle classes.

All cities were originally dependent upon a lord of the manor. But at quite an early period representatives of the citizens took part in the judgment-courts, and at a later date in the councils also. It was in the nature of things that they should seek to restrict, and finally do away with, the co-operation of the feudal officials. Step by step the citizens' 'council' extended its influence from judicial and commercial concerns to the whole round of civic affairs: a burgomaster was set at the head of the council, and the wealthy vassal families of the lord of the manor were absorbed into the councillors' families. But even when the evolution had been so far happily accomplished, the relationship to the feudal lord frequently remained indefinite. For the majority of the chief cities, the decisive moment came in the course of the thirteenth century. In most cases union was amicably achieved, because the citizens had the advantage of their wealth upon their side; in other places, bloody conflicts arose, in which victory fell first to one side and then to another, as in Cologne and Strasburg, the two greatest cities in the empire. Here and elsewhere, the episcopal head of the city forced matters to a trial of

Cities and Principalities

strength. The emperor Frederick II, like all the Hohen-staufen, supported the bishops in their war against the towns. In 1232 he put an end to the existing town councils as being contrary to law, and forbade the formation of city unions. If the law had been carried out, it would have meant the end of civic liberty, but the Bishop of Worms, who had brought about the prohibition, failed in the attempt to put it into practice. The citizens of Strasburg won their right of self-determination in the fight on the Haus Mountains, and the men of Cologne at Worringen in 1288. By the end of the century, the greater German cities, with few exceptions, were managing their own affairs in virtual independence.

Their monarchical constitution—if the expression may be allowed—gave place to an aristocratic government. The bulk of the population exercised no influence upon the city government. The council, to which was entrusted the direction of the affairs of the city, usually consisted of members of the rich merchant class, together with the successors of the feudal vassals. These latter possessed property within the city, had intermarried with the merchant class, and were themselves engaged in trade. Yet there were cities, in which the families who were allowed to furnish members to the council, belonged almost exclusively to the merchant class: indeed this may have been the case in the majority of the cities of the empire. Yet whatever might be the origin of the councils, they were all distinguished by an aristocratic class-consciousness which divided them from the 'common' people—'the infected masses.'

Knightly manners and ideas were early grafted on to middle-class occupations. Gottfried von Strassburg was a *bourgeois* by birth. The city festivals, such, for instance, as the welcome of Frederick the Second's English bride by the citizens of Cologne, were sometimes carried out altogether in the traditions of chivalry: it happened in the thirteenth century that in one day a hundred sons of the citizens of one city were dubbed knight by a German king.

But these knightly merchants had more at heart than their own prosperity. They gave a shape to urban life, which became before long the pattern for the whole State, and is still influencing the life of the towns of Germany. Many of their regulations belonged to a period when the council had to suffer the co-operation of feudal officials:

The Townsfolk

others were not drawn up until after the city had freed itself from the feudal lord. One of the most important tasks was that of insuring the city food-supply. Because of the bad state of the roads, and the uncertainty and costliness of traffic, the city population was obliged to draw its supplies from the immediate neighbourhood. Occasionally they succeeded in compelling the surrounding inhabitants to sell their farm produce exclusively in the city market. The 'staple-law' was more universally applied. It compelled not only the vendor of foodstuffs, but every merchant who passed the city within a certain radius with a cavalcade of goods, to bring his wares to the market and expose them for sale for some days. The right of 'Footing' allowed the citizens to buy as many goods as they required, even against the will of the merchant. On the other hand, the search for a market was not one of the anxieties of that time. Artisans worked essentially for local customers, and those who frequented the market. The increasing cultivation of a single industry, as for instance in the linen towns of Constance and Ravensburg, or the metal city of Nuremberg, made outside markets a necessity: as a general rule the Council could do no more than protect its merchants in foreign countries to the utmost of its power.

The chief field covered by the legislation of the council was the regulation of economic life within the city. It was guided by the idea of insuring to every citizen his 'nourishment,' i.e. a sufficiency of the rudiments of existence. This principle arose from the limited nature of trade, which we are too apt to forget in the presence of brilliant exceptions. As we have seen, the urban craftsmen and merchants could in general count upon constant custom, within the city and its immediate neighbourhood alone. Only a small proportion of the master workmen employed one assistant, and very rarely more than one. A dozen masters formed quite an important guild; the largest guilds had seldom more than thirty or forty members.

The whole of the year's traffic across the St. Gothard Pass may have amounted to the lading of from one to two modern goods trains: the grain dealt with in one year by the Hamburg merchants, even after the commencement of modern history, could have been stowed in the holds of two modern ships. Besides the great merchants, this trade provided a living for innumerable small and lesser dealers.

Cities and Principalities

No less than sixty-one merchants from Basle, from the greatest down to the smallest, had a share in the train of merchandise which was plundered by robber barons in the fourteenth century on the way to the fair at Frankfort. When three ships from Riga were wrecked about the same time, hundreds made good their claim to compensation. The profits of merchandise were very much greater than they are to-day; a man could gain a living out of even the smallest business, if he were protected from unfair competition.

This task was early taken in hand by the craftsmen and merchants themselves. From the twelfth century onwards, corporations or guilds were springing up, now here, now there. What the manorial fellowship offered to the peasant on the land, the immigrant was to find amongst the members of his craft: assurance of a competence, co-operation in the regulation of business which was shared by all, and brotherly support. Not an increase in sales, but as fair as possible a sharing of 'nourishment' was the essential aim of the guilds' regulations. No man who did not belong to a guild was allowed to follow a craft or business. The buying-in of raw materials was regulated: the master was permitted to purchase on market-days only and at prices fixed by the authorities: the number of assistants and apprentices was settled by the guild: the quality of goods and the range of prices supervised. The guilds also regulated social intercourse and appearance in public. They called their members together for evening drinking parties and for great feasts; they appointed them their seat in church and their place in processions. The guilds formed a military unit, and the burial of their deceased members was part of their care.

The guilds certainly required the co-operation of the city authorities in order to carry out this strict system. In the course of the thirteenth century, when the council obtained a free hand, the guild system also reached its full development. The idea of associated self-help, which inspired the rules of the guilds, was not, as we have seen, a new one; it was deeply rooted in German life. But the adoption by the city authorities of the idea of comradeship, and its shaping into a publicly recognized corporation, was an act of far-reaching importance. The path which was then marked out could not long be followed under a

The Townsfolk

monarchical government. Not till the reconstruction after the Napoleonic wars, did this ideal again meet with acceptance: the present life of city and state is built up in great measure upon associated self-government.

The individual tasks of the jurisdiction and government of the city were discharged by the citizens in the same far-seeing spirit. In place of legal proceedings of an essentially formal nature, amongst which the so-called 'Judgment of God,' which frequently took the form of a duel, was the highest court of appeal, the towns were the first to institute a judicial investigation of the facts of the case, coupled with free weighing of evidence. The evolution of city government has two leading characteristics: firstly, the endeavour to comprehend the total sum of the community's requirements, and, secondly, the early development of officialdom. The council's sphere of action grew steadily more comprehensive. In addition to matters of trade and commerce, the administration of justice and the policing of the city, with the help of public taxation they undertook the development of the city's finances, the improvement of military administration, and the beginnings of a public service for the care of the poor and sick, and of education. A system of public service arose which had many ramifications, from the councillors down to the sworn brokers and surveyors, the weigh-masters and policemen. As early as the thirteenth century business began to be transacted in writing: lists of citizens for many of the towns survive from the fourteenth century: the annoyance that 'the town's laws were written on many letters and memoranda, which could not be found when they were wanted,' was removed by legal documents, which after the middle of the thirteenth century were for the most part written in German.

If the usefulness of the city government were in need of proof, it can be found in the flourishing state of the city community. At a very early date, at latest by the middle of the fourteenth century, the majority of the German cities had already reached the dimensions which they maintained up to the last century. Exceptions to this rule are only to be found in a few cities, such as the great seaport towns, and the residences of the princes, whose development was determined by special circumstances. As a matter of fact, the numbers of the population still

Cities and Principalities

kept within narrow limits: about the middle of the fifteenth century Nuremberg numbered some 20,000 inhabitants, and Frankfort-on-the-Main, the half. Nevertheless, seeing that trade and commerce were in general much more profitable then than now, one must suppose that the prosperity of the cities grew much more rapidly than their population. Costly buildings were the visible result of this growing opulence; or the citizens who had not yet done so built stately walls to replace the old fortifications, which were almost useless for purposes of defence.

Not less important than the safeguarding of existence was the transformation of human beings, under the influence of civic work and order. The craftsman who made an implement by the patient work of his own hands, stood on a higher creative plane that any that could be attained by the countryman of his own time, or by a man of the same trade at the present day. The merchant could cultivate courage and the love of enterprise in a different field, but in much the same manner, as the knight of a vanishing epoch. Both, as fully privileged members of their professional union, learned to feel themselves citizens and pillars of an ordered society. Meantime the peasant dragged on his monotonous existence, disunited from his fellows and living under conditions of dependence which were regulated according to individual circumstances, and formed no part of the recognized public system. And, at the other end of the scale, the knight watched the ground cut away from under his feet.

All this was accomplished by the citizens while engaged in conflict with an unfriendly world around them. Again and again they made an attempt to establish peace and good government outside the city walls, if only with the object of safeguarding their economic relationships. These were in constant danger through the robber barons: if there were no caravans to be intercepted, the knight would content himself with stealing the linen from the citizen's bleaching green. The cities tried small expedients to help themselves. They purchased safe-conducts from the robber barons, or they bribed counts and noble lords to protect the city, making them patricians by letters patent, which yielded a good income to those who were so honoured. But co-operation held out more promise of success. During the Interregnum, when the royal authority was entirely

The Townsfolk

in abeyance, the League of the Rhine Towns was formed in 1254. It embraced towns which were widely separated, such as Lübeck, Berne, and Regensburg, with princes spiritual and temporal, counts and lords. King William of Holland encouraged the aims of the League. But his early death, and the confusion which set in with the dual government, broke up the union which had seemed to hold out great prospects for the future. City leagues of a still more comprehensive nature were repeatedly formed in later times: the Hanseatic League alone endured for any length of time, or possessed real power.

The Union of the Hanse Towns forms part of the great movement of expansion, which was in full force in the thirteenth century, and continued with almost undiminished vigour till far into the next. Its beginnings may be traced back to the time of the first Hohenstaufen. A Polish campaign undertaken by Frederick I in the year 1157 gave a great impetus to German expansion in Silesia. For the rest, the enterprise was only half-heartedly encouraged by the emperors: but their acquisitions in other parts of the world strengthened the people's self-confidence and thus prepared the national mind for colonization. The princes of the border territories and the Church pointed out the goal and the path which led to it, but our appreciation of their services should not lead us to underestimate the share in the work which was taken by the settlers. Their enterprise, their tireless industry, their varied skill, and their spirit of fellowship decided the fate of the great undertaking, which was destined to change the face of Germany and even of eastern Europe.

The Germanization of Holstein, Mecklenburg, Pomerania, Prussia, Brandenburg, Saxony, Silesia, and Austria meant a great extension of the area of German soil. Two-fifths of the empire, as it stood before the World War, was acquired during the expansion of the twelfth and thirteenth centuries: in pre-war times their inhabitants formed far more than a third of the population. The solid German block in the centre of Europe had henceforth sufficient size and weight to prevent its existence being permanently jeopardized, either by internal rupture, or by the impact of foreign States. Since the area expanded in one direction only, the forces of national life were turned into another channel. The linking-on of the wide eastern territory shifted the position of the provinces which were eastern at the time of the early emperors to the centre of the empire. The districts watered by the Elbe henceforth became the medium of interchange between the industrial west of Germany and the east, which was predominantly agricultural: for the future they occupied a position of importance such as the Rhineland provinces had held in former centuries. Side by side with the old tribal communities, new national units were formed through the mingling of various German and Slav nationalities on colonial soil: receiving, and, in increasing proportion, giving also. The eastern provinces quickly took the lead in political life, for there was no burdensome inheritance of past history in the newly colonized districts. Here, as never before, a determined autocracy could spread and take root, grouping wide stretches of land into one strong political entity.

Every class in Germany co-operated in the work of colonizing the east: but the share taken by the middle class noticeably increased after the thirteenth century. At that time a great number of cities were founded by the German princes in the eastern provinces: they may still be recognized as new foundations by the regularity of their plan.

It is true that they lay much farther apart from each other than was the case in the west and south, and in most cases they remained more backward in development than the cities of the mother country: for that very reason the local prince was able to maintain his authority over them. The spread of town life was also the chief benefit bestowed by the settlers upon the countries which were not under German rule. The peasant occupation was also of great importance in Bohemia and Moravia. The political inclusion of Bohemia within the empire, which took place when Frederick II invested the House of Przmyslid with hereditary royal dignity, created specially favourable circumstances within that area. German nobles and vassals came into the country in the train of German princesses. The officers at the Court, the feudal system, the building of castles, all developed after the German fashion: and German monasteries were also able to extend their sphere of influence.

The frontier mountains were won almost entirely for Germany: the mines lay exclusively in German hands, and occasioned the building of purely German towns such as

The Townsfolk

Iglau and Kuttenberg. The influx of immigrants in the thirteenth century covered the wide plain more thickly with German settlements, and here also it introduced the new habit of living in towns. Prague, Brünn, Olmütz, and many other cities where Germans had settled in large numbers, were granted city rights, and became the pattern for the markets of Slavonia. Affairs in Hungary followed a like course. Here, too, German immigration profited by powerful though not equally lasting patronage on the part of the Court. Here, too, a self-contained peasant settlement with extensive rights was founded in Siebenbürgen, and a German mining district in the county of Zips. The evolution of city life in Hungary also dates back to the Germans. The civic law-book of the town of Ofen stated at the beginning of the fifteenth century that the Germans had the right of choosing ten councillors and the Hungarians only two: while judges, scribes, and treasurers must be of undoubted German extraction. But it is only on the advanced posts in the south of Siebenbürgen and in Burzenland that the cities, such as Hermannstadt and Kronstadt, have preserved their original characteristics intact.

Conditions similar to those in Ofen prevailed for centuries in Cracow and Lemberg: for city life in Poland also is of German creation. Before and after the middle of the fourteenth century, nearly eighty towns possessing German rights were founded in Poland, together with two hundred and fifty German villages. Many such as Gorlice=Görlitz still bear the name of the German city from which their founders came. Before long they met with strong opposition at the hands of the nobility and the Church. For this reason, the German settlement in Poland could not achieve the permanent form which it obtained in other lands. But even during the period of Polish ascendancy, economic and intellectual relations with Germany were still maintained both in country and town.

Dürer lived for a time at Cracow, Veit Stoss worked for more than thirty years in the same city, and German humanists taught there. Merchants and craftsmen carried German institutions far into the territories of Russia. Russian princes granted German civic rights to many of their townships: German guild rights can be traced as far as Charkow.

The church of the German Merchants' Company at

Cities and Principalities

Novgorod was consecrated as far back as the reign of Frederick I. Even at that period, the most ancient and most modern methods of German expansion united to found the first overseas colony in the north. A prebendary from Holstein travelled with the merchants to the coast of Livonia, and there became bishop of a little community. In the year 1202 one of his successors, a canon of Bremen, founded the town of Riga with the support of the merchants, and instituted the company of the Knights of the Order of the Sword. At the end of a few decades, Livonia, with the greater part of Esthonia and Courland, was under the rule of German lords spiritual and temporal: Riga, Reval, and Dorpat were the centres of their trade. But it was not possible to Germanize a territory so distant: communication with the mother country was lacking. Danes, Russians, and Lithuanians were formidable foes. Help, however, came opportunely through the knights of the Teutonic Order, who were advancing northwards out of Prussia.

It was not till a much later period that the name Prussia was transferred to the largest State of northern Germany. But the growth of the supremacy of the Teutonic Order exhibits some of the essential features to which the State of Brandenburg owes its rise. Unquestioning military obedience, and a strict government by functionaries, were assured by the oath of knighthood. The Order also exercised a kind of ecclesiastical government in the country: it filled almost all the bishops' thrones and the cathedral chapters with its own members, and obedience was as much a matter of course in Church government as in other spheres. An ambitious policy was possible on these foundations and in this respect the Masters of the Order, during its best period, were no whit behind any of the rulers who raised the State of Brandenburg to a commanding position. Many of the Great Elector's political moves are called to mind by the method which they employed to rid themselves of the troublesome Duke of Poland, who had invited the presence of the Order, and afterwards urged his own pretensions. In the same way, the formation of a great mercantile power is reminiscent of that ruler's intentions, which it is true he never succeeded in putting into practice. Frederick William I was not more adept at bringing a great thing out of an insignificant, and bestowing the same care upon both: not Frederick II could have proved more steadfast amidst the storms of unceasing war than were the first Masters. In these battles, the Lettish population south of the Memel was almost annihilated: their place was taken by German immigrants, and in the flat lake district, by Masurian settlers. North of the Memel the old population persisted, thinly overlaid by a German ruling class. Before the end of the thirteenth century the Order had gained command of east and west Prussia, Courland, Livonia, and Esthonia: the Grand Master was in the first rank of German princes.

The subjection of the coast territories went side by side with the conquest of the sea. The German merchant, who was beginning in the twelfth century to dispute the Baltic with the Danes, could not reckon upon the support of the empire, and there was never any question of military backing for his enterprise. It was not till a later period, when German supremacy was no longer in doubt, that the cities formed themselves into a closer union. Groups of merchants from various places began the peaceful contest, and carried it to victory. As early as the twelfth century a union of 'the common merchants' was formed in the town of Wisby in Gothland: a strong city wall with thirty-eight towers, and the well-preserved church of Sancta Maria Teutonicorum, with the ruins of ten other churches, still bear witness to its former glory. The road led hence to the East, across the coasts of Livonia and Esthonia towards Novgorod, the great exchange for goods drawn from Russian territory as far back as the Ural. Gradually the itinerary was extended. In the West the peninsula of Schonen, the great market for herrings, was included in the regular course of business traffic: then the merchants penetrated into the North Sea till they reached Bruges. This brought about an interchange between the greatest markets of the West and East: Russian furs and Flemish cloths were the chief articles of commerce. Branches from the chief trade route led to Norway and England. The consequence of the extension of trading connections was that the native cities of the traders began to act in concert. The 'Hanse,' i.e. the League, spread rapidly, and in the second half of the fourteenth century it included all the important ports from Amsterdam to Reval, as well as towns lying far inland, such as Cologne, Halle, and Breslau.

On account of its situation midway in the voyage between

Cities and Principalities

East and West, Lübeck succeeded to the position held by Wisby, and became the head of the Hanse. The usual weapon of the League, the economic boycott, always proved adequate in the case of the members. But they were obliged to fight the Danish king, who made a sudden attack upon Wisby. In the year 1370 the Peace of Stralsund laid down the prerogatives of the merchants and even gave them a voice in the election of the Danish king.

The German people had drawn wide tracts of land in the east and north within their sphere of influence. Vital acquisitions were being won while the emperors were still fighting in Italy. The French victory over the English at Bouvines in 1214, which smoothed the way for the Staufen Frederick II to the German throne, Crusades, and Italian battles, followed thick and fast within the space of a few decades upon the gain of Livonia, the foundation of the Teutonic Order in Prussia, and the spread of German commerce across the Baltic. An endless stream of stimulation flowed into Germany, quickening every department of life. All that they gained and made their own they carried with them into foreign countries. As a consequence of the collapse of the economic formulas of the Middle Ages, wide classes of the population of southern and western Europe also had been borne upwards in the development which followed: the Crusades and their aftermath had quickened intercourse and made the intellectual needs of the nations akin. Interchange between nation and nation, and an international consciousness were being evolved, at the time when the form in which the emperors had moulded central Europe was being shattered. Taking and giving, the German people could now in a new sense work out the destiny marked out for them by their situation in the heart of Europe.

Chivalry and the Church were the most active exponents of the cosmopolitan spirit. Germany had adopted chivalry from the West, and passed much of it on to the East. As early as the first decade of the fourteenth century a Slav prince, Wizlaw von Rügen, was composing German love-songs. But, in general, preference was given to more robust and entertaining fare, such as aphorisms with a broad outlook on life, composed in the impressive style which Freidank had invented—instructive matter, riddles, and funny tales. The taste for narrative poetry was served by innumerable sequels, by imitations and expansions of the romances of chivalry and the popular epics. Wolfram's *Parsival* was expanded to order by an honest goldsmith, and his additions were twice as long as the original work. Matter was everything, form nothing. This was almost universally the case. In addition to the play upon the wise and foolish virgins, which goes back to the beginning of the fourteenth century, and is artistically complete, there are others in which the sacred and the farcical are curiously mingled, as for instance the Easter play, in which the Apostles organize a race to the sepulchre. But it must not be forgotten that this period of formlessness marks the entry of German prose into literature. Ottocar von Steiermark, who at the beginning of the fourteenth century wrote an Austrian rhyming chronicle of 80,000 verses, was also a master of the poetical style: yet the prose chronicles of the cities, which were now gradually becoming more numerous, produce a scarcely less lively effect.

While the spirit of chivalry was disappearing, ecclesiastical learning attained its final shape. Earlier times had been content faithfully to accept and pass on the traditional views. But when portions of the Greek philosophy came to be known through the Arabs, intellectual independence awoke, and an attempt was made to prove the reasonableness of Church doctrine. Aristotle, parts of whose writings had become familiar through Latin translations, was employed as a model. After the pattern of the Greek philosophers, scholars began to separate theological dogma into its individual conceptions, and to demonstrate their validity: to bring intelligent criticism and religious faith into agreement. This 'Learning of the Schools'—scholasticism—does not represent what we understand by unfettered research, and in its later stages it led frequently to an overestimation of pure thinking and a toying with empty notions. But as a school for thought, scholastic learning was extremely important, and represents an attempt which is still worthy of admiration, to group all branches of knowledge into one united whole.

France was its birthplace, and in the twelfth century countless Germans had journeyed thither, to drink their fill of the new spirit. But it was not accepted by German theologians as a whole. It was about the middle of the thirteenth century, by the agency of Albert the Great,

Cities and Principalities

that scholastic science first took firm root in Germany. This Swabian noble was a born scholar. He was nominated as Bishop of Regensburg, but after a few years resigned the office, in order to follow his own bent, investigating and teaching, now here, now there. In addition to ecclesiastical learning, his broad mind embraced the whole of the profane sciences, and could hold its own also in questions of practical life. In Cologne, where he worked for many years, he repeatedly acted as mediator between the archbishop and the inhabitants. The aim of his life was to raise the edifice of Christian dogma upon the works of Aristotle and the annotations of his Arabian commentators, which signified for him the sum-total of all secular knowledge. He pursued this aim by innumerable writings, which brought the Greeks and their expounders nearer to the West than did the inadequate attempts of earlier scholars. But his chief instrument was the spoken word.

Thomas Aquinas, the perfecter of Scholasticism, was Albert's pupil. Like the Gothic cathedrals, the edifice of scholastic thought still towers across the centuries: it is built, like them, upon firm foundations, and raises towards heaven the same clear-cut and consistent superstructure.

Scholastic learning and Gothic architecture mark the highest peak of ecclesiastical supremacy. Just at the time when Scholasticism was entering upon its triumphant course, the Papacy created a powerful tool for itself in the Mendicant Orders. Francis of Assisi had recognized his call to win souls, and had rejected the idea of founding an Order. But when the community which he had founded received the papal sanction, it was transformed into an Order which had little in its system to distinguish it from others. Yet the Mendicant Orders were a novelty in the mediaeval world. They worked no longer in the country, but in the towns: they placed the service of one's neighbour at the heart of the religious life, and practised it through preaching, the cure of souls, and the care of the sick. They enjoyed privileges which seriously encroached upon the prerogatives of the bishop and priest, such as the right of preaching and hearing confession without episcopal permission. Thus they became the pope's picked troops, in direct contact with the city masses. Through their means the Papacy succeeded for long years in suppressing the movements which were working underground.

137

The Townsfolk

Walther von der Vogelweide and Freidank complained, even at their early date, of papal blunders and unworthy priests: as time went on, such complaints became clearer and more general. They were founded in part on actual improprieties, in part on a new moral standard by which men judged the duties of the Church and her servants, and on a deepening intensity of religious feeling. In many places, men and women went so far as publicly to renounce the secularized Church. In the year 1211, eighty heretics are said to have been burnt in Strasburg: the persecution between 1231 and 1233 dealt with many hundreds of heretics. Conrad of Marburg, who was its chief leader, was slain. But the activity of the Inquisition was not checked: the pope entrusted it to the Mendicant Order of Dominicans. From their ranks came one of the most prominent of German preachers: Berthold von Regensburg. No one had ever spoken as he did to the German people, drawing his matter straight from life, and gripping the life of his hearers. His heart yearned over the poor 'who eat scarcely better than their cattle, and are pale and thin'—and was furious with the avaricious 'whose Amen sounds in God's ears like the barking of a dog'—the noble oppressors, who 'like to build houses at the cost of others,' and the rich merchants. His words were very powerful, and thousands flocked to hear him, so that he was frequently constrained to preach in the open field.

But there were other movements which scorned all direction. In the second half of the thirteenth century, defying all dissuasion from the Church, the Flagellants began to travel through the country: a century later, under the terrible scourge of the Black Death, the frenzy reached its climax. And, unobserved, a different view of religious things was quietly making its way among the German people. At first mysticism followed the road of orthodox piety, but of necessity diverged from it, as it grew and developed. He who closed his eyes in pious meditation— the Greek word μυειν means to close the eyes—looked no longer upon the stately building of the Church, but upon the One Thing, which Johannes Tauler, about 1350, enshrined in these words: 'The Soul hath more of God than all Heaven and than all temples which are made of wood and stone, and decked never so beautifully with gold, silver, and precious stones: for our soul is the Heart of God, which includeth all fatherly love and fidelity, as well as all divine joy and bliss. Because therefore the Almighty God hath set all His Love upon the Soul, He dwelleth far more truly in the Soul than in Heaven and in all earthly Temples.'

Tauler emphasized the moral demands of the same mystic way of faith which was acknowledged by his predecessor Master Eckhart of Strasburg, and expressed in poetry by his Germanic contemporary Heinrich Seusa. All three belonged to the Dominican Order.

Like Scholasticism, Gothic architecture found its way at a comparatively late period into Germany. It was not the result of any flagging of the creative impulse. The completion of the great Rhenish cathedral, the building and rebuilding of innumerable Cistercian monasteries, the renovation of many old churches in the towns, together with the building of princes' castles, rather point to the conclusion that joy in architectural creation was keener in the thirteenth century than ever again until the century of the Baroque. But it was the abundance of occupation which induced the builders to exercise their native dexterity to the full. Western forms were at first adopted one by one, cross-ribs and pointed arches introduced, where they suited the plan of the whole. Architects who had studied for a long time in France, and had grasped the idea of the new architecture in all its profundity, were able to change entire buildings in such a way that the works resulting from the union of the foreign with the indigenous were complete in themselves.

In the Cathedral at Bamberg the two west towers are Gothic. Yet they are most exquisitely assimilated to the rest of the building. The Cathedral of Limburg has Gothic upper storeys upon the Romanesque substructure, and betrays in the form of the towers the influence of the Cathedral at Laon. But the master who brought the work to its conclusion, blended the older ideas of building into the new, to produce a uniform creation.

What German builders sought and found in France, was not a new world of ideas, but the final embodiment of their own endeavour. In the north of France, the problems of vaulting had been solved, and as early as the middle of the twelfth century it had been employed in pioneer structures. The introduction into the arch of ribs and moulding

The Townsfolk

lightened the weight of the vaulted roof, and made it possible to support it still more definitely upon the four corners. The pointed form of the ribs brought relief from the tyranny of the right angle. Pinnacles and flying buttresses received the lateral thrust of the vaulted roof. Thus the problem was solved on the technical side. Construction became more mobile: in place of ponderous masses the chief impression was produced by the interplay of forces. Windows, towers, plastic decoration, the greatest and the most minute, were all enlisted in this play of forces: all aspired towards heaven, leading the mind of the spectator heavenwards. Out of the blending of mathematical exactitude and pious fervour there arose a new fashion of building, which was to affect all the countries of Europe and to leave its impress on every branch of artistic activity: the Gothic style. Its forms are already visible in the pure austerity of line which distinguishes the Elizabeth church at Marburg—one of the first of the *Hallenkirchen* which have the nave and aisles of equal height, such as were frequently to be met with in Westphalia in the Romanesque period, but infinitely lighter and more charming, by reason of the vista which they present. The choir of the Cathedral at Cologne and the nave at Strasburg Cathedral show the ripe development of the Gothic style, about the year 1250.

Through the breaking-up of wall surfaces, and the high relief of piers and mouldings, the painter tended more and more to resign his task to the sculptor: innumerable niches had to be filled with free-standing examples of plastic art. It is in the nature of plastic art that it endeavours not only to grasp the truth, but to embrace it on all sides. Inspired by that joyous acceptance of life in its entirety which was characteristic of the time, the sculptors threw themselves with devotion into their new task. The apostles on the choir screen of Bamberg Cathedral are no longer ranked side by side in monumental peace, as in the representations of earlier times: one turns to the other in animated conversation. The artist tries to render the diversity of character and the conflict of opinion. He is not content with the play of gestures and of hands. Victory swells the robe of the triumphant Church, while that of the vanquished Synagogue hangs smoothly down. Heroic strength, controlled by 'moderation,' is embodied in the famous

Cities and Principalities

Rider of Bamberg. Maidenly nobility breathes from the figures of Church and Synagogue at the doors of Strasburg Cathedral. The Founders' figures in the Cathedral of Naumburg are nearer to reality in bearing and expression, and harsher in the treatment of the clothing. There was a long road to travel from the abstract representations of earlier painting to the joyous attitude of acceptance, the truth to nature which characterized this period. German art had covered it in the space of barely half a century.

The East was not yet capable of producing statues like those in the great cathedrals of the mother country. For a long time Austria was faithful to the Romanesque style of building, and developed its decorative forms in the richest abundance: the eminently beautiful Golden Gate in the mining city of Freiberg is likewise Romanesque. But at last the Gothic style gained an entry, and its transformation into 'Brick-Gothic' meant little less than a new creation. The eastern districts also developed a wealth of local and personal characteristics. Chorin and Pelplin possess Cistercian churches. But while the more westerly breathes something like secular elegance, the church at Pelplin bears the stiff military impress of the Teutonic Order. Marienwerder plans castle, church, bridge, and tower in a defensive group of singular beauty: the architecture of Bohemia and Moravia exhibits more uniform features, and here the Premonstratensians and Cistercians were chiefly responsible for the building.

The mightiest effort of Gothic architecture in Germany is the Cathedral at Cologne. The presence of a king lent special splendour to the festival of the laying of the foundation-stone. But it was not Conrad IV, the son and representative of the emperor Frederick II, but his rival, King William of Holland, whom a fraction of the princes had set up at the instigation of the Archbishop of Cologne. The dark decades of the Interregnum were throwing their shadows before. While the cosmopolitan spirit of Gothic architecture was taking the lead in the world of art, the age of imperial world-politics was drawing to a close. It is true that at the beginning of the fourteenth century Henry VII, the first king of the House of Luxemburg, attempted to renew his imperial claim upon Italy, and his successor, Ludwig the Bavarian, went so far as to set up a rival pope, and so gave rise to fierce fighting. But

The Townsfolk

then the bond which united Germany to Italy was snapped for ever. In 1338, at the Electoral Assembly at Rhense, the electoral princes declared that no king elected by them required the papal ratification for his election. Two journeys to Rome undertaken by Charles IV filled the imperial coffers, but actually signified the final renunciation of the dream of empire.

The renunciation came too late to be of service to the royal authority. Even Frederick I had thought it expedient to obtain the consent of the princes in important matters of State. After his time, the opinion gained ground that the empire was composed of the princes together with the king. Finally the representative of monarchical government took rank only as the first amongst his peers. The empire became a federal government: Bismarck himself was to found the empire upon the union of the Federal States. The internal government of the German States at the present day has its roots in the thirteenth century, and has been evolved from the sovereignty of the princes.

But even the student of history who is inclined to judge of political life by other standards than the personal, will derive no satisfaction from the manner in which the princes pursued their ends. How entirely they were lacking in the feeling of responsibility towards the community is perhaps most clearly seen in the behaviour of the most eminent amongst them, the electoral princes, at the king's election. He who offered the richest bribe to the determining body would have the best prospects of success. The choice of a Frenchman to be the King of Germany, which was a part of the Italian policy of France about the turn of the thirteenth century, was actually prevented only by the fact that the necessary cash was not forthcoming. Greed for gold, for land, and for authority was the spring of all action and want of action: this rule of conduct is not excused by the fact that it concerned itself, especially in the early days, with none but trivial ends. Territories which lay far apart from each other were united under one head by chance or accident—those which formed part of one whole were divided by right of inheritance. This resulted in the disruption of the old tribal communities, which might otherwise have been of service in the evolution of national consciousness. But as princely government developed a set form, it substituted the individual life of the princi-

Cities and Principalities

pality for the individual life of the tribes: and this up to the most recent past opposed what were perhaps the strongest obstacles to the national union of Germany. Yet there is hope for the future, that such hindrances, as they are of purely dynastic origin, may lose their force with the disappearance of the dynasties.

The sovereignty of the princes was not the immediate result of the collapse of royal authority; its origin is to be found rather at the period of the development of the feudal system. The great lord of the manor, when he passed on to his son the public rights which were bound up with his fief, was taking the first step towards princely sovereignty. As early as the twelfth century all the king's rights which were connected with cash revenues had been transferred almost without exception to the princes: rights of market and toll; the mint, mining, safe-conduct, and the protection of the Jews.

In the thirteenth century the princes' ambitions looked beyond such isolated benefits, and when the Staufen were in need of their help in the Italian wars, they obtained comprehensive concessions of a fundamental character: and it was agreed that, in the future, every man should enjoy undisturbed the rights he already possessed. In particular the king, Frederick II, resigned his claim to erect castles and custom-houses within the princes' territories, and to encroach upon their right of coinage. Thus the sovereignty of the princes, which had long been attained in fact, was legally recognized: in 1232 this recognition found expression in their title of 'Lords of the Land' (*Landesherren*). Somewhat later the electoral princes were distinguished from the rest, and the election of the king became henceforth the prerogative of the electoral college. In 1356 their power was further strengthened through the provisions of the Golden Bull, by which their lands were to be preserved intact, and supreme jurisdiction ensured to them over their vassals. This signified the achievement of their sovereignty, and at the same time it acted as an incentive to the others, to strive for the same end.

The sovereignty of the princes took its rise in various sources. Much older than the rights already mentioned were those which treated the prince as count and duke: as lord of the land over his tenants, as feudal lord over his vassals, as magistrate over those who were placed under

143

his jurisdiction. These rights also were for the most part connected with receipts. A reckoning for the Principality of Upper and Lower Austria shows the composition of the revenues in an individual case. Tolls and customs stand at the head: then follow the revenues from landed property, of which the greater half are natural products: the dues from the Court of Justice come directly after, and, at a further remove, the revenues from the Mint. Regular taxes were gradually added, beginning with a ground tax, which fell of course most heavily upon the peasants, for at that time, as a general rule, the countryside offered least resistance to the advance of princely government.

Princely government was founded on these beginnings. From the steward of the castle was evolved the official, with purely local powers of police, jurisdiction, and government: he was frequently assisted by a treasurer—the paymaster or 'cellarer.' The higher ranks at the prince's court were slower in taking shape, and were in all essentials a copy of the Royal Court with its Court officials, its Chancellor, and its Privy Council. Since the fourteenth century the Roman Code had been introduced into the Law Colleges from the court of the Luxemburg king, and provided a favourable atmosphere for the development of princely sovereignty.

As might be expected, the evolution of the sovereignty of the reigning princes exhibits great diversities. The east, which had been newly opened up, offered much more favourable conditions than the west and south of the empire. After the threatening advance of the Danish king had been checked by the victory gained by the northern towns and princes at Bornhövede in 1227, the Ascanians were able to develop a fairly compact territory between the Elbe and the Oder, and even, through the acquisition of the Neumark, to expand across the Oder. All judges pronounced judgment in the name of the Margrave, at whose court converged all the threads of a well-ordered government. The cities flourished under an active trade. The dynasty of Babenberg in Austria gained Styria by inheritance, and shortly afterwards Carniola also. Their wide territory extended from the Danube as far as Adria, and the duke ruled as an almost independent prince. Earlier than in other German provinces, a popular school of poetry developed in Austria, coloured by chivalry: here Walther von der Vogelweide learned 'to sing and speak.'

Cities and Principalities

The Nibelungenlied took its final shape on Austrian soil. The last of the Babenbergers could strive for the crown with good hope of success. He was forestalled, however, by his Bohemian neighbour (p. 131). After the extinction of the House of Babenberg, King Ottocar II raised Bohemia to the first rank in the east, adding to his dominions by warlike or by peaceful means Austria, Styria, Carinthia, and Carniola. In the mother countries of Bohemia and Moravia the king, whose mother sprang from the House of Staufen, encouraged the German immigration. Through the labour of the German miners he became 'the richest prince' of the empire.

Bohemia, Austria, and Brandenburg were the nurseries of the ruling dynasties, which in turn took over the government of the empire.

Bohemia's great hour seemed to have come when in 1273 the Electoral College assembled to elect a king. They came together at the behest of the pope, who hoped through the re-establishment of the German throne to gain support for the intended Crusades, and help against the menace of France. Yet Ottocar's powerful position stood in the way of his election: for the electoral princes did not desire a strong lord over them. This point of view also decided the subsequent elections. The choice fell repeatedly upon men who were possessed of little landed property. Ruling families succeeded each other six times in eight decades, so that it was impossible for the reigning monarch to build upon the work of his predecessor. From the middle of the fourteenth century, the family of Luxemburg remained for about ninety years in almost undisputed possession of the royal dignities, when they in turn made way for the Hapsburgs.

The property of the empire, with the exception of a small residue, had melted away in the wars of the Staufen against their rival kings: the royal authority had been almost entirely suppressed within the principalities: only the taxes from the imperial cities still brought some revenue to the king. The king's position depended entirely upon the fact that he possessed great domestic power: this fact explains the efforts to attain domestic power which were made by every ruler during the Middle Ages which were now coming to an end. Such power has earned a bad name: but the fact must not be overlooked, that without it even the most modest exercise of kingly prerogative would not have been possible.

The Townsfolk

When Rudolph of Hapsburg succeeded to the kingly
dignity, he was faced by the difficult task of making his
peace with Ottocar of Bohemia. His way was made easy
by the aversion of the other princes for the most powerful
amongst them. When Ottocar refused to take the oath
of allegiance, they declared him an outlaw. It was the
king's part to give effect to their resolution. By a series
of clever negotiations he won allies in the west and east
of Bohemia. A warlike advance upon Vienna was favoured
by a rising of the Austrian nobility, and forced Ottocar
with surprising swiftness to own himself beaten. He remained
in possession of his hereditary lands, but Rudolph kept his
hold upon the Austrian dukedoms. This aroused enmity
against him within the empire, which the King of Bohemia
was able to turn to his own advantage. Two years later,
in 1278, the armies faced each other once more on the
plain of the March. Rudolph was now almost entirely
dependent upon his own troops and the allied Hungarians,
but by throwing in reserves which he had carefully held
back till the right moment, he decided the battle in his
favour. Ottocar was slain. Rudolph left Bohemia and
Moravia to the son of the dead man, who was still a minor;
but he obtained the consent of the Electoral College to
the cession of the dukedoms of Austria and Styria, together
with Carinthia, to his own son. With careful preparation
and determined handling at critical moments, and with
wise self-restraint in the hour of success, the sixty-year-old
monarch laid the foundation of Hapsburg greatness. His
efforts for public peace restored the throne to its lost
popularity. By a fortunate choice of his connections by
marriage he opened wider prospects to the House of Hapsburg: all the secular electoral princes, including the heir
to the throne of Bohemia, were Rudolph's sons-in-law.

His immediate successors attempted to follow in his
footsteps, but with less success. After a few years, the
princes deposed the brave Count Adolph of Nassau and set
up Rudolph's son Albert in his place. Albert I worked for
the creation of a Greater Austria which was to include
Bohemia and Hungary, but his life was cut short by an
early death. Henry VII, Count of Luxemburg, had no
difficulty now in gaining Bohemia for his own house. But
he too died in the flower of his age, while he was attempting
to make the imperial authority once more effective in Italy.

Cities and Principalities

Fear of the Hapsburgs placed Lewis of Wittelsbach on the throne. In his contests with the pope, the electoral princes and the majority of the people were on his side. The exaggerated ambition of his domestic politics, however, aroused so much opposition, that the princes set up the Luxemburger, Charles IV to be king.

This grandson of Henry VII was the first and the most important Bohemian king to sit on the throne of Germany, and doubtless the most remarkable man to wear the crown in the interval between Frederick II and Maximilian. He was a deep student and man of active life; a true son of the Church and a friend of the Humanists, intellectually versatile and yet never satisfied: in all things a child of his paradoxical century. He began his life's apprenticeship at a very early age. After spending seven years of his childhood at the court of his uncle the French king, he was constrained, while little more than a boy, to represent the doubtful pretensions of the Luxemburgers in Italy. Afterwards he was made ruler over Moravia and Bohemia, suspected and victimized by his restless father, who was in perpetual need of money. The qualities which distinguish Charles's statecraft were formed by these experiences: the deliberation, the habit of counting upon the slight advantage, or the small deception, but in addition the indefatigable tenacity which is the earnest of success.

Charles IV realized that even the most successful policy of domestic aggrandizement must fail, if affairs in Germany could not be placed to some extent on an orderly footing. Free from all self-deception, and with a calm recognition of accomplished facts, he pursued his aim, and by the grant of special privileges he won over the most powerful elements in the empire to the side of the new order.

So in 1356 the famous Golden Bull became the law of the empire. It ensured the privileged status of the princes who formed the electoral college, and laid down the conditions of election and the manner in which elections were to be carried on. Through these and other regulations, it became the basis for the further development of the imperial constitution. The king endeavoured to foster the cause of public peace, by promoting treaties of peace between the lords and the towns of various principalities. Although these treaties were limited in time and place, yet they indicated an advance, and became the model for later efforts in the same direction. Charles also dealt with the foreign relationships of the empire, as far as it seemed feasible to him, without giving rise to complications. He was crowned as Emperor and King of Burgundy: but this was no longer indicative of an increase in power, nor from Charles's standpoint was it intended to be so. Like his predecessors, he knew that the real source of his authority was to be found in his domestic power: and this he succeeded in extending and completing. His second marriage brought him the Upper Palatinate, the third the remainder of the dukedoms of Silesia, the fourth offered prospects in Pomerania. His most difficult task was to wrench Brandenburg out of the hands of the Wittelsbachs. In this case Charles exerted every means at the command of his politics: he gave his daughter in marriage to one of the heirs apparent: he agreed to a settlement of the succession: he employed not only the meshes of diplomacy, but military campaigns and a great expenditure of money. With these he finally attained his object. In the east of Germany a State was in process of formation which, starting from the Bohemian Bastion, embraced the territories on the Elbe and the Oder as far as the Baltic Sea. It was of the greatest importance, from a military, economic, and political standpoint. Prague extended its borders, and became the brilliant capital of this kingdom. Here, as early as the second year of his reign, Charles had founded the first university on the soil of the empire: he lived to see the number of its students increase to more than ten thousand. The royal palace, the Hradschin, was rebuilt after the pattern of the Louvre: the cathedral which was being raised for the newly founded Archbishopric of Prague was to surpass that of Cologne in size. A French master-builder had begun it, the Swabian Peter Parler gave it its character, and his influence extended far beyond the capital. In other spheres also, German artists upheld the honour of their country amongst the great number of those whom Charles summoned from various nations.

The emperor accomplished the election of his son Wenzel by the electoral princes and by the pope. Then indeed it seemed as though his successor would be able to reach the goal, which was pointed out to him in a memorial probably composed by Charles himself, and 'again set up the commonwealth which had long lain prostrate on the earth.'

THE EMPIRE AND THE REORGANIZATION OF EUROPE

AFTER a long interval Germany once more had a king, who was not compelled to spend the strength of his best years in acquiring domestic power. Yet, even for a man with great resources at his command, it was an almost impossible task 'to gather up the scattered portions of the empire into one whole,' as the memorial already mentioned expressed it. Charles IV had succeeded in winning the consent of the electoral college to his measures. But other princes were striving for similar favours; cities and knights united to make their demands heard: foreign developments called for delicate handling and increased the difficulties of the situation. The same year, in which Wenzel took over the government, marked the beginning of the schism in the Church. While the nations were being forced to reach a common decision upon pressing Church problems, the whole empire was becoming conscious of many and various ties of quite a different nature, which connected the States in the west, east, and south. In addition to the economic and intellectual intercourse between the nations, inter-State relations had become closer and more intimate than in earlier times, and began to fill an important rôle. A State system was in process of formation in Europe: foreign affairs exerted an ever-growing influence upon the shaping of conditions in Germany.

Wenzel of Bohemia was not the man to solve the problems to which these circumstances gave rise. In the conflict between towns and princes, of which we shall hear more, both parties gave the king to understand that they were dissatisfied with his attitude. For this reason he gradually lost all desire to intervene in the affairs of the empire, the rather that he was greatly preoccupied with the cares of his domestic power in Luxemburg.

Charles IV had divided his estates among his sons in such a way that Wenzel received Bohemia and Silesia, and became heir-apparent of the Duchy of Luxemburg, while Sigmund was raised to the dignity of Elector of Brandenburg: a younger son was provided with portions of

The Townsfolk

Brandenburg and Lusatia. Brilliant prospects were offered to Sigmund by his betrothal to Maria, a daughter of King Louis of Hungary and Poland. But the estates of the realm of Poland dissolved the union between the two empires and compelled Louis' second daughter to marry the Archduke Jagello of Lithuania, who embraced the Christian faith.

Neither in Hungary was Sigmund's succession carried through without difficulties. Maria was forced to submit for a time to a betrothal with the French king's brother, and even after her marriage with Sigmund she was kidnapped by the followers of a third suitor into a fortress on the Dalmatian coast, and threatened with death. It was only through Wenzel's vigorous support that Sigmund was able in the end to occupy the throne of Hungary.

But he made an ill return for his brother's sacrifice, and the electoral college had good ground for complaining of his neglect of the affairs of the empire. At that time the French king's occupation of the territories on the Lower Rhine was only prevented by the bold stand made by the Duke of Geldern. Finally, Wenzel absented himself from the empire for eight whole years. He quarrelled with the estates of the realm in Bohemia, and with his nearest relatives. Meantime the evil side of his nature—laziness, drunkenness, and cruelty—got the upper hand. When all their warnings to the 'Pig in the Stye' were of no effect, the Rhenish electoral princes united, and set up Rupert of the Palatinate to be king. He died, however, after ten years of uneventful rule, whereupon the votes of the four western electors were divided. To gain a majority it was necessary for both parties to treat with the House of Luxemburg, who disposed of the votes in Bohemia and Brandenburg, and could count upon that of Saxony. Under these circumstances, both Wenzel's brother Sigmund and his cousin Jost von Mähren were elected. As Wenzel had not abdicated, three Roman kings reigned together for a year, when Jost's death simplified the position.

Sigmund was as unlike his brother as possible. A cheerful, wise, and clever man, he was nevertheless unstable and too careless in money matters. His plans and projects were never successful in Germany. After his election, he allowed four years to pass before making his appearance, and later devoted little of his time to the empire. As King of Hungary, he had been early acquainted with the terrible menace

The Reorganization of Europe

which was advancing from the east with the Turks, and in 1396, as a young man, he had fought bravely but unsuccessfully against them at Nicopolis. He hoped that his election as King of Germany would enable him to unite the Christian peoples against the common foe; but this could only be accomplished after an end had been put to the schism in the Church, which also implied division between the nations. Sigmund laboured at this task with skill and success, until he became entirely preoccupied with the difficulties which overwhelmed him in Bohemia.—Thus he too proved unequal to the royal task of putting German affairs in order. Yet, unlike former rulers, he did not employ his position as king for the aggrandizement of his domestic power, but he made the name of King of Germany respected again among the nations through the invaluable service which he did to the Church.

The enhanced power of the Papacy had won its greatest secular triumph in its victory over the imperial crown. When towards the end of the thirteenth century, Boniface VIII uncompromisingly asserted the rights of papal supremacy, he encountered the opposition of the native French monarchy. A profound antagonism between Church and State grew out of the question whether the king had the right to tax the national Church. 'Let no one persuade thee that thou hast no Lord over thee,' wrote Boniface to the French King Philip IV, and again: 'To obey the Roman Pontifex is necessary for every man who would win salvation.' No former pope had advanced so uncompromisingly the doctrine of papal omnipotence.

Philip was threatened with deposition and excommunication: but he could rely upon his people's support, and the clergy were obliged to follow the example of the other estates of the realm. King and people demanded a general council for the deposition of the pope, whose conduct was open to attack on many sides. While opinion in foreign countries was still being worked upon, the king's chancellor set out for Italy. The pope's enemies in Rome delivered the old man into his hands, and he died in a few weeks. The swing of the pendulum was evident in the cardinal's election of a French archbishop, and the removal of the papal residence to Avignon: the Papacy had become a tool of French imperial politics.

During the seventy years of 'Babylonish Captivity' from

1309 to 1378, the popes found compensation for their loss
of independence in the discovery of new sources of revenue:
what their predecessors had introduced in the thirteenth
century was now brought to completion. While the papal
right of jurisdiction was extended, an ever-increasing
income was derived from the confirmation of the appoint-
ments of bishops and archbishops: the offices of bishop,
canon, and parish priest were in steadily growing numbers
reserved to the pope. No secular ruler had such a wealth
of offices and honours at his disposal, and none understood
better how to translate his powers into ready money.

Once again the spiritual office sank to the level of a pawn
in the game of usury: the freedom of canonical election
threatened to disappear: all the abuses, for whose removal
the popes of the early Middle Ages had struggled so
vehemently against the Crown, were openly practised under
their successors. Yet dissentient voices could be heard from
the ranks of the misgoverned Church: increasing numbers
of the laity bound themselves together to check the scandal.

The first German kings, elected after the Interregnum,
had willingly recognized the papal pretensions to confirm
their election. But Henry VII's march on Rome, which had
originally been supported by the pope, led to a clash
between the two Powers. The pope made use of the ensuing
double election in Germany to postpone his recognition of
either king to the latest possible date: when Lewis the
Bavarian had overthrown his opponent of Hapsburg, he
was met by excommunication. His conflict with the Papacy
resembled that of the French king in the fact that the
majority of the German nation ranged themselves on the
king's side. But the effects of the new quarrel were much
more widely felt, and raised the most momentous questions
of principle. Lewis won support even from the ranks of the
mendicant monks, who were the picked troops of the
Papacy. The ideal of poverty upon which their Founder
had established his order was taken seriously by the
Franciscans; they publicly resisted the secularized Papacy,
and even for a time defied its authority. The opposition of
the Order collapsed: but the influence of its learned member,
William of Occam, lived on in his writings.

He did not attack the teaching of the Church: but he
distinguished between the province of knowledge and that
of faith, which were counted as one by the schools. Neither

The Reorganization of Europe

did he on principle break with the existing constitution of the Church: yet he demanded for the members of the Church the right, in case of need, to defend the faith: a general council, from which women were not to be excluded, was to be set over the pope. Marsilius of Padua agreed with the Englishman in demanding a general council. But he based his 'Refuge of Peace' on considerations which were yet more profound, and he spoke a sterner language. As the State is not a creation of the emperor, but has been established by the community, which may demand a reckoning from those who wield its authority, so, in the view of Marsilius, is the Church the creation of the community of all the faithful, in whose power lies the appointment and deposition of the priests, even of the highest. The authority of the priests is of divine origin, but it has its limits. Secular supremacy is not within their province. Many of the ideas, which were powerful at the time of the Reformation and the Enlightenment, were first formulated by Marsilius.

King Louis, at whose Court these men lived, was very far from translating their ideas into deeds. His ultimate desire was for peace with the Church: and his two successors also went a long way towards meeting the papal wishes. But his dispute with the Papacy had this immediate effect, that the pope's pretension to ratify the king's election was expressly rejected by the electoral princes at the Electoral Diet at Rense in 1338, and was passed over in significant silence in the Golden Bull of 1356. The idea of a council also gained ground as confusion grew within the Church.

The return of the Papacy to Rome led to the nomination of a French rival pope, and to a schism in the Church which lasted for nearly forty years. The dispute of the popes, and the division of Christendom into two camps, intensified the abuses under which the Church was suffering. It was at this time of distress that the Englishman Wyclif began to deliver his message.

While Marsilius himself had approved of the dominant position of the priests, and of the ecclesiastical hierarchy, Wyclif recognized human agency alone in the distinction between clerical and lay, and to him the veneration accorded to the pope was pure idolatry. He arrived at these deductions through his basic idea that the whole truth was to be found in the Bible alone. He anticipated much that

153

was essential in Luther's train of thought: yet it was not the Englishman, enjoying the protection of his university and his sovereign, but the German, who had to fight his own battle, who became the author of the Reformation. John Huss, the Prague professor, took his stand upon Wyclif. He was not an original thinker, but a man of arresting eloquence, who was able to inflame his people, no less against the privileged position of the Germans, than against Roman misrule: a man who was so true to himself that he preferred death at the stake to a denial of his convictions.

The sensation which was aroused throughout western Europe by the speeches and writings of these men widened the scope of the tasks which were awaiting fulfilment. In 1409 a General Council was called by the cardinals at Pisa 'For the Reform of the Church in Head and Members': but its only result was that from that time forward there were three popes instead of two.

It required courage to make another attempt. King Sigmund possessed that courage. He turned to account the embarrassments of the pope who had been set up in Pisa, by forcing him to summon a new council in the imperial city of Constance. At the same time, by a personal written appeal, Sigmund made a bid for the followers of the other popes. Some five hundred princes of the Church, representatives from thirty-seven universities, ambassadors from every European State, hundreds of secular princes and lords, made, according to the reckoning of a citizen of Constance, a total of over 70,000 men at one time. These were all assembled in the little city, which became for some years the centre of events in Europe, as well as the scene of questionable gaieties. The members of the council which lasted from 1414 to 1418 were divided into four nations, according to the custom which had been adopted at the universities. Sigmund took part industriously in the sittings. The attempted flight of the last elected pope would have broken up the assembly, but for the king's firm attitude. When this pope had been deposed, Sigmund in person arranged the abdication of another. After this, he visited the French king in Paris, and the English king in London, in the hope of mediating between them. But when, after eighteen months, he returned from his travels, he found that a complete understanding had not even yet been

The Reorganization of Europe

arrived at with the former popes. Sigmund's attempt to set on foot the reform of the Church was wrecked by the counter-proposal of the French and Italians, and in the end, of the English also, that the first step must be to give a new head to the Church. The 'Union of the Church' under a newly elected pope was thus the solitary achievement of years of toil. The no less important 'Improvement of the Church' was postponed, and an ill service was rendered to the 'Cause of the Faith' by the condemnation of John Huss.

The Hussite Wars formed a sorry sequel to the Council of Constance. The Bohemians, who revered in Huss their national and spiritual leader, fought for their nationality and their faith. Sigmund, who was heir to the throne after Wenzel's death, was powerless. The electoral princes appealed to the forces of the empire. But the imperial troops were beaten, and the help of the armies of the Cross proved of no avail: the Hussites advanced as far as the Baltic, leaving frightful devastation in their train. There was no other remedy: the Council of Basle which sat from 1431 to 1439 had meantime begun its deliberations upon the reform of the Church: it negotiated with the most moderate among the leaders of revolt, and acceded to their principal demands. A breach had been made in the unity of the Church.

At last Sigmund was able to enter Prague. He died in the following year. His project of leading all the Western peoples to war against the Turk had been frustrated. In like manner, all hope had vanished of the drastic reform of the Church which he had so strongly pledged himself to accomplish, though it is true that the Council of Basle removed some of the most crying abuses. Certain of the princes were soon on the spot, to secure privileges for their national Churches by direct negotiation with the assembled fathers. But little by little the supporters of the most drastic demands gained the upper hand. This cleared the way for the pope's counter-attack. For a time two councils and two popes fought with each other, till Rome won the day. The idea of a council had lost its efficacy.

In one sense, the history of the empire also comes to a close with Sigmund's reign. As he left no male heir, he nominated his son-in-law Albert of Austria to succeed him, in Bohemia, and Hungary, and in the empire. The electoral college actually chose the Hapsburger, being well aware that no other king would have had a chance against the lord of the eastern territories, who united the Hapsburg inheritance with that of Luxemburg. This consideration was more in evidence in the succeeding elections: in the end the imperial crown became in a sense the heritage of the Hapsburgs, and remained in their family till the dissolution of the empire in the storms of the Napoleonic period.

This power, which was to grow so mighty, rested at first upon an unstable foundation. Albert II, who reigned scarcely two years, was succeeded by his eldest cousin, Frederick III of Styria and Carinthia: he wore the crown for more than half a century, longer than any other of the German kings. But an indolent successor dissipated the patrimony which had been carefully accumulated by former generations.

Led by self-elected princes, Bohemia with its neighbouring territories, together with Hungary, revolted from the heir of the Hapsburgs. Sore dissensions in the family tore Austria and the Tyrol for a time out of the king's hand—in his old age, the King of Hungary robbed him of almost the whole of Austria, Carinthia, and Carniola, and for years kept his court in Vienna.

Yet even in these straits the old man prevented his son from relinquishing Lower Austria. He was supported by a mystical faith in the mission of his house. Though his own kindred and strangers also might plot against him, and conquer his lands, he must carry his point in the end. And he did carry his point: he outlasted them all. He became the heir of the childless among his kin: settled for his family the right of inheritance in Bohemia and Hungary, betrothed his son Maximilian to the heiress of the Duke of Burgundy, and lived to see the Hapsburg possessions increased by Burgundian territory. Thus Sigmund the Inactive must take first rank amongst those who raised the House of Hapsburg to the position of a world-power.

The empire was the sufferer. Frederick III left to the Hungarians the task of carrying on the war against the Turks. In his hands the Reform of the Church became the task of the House of Hapsburg, from which they reaped great profit, while the empire paid the costs. In common with other sovereigns, the electoral princes had been granted concessions from the Council of Basle, which, it must be admitted, required further guarantees. But instead

The Reorganization of Europe

of pleading the cause of the empire, the king helped the pope out of his difficulties, and sowed dispeace amongst the estates of the realm. In 1448 the Concordat of Vienna brought to Hapsburg a considerable premium in ready money, and the right of disposal over six bishoprics and one hundred benefices. But as far as the other parts of Germany were concerned, it meant that the papal financiers would continue to draw a profit from them. Why should not the estates of the realm lend themselves to conquer Switzerland for Hapsburg? But at this point Frederick encountered opposition. When the bands of the French king's mercenaries summoned by him brought frightful devastation upon Switzerland and Alsace, indignation broke into flame. Frederick retorted by attending no diet for twenty-seven years. And afterwards he intervened so rarely, that for all practical purposes the empire was entirely deprived of its head. Cities, knights, and princes quarrelled amongst themselves, while one territory after another was lost along the frontiers.

In the last years of Charles IV, the imperial cities of south Germany entered the league of Swabian cities which was directed primarily against the princes. A few years later the Rhineland cities allied themselves against the knights, who on their part had formed confederations: two thousand knights are said to have belonged to the League of the Stars. The similarity of their aims soon led the towns to unite: the knights' leagues were worsted and their rôle was played out.

The quarrel with the princes still smouldered on. For years the two powerful parties opposed each other, and strove with King Wenzel for the fulfilment of their demands. In any case, these towns could not pretend to represent the common cause of the middle classes. Those which were under sovereign authority (and the great majority of all urban communities belonged to this class) stood aside from the Unions, as did the cities of the Hanseatic League. These Unions cherished no stronger desire than to shake off the oppression and menace of their noble or royal masters. They were drawn together, amongst other things, by the insecurity of the roads, the struggle with the princes for supreme rights, and the fear lest the king might deliver them as a royal pledge into the hand of the princes. They had no far-seeing and uniform aim, and each step they took was hampered by every kind of dissension. But when we are inclined to blame the towns, we should remember that at that period things were in no better case amongst the princes.

In spite of all defects in the towns' leagues, there might then have been a possibility, if indeed it was not even then too late, of strengthening the royal authority by the help of the towns, and of counteracting the tendency of Germany to split up into a number of separate principalities. The defeat of the Duke of Austria at Sempach by the Swiss confederates allied with the towns, which took place in 1386, immediately before the outbreak of the towns' war, might have encouraged a resolute king to a similar attempt. But Wenzel of Bohemia had no desire to risk his skin for such remote objects. His policy extended no further than playing the towns against the princes and, in concert with them, in cheating the Jews of the Swabian League out of their bonds.

In the year 1388 the storm broke out in Bavaria Franconia, and Swabia. In Wurtemberg the towns were defeated by the old Count Eberhard at Döffingen: it was the greatest battle which had been fought for many decades on German soil. But it brought about no settlement. The strength of the combatants was dissipated in isolated fights: the trading routes were deserted and 'overgrown with grass and thistles.' This fell more hardly upon the towns than upon the princes. Their enterprises were hampered by a disinclination to further sacrifices. When the king at last intervened, they were forced to dissolve their leagues. Their attempt to meet the princes as a united force had been shattered: but the princes, on their part, had not succeeded in breaking the economic and legal independence of the towns.

About the middle of the fifteenth century, serious fighting broke out again. Nuremberg, the chief city of Franconia, had to defend herself from an attack launched against her by the Hohenzollern Margrave Albert Achilles, with more than twenty princes. The Swabian towns fought against the Count of Wurtemberg and Duke Albert of Austria. At this time the idea of a League of the Country's Peace was revived, to include the towns, the knights, and the princes: this again brought up the question of imperial reform. These subjects were discussed through many following decades. But what could be accomplished by such a Union was already obvious; in a short time the Swabian League had brought order into the storm centre of the empire; and in 1488, the very year of its founding, it released the young King Maximilian from his captivity in the Netherlands. As the towns were indispensable for the reform of the empire, they could not well be excluded from the diets.

In 1489 the imperial cities took their place for the first time as a complete 'college' beside the colleges of the electors and princes. The citizens had fought their way to regular participation in the affairs of the empire.

Another step was taken to reform the Germanic Constitution when, in the course of the fifteenth century, the power of the sovereign princes took a fixed shape. About the year 1500 the majority of the great principalities had already reached the dimensions which they were to retain until the eighteenth and nineteenth centuries. The rise of the Houses of Hohenzollern and Wettin dates back to Sigmund. After the extinction of the Ascanians in 1319, the Mark of Brandenburg had had many varieties of rulers from the Houses of Wittelsbach and Brandenburg. What Charles IV had accumulated was scattered by his nephew, Jost von Mähren. In 1415, Sigmund invested Frederick of Hohenzollern with the electorate of Brandenburg. He was that Burgrave of Nuremberg to whose zeal and cleverness Sigmund chiefly owed his election to the throne.

Upon him and his immediate successors fell the difficult task of re-establishing their authority. The first Hohenzollern subdued the knights, and the second the cities: the fourth broke the ties uniting him to the family possessions in Franconia, which had been a constant source of trouble to his predecessors. This prince was the first to take up his permanent residence in the Mark, and he directed the co-operation of the estates of the realm into organized channels. In time to come the country profited by the domestic legislation enacted by Albert Achilles in 1473. It made impossible in the Mark those partitions which proved fatal to the neighbouring electorate of Saxony, and to other principalities. After the extinction of the local Ascanians, the dukedom of Saxe-Wittenberg had been bestowed by Sigmund upon Frederick the Quarrelsome of Meissen, in gratitude for his services in the Hussite Wars.

The Townsfolk

About the middle of the fifteenth century the House of
Wettin was involved in a disastrous fratricidal war, and in
1485 it split up into two reigning houses. The Ernestiners
retained the electoral dignity, together with Saxe-Wittenberg and the greater part of Thuringia; the Albertiners
obtained Meissen and the territory of northern Thuringia
with Leipzig. In the first half of the century, the endless
quarrels between the three reigning houses of Wittelsbach—
Munich, Ingolstadt, and Landshut—had a still more
devastating effect upon the land of Bavaria. It was not
until 1500 that Bavaria was united once more under one
ruler, as was the Landgraviate of Hesse, which for a
considerable period had been partitioned between the two
Governments of Marburg and Cassel. Somewhat later
Wurtemberg, which had suffered little from partition and
had been growing steadily from small beginnings, was
advanced to be a dukedom.

Towards the end of the century, certain limits had been
set to the growth of princely power. Originally, the territorial
prince had considered it his right to summon the higher
clergy, the vassals, and the bond vassals of the principality
to his councils. The right of summons became an obligation,
and the obligation of summons gave rise to a right of assent.
As the sovereigns required more money to keep up their
court, and to pay their officials and their mercenaries, the
towns grew in importance, for the heaviest of the burden
must fall on their shoulders. In the end it came about that
the assent of the 'estates'—clergy, nobility, and townsmen
—was required not only for new and extraordinary taxation, but also for territorial legislation, the regulation of
inheritance, and other matters. The princes, who had
almost entirely freed themselves from dependence upon the
emperor, had to be content to work in concert with the
corporations of their subjects.

This situation was the result of a long and occasionally
stormy process of evolution. Neither the knights nor the
towns showed any inclination to submit to princely
authority. The prince could frequently count on his towns
for support against the knights: the history of the first
Hohenzollerns in the Mark offers a well-known example of
this fact. But taken as a whole the towns presented still
more serious difficulties. The citizens of the chief town of
Westphalia, for instance, renounced their allegiance to their

ruler, the Archbishop of Cologne, put themselves under the government of the Duke of Cleve, and gained their point at the end of a five years' war (the Feud of Soest, about 1450). As a rule, however, the ruler retained the upper hand, either by his own strength, or in alliance with neighbouring princes. Nevertheless, as he was obliged to grant the estates a share in the government, the result was not unlimited authority for the prince, but an equalization of forces. On this basis the principalities were able in time to gain internal autonomy.

In this respect the towns were still for a long time in a more advantageous position than the princes, but during the fifteenth century they too were troubled with internal unrest. As in the empire and in the principalities, so in the towns, those who up till that time had been excluded from political influence were striving for a share in the government. It was not through any lack of the necessities of life, but through an enhanced sense of their own importance, that the masses of the craftsmen were driven into conflict with the hereditary patricians. The movement began in the industrial cities of Flanders and the Rhine, and embraced almost the whole of Germany. The hereditary patricians were accused of excluding the rest of the citizens from the council, of oppressing the poorer class, and of wrongfully employing the administration to their own advantage. Whether these charges were capable in every case of practical proof must remain in doubt. In any case, they gave evidence that the artisans had been trained under the discipline of the guilds to aspire to political influence. For however varied were the circumstances, the object was everywhere the same: participation by the guilds in the city government.

In many cities the hereditary patricians yielded the point without great resistance: in other places it gave rise to a protracted struggle, carried on with varying fortune. In Strasburg the Constitution was altered twelve times in barely one hundred years. Death by fire and sword threatened the vanquished, especially when the patricians came off victorious. The results of the movement were as varied as its course. In some cities, the council was without more ado divided up amongst the guilds, so that the patricians exercised no further influence save as guild members. In other places the guilds were satisfied with having a small number of their members received into the council, or with forming a new council 'from the community' in addition to the old. The rule of the patricians continued almost unchanged in the great Hanse towns, where craftsmen were of small account compared with the merchants. In Nuremberg also, and some other towns, the patricians retained their authority. As far as we are able to judge, it was usually a matter of small moment to the well-being of the community whether its Government were aristocratic or democratic.

The forces of the future were struggling for the mastery, in the lowest as well as the highest class. In the tumult of this conflict, it occurred to no one to estimate the loss which the empire, as a whole, was suffering.

To counter the efforts made by the House of Hapsburg to attain a position of princely power, the League of the Swiss Confederacy was maintained and extended, without, however, in any way impairing its relations with the empire. For during the century and a half which followed the death of Rudolph, the men who wore the crown were almost without exception ready and willing to add to the difficulties of their fellow aspirants of the House of Hapsburg. One Hapsburg, it is true, succeeded in persuading King Charles IV to a joint attack upon Zurich, but when the citizens hoisted the imperial standard, the king withdrew and arranged an advantageous settlement.

But when the crown passed from the House of Luxemburg to the hated Hapsburgs, the relationship of the Confederacy to the empire was changed at one stroke. In 1444 Frederick III let loose upon the Swiss the savage French mercenaries of the Armagnacs. After that the Confederacy sought to break away from the empire: when Maximilian tried to reform the imperial constitution, they refused to accept any further obligations towards it. Maximilian's military expedition had no terrors for the conquerors of Charles the Bold. Even before the century had come to an end, the Swiss were actually released from the imperial alliance.

By her victory over the Duke of Burgundy, the empire was freed from a serious danger which threatened her from the west. In the course of one century the dukes of Burgundy had accumulated great territorial possessions. In the south they owned Alsace, and the territories west-

The Reorganization of Europe

ward as far as the Loire; in the north, Belgium and the Netherlands, almost as they stand to-day, and in addition other French territories and Luxemburg. Charles the Bold determined, by conquering Lorraine, to unite the northern and southern halves of his dominion, and thus gain a royal crown. He won the co-operation of Frederick III for these plans, by holding out a prospect of the betrothal of his heiress to Frederick's son, Maximilian. Now, after a quarter of a century, the Germans were again allowed a sight of their emperor. The two princes had an interview at Trèves. All the preparations were already made for the ceremony, and the crown exhibited for public admiration. Suddenly, on the eve of the day fixed for the coronation, the emperor left the town secretly with his son, for he dreaded the difficulties which would inevitably arise from the opposition of the electoral college.

Charles made a second attempt by force of arms. Geldern was already in his power, and he turned against Cologne. Only the heroic defence of the citizens of Neuss prevented his occupation of the archbishopric. The emperor saw to it that no advantage should be reaped from this success: he made sure of the desired marriage for his son by betraying the empire. In a short time Charles was master of Lorraine. But his luck forsook him in his war with the Swiss. After his death at the Battle of Nancy in 1477, war broke out between France and Germany over the reorganization of the western frontier.

In the north, the rule of the Danish king was extended into the imperial territories without recourse to arms. On the extinction of the House of Schauenburg, Schleswig, being a Danish fief, would inevitably be reabsorbed into the northern empire, and there was a danger that it might be separated from Holstein. To avoid this, in 1460 the estates of the dukedom of Schleswig-Holstein elected the Dane to be their duke.

By the change of Government in Schleswig-Holstein, the Danish frontier was advanced almost as far as Lübeck. At the same time, changes in the west and east weakened the internal strength of the Hanse: the Dutch towns were supported by their Burgundian master: the Prussian seceded from the league upon their incorporation with Poland. Little by little the league became conscious of the rivalry of neighbouring states which had grown out of

The Townsfolk

their tutelage. The Danes seized upon every means of embarrassing the trade of the Hanse: they gave the preference to Dutch and English merchants; they incited the Tsar to plunder Novgorod, offering him in return their help against Sweden. Upon this, the Hanse again supported Sweden in her revolt against Danish rule. The Hanse were continually successful in battle. The English, who were already formidable rivals in the North Sea, and as early as the fifteenth century had temporarily closed the Steelyard, were obliged to restore German trading privileges in their former extent. In 1524, the King of Denmark, the last sovereign to rule over a united Sweden and Norway, was driven out of his capital. As late as the first decades of the sixteenth century, the Hanseatic towns still maintained their sovereignty, but their internal force was failing. Their undertakings were hampered by dissensions between the western and eastern members of the league. In the long run, the Hanse were unable to compete with the merchants of neighbouring states, who had the advantage of the powerful support of their rulers, while the empire, on the other hand, was indifferent to the fate of its merchants, and a number of towns were even forced by the princes to resign from the league. The turning-point came in 1536, with the ill-starred attempt of Jurgen Wullenweber, the Burgomaster of Lübeck, against the successor of the last king of the Union: from that time the collapse of the Hanse was rapid.

The position in the east was even more threatening than in the west and north. During the course of the fourteenth century the German race encountered strong national opposition in Bohemia, Hungary, and Poland. This was connected with the advance of the nobility who, like the princes in Germany, were robbing the Crown of one right after another. Poland enters modern history as a republic of aristocrats, and here the anti-German movement first made itself felt. The union of Poland with Lithuania under Ladislaw Jagello (p. 150) transferred the old enmity which existed between the Lithuanians and the Teutonic Order to the whole empire, and at the same time it increased the offensive strength of the united peoples so that they were able successfully to strive for an outlet to the sea. In 1410, at the Battle of Tannenberg, the Order succumbed to the superior power and better leadership of its opponents: yet it retained the Marienburg. At that time King Sigmund interfered in its favour, and was able skilfully to make use of the strained relations which existed between the Polish duke and his cousin, to whom he had been forced to resign the government of Lithuania. Hence the conditions of peace were more favourable than might have been expected.

The knights had proved in the battle that they still knew how to die: but they no longer knew how to live. They were powerful; yet they did nothing to reconcile their subjects to their government, which, for the great majority of the population, was the rule of a foreigner. They were rich: they had complete control of the valuable amber market, and to a great extent of the export of grain; their ships sailed as far as Spain. But they made no friends of the mammon of unrighteousness. The sovereigns were everywhere consenting to the co-operation of their estates in the Government—but the Order desired to be unquestioned master. This aroused resentment amongst the provincial nobility, the clergy, and the citizens, whose enterprises were already hampered by the important trade of the knights. After the Battle of Tannenberg, many great towns had already surrendered to the enemy: but the knights refused to take the lesson to heart. Their Grand Master— the hero who had saved the Marienburg in the midst of overwhelming disaster—had to lie ten years in a dungeon because he had granted certain rights to the towns and the provincial nobility. Finally, the Prussian confederation broke away from the towns and the nobility, and applied for help to the King of Poland. A twelve years' war laid the land waste and exhausted the resources of the Order. Mercenaries, left without pay, sold the castles of the Order to the enemy. In 1466, at the second Peace of Thorn, west Prussia with Ermland fell to Poland, and the Grand Master became a Polish vassal. Henceforth east Prussia was divided from the rest of Germany by a wide strip of territory under Polish government where, as an almost invariable rule, the German nationality maintained its footing in the towns alone.

During the decades which followed, the danger which threatened in the east became more menacing. Albert II had united Bohemia and Hungary, Sigmund's legacy, with the Hapsburg possessions. But the countries struggled from under the yoke of the Hapsburg. The Bohemians, who ten

The Townsfolk

years earlier, in the Hussite Wars, had turned their fury against the Germans, now desired a Hussite Government, while Hungary looked for a strong leader against the Turks. Frederick III, who acted as guardian to Albert's posthumous son, allowed matters to run their course too long. When Albert's heir died in early youth, the actual rulers ascended the throne: in Bohemia George Podiebrad; in Hungary John Hunyadi, the conqueror of the Turks, who was succeeded shortly after by his son, Matthew Corvinus. These were resolute men of action, striving after high aims, and befriending art and science—men of a new age. It was not long before Bohemia found herself hampered by the conflict between the Hussites and the Catholic inhabitants. This gave the King of Hungary the more freedom of action. He forced the estates of the realm to do his bidding, and raised the most powerful army in the west, besides a considerable fleet. At the age of sixteen he had been elected king. At the age of thirty he had won from the Turks Bosnia, Moldavia, and Wallachia, together with Moravia, Silesia, and Lusatia, portions of the Bohemian heritage.

Twelve years later he marched into Vienna (p. 156). The Sudeten countries were now to be united with Austria, and their sovereign crowned with imperial honours. His early death in 1490 shattered these plans, but opened the way for a union of the great Eastern empires. This came about when Hungary chose for his successor the Bohemian king Ladislaw, the son of that King of Poland who had vanquished the German Order. Poland, Bohemia, and Hungary were now under the dominion of the House of Jagello, and formed a territory greatly superior in size to the German Empire.

Fortunately for Germany, this powerful group of countries was lacking in internal unity. The three empires pursued quite different objects. Their king was never anything but a stranger to the great majority of Bohemians and Hungarians; on every hand the nobility were wresting authority from the throne.

To Maximilian I, son of Frederick III, fell the task of winning back the countries which had been estranged under his father from Hapsburg rule. While Frederick was still alive, Maximilian had been elected King of Rome—a step which the electoral college had been induced to take after the capture of Vienna by Matthew Corvinus. After the

The Reorganization of Europe

death of the King of Hungary, he won back the lost Austrian provinces. His assault upon Hungary was so far successful as to lead to an Act of Succession, which gave Maximilian the prospect of inheriting that country, and of the support of the king in his attempt upon the Crown of Bohemia. Thanks to a clever marriage policy, and to the favour of fortune, these hopes, after many vicissitudes, were later fulfilled. As the Tyrol also came by inheritance to the reigning Hapsburgs, the south-east of Germany, with Bohemia and Hungary, which Bohemia in the thirteenth century, and Hungary in the fifteenth, in vain tried to co-ordinate, were at last at the beginning of the modern period united under German leadership.

This did not come to pass till after the death of Maximilian. The great object at which he aimed was a Turkish campaign, which he proposed to undertake, not as a Hapsburg, but as the leader of Western Christendom. But in regard to this plan, he had the same experience as Sigmund of Luxemburg: more urgent duties pressed upon him, and in the end his intention was not carried out. But the hindrances which the two men encountered were not of the same nature, and their difference is significant of the change in the times. Sigmund was turned aside by his efforts in connection with the council, and by the Hussite Wars: Maximilian had to defend himself against the reigning House of France.

In contrast to the course of evolution in Germany, the power of the French king had grown almost uninterruptedly from small beginnings. He was supported in his struggle with the great vassals by the Church dignitaries, who did not possess the same secular power as the German princes of the Church, and the towns which had begun to flourish at a much earlier date than those of Germany. As the ruling family was changed only once in six hundred years, when the Valois succeeded the Capets in 1328, the hereditary character of the Crown had become established. Two 'Hundred Years' Wars' against the English, while they put the throne into the greatest jeopardy, strengthened the national sentiment of the people. With Charles the Bold, the last feudal lord who was not subject to the throne had been deprived of his power to hurt. The internal authority of the kings then stood on so firm a basis, that they were able to devote their whole strength to the pursuit of those objects for which their predecessors had repeatedly striven, but always in vain—the extension of the power of France, and the acquisition of the imperial crown.

In the inscriptions upon the banners of his troops, Charles VIII was proclaimed as 'God's Ambassador.' In 1494 he directed his attack upon Naples and Milan, to which he was not without hereditary pretensions. Sicily was at the time under Spanish rule, and was held to be indispensable for Spain's grain supply. Without Naples, whose throne was occupied by a collateral line of the Spanish dynasty, this possession could not be defended. It was not long since the Spanish royal house had united the dominions of Aragon and Castile; and only a short time since she had driven the Moors from the Continent and sent Columbus on his voyage to India. Now she turned the whole force of her arms against France. Maximilian, who had married a princess of Milan for his third wife, claimed feudal rights over the city. At a later date, England also became involved in the controversy.

The clash of these contending Powers led to a wearisome and indecisive struggle, which even at that early date shows all those features which distinguish the long catalogue of later European wars. It was not confined to the immediate actors, but drew many other States, both great and small, into its vortex. It was not waged in order to acquire land to live in, nor to defend the rights of contending nations, not even to settle the differences between Church and State; its sole purpose was to pander to the reigning houses in their lust for power. Without any clear conception of the resources of their countries, without regard to the natural homogeneity of territories, they endeavoured to seize all that could be seized, and sowed hate amongst the nations. The war gave rise to multiple alliances, which were announced in lofty words and as lightly betrayed; treaties of succession, and marriage contracts, which were frequently opposed to every natural sentiment. The scale was turned, not by national force of arms, but by native and foreign mercenaries. In the last resort money was the decisive factor, wrung out of the peoples, and accumulated in the pockets of a few money lords.

So far as the human worth of the participants is in question, there is no doubt that Germany produced the best man. Maximilian was more than a selfish politician,

The Reorganization of Europe

caring only for his family's aggrandizement: he gave his heart and mind to the needs of the empire. He united restless energy with the brilliant talents and extreme intellectual versatility which he inherited from his Portuguese mother. And yet he was not a man of action. His inexhaustible imagination led him constantly to seek after the better, and thus to miss the good which he already possessed. Often also 'the evening scattered what the morning had resolved.' He lost much by the instability of his will. He was hampered still more by the insufficiency of the means at his command. When the results of his life are taken into consideration, the German people have no reason to think of him with gratitude. Yet he won all hearts, and even the modern observer can feel the charm of his attractive personality through all that he did and furthered, accomplished and left alone. We are conscious of his cheerful acceptance of life, and of the thirst for knowledge, which drove him to seek the society of learned men, and to study the stars: his joy in all creative work which made him at home in the studios of painters and woodcarvers.

When he succeeded to the throne on the death of Frederick III, he had already served his apprenticeship in politics. His father's tenacious marriage policy had made him master of Flanders: at a later date marriage plans played a leading part in his own calculations. After a short period of wedded happiness with Mary of Burgundy, he became suitor on his own behalf and that of his son for two daughters of the Spanish king and queen, but was rejected with scant ceremony. He got as far as a marriage by proxy with the heiress of Brittany, but the French king then forced his betrothed to become his own wife. Maximilian was more successful with the niece of the Regent of Milan: she brought to the marriage some hundreds of thousands of gold florins, and pretensions—very shadowy, it must be admitted—to the dukedom itself.

Maximilian was no less experienced in warfare than in courtship and marriage. In his wars with France, the Netherlands, and Hungary, he had proved his bravery, earning the title given him by his contemporaries of 'The Last of the Knights.' Even at that period he did a great deal to encourage the development of a troop of lansquenets (foot soldiers) and of firearms. Untroubled by the prejudices of his peers, he marched into the proud city of Cologne at

The Townsfolk

the head of his foot soldiers, with his long spear on his shoulder. In process of time he gave the soldiers a kind of self-government: they looked up to him as the founder of their 'Order.' He had his cannon mounted upon wheels, and sometimes served it in battle with his own hand. He was even practised in the difficult art of making money, though all his life long he was never successful in it. If he ever possessed money, it took to itself wings, though neither he nor anyone else could say how it had gone.

Exactly a year after the death of Frederick III, Charles VIII marched across Italy and took Naples at the first assault. Without hesitation, Maximilian joined the 'Holy Alliance,' which leagued him with the pope, the Spanish king and queen, Venice and Milan. The empire was to provide the money and the troops. It was a favourable moment for the estates of the realm to bring to a point the long-debated reform of the Germanic Constitution as they conceived it.

Claim and counter-claim were dealt with at the Diet of Worms in 1495. The estates were inclined to agree to a universal tax of the empire, 'the common Penny'—it was to be both poll-tax and property-tax, and to be collected not by the nobles but by the parish priests. This was a great concession, but now came the counter-claim: the appointment of an imperial council with such extensive powers that little was left to the king beyond the supreme command of the army, the right of the bestowal of fiefs, and the sanction of ennobling. It cannot be said that princely self-interest alone was voiced in this demand. The princes' representative, Berthold von Henneberg, Archbishop of Mayence, took in all seriousness his duties as the German chancellor of the empire. He hoped to give the languishing empire a new lease of life by raising the princes, in whose hands lay the actual authority, to the position of constitutional supporters of the whole edifice, and thus making them responsible for its welfare. He hoped nothing more from the rule of the Hapsburgs. But Maximilian defended himself most resolutely against the infringement of his rights: it seemed to him that he was about to be 'bound hand and foot and hung on a nail.' He adjured the princes to postpone the hateful question of reform, in face of the threatening danger: but his prayer fell on deaf ears. One cannot refuse sympathy to either party—neither had all the right on its side: their disagreement was not their fault, but the fruit of a century of evolution.

Unity was reached upon other points. Perpetual public peace took the place of the public peace limited by time and place, which was the utmost that had hitherto been attained. A supreme court of justice was to adjudicate in cases of breach of the public peace, and in disputes between nobles in immediate dependence upon the emperor, and also to act as the final court of appeal in other specified cases. It possessed, however, no military or political compulsory powers. An insufficient substitute was provided by the subsequent division of the empire into ten districts, for the suppression of unruly elements. But even so, a great advance was marked by the decision to do away entirely with the right of armed self-help, and to recognize the idea of the legal state. The reform of the administration and of the taxes went no farther than a commencement. For the moment, the estates dropped the imperial council, and agreed to an assignment upon the receipts from the imperial tax. But out of the 150,000 florins assigned, only a small fraction was collected, although with three exceptions all the towns made punctual payment. Yet there was no lack of money: a single papal year of jubilee, in 1502, brought in 400,000 florins. No more was accomplished by subsequent diets. When success came to Maximilian, the French king was no longer so dangerous: when difficulties overwhelmed him, the emperor was forced to reduce his demands to the lowest point.

For a few months Milan and Venice provided all that was needed. As captain of his allies' mercenaries, Maximilian marched for the first time into Italy, but was unable to accomplish anything. Meantime, in France Charles VIII had been succeeded by Louis XII. He found willing allies in the Swiss, and enticed the members of the Holy Alliance one by one to his own side, and conquered Milan. Now a league of Italian States was formed with France against Venice, quickly countered by another 'Holy Alliance,' which drove the French for a time from the peninsula. But in the end the French king maintained his hold upon the dukedom.

In all these wars Maximilian played his part, now on one side and now on the other. His instability admitted of the most extraordinary schemes. At an early stage of his career,

The Townsfolk

he meditated an exchange with the King of Hungary: he was to represent him in the empire, while he himself kept an eye upon Hungarian affairs. In later years he planned in all seriousness to become the successor of the sickly pope Julius II. In his old age, he dreamed of ending his life in peace as King of Naples. But such ideas went as quickly as they came. All he brought home from his various enterprises was a heavy burden of debt. If he missed the coronation, he at least gained the title of emperor. When he saw that the march upon Rome which he had planned was frustrated by the Venetians, he provided himself by his own authority with the dignity of 'Elected Roman Emperor.' His successors kept up the title.

The success of Maximilian's marriage policy was all the more striking. While affairs in the east continued so stationary (p. 166) that he could safely count upon them, fortune came to his aid in the west in a totally unexpected fashion. The alliance with Spain dated from the time that the French king's attack upon Naples had united the other Powers against him. At that time Maximilian's son Philip had married Joanna, a daughter of the Spanish king and queen; it was a good match, and nothing more. But afterwards Joanna's brother died, and then her elder sister, and finally her sister's son. Joanna became mistress of the whole wide realm with its colonies, and Charles, her son and Philip's, the heir.

A powerful Hapsburg realm now came into being. It encircled the French rival on the west and east, and carried on the traditional struggle with greater prospects of success. It began meantime to fight against the advancing Turks. But the head of the Hapsburg dynasty was at the same time German emperor. Hence the German people were plunged into international conflicts at a moment when the most serious endeavour for the reform of the empire's Constitution had failed, and when the religious war broke out, which was to cause a new and fatal division.

THIRD PART

MASSES AND MEN

THE struggle for political power in the empire was part of the great war waged simultaneously throughout Europe for the overthrow of the feudal State. Alike in the west and in the east the issues were clearly decided before the opening of the modern period, but in a contradictory sense. While in the east the nobles were bringing Crown and townsfolk into dependence upon themselves, in the west national monarchy was being gradually evolved.

The French king owed it principally to his alliance with the towns, that he was able one by one to subjugate his refractory vassals. What was accomplished in France by the hard labour of many generations, came to pass in Spain in the course of one.

In both these countries, the Crown itself obtained the conditions which were required to raise it to unlimited power. It was otherwise in England. There the nobility as a whole were opposed to the Crown, and received the support of the other estates of the realm. The outcome was a division of executive power between the Crown and Parliament, representing the estates of the realm. This position in no way precluded the struggle for mastery, but it was exceptionally fitted to produce the true spirit of citizenship. The large-scale alliances of grouped forces, the sanguinary conflict, the ultimate settlement, are common features of all these historical processes.

We find nothing comparable to them in German history, outside the restricted spheres of the principalities and the towns. Here it was possible to overturn the feudal Government and to evolve new forms. In the empire, on the other hand, the struggle for power resolved itself into a number of small conflicts, while decision remained in the balance. Like a deadly disease, the endless quarrels between the opposing powers attacked the body politic, and were never fought to a conclusion.

While the German nation was gradually losing its political importance, it had attained a position in the economic and intellectual life of Europe equal to that of the leading

The Townsfolk

nations. This was the work of the thousands who had cast off feudal customs, and within the walled and protected towns had won hearth and home, an active calling, and the respect of their neighbours—the work of a nation of citizens. It was the result of a countless number of single achievements which, depending entirely upon private capacity, had developed the powers of the individual and gradually transformed his attitude towards the world of the senses and the spirit.

How closely the economic evolution was bound up with the new social system, which the middle classes had founded and brought to recognition at the zenith of the Middle Ages, is most clearly shown in the rise of the handicrafts. Every kind of profit and stimulus was offered to the enterprising merchant. The master craftsman, on the other hand, when he had finished his years of travelling, was confined to the little circle of the fellow members of his guild. Yet it was no exception for him to produce works which rank with the most perfect ever created by professional labour.

Such achievements were, of course, only possible because customers were available in sufficient numbers, to order and purchase. Within the city population, which was still growing steadily, the great majority of commissions were given by the merchants, who had all kinds of personal requirements, and undertook the sale of the craftsmen's products in foreign markets. To these were added a growing number of commissions from city governments, which gave employment chiefly to the building crafts: together with the demands of the lords of the manor in town and country, of the monasteries and chapters, and of the nobles and the princely courts. For, because the craftsmen working in the service of a feudal lord were inferior to those of the town, the lords of the manor showed a growing preference for city products: even work which was so closely bound up with the life of the monastery as that of the making of parchment and the painting on glass, passed into the hands of city masters. More demands were made upon life with the increase of wealth: in its turn, growing luxury made men more exacting in regard to the nature of the things produced. An important commission sometimes led to detailed debate upon artistic questions in the council: when Riemenschneider was to represent our first parents in the lady chapel at Würzburg, the majority of the councillors gave their votes for a beardless Adam.

But however favourable the general economic situation might be, it provided no more than the outward conditions necessary for the flourishing of the handicrafts.

The fact that the workers were equal to these greater demands is explained in great measure by their self-imposed rules. Shielded from the irritating competition of our own day, the master was able to work in peace: if he required a fortnight to make a good lock for a door, months for a cupboard, and years for some mechanical work, he was certain of being paid for his labour. In many cases the object grew from its commencement to its completion, in the same workshop. Owing to the small number of assistants the master was frequently obliged himself to perform a great part of the work. The master's method of working, and the instruction given by him, together with the close comradeship of his fellow guildsmen, combined to give the workman the feeling of intimate union with the work of his hands. 'He who seeks only to gather money and wealth by his labour, is acting ill and his labour is usury.' This sentence, taken from one of the guild rules, shows the spirit which inspired the craftsmen.

To work as member of a guild, and to produce work passed by the guild's authorities, seem scarcely reconcilable to-day with true artistry. Yet so far as we can see, the community spirit was so powerful at that time that the most illustrious artists accommodated themselves without question to the rules of their craft. On the other hand, at the most flourishing period of the guilds, the masters were far-seeing enough to grant liberty of action to the most eminent members. Tilmann Riemenschneider, to mention only one amongst the sculptors, worked in stone and in wood: Dürer left the workshop of his father, who was a goldsmith, to learn from a painter, and at a later period of his life his wood and copper engravings were far more numerous than his pictures. He also practised carving, and many other arts. But such versatility was not very common at that period. The trend of the time was rather to incline the craftsmen to occupy themselves more and more exclusively with the production of a special class of article. The increase of commissions, as well as the possibility of profiting by mechanical discoveries, fostered this development, which led to a widespread division of labour, and the branching-off and reconstitution of numerous guilds. There were not a few guilds which consisted entirely of women (such as carpet-weavers and silk-embroiderers), while the married women frequently helped their husbands in their profession, either by co-operating in the production, or by selling the finished goods, as may often be seen in the woodcuts. The subdivisions of the smith's craft were specially numerous. Under this head it would be easy to name half a hundred independent guilds, down even to the makers of spoons. As the distribution of departments of labour was most thoroughly carried out amongst the smiths, so was the subdivision of stages of production amongst the wool-workers. This tendency to specialization explains the fact that about the middle of the fifteenth century a city like Frankfurt am Main, which was not one of the largest, numbered nearly two hundred independent professions, of which over forty had sprung up during the previous fifty years.

The fact that certain districts and towns produced a special quality of goods in a specially large quantity (see p. 87) brought about a new kind of division of labour. Whereas modern goods travel to and fro in an unfinished state from one factory to another, in those days they were worked up, as far as possible, in one place, from the preparation of the raw material to the completion of the finished article. Specialization depended chiefly upon the neighbourhood of districts which produced the raw material, upon the perfecting and transmitting of advanced methods, and upon good trading connections. The metal industry of Nuremberg was favoured by all these conditions, so that it won its way to the leading position amongst German industries: the cloth industry, which gave its character to a great part of the city, was almost equally important. The supremacy of these industries explains the fact that specialization was carried out in Nuremberg to the most minute detail. The men of Nuremberg had for rivals the metal-workers and weavers of Augsburg: yet the cloth industry had a less prominent place in that city than the production of fustian. This was as important for Augsburg as linen-weaving for Ulm. Flanders was its chief seat. The production of woollen stuffs took first place almost universally in the Rhineland towns.

Metal and textile industries, which as far back as the Middle Ages provided the livelihood of many citizens, became of vital importance for our economic system as a whole, on the introduction of machinery. But the quality of goods did not keep pace with the measure of production, so that we are filled with envy and admiration by the solidity and delicacy of handmade creations—the carvings on beams and panels: the artistic locks, the elegant cupboards and chests with inlaid decorations, the noble vessels for table and kitchen, the richly chased armour, the carved cross-bows, and many other things.

The technical skill of the guild masters was cultivated in connection with the arts, and at that early period as in later times Germans proved themselves skilful engineers. As early as the fourteenth and fifteenth centuries, mills of the most varied kinds were already being built, including hammer mills and wire mills, and the first paper mill at Nuremberg. Before the middle of the fifteenth century, the first muskets were cast at Augsburg; about the year 1500 a citizen of Nuremberg invented the pocket timepiece, and a few decades later the spinning-wheel was invented by a Brunswick master.

But no discovery ran so triumphant a course, nor worked such a revolution, as the Black Art of the Mayence patrician, John Gensfleisch of Gutenberg: it threw open the portals of the New Age.

Before long the German printer was a guest as much courted in foreign countries as the German miner, who from old time had wrung its treasures from the soil in the east as well as in the west of Europe, and even found his way to the American colonies. German work and the German worker were especially valued in those countries which had a high standard of living. This fact can be gathered no less from the casual remarks of German merchants abroad, than from the enthusiastic descriptions of Italian and French visitors to Germany. Such witnesses testify that the much-travelled monk Felix Fabri of Ulm did not stray too far from the truth when towards the end of the fifteenth century he wrote in the fanciful style common among the scholars of his time, of the respect accorded to German craftsmen in foreign lands.

'With the divine art of printing books, there has been connected an improvement in the ordinary arts, such as manual work in all metals, in all woods, and in every material. The Germans are so industrious in these crafts that their works are famous throughout the whole world. Therefore, if anyone desires a magnificent work in metal, stone, or wood, he applies to the Germans. I have seen German goldsmiths, jewellers, stonecutters, and cartwrights producing miracles among the Saracens, and noticed that they—especially the tailors, shoemakers, and masons—excelled the Greeks and Italians in dexterity. Only last year the Sultan of Egypt surrounded the harbour of Alexandria with a wall, a work which was the wonder of the whole East: and employed for this purpose a German who is said to have been a native of Oppenheim. And, lest I should become tedious, I say that Italy, although she is renowned above all the countries of the world, and blessed with corn in superfluity, has no tasty, digestible, or eatable bread except that which is baked by German bakers. Therefore the pope and the high Church dignitaries seldom eat bread unless it is made in the German fashion. Biscuits too they make in such a masterly way, that the Venetians have none but German bakers in their public bakeries, and send the baking far and wide throughout the Hellespont, Greece, Syria, Egypt, Libya, Morocco, Spain, and France, and even to the Orkney Islands and the English and German ports, for the nourishment of their sailors and for others to buy.'

And why was there no mention here of the German merchant? As we shall see, the fact that he abandoned this trade to the Venetians cannot be accounted for by a lack of enterprise. On the contrary, the craftsman had every reason to be heartily grateful to him. He conducted the sale of German products both at home and abroad with exceptional ability: his carrying trade in foreign goods also brought a great deal of money into Germany, by which home industry was the gainer.

The agency for Oriental goods, which was the most profitable part of the carrying trade, was first put in train through the Crusades. Even after the last coast towns of Syria had been finally lost by the Christians, Italian merchants were able to carry their mercantile pre-eminence still farther afield. They possessed numerous colonies on the Black Sea, maintained friendly relations with the Mongolian lords of central Asia, and penetrated to the gate of China. At the time of the Hohenstaufen, the markets of Champagne were the only considerable place of exchange for Oriental trade. When about the year 1300 they fell into decay, the Italians brought their wares to Bruges, which thus became the chief market of western Europe. In this 'Venice of the North' the Hanseatic merchants accepted Oriental goods for sale in the markets of England, the Scandinavian peninsula and the East. In exchange they brought chiefly wax, furs, and fish, timber and grain, flax and hemp from the eastern districts, iron and copper from Sweden, salt from the west coast of France, Rhine wine and other products of the German soil. These were thus, in the main, mass products, the fruits of the cultivation of land and forest, of fishery and mine, in northern and eastern Europe, with metal and woodwork from Germany. Sea-trade with its many risks inclined the merchants to close their ranks. As the eastern and northern countries were comparatively backward in economic development, the Hanse obtained the command of trade in the districts between Novgorod and the French coasts, together, as we have seen, with considerable political influence.

The Hanse merchants made their appearance in foreign countries as masters rather than guests: and they took it for granted that they should maintain discipline and order in their ranks without outside help. This was not an easy task; for in many of their foreign houses the merchants and their assistants were numbered in thousands, and there was heavy drinking after the hard day's work. They were a race familiar with trouble and danger of every kind: what was said of the North Frisians was true of them in every particular. 'They are rough in their manners, seeing that they greatly frequent the sea.' The roughness with which they treated their recruits went even beyond the tests for journeymen which were customary inland, and these did not err on the side of gentleness. The manners were roughest in the warehouses at Novgorod, Schonen, and Bergen; more decent in the Steelyard in London and in Bruges, where the merchants lived in lodgings with the townspeople. Everywhere the Hanse merchant proved himself to be a true man, aware of his mastery, bold and enterprising, though not, strictly speaking, refined. As a rule, the hunger for gain had set its stamp more clearly upon him than upon his south German compeers. His taste for intellectual riches was less developed, while the material joys of life made a much stronger appeal to him.

The overland trade with Italy presents a very different picture. For centuries, German and Italian merchants had been making use of the Brenner Pass, the Great St. Bernard, the Septimer, and the Semmering. The road across the Brenner to Augsburg and Nuremberg formed the closest and most important link between Venice and the cities of southern and central Germany. From thence the goods were despatched either northwards through Erfurt, or north-westwards through Mayence and Cologne: the road eastwards led from Augsburg through Regensburg and Prague.

Direct intercourse between the upper Rhine and Milan threw open the Pass of St. Gothard, which was made permanently fit for traffic in the first half of the thirteenth century: the trade of the Rhine made its way to England through Basle, Mayence, and Cologne. The exchange of goods between the west and east was mainly served by the Danube in southern Germany, and in the north by the road from Cologne through Cassel and Erfurt to Leipzig.

Goods in bulk were not suitable for despatch across the mountains, but only those which were comparatively costly. Hence the south German merchants were for the most part restricted to the export of native productions. Moreover, in contrast to the Hanse cities, they had to deal with a people who were highly developed both economically and intellectually, in whose presence they felt themselves not masters but pupils. Venice was considered —not only amongst the Germans—to be the University of Commerce. It was the only city in Italy where the Germans lived together in a merchants' hall. But there was an immense difference between the life in the *Fondaco dei Tedeschi* and the doings in the commercial house at Novgorod. The spacious premises belonged to the State: its officers exercised a strict oversight, and also judged the disputes which arose amongst the visitors. State brokers negotiated the trade between inhabitants and foreigners, and saw to it that the proceeds of the sale were expended again upon Venetian goods. Nevertheless, the number of guests increased almost uninterruptedly during the later centuries of the Middle Ages: for the Italian market was not only of the greatest importance for the exchange of goods, but in other respects also it gave the strongest impetus to the trade of middle Europe.

Italy was the native land of ready-money economics, and of money transactions, and here first the proverb came true that money breeds money. Commerce and handicrafts, and a rise in the price of land, altogether had led to the accumulation of larger fortunes, which were employed in all kinds of business undertakings. Florentine financiers in particular made great sums by lending money to the landed proprietors, both lay and clerical.

As early as the thirteenth century, banking companies were formed in Florence, which also received investments of various kinds from outsiders, and carried on their business sometimes in goods and sometimes in cash. The Church might forbid the taking of interest, but it was the clergy themselves who made the greatest use of the banks. The Papacy above all employed them, not only as go-betweens in the debit and credit transactions of their world-wide empire, but also in the taking up of credits. For in spite of the increase in the papal income, it did not always keep pace with the rapidly increasing expenses of diplomatic and military undertakings. The connections and influence of the Florentine bankers extended beyond Italy, over the whole of western Europe. The names of kings and princes, lords spiritual and temporal, were entered in their ledgers. They seized upon the public revenues, the mines, the exports and imports, and such of the industrial enterprises of individual States as offered a prospect of success. Cosimo de' Medici and his nephew Lorenzo, the Treasurer of the Holy See, were not only the masters of Florence, but took their place amongst the mightiest of the Western world.

Close business ties with Italy fostered the growth of capitalism in Germany, where it found a ground prepared for it. As the arable land had been completely appropriated towards the end of the Hohenstaufen era, a great increase in ground values took place, and a corresponding diminution in the burden of rent. This meant increasing scarcity for the king, the princes, the Church, and the knights, in so far as they, being landed proprietors, were dependent upon rents. They experienced a growing need of ready money: the lords temporal required it, to pay their hired soldiers and their officials: the lords spiritual needed it, to meet the sums which were sometimes very heavy, which were due to the pope on the transference of both greater or lesser offices. At the same time, during the latter centuries of the Middle Ages, the sources from which great fortunes were accumulated began to flow more freely. Trading profits rose, together with city ground rents, while the increasing output of the mines added considerably to the sum of ready money. After a temporary period of exhaustion, the production of precious metals reached its highest level by means of new discoveries and technical improvements, so that from the middle of the fifteenth to the middle of the sixteenth century, Germany actually represented the 'Mexico and Peru of Europe.'

Towards the end of the Middle Ages, capitalism became a power in Germany, not only in mining, but in other branches of industrial work. It carried on an increasing struggle with the limitations imposed upon it by the economic policy of the towns, with its guild rules, its staple rights, its fixing of prices and other market regulations. The merchant aimed at engaging a number of master craftsmen to work for him alone: he delivered the raw material, paid the wages, and took over the finished goods to sell them to the middleman or the consumer—he became a 'publisher' (*Verleger*). In the fifteenth century this system of 'publishing' raised the manufacture of woollen material in Flanders to the status of a great industry. In Germany it made its way also into the highly developed weaving industry, and in particular took possession of the new industry of printing: to this day we speak of 'publishing' books (*Buchverlag*).

In Germany, for a long time, the actual money transactions were in the hands of foreigners. As early as the thirteenth century, money dealers from Lombardy were established in many of the cities. They undertook the business of money changing, which was of great importance in view of the endless variations in coinage at that epoch.

Masses and Men

They also acted as bankers to the See of Rome, and transacted loans on a basis of security and interest. The Jews were more numerous and more influential than the Lombards, and were at first made equally welcome. But after the first persecutions at the time of the Crusades, they lived in hourly jeopardy as unwelcome guests, whose presence must be endured because it is indispensable. The tax which they had to pay for the right of protection formed a considerable source of income for the wearers of the Crown, till the right of protecting the Jews passed over, like so much else, to the princes and towns. This brought about a great change for the worse in their situation, while their business as dealers and craftsmen was more and more restricted through the development of the guild system. In the end nothing remained to them but money dealing. Here it is true they could reap a rich harvest, which could more easily be concealed or conveyed away in the hour of danger than any other kind of property. They were not bound by the Church's embargo on usury. Although this prohibition was defied by Christian financiers and even by churchmen themselves, yet it did on occasion exercise a restraining influence upon them. The shyness with which the undisguised reckoning of interest was avoided is significant in this connection: the amount was either deducted when the loan was made, or else the sum was given gratis for a short period—it might be only a few days, so that the interest figured as compensation for the postponed return of the capital.

The considerations which gave rise to such proceedings were lacking in the case of the Jew; his own cleverness did the rest. Certainly the business of short-term loans was in most cases very precarious, a fact which explains what to our ideas are the fantastic rates of interest usual amongst money-lenders not of the Jewish race alone. Yet because the Jews confined themselves entirely to money lending, the expiring Middle Ages are full of bitter complaints against the Jewish usurers. 'The Princes and all the Estates of the Realm,' so runs a royal decree at the end of the fourteenth century, 'are so oppressed by the exorbitant demands of interest, that in the end they are obliged to flee from their country and kin, and turn their back upon them.' What is here told with calculated exaggeration of the estates of the realm, is literally true of a portion of the humbler inhabitants of town and country. The possession of innumerable debtors' bonds 'was the poison which killed the Jews,' so wrote a chronicler of Strasburg. Bloody persecutions of the Jews recurred continually upon the most absurd pretexts. Those who met their death were the representatives of the dawning reign of capitalism, and were hated also for other reasons.

It was not practicable to treat the merchant class with equal violence, but at the end of the Middle Ages the dealers were universally execrated for raising the price of goods. Great fortunes in Germany seem to have been principally built up on trade profits, and through the prices of merchandise the Germans first became aware of the power of capital. As early as the fourteenth century there were many merchants who commanded a fair amount of capital of their own; this is proved by the considerable payments which they were able to make for orders which they had given. But not until individual resources were united into a company, after the Italian model, was the way opened for capitalism to dominate business. Originally such companies were restricted to the members of one family: they were formed for a short period, to serve some definite end. But the circle was enlarged with time: several merchant families would join together, outsiders were admitted upon taking shares, and the methods of profit sharing became more clearly defined. Men and maid-servants brought their savings to the Höchstetters of Augsburg, hoping to make their fortune quickly, and merchants who were good business-men would make their acceptance of an apprentice dependent upon whether he invested his money in the business.

The method in which business was carried on even in the large companies was influenced in many ways by the narrow conditions in which the merchant class had developed. As a rule, the wholesale merchant still found the retail side of his business to be the most profitable. Thus the great merchants of Cologne obtained a special privilege from the English king, allowing them to sell wine by the quart. The sciences of accounts and book-keeping were still in their infancy. As the use of Arabic numerals did not become universal till near the end of the fifteenth century, all reckoning was made by means of tally-boards, and that was a laborious task. The notebooks kept by the

merchants upon their travels are not remarkable for suc-
cinctness. We are amazed to find this entry. 'Item, and
there is yet another man, who bought at the same time
as the above-named, he owes me 19 florins to be paid
for Paternosters, at the autumn market: I have forgotten
his name.' Of course, the merchant was not confined to
such chance descriptions for the balancing of debit and
credit: but it must be admitted that about the year 1500,
book-keeping was as primitive as possible.

All these handicaps were overcome by south German
trade, thanks to its close connection with the industrial
production of its own country. The fustian-weaving industry
of Ulm, with which the prosperity of the town was bound
up, depended as much upon foreign trade for its supply
of cotton as for the sale of finished goods, which was
very extensively carried on in Lübeck, Antwerp, and the
Spanish markets. In addition to cloth weaving and the
metal handicrafts, the manufacture of fustian held an
important place in Augsburg: to a citizen of Augsburg,
Burkhard Zink, we owe a clear picture of the way this
business was carried on about the middle of the fifteenth
century. In Venice he sold the cloths, which had been
woven for his master by the Augsburg weavers. In exchange
for these, he bought cotton, and 'carried the bales from
Venice' over the Alps to Germany. He had scarcely reached
home, before the wagons were packed again with cloths
and fustian. Zink conducted the cavalcade to Nuremberg,
and to the Frankfort market, bought and sold, and then
rode back to Venice by way of Augsburg.

The favourable position which Nuremberg occupied for
foreign trade, was utilized in the same way by the merchants of the city, to dispose of their toys, and other
native products (p. 180). No other German city, with the
exception, perhaps, of Cologne, obtained in process of time
so many exemptions from customs. In the *Little Book of
my Family and Adventures*, written by the Nuremberg
merchant Ulmann Stromer, he sets down the weights and
measures used in many foreign markets, from Azov and
Lemberg to Bruges and Barcelona. The Nurembergers
also kept up active relations with Italy, and in Danzig
the dealers complained of their competition—and all this
before the end of the fourteenth century.

The merchants of the Rhineland also dealt in many

The Townsfolk

kinds of native wares with Italy and the Netherlands. The convenient Rhine thoroughfare assured them the lion's share of the market in Bruges, where the merchants of high and low Germany did their business. Their close connection with this market fully compensated the men of Cologne for the fact that since the thirteenth century they had been forced to share the trade of the English markets with the Hanseatic towns. The city aimed at the realization of the old staple-right, whose strict application would have split the Rhineland trade into two parts, and given it entirely into the hands of the men of Cologne. In spite of all ratifications on paper, they failed in their object, fortunately for German trade: but Cologne remained the powerful trading centre for the cities of west Germany.

While trading companies in the west and north scarcely developed beyond the simplest forms, they took the lead in the High German cities, and opened the way for far-flung enterprises. Ravensburg was the seat of the Huntpiss Company: it kept its own representatives in Barcelona and other Spanish cities, and drove a wide and lucrative trade, partly by land, and partly by the sea routes, through Genoa and Marseilles. After the middle of the sixteenth century the company of 'Dettigkofer and co-partners' in Memmingen, had a 30 per cent. share in the profits of a great undertaking in the Levant, which was carried on through their own vessels with depôts at Cyprus, Alexandria, and Tripoli. Ravensburg and Memmingen are scarcely known by name to many to-day: when we think of Augsburg the proud past lives again before us.

Augsburg became the seat of the greatest trading companies, the city of the wealthiest inhabitants. In the second half of the fourteenth century, Hans Rem began his career with 500 florins and ended with nearly 30,000. Lucas Rem, the younger, his great-grandson, made an acceptable son-in-law to one of the Welsers. His journal gives us a glimpse into one of the most important chapters in the history of this world-famous house. At fourteen, Rem learnt Italian in Venice, and trading and book-keeping at home. When he was fifteen, he was sent to Milan to put in order the books of the Welsers' representative, 'who was out in his reckoning.' He finished his apprenticeship in France. At two-and-twenty he took over the management of the

Masses and Men

Welser factory in Lisbon. There he arranged a treaty with the Portuguese Government, for the despatch of three ships to India in the year 1505, in which shares were taken by the Fuggers and some great Nuremberg firms in addition to the Welsers: the enterprise brought a profit of more than 150 per cent. Rem's employment was so exhausting that he would gladly have exchanged it for another. But the Welsers knew his value. After a short stay in Italy and the Netherlands, he had to return to Lisbon and set in order the Welsers' business in the plantations of the Canary Islands and in Madeira. When he had accomplished this task also, he at last succeeded in taking leave of the king, on which occasion the king brought 'the queen and all his children, most richly dressed, into his chamber.'

The opinion is sometimes thoughtlessly repeated that the German merchant slept through the new day which dawned with the age of discoveries. To this charge, the *Journal of Lucas Rem* is in itself a sufficient refutation. The German merchants' close connection with Portugal was nothing less than an alliance with the economic power, which had newly risen to the leading place in the Western world, and it was concluded almost in the same hour that the glory of Venice began to fade. The first heavy blow which she sustained was the conquest of Asia Minor by the Turks. When the Portuguese were in a position to suppress the maritime trade of the Arabs in the Indian Ocean, they crippled the trade between Venice and Egypt. The establishment of the Turks in Egypt meant the fall of Venice. Henceforth the treasures of India were brought in Portuguese ships to Lisbon, and thence to the Netherlands. There Bruges had lost her original importance, because her harbour was filling up with sand, and Antwerp had succeeded to her position. Here too the Germans were quickly upon the spot. High German trading companies set up their factories, and the Hanse merchants opened a new business house, after the middle of the sixteenth century, shortly before the Duke of Alba entered with his troops. The first successful attempt to trade directly with the country 'where the pepper grows,' was followed by others. But one can readily understand that the Portuguese kept their eager competitors at a safe distance. Spain followed the same tactics. Charles V stood in close business relations with the Welsers, and could not refuse to allow them to journey to Venezuela and settle there. They established over one hundred plantations and mines, and German captains pressed forward into territory which was not trodden again by Europeans until three hundred years later. But when the Germans proved unable to meet their obligations, the land was taken from them.

During a long period the goods trade was the one branch of capitalist activity pursued by the Welsers, while it represented the entire business of other trading companies for the whole course of their existence. The Fugger family followed the profession of financiers in the grand manner. The grandfather had emigrated to Augsburg, where he exercised the craft of weaving: his sons made a fortune by trading in goods. Jacob Fugger, of the third generation, worked the mines on a capitalist basis, and turned his attention to pure finance. Towards the end of the fifteenth century, in association with other financiers, he seized upon mines in the Tyrol, Carinthia, Hungary, and shortly afterwards in Spain, whose rich output made the Fugger family masters of the metal market.

Emperor and empire were forced to surrender to their superior strength. The trade in metal carried on by the House of Fugger was expressly exempted by Charles V from the ban on monopolies, which was applied to all other goods. The emperor was not less dependent upon the support of capital than the Papal See, to whom the Houses of Fugger and Welser were as indispensable as the Florentine bankers of former times. Lords spiritual and temporal, both small and great, were all under obligation to capital. Can it then be wondered at if all complaints of the usury of the merchants fell on deaf ears? In fifteen years the House of Fugger multiplied its capital by ten: towards the middle of the sixteenth century it reached its highest level with five million florins. Others followed at a great distance. In Augsburg, however, there was a considerable increase in the number of great fortunes of more than 3,600 florins, which in the year 1540 had risen in barely seventy-five years from 39 to 278.

If former generations had worked in order to live, and to live as well as possible, men now began to work in order to grow rich. Young men thronged into the merchant class. 'The principal cities of Germany,' laments a learned man, 'allow no man now to learn arts and languages. But as soon as a boy can write and read German he must go to Frankfort, Antwerp, and Nuremberg, and learn reckoning and the business of commerce. Yes, there is no help for it, he must be a trader or a merchant.' At the same time the prentices and assistants served almost as hard a probation as in the craftsman class, and even the independent merchant had to contend with all kinds of difficulties. The bad state of the roads itself was accountable for various disasters. Through the operation of ancient laws, the owners of goods were exposed to the constant danger of losing their whole load when an axle broke or a ship was wrecked. The new age had given rise to innumerable staple rights and custom houses, of which, for instance, there were forty-seven on the Elbe between Hamburg and the mouth of the Moldau. The merchant suffered by these institutions, in a somewhat humaner fashion, but no less painfully. The worst evil that he endured was from the highway robbery of noble and commoner, upon which neither the Leagues for the Common Peace nor the reform of the empire had much effect. The merchants, therefore, were quite justified in referring to their trade as an 'adventure.'

They were obliged to encounter most of these difficulties and perils in their own person. It was something to boast of when the thirteen-year-old Lucas Rem rode in ten days from Augsburg to Venice, or Zink, who was growing old, accomplished the journey from Augsburg to Trent in five days, though he was already tired 'from riding so fast on the roads.' In their travels from market to market many must have sympathized with this brave man, who wrote: 'I had no peace, and the saddle nearly burned my hinder parts.' In addition to bodily vigour, and dexterity in the use of weapons, the merchants' calling demanded not only the knowledge and capacity which are still indispensable, but a great number of other accomplishments; above all, an exact acquaintance with the extremely varied standards of measurement, coinage, and weight, with the commercial routes and the rights of toll and market, and many others. A knowledge of languages must have formed an even greater element in success than at the present day—for even within the empire itself business was transacted in various languages according to locality—in St. Gall, for example, in Spanish, French, Lombard, Hungarian, Bohemian, and Polish. We must keep in mind the toils and dangers inseparable from this life, if we are to form a correct estimate of what was achieved by the German merchant in the Middle Ages.

It was chiefly to his activities that the whole body of townsfolk owed the means of making their houses habitable, and of building their cities beautiful and strong against assault. It was to his opulence, pride of citizenship, and love of beauty that these turreted cities owed their erection. In the Middle Ages they were gazed upon with delight by the *blasé* travellers from foreign lands. They were described in loving detail by Gustav Freytag, Riehl, and later writers, while the present generation has learnt to know them more intimately through the development of photography and the growth of facilities for travel. The careful student, however, will find plentiful indications of the presence of a number of poverty-stricken inhabitants amongst the few who were rich, and the mass of the middle class. They lived side by side, and sometimes, even at that early date, over each other, in circumstances which were mean and depressed even by the standard of that time. We are unfortunately so much accustomed to this phenomenon that we see nothing remarkable in it: but it does not fit the age of strict guild regulations, whose aim was to ensure to every man his 'nourishment.' How is one to account for the striking discrepancies in the conditions of living?

Every handicraft did not, of course, provide an equally good living to the man who practised it. The most lucrative industries were either those which demanded special abilities, such as those of the gold and silver smiths and platers, or else those which could count upon a regular clientèle of daily customers. In a fifteenth-century schedule of the property of the handicraftsmen of Heidelberg, the butchers and bakers head the list, the weavers have to be content with less than a third, and the wine-merchants' porter with a seventh of the butchers' fortune. It is more difficult to explain the extraordinary diversity in the extent of business transacted by one industry in the fourteenth century at a period, that is to say, when there can be no question of a highly developed capitalist system of economics. In Frankfort on the Main, the eleven greatest weaving industries had the right to bring to market more than twice as many pieces of cloth as all the forty-nine masters together, who were the smallest producers. Besides such small guild masters, there was a fairly large number of people who earned their living at a handicraft, without belonging to a guild. There were besides free day labourers who were indispensable, for instance, to the farming industry of the city, underpaid town officials, and wandering folk.

In the wealthy city of Augsburg, and at the time of its greatest prosperity, the number of those who were almost or altogether without means was established as about the seventh part of the inhabitants. This class was most painfully conscious of the fall in the purchasing power of money, and of the increased cost of the necessaries of life, which had been brought about by commerce. While it was not till the period of the Reformation that unrest began in the unorganized masses: as early as the fourteenth and fifteenth centuries, the economic war between journeymen and master craftsmen had already broken out in many places. They were chiefly concerned with wages and hours of labour, but also with such fundamental questions as the right of journeymen to form regular 'brotherhoods.' The union of workmen throughout wide districts, the strike and the boycott, already proved powerful weapons, and the journeymen frequently succeeded in obtaining their demands.

More important than the tension within the ranks of the city population, were the universal conflicts between the estates, which became very bitter in the later centuries of the Middle Ages. The nobles esteemed themselves better than the citizens, and yet looked with envy upon their riches. There were many of the wealthy citizens who allowed themselves to be dazzled by the glitter of the knightly name and profession; there were even great cities in which the merchant's calling was no longer considered well-bred. Then the patricians laid out a portion of their fortune in landed property, the merchant retired from business, gained a noble son-in-law, or himself became a knight: it cannot be denied that the nobility, who now more than ever valued a descent from noblemen, knights, and squires, turned the cold shoulder upon such upstarts. But there was still plenty of healthy pride in citizenship.

The Townsfolk

The Fuggers, even after they had been raised to the rank of counts, clung to their occupation as merchants, and the same spirit obtained in Hamburg and Lübeck.

Side by side with the townsfolk, who formed perhaps the tenth part of the whole population, stood the mass of the peasants, who were shut out, not only from business life, which made the fortune of so many citizens, but also from political freedom and the growing culture of the cities. Taken as a whole, their economic position was less favourable than before. For the development of capitalism brought with it depreciation in the value of land, and the prices of agricultural produce fell beneath those which were demanded by craftsmen and tradesmen. Any levelling-up was prevented by the fact that the prices of food were fixed by the city authorities. Yet as a rule, no actual economic distress was felt, except where the peasants' property was split up by inheritance into minute portions, as was the case in many districts of south Germany. The complaint was more general, that the lords of the manor and the reigning princes were trying to add to their share of the common pasture-land, to extend their rights, and to increase the obligations of the peasants, and in many places the alien Roman law, which was gaining ground at that time, favoured their aims. The pressure was felt most heavily in the tiny political structures of the south-west, where the State was scarcely distinguishable from a large seignorial manor. The peasant actually suffered from the so-called 'new discoveries' of the legal claims of government, and from the interference and encroachments of government officials, because they made him most keenly aware that he alone had no share in the estates system which protected the rights of other classes. His indignation must have been fanned by the profound contempt which he endured from nobles and citizens. The religious unrest of the time was not without its influence. 'To defend righteousness and divine justice,' the 'Laced-shoe' (*Bund-schuh*) summoned the peasants to battle. A peasant man and woman and a peasant's shoe with golden thongs were portrayed upon their banners, while others showed the image of the Crucified, with that of the Virgin and St. John. Throughout the fifteenth century, and at the beginning of the sixteenth, the peasants continued to revolt, now here and now there, in the Alpine districts, in Swabia, in

Masses and Men

Franconia, and on the Upper Rhine. More than once they were joined by the lower townsfolk. Everywhere the risings were suppressed, but the leaven worked on.

This state of unrest was, to a certain extent, an effect of the intellectual revolution, which went hand in hand with the evolution of economic life. The masses began to take an interest, not only in the business of industry and commerce, but also in intellectual matters: and as the blessing of daily work set the individual free from many of the chains which bound him, his personality shook off the traditional limitations of feeling and thought. The education of the masses and the development of personality are the distinguishing mark of intellectual life at the end of the Middle Ages.

Intellectual hunger sought its satisfaction along many channels. It was a golden age for copyists and dealers in manuscripts, till Gutenberg's discovery dealt a heavy blow to their industry. Woodcuts and copper engravings exercised an influence which was scarcely less powerful than the written or printed word. Men read and gazed for their entertainment and edification, but not less for their instruction in the life of man and nature, and in past and present history. And they were not content with absorbing—they desired to co-operate as far as they were able. Carnival plays offered a welcome opportunity of giving free rein to the roughest humour: the presentation of miracle plays sometimes provided employment to hundreds of actors, and from day to day the whole town would look on. In many cities of west and central Germany, craftsmen who were master singers devoted themselves to the noble art of poetry: journeymen, squires, writers, and young girls composed popular songs. The woodcuts which were offered for sale in the markets, the carved altars and decorated fountains which were springing up in great abundance, the paintings on the external walls of the houses, made all classes familiar with the works of creative art.

Chroniclers began to record the work of prominent artists amongst the other important events in the life of the cities. The citizen made a point of having at least one room in his house, which he adorned with carved chairs and artistic utensils. The people flocked in crowds to the great preachers, and at no period were so many churches built in the

The Townsfolk

German cities as at the close of the Middle Ages. The citizens gave money and goods: they collected the building materials, they presented costly gifts for the furnishing of the interior and the support of the priests.

The participation of such different classes of the population gave a popular turn to all departments of intellectual life. Even amongst the most learned, alchemy and astrology found eager disciples. Many writings of a popular character, amongst which descriptions of travel were chiefly in demand, provided for the dissemination of scientific knowledge. All feeling for style vanished from literature: authors cared for nothing but the subject-matter. The old romance of chivalry was not yet dead; it survived as a prose narrative, enriched with all kinds of additions in a popular style. Up to the time of Goethe's boyhood the folk-story book was the favourite reading of the uneducated class, while the more cultured, including the princes, delighted in allegorical variations upon the old love-poetry. In *Teuerdank*, which tells the story of the emperor Maximilian's wooing, the hero falls into great dangers through three evil companions—Impertinence, Misfortune, and Envy. *Teuerdank* was the last word of an expiring era. There were far more readers for the collections of rude jokes and the innumerable satirical works in verse and prose, in which individual foolishness and crime, as well as whole classes of the population, were held up to ridicule. The Low German *Reinke de Vos*, which appeared in print about 1500, is, according to Herder, 'a fable of the world with all its professions, classes, passions, and characters.' Sebastian Brant's *Ship of Fools* was for some decades the most widely read work in German literature. Such writings held the mirror up to the people as they were: undisciplined, rude, unpolished, but with a keen sense of reality. Natural feeling found its suitable and straightforward vehicle in the folksong. There one can hear the full *motif* of robust joy in life, mingling with the wistfulness and melancholy of love, in tones which recall the intimate tenderness of the best middle-High-German period.

More inflexible than language, stone imperiously demands a fixed form. Yet in architecture also, the intrusion of the popular spirit made itself felt: creative power was flagging, while highly developed technical dexterity made a parade of skill. The clearly articulated cross-shaped vault became

the reticulated vault with its bewildering maze of inter-
lacing; the delicate tracery of the window arches lost in
noble beauty what it gained in ingenuity. Late-Gothic
architecture is famed not for the perfection of structural
detail, but for the new method of planning the whole. The
great churches which it produced had a more uniform
exterior. They omitted the transept, brought the buttresses
into the interior, and formed the spaces between them
into chapels. In the interior, the eye of the spectator,
which in Cologne Cathedral is drawn inevitably upwards,
now wanders from the dusky nave to the side aisles, which
are one with it in height, lingering on their slender pillars
and the many-coloured glass of their windows. Love of
the picturesque has triumphed over the movement which
strove mightily towards heaven. All the more powerful
is the feeling of upward-striving expressed by the architecture of the towers: the Late-Gothic towers at Ulm and
Vienna exceed everything which has been achieved by
architecture before or since. The town house, being still
cramped in its proportions, offered less space for the
development of the Gothic idea of architecture than the
public edifices in which the expiring Middle Ages are so
rich—the massive gateways, the towers upon the bridges,
the guild, and council houses.

The tasks allotted to the sculptors were equally numerous and varied: but the flagging of the great impetus
which had inspired the thirteenth century was most
evident in this field. On the other hand, painting, which
could no longer be employed upon the broken wall-spaces
of Gothic architecture, conquered new fields of art in panel
painting and painting on glass. Master Wilhelm (*circa*
1350) is one of the oldest German panel painters: he is
the first German artist whose work is mentioned in a
chronicle. Delicate, over-slender figures with large soulful
heads are grouped before a glittering golden background:
a gentle gliding movement pervades all his pictures of the
Life of the Virgin and of the Passion. Stefan Lochner,
about the year 1430, unites tenderness with virile strength,
reflection with acute observation of nature. In his *Adoration of the Three Kings*, the aspiration of the German soul
to the divine is most purely and beautifully expressed.
But, even in his time, Low and High German masters were
inclining more to the rendering of reality, and the highly

The Townsfolk

developed art of the Netherlands acted as a powerful reinforcement to that tendency. The altarpiece of the brothers Van Eyck at Ghent (about 1430) opened a new era for German painting, no less than for Flemish. These masters did not seek to portray the gentle beauty beloved of the Rhineland artists, but the angular reality: the sober life of the townsfolk rather than the lofty play of sentiment: in the numerous execution scenes, low life was depicted with astonishing verisimilitude. So the donors of commissions were pleased, and industrious masters, such as Dürer's master, Michael Wohlgemut, could scarcely employ enough journeymen to carry out their orders.

Together with the loss of feeling for form, the last years of the Middle Ages were marked by the increasing secularization of intellectual output. The Church still exercised a powerful influence in all departments of life. But in science, culture, and the exercise of the arts the secular spirit was gaining ground and beginning to supersede the religious. The universities were still far from becoming places of unhampered research: yet they offered a learned education to a growing circle of laymen, and little by little their teachers relaxed their intimate connection with the Church. While two out of the five universities of the fourteenth century were founded by cities, city schools, which included schools for girls, were founded during the same period in increasing numbers, competing with the cathedral and monastery schools. The instruction was not better in one than in another: whatever its quality, it gave to growing classes of the population the opportunity of sharing, if only in a modest way, in the intellectual life of the time. In ever-increasing numbers, the artists depicted secular subjects in which the rough humour of the populace came to its own: the banter and mockery of the stonemasons flourished, even without and within the walls of the House of God.

The knightly distinction of the age of the Hohenstaufen was gone, never to return. Even the rulers witnessed the reflection of their own life in the creations of contemporary artists: the people's festivals were equally the festivals of those of higher rank, and the frightful punishments which were dealt to evil-doers were a spectacle for high and low. But the loss in form and dignity, and the cultural decadence of the higher classes of society, was

Masses and Men

balanced by an increase in living energy—and by the elevation of the lower classes of the population. The upper and lower classes had drawn closer together, and the fine fruit of this approach was a uniformity of feeling and of manners, such as the nation had never possessed before, nor was ever able to attain later. At that time the prince thought and spoke not very differently from the peasant: and the peasant saw in the prince a man of like passions with himself. It was not till later that the consciousness of life lived in an alien world came to poison the relations between the members of the different classes of society.

The mutual approach of the different ranks within the life of thought and feeling was not incompatible with a clearer definition of individual traits. The occupations of the middle class were in themselves favourable to the development of personal characteristics. The craftsman and the merchant were obliged to trust to their own ability in a far greater degree than the countryman. Their lives were shaped far more swiftly and decisively by zeal and aptitude, and, as we have seen, they frequently broke the fetters with which superior authority, bent on the good of the many, had hampered the work of the individual. Political warfare within the city played its part in bringing the citizen to maturity: it has been remarked with justice that the description of the guild battles in Cologne in the thirteenth century gives, for the first time, a clearly outlined character sketch of the various personalities engaged in them. Moreover, the towns were the centre of the new capitalist system, which more than all other influences promoted the development of the individual: capital overstepped all the limitations which had been set for the protection of the masses; it forced the princes, both spiritual and temporal, to bow to its authority. There were no limits to the activity of the man of action beyond what were set by his own desires and his own strength.

The same attitude to life, which for the daring merchant took shape out of the conditions of his existence, inspired the scholar in his quiet room. The discovery of the sources of the life of antiquity had given birth in Italy to the Renaissance and to humanism. Men turned away from the exclusive worship of the Church ideal of otherworldliness, and began to appreciate the worldly. Nature and man seemed the objects most worthy of contemplation and

The Townsfolk

endeavour: while man was regarded, not as the member of a community, but as an individual in whom existed an unlimited capacity for perfection. In Italy amongst the princes the newly acquired ideal revealed itself in an unbridled lust for power, and amongst the cultured classes in a boundless thirst for pleasure. But there was little evidence of this among the German humanists. Sons of their nation, inclined to a pedagogic attitude, they cultivated above all else the idea of the possible perfectibility of mankind: by the instruction they gave in schools and universities, they instilled it into the nation, and produced an effect which was at least equal to that of their work as students.

Nourished from so many different sources, the struggle for personality showed itself under the most varied conditions. The growing urge to self-portraiture is typical of this development. It is true that the personal revelations of the fifteenth century have nothing of the charm which still clings to the letters of distinguished women of the previous century: and there is no trace of the emotional life cultivated by the mystics. Even the records of well-instructed and widely travelled men are dominated by sober reality. But the fact that an ever-increasing number of people felt the need of seizing the events of life and imparting them to others, is eloquent of the awakening consciousness of personality.

'Men of education' now began to participate in the life of the city: students and teachers, doctors, lawyers, who differed considerably both in their nature, their conception of life, and the results which they obtained from it. What a contrast between that bird of passage Conrad Celtes and the many who, after a few years' wandering, settled down as headmasters of schools: or between Mutianus, the leader of the Humanists of Erfurt, whom we know only by his letters, and the uncrowned king, Desiderius Erasmus, who ruled Europe with his pen. In many ways practical work, and work which was purely intellectual, influenced and interpenetrated each other. When no post happened to be vacant, wandering humanist teachers would accept employment in the government offices, either royal or civic. Cardinal Nicholas of Cues was at the same time a deep student and a wise statesman. Charles IV and Maximilian were penetrated with the new ideas. Hutten the Knight was also a knight of the pen. Willibald Pirckheimer, who had acquired the finest mental culture during his seven years in Italy, entered the service of his native Nuremberg as a councillor, captained her levies in the Swiss war and chronicled its battles. Reuchlin was for many years employed in State affairs for the Count of Wurtemberg and the Swabian League. Such men were the embodiment of all that the New Age demanded from its sons: a fully developed personality finding its work within the given conditions.

The new spirit not only broke down the barriers of rank and profession: it overstepped the traditional frontiers of knowledge and feeling, and claimed for its own the whole world of things visible and invisible, present and past. The sensation of soaring power informed the whole of life like the brightness of a spring morning. While the voyages of bold discoverers were enlarging the globe's surface, men's eyes were opened to see the world immediately around them—the gay multiplicity of village life, the ranked order of city government, the variety of costumes, the whole wealth of human peculiarities.

Learned men were seeking, along new paths, to rob nature of her secrets. To scholastic learning, God-given truth was like the light by whose beams the student was led to penetrate the world's darkness. Men were now striving out of the darkness of material things towards a light which they divined rather than saw. Truth was no longer a gift, but a quest. The path had now been struck out, along which critical students of a later period were to win their victories. Astrology and alchemy stood at the beginning of that pilgrimage: but by the middle of the sixteenth century it had led Copernicus, a canon of Frauenburg, to the revolutionary perception of the movement of the heavenly bodies, and his contemporary Paracelsus to an insight into the nature of diseases, which was as surprising as it was extravagantly expressed.

The fruits of the new methods of research ripened first in the fields of philology and the study of history. Numerous editions of Latin authors had already appeared when Erasmus published a complete edition of Aristotle and of the Greek New Testament, and Reuchlin instituted the scientific study of Hebrew. The inadequate grammar and translations of the Middle Ages gave place to better. Still

The Townsfolk

following the footsteps of their beloved antique authors, these Germans, with names recast after a Latin-Greek model, plunged into the study of their nation's past.

Soon after 1500, the first German history drawn from original sources was written by Wimpfeling of Strasburg, from the earliest times down to his own period; can we blame him if the bright light which shone upon him blinded his eyes to the shadows? Town chronicles too began to be written in a more lively style. But most characteristic of the nature of humanism are the undertakings which took a really comprehensive sweep. Such were the new *History of the World*, written in Latin and German by Hermann Schedel, the city doctor of Nuremberg, with two thousand woodcuts from Wohlgemut's studio: and Maximilian the First's magnificent plan for a *Germania Illustrata*, in which the most eminent scholars and artists were to collaborate—a truly royal project which, like so much in Maximilian's life, remained a project only.

The same breath of life which wafted the scholars to new shores swelled the sails of the artists. What a task was theirs, to give an artistic form to all the boundless aspirations of their time! Many undertook the task and vindicated the right of the individual with more determination than in former times. The great artists of the thirteenth century worked anonymously: if Dürer had not entered the name in his travelling journal, we should not even know who had painted the famous *Adoration of the Three Kings* in Cologne Cathedral (p. 195). But now artists publicly acknowledged their works. The self-representations of brassfounders and woodcutters kept pace with Dürer's self-portraits. This was more than a superficial change: it was the expression of the changed attitude of the artist towards his work.

It is more possible for the painter and draughtsman to render the whole content of his vision, than for the worker in another medium. One of the most ingenious of German artists, who wrestled at the same time with the secrets of life and of art, worked as draughtsman and painter. Albrecht Dürer first won fame by his woodcuts and copper engravings. Under his hand the woodcut gains an unsuspected power of expression. Movement breathes through every line of his design. Nature's will to live works in the grass and trees, even the dead stone is caught up into the circle of living energies. So the woodcut becomes the medium by which he gives shape to inward visions of overwhelming import. The four Riders of the Apocalypse leap forward with resistless might, bringing death upon the world by pestilence, hunger, and sword. The manes of the horses float in the wind: the garments flutter: on the ground, dying men writhe in terror. Side by side with this awe-inspiring revelation of the last things we find the gentle serenity of the *Life of Mary* with its lovely representation of daily life. As an engraver on copper, Dürer renders the extremest refinement of artistic perception, the intricate interweaving of light and shade. In a plate of the Passion, the struggle between darkness and light becomes an arresting allegory of what was passing in the soul of Him who was to the artist, 'Christ the Lord, the Fairest in all the world.' Again and again, in contrast to the painters of the Middle Ages, he represents Him as an heroic conqueror. A stay in Italy is intended to throw light on the secret to which the Italian pictures owe the perfection of their effect and their lifelike splendour. The pictures which Dürer paints after his return show the influence of this study: but once more he attains a still higher level in his work on the copperplate. *St. Jerome in the Cell* is irresistibly attractive in the enchantment of its sacred quiet. *Melancholia* announces the bitter discovery of the fruitlessness of man's search for knowledge. Defying all the forces of evil, the *Man in Armour* rides in peace through the dark valley. His home lies before him gilded by the light of heaven. The sparkling drawings for Kaiser Maximilian's Prayer Book, portraits, woodcuts, the plunge into the gay social world of Flanders: life and work together flow onward like a wide stream. It grows calmer in the latter years. Scientific labours on the problem of form call for completion. The *Four Apostles* are finished as his last piece of painting. They are the spontaneous creation of the artist, who presents them to the council of his native city. The harmony of their heads, their attitudes, their garments, is unexampled in its expressiveness. Dürer's Apostles are not heralds of the triumphant Truth, but images of striving humanity. The eye of their creator has penetrated the motley disguise of the world of appearance, and come to rest upon the eternal foundations.

The Townsfolk

Grünewald, the daemonic, offers a sharp contrast to the virile Dürer, who has the dark forces under his control. We know practically nothing of the life of the artist: his contemporaries counted him as one of their greatest men. His altar at Isenheim is like a spring of water gushing from primeval depths. Horror blunts pity before the picture of the Crucifix: colour runs riot in such a mastery of lighting as had never before been seen when the transfigured body of the Risen Lord is rapt to Heaven. Hans Holbein the younger, on the other hand, paints what reality presents, with unswerving eye and a hand sure of its colours. The *Madonna of Burgomaster Meyer* is the distinguished wife of a citizen, surrounded by a middle-class family. The German merchants in the London house, the English king and the nobles of his country—they are all men of flesh and blood, but without the refinement of mind which breathes from Dürer's portraits.

The same versatility in creation and in the personality of the artist is present in plastic art. As the painter enlarged his possibilities of expression by woodcutting and engraving upon copper, it was a common thing for the sculptor also to employ the carving tool and the pencil. Carved altars were a very favourite decoration for churches in the late Gothic period, and were achieved by the united labour of sculptors, painters, and carpenters, unless one master could practise all these branches of art. Their close connection had this result: that painting, which was the leading art of the period, exercised a powerful influence upon the shaping of the work. The picturesque style of carving is specially evident in the altars of Veit Stoss of Nuremberg, clear cut, extremely animated figures, fluttering garments, inexhaustible riches of form. The best works of Tilmann Riemenschneider are distinguished by a nobler proportion; he made a great number of altars and tombs in Taubergrund and Würzburg. Adam Kraft, working in stone, united simple truth to nature with the most highly developed delicacy of treatment. His pyx in the Lorenzkirche at Nuremberg is a fragile miracle of late Gothic sentiment, while the masterly brassfounding of Peter Vischer already speaks the language of the Renaissance.

The work of the artists reveals how largely the sentiment and thought of the period were governed by religious motives, but at the same time it shows how personal a form was already given to religious experience.

The tension between private sentiment and the governing powers necessarily made itself felt more powerfully and universally in the religious life, than in any other field: for here it was a question of matters which penetrated more deeply into the innermost being of the individual, and were of incomparably greater importance to the community than other intellectual questions. The piety of the common people was never more active, as is proved by innumerable foundations and brotherhoods, of which there were nearly one hundred in the larger towns, pilgrimages, and pious exercises of every kind. The very fact that this activity was so universal introduced an element of superficiality which sometimes took questionable forms, as for instance the hunt after wonder-working relics, in which the elector Frederick the Wise took a leading part: he collected about five thousand objects in the monastery of All Saints at Wittenberg.

Although a general condemnation of the clergy of that period could not in any way be justified, yet in certain places the worldly spirit had reached an alarming height. It is true that little might be heard on the other side of the Alps of the unworthy life of many of the popes, yet the Germans experienced only too keenly in their own persons the evils of the papal system of finance. The appointment of bishops and canons lay almost exclusively in the hands of the nobles; the wealthy abbeys were known as 'Hospitals of the Nobility,' and in the cathedral chapter there were many who led a most worldly life, of which their hunt for benefices is an evil instance. One must admit that the union of many benefices under one head was often rendered necessary through the depreciation of money. But it was fatal to the cure of souls: for the incumbents deputed their obligations to poor, uneducated priests, who were unequal to the demands made upon them for spiritual guidance. The soul's hunger felt by wide sections of the people had the effect of leading many among the numerous secular-religious communities, such as the Brothers of the Lay Community, to seek a path outside the Church.

'We are not monks, but our aim and desire is to live piously in the world,' such was the declaration of the Brothers of the Lay Community. The high value set upon secular work which is evident from their words, was essentially a fruit of the professional life of the towns. In the building of churches and pious foundations, in the beginnings of secular education, in the care of the poor and sick, the citizens had taken over tasks which at the height of the Middle Ages had been discharged by the Church alone. The reigning princes also began to intervene more and more in Church affairs. After the Imperial Concordat had been shattered at the time of the Council of Basel, the Papacy had been gradually forced to make concessions to individual princes. Long before Luther's time, the path was already marked out which led to the formation of the territorial churches by way of the taxation of the clergy, the suppression of decayed monasteries, and the disposal of Church property.

The higher clergy were united together by similar aims, which were not hostile to the Church, yet certainly not in accordance with it, where they were concerned with Church reform and the limitation of the pope's financial authority. In the diets which sat towards the end of the fifteenth century, the ecclesiastical grievances (*gravamina*) of the estates of the realm played a permanent rôle, and lords spiritual, like Berthold von Henneberg, were amongst the supporters of the agitation.

The fruitlessness of such exertions aggravated the internal unrest, which we meet with in countless utterances by secular and religious speakers. The writings of those men who represented the new secular learning, are the most illuminating. The earlier humanists had succeeded in reconciling their learned endeavour with the opinions of the Church. Gradually, however, the aristocratic features of the new culture became more pronounced, the sentiment of inward independence grew stronger, but with it contempt for the illiteracy of the clergy, and criticism of ecclesiastical organizations and dogma. When the much respected Reuchlin quarrelled with the theological faculty at Cologne over the suppression of the Talmud, humanist circles produced a work which most wittily held the degeneration of the lower clergy up to ridicule: 'Letters from the Men who love Darkness rather than Light.' It was the aim of the letters to kill by laughter: with grim fury Hutten fell upon immoral monks and the avaricious Papacy. He was full of warm love for his German compatriots, but there was no limit to the violence of his onslaughts. The fight was to be carried on, not only by the little band of scholars, but by the whole nation, so he began to write in German:

> Now I cry to the Fatherland—
> The German nation in her own speech,
> To bring vengeance upon these things.

The cry rang distastefully in the ears of the refined Erasmus. He too met clerical ignorance with the bitterest mockery, and attacked the superficiality of the religious Church life; indeed, he could claim the credit of having done more to further the cause of the pure Gospel by the unlocking of its sources than any other of his fellow combatants. Yet he consistently maintained that reform was the affair of the scholars. For him the essence of the matter was nothing less than to set free 'the simple philosophy of Christ,' and to recognize the agreement between that philosophy and the teaching of the most noble amongst the heathen.

Such breadth of thought was granted to few. Yet Erasmus did not stand alone in his views, and the demands which he deduced from this recognition were on a par with those which were urged upon the plain man by his religious feelings. In the desire to set religious experience on an independent footing, and to simplify the mediating function of the Church, the keenest intellect in Germany was at one with the simple sentiment of many.

This wish did not betoken alienation from the Church —not even alienation from the Papacy. The bounds of the existing community of believers seemed to be wide enough to afford space for the new development. Hence even the profound religious excitement could not lower the pitch at which life was being lived, which inspires so many utterances at the beginning of modern times.

'If one should read all the Chronicles,' wrote Luther, some years after his first public appearance, 'he would find naught in this world from the time of Christ's birth which can be compared at every point with this century. Such building and planting hath never been so general in all the world, nor have such riches and variety of eating and drinking been so general as they now are. And who hath ever read of such a body of merchants as those who now journey round the world, devouring the whole world? All manner of arts are arising and have arisen: painting, etching, engraving, so that the like hath never been seen since the birth of Christ. Moreover, some there are now of such keen intelligence that nothing is hidden from them, and a boy of twenty knoweth more now than twenty doctors knew aforetime.'

But this universal exaltation itself produced a state of tension in every department of life. There was an abundance of views and sentiments, existing side by side and struggling for the mastery, and political evolution was thrusting Germany with all its fermentation into new and complex international relationships. Luther's appearance launched a movement in which economic, social, political, and intellectual problems were intertwined in a manner never before known.

THIRD BOOK

THE PRINCIPALITY
1500–1800

PREFACE TO THE THIRD BOOK

THE Reformation gave a powerful impetus to the movement for harmonizing religious experience with the growing consciousness of personality. For centuries to come, religious questions and their discussion once more dominated intellectual life: one may cite the last works of Lessing, who died in 1781. Moreover, the attitude of princes and people in the religious contest played a decisive part in the inward culture and mutual relations of the State. Absolute government would have been unthinkable, either in Catholic or Protestant countries, without the Reformation movement. During the period of absolutism, the great States strove together for supremacy, and especially for the command of the ocean, which had become the medium of world trade, with a concentration of national forces which had been hitherto unknown.

Even before a decision had been reached in the rivalry between France, which was victorious on the mainland, and England, which was striving for the command of the seas, the French Crown had to pay the price of the exhaustion of her national strength. In the French Revolution, the absolute power of the king succumbed before the conception of democracy. Through the Revolution, the subject rose to be the pillar of the State, and the principality was transformed into the Fatherland.

As the birthplace of the Reformation, Germany became for some decades the focus of European development. In the Peasants' War the religious movement was merged in a great endeavour after social reconstruction, which, if it had succeeded, would have brought about a fundamental change in public life. But the peasant rising was suppressed, and the princes reaped the political profits. Before long, however, intellectual, economic, and political life were cast in a rigid mould. During the Thirty Years' War, Germany became the theatre of the struggle for supremacy in Europe. The

The Principality

princes founded their absolute power upon the stricken field. The history of the German people became the history of the principality, and was largely determined by the relations of the territorial Governments to the Great Powers: even the contention between the old imperial power of Austria and the aspiring Prussia came under this head. Not until the collapse of the empire during the Napoleonic period, could the idea of the Fatherland prove, even in Germany, its capacity for making history.

FIRST PART

RELIGIOUS WAR

MORE truly than any other revolution in German life, the religious movement at the beginning of modern history may be regarded as the work of one man. Without Luther's conscientious struggle, and the conviction which he won so hardly and proclaimed so bravely, there would have been no Reformation. But the fact that his voice prevailed can only be explained by the circumstances of the time. Sufferers from every kind of ill, both mental and physical, thronged to him as to a saviour; in the council chambers of princes, the monk soon came to be valued as a piece upon the political chess-board. These conditions created a favourable atmosphere for the preaching of the new doctrine, but they themselves had to be reckoned with. Decades of struggle followed the years of hope; the change is marked by the Peasants' War.

Luther faced the world in the freshness of his young manhood, but already matured through the stress of inward conflict. As one active, merry lad amongst others at the Grammar School of Erfurt, he had followed the course of study desired by his ambitious father. Then, acting on a sudden resolve, but not, as he afterwards confessed, 'heartily and of free will,' he begged for admission into the Augustinian monastery. Yet he had no vocation for monastic life, and found no peace, either in the Church doctrine of grace, or in the performance of the penances, to which without the order or knowledge of his superiors he now devoted himself. This peasant's son was living again in all its primitive force the experience of the prophets of the Old Testament, when they looked upon God in His terrible anger. 'There is no escape and no comfort either within or without—nothing but accusation and condemnation for all.' An awful gulf yawned between the angry Creator and the sin-laden creature: all that wretched man considered as his merit, and all the help offered by the Church, was swallowed up in it. Only the determination to recognize the God of Love in the God of Wrath, only the wings of faith, could bear the soul across it to the throbbing heart of Him who has promised His grace to all who love Him. He who is certain of his salvation by faith does the works which please God, as the good tree brings forth good fruit, by inner compulsion, without admonishment and precept.

Luther set himself to awaken the new type of religious man: he remained too long without a right understanding of the need of his followers for a rule of conduct by which to order their daily life; and his work suffered in consequence. His religious belief was only won after long conflict. Clear conviction came when he had already worked most successfully for several years at the University of Wittenberg, where his far-reaching activities as teacher and student, preacher and pastor, obliged him to occupy himself with the problems of theological learning, no less than with the needs of the human heart.

The experience which he had gained as a pastor aroused his scholarly zeal, to fight against the abuse of the proclamation of papal indulgence, which was being practised by the Dominican monk Tetzel on the frontiers of the electorate of Saxony. When Luther nailed the 95 Theses to the door of the Castle Church of Wittenberg, he had no idea of breaking with the Church. His Theses were nothing more than a challenge to a learned debate on the nature of indulgence: his intention was to expound the doctrine of the Church, and thus put a stop to the degradation to which she was being subjected for the sake of gain. But events fell out otherwise. The Theses were rapidly printed and translated, and universally disseminated and discussed; here and there they were even brought to public notice by command of the sovereign. When Luther was attacked and brought to book, he came gradually to see that his religious convictions were irreconcilable with the Church doctrine; when he examined Church doctrine scientifically and defined his convictions with growing clearness, a new doctrine was the result. The 'Monk's Quarrel' grew in a way undreamed of, in breadth and depth. The dispute about indulgence became a Church dispute.

His opponents were better able than himself to estimate the importance of his first step. But the political situation made caution necessary. The election of the emperor was about to take place, and the Papal See wished to prevent the election of Charles V, who, as occupier of the imperial throne, would be capable of becoming a most unpleasant neighbour in Naples. Efforts were therefore made from

Religious War

Rome to gain the support of the Elector of Saxony for the candidature of the French king Francis I, and he was even urged to become himself a candidate. On the first occasion, Luther was protected by the elector's intercession from the stern measures recommended by Tetzel, and others more powerful than he, and later Frederick the Wise also stretched his protecting wing over his professor. It was not a small matter to lend a helping hand to the acknowledged heretic, in the face of pope and emperor: and Luther did nothing to make it easier for his sovereign. Frequently, it was desperately hard to find a way out. After the great day at Worms, the prince never saw the proscribed monk again; it is impossible to say how far he secretly agreed with him. But he and his counsellors never faltered in their prudent policy.

So time was granted to the harried reformer to work out his ideas. Only three years after the nailing of the Theses he published his great works upon reform. He sought 'The improvement of the Christian profession' primarily by doing away with the privileged position held by the priest in the Church and in the world: 'All Christians are really of the priestly class!' But leaving the ecclesiastical field, the tract goes deeply into the pressing secular problems of the time; it calls for measures against the flowing of German money into Rome, for the setting up of a national Church, and for the freedom of the State from the authority of the Church of Rome: it proclaims war upon the usury of the merchants and upon the state of beggary: it offers suggestions for the reorganization of education, for the care of the young, and other similar matters. In face of the Church's refusal, he calls upon the members of the State Government, the emperor, princes, and lords, the 'Christian nobility of the German nation,' to carry out the necessary reform. Never again did Luther enter so deeply into the secular needs of his people.

His later writings are the work of a totally different man; he wrote them in the Latin tongue, for scholars. They are full of bitterness against the sacramental teaching of the Church ('Upon the Babylonish Captivity of the Church'), which had been left untouched even by Wyclif and Huss. He had roused the nation; the axe was laid at the root of the tree, and it was doomed to fall; bright visions of the future now rise before him; how the true Christian is blessed by God ('Of the Freedom of a Man of Christ') and how he is proved true in every situation, in every hour of his earthly life ('Of good Works').

Luther was still pouring forth this flood of constructive ideas, set out with powerful eloquence, when the danger which had long threatened him became a certainty: Dr. Eck brought the papal ban to Germany. Again the fires flamed up, and reduced the apostate's writings to ashes. In December 1520, Luther replied by casting the papal bull, and the book of ecclesiastical law, into the flames. This revolutionary act before the Elster Gate at Wittenberg cut him off irrevocably and publicly from union with the Church. It was time for the secular power to make itself heard.

Some weeks earlier Maximilian's grandson, Charles V, had been crowned Roman king, and acknowledged as emperor by the pope. Francis I had tried in vain to hinder this aggrandizement of his fellow competitor, whose possessions encircled France in the west and east. His own candidature was finally wrecked by the princes, who considered that the French king might prove a greater danger to the freedom of the estates—'German Liberty'— than the Hapsburger, whose forces were much less concentrated. But before the decision was made, both candidates had to pay great sums to the princely electors. Only the Elector of Saxony disdained to bargain: the possession of his silver mines may have made it easier for him to reject the foreign money. The German people gladly acclaimed the emperor's grandson: Luther himself built his hopes upon 'the noble young blood.' But the princes could not be under any illusion. They knew that they were choosing in Charles not a ruler who would help the empire in distress, but only the lesser evil: the engagements to which they made him subscribe for the safeguarding of their 'Liberty' speak with no uncertain voice.

As a matter of fact, there is scarcely a moment in German history in which Fate worked together with man to produce more disastrous results. Charles had grown up in the Netherlands, under the influence of Romano-Burgundian culture. At seventeen he had accepted the crown of Spain: as a foreigner, not even acquainted with the language, he met with considerable difficulties. When his presence was needed in Germany, he left Spain in open rebellion. As a

Religious War

stranger in Germany also, he encountered extremely difficult conditions. The fixed point in his political thinking and striving could only be to establish the world-power of the House of Hapsburg, and to make the separate countries under his dominion serviceable to this end. He was well aware of the need for reform in the Church of his day. Yet, apart altogether from the personal obligations which rested upon him as a true son of the Church, his political efforts must include the defence of Church unity.

But the Germans were no longer confined within the limits of these ideas. The growing power of the princes led them to see an infringement of their rights in every command of the emperor: Luther's attack upon the unity of the Church found an echo in the widest circles of the people. The direction in which their will was bent was the inevitable outcome of the German nature, both present and to come, as Charles's efforts in the contrary direction were inherent in the nature of Hapsburg authority and the personality of its representative. Charles was obliged to witness the destruction of his lifework, and was the only one in the long line of German emperors voluntarily to lay down his crown—while Germany, thrown into deeper confusion than had ever been known before, went forward into the dark.

In the first diet which the young emperor summoned at Worms, the wishes of the House of Hapsburg and of the German nation came at once into collision. He needed troops for the imminent struggle with France. The estates, amongst other things, demanded a discussion of Luther's cause, and in this they were actuated in no small degree by their fear of 'the common man.' Instead of adding the sentence of outlawry to the ban of the Church, Charles agreed to have Luther summoned before him. His appearance on the first day, his request for time to consider the demand for recantation, discouraged his friends. But on the second day, he gave his 'simple answer' which ran through the whole of Germany. The emperor too, as a Hapsburger and as a defender of the Church, had no choice but to act as he did; the Edict of Worms, which was published after the close of the Parliament, pronounced a sentence of outlawry upon Luther and his adherents. But its execution remained in abeyance. Foreign complications caused the emperor's absence from Germany for nearly nine years: Luther found an immediate refuge in the Wartburg, and afterwards lived on in Wittenberg unmolested.

In the Wartburg he began the two works which were to serve from that time forward as a basis for the preaching of the Gospel. The collection of his sermons for all occasions of the Church year was his favourite amongst all his books, and gives a deeper insight into his nature than any other, with the possible exception of the Larger Catechism. But while the *Kirchenpostille* (Collection of Sermons) could actually affect the Protestant Church and family alone, the translation of the Bible, with its formative influence upon the language and its intimate fusion of true German sentiment and Christian piety, was fruitful for the whole nation. Yet even while he was straining every nerve in his creative work, his inward conflict never ceased: 'Art thou the only wise man? What, if thou errest and art leading these multitudes into error, who will all be damned to all eternity?' Yet Luther was no more paralysed by these attacks of doubt, than by that most painful disappointment caused him through the behaviour of the iconoclasts in Wittenberg. Melanchthon, the elector, and his counsellors— all were at their wits' end. Before Luther's wrath, the spectre vanished.

While he was still working upon the foundations of the new doctrine, his words were gaining more and more disciples, even beyond the frontiers of Germany. The number of publications which dealt with the subject multiplied enormously; from 1516 to 1529 it increased ninefold, and the great majority took his part. But it was not till the year 1525 that he was first publicly joined by two princes of the empire, the landgrave Philip of Hesse, and the elector John, the successor of Frederick the Wise. For the rest, the princes held back, if they did not definitely reject him, like the emperor's brother Ferdinand, the ruler of the Austrian territories, or Duke George of Saxony, the Prince of Brandenburg and the House of Wittelsbach. As the years went on, many other influential men, especially amongst the Humanists, are known to have turned away from Luther. But the majority of the nation still clung to the idea that a Reformation of the Church, as they understood it, must be the work of the empire. The Imperial Government, which ruled the empire under Ferdinand's presidency, refused, sometimes formally, sometimes evasively, to carry out the Edict of Worms.

Yet the estates were not of one mind amongst themselves. The south German princes united under papal influence to combat secession: the emperor entered the strongest protest against a diet planned with the object of reform. So everything remained in the balance.

But the time of ferment called for action. Because Luther, working for the spread of the new spirit, did not comply with the necessity for new forms, iconoclasm was able to gain the mastery in his own town. For centuries, temporal had been most closely bound up with spiritual: Luther himself had attacked economic, social, and governmental problems. The time of waiting had been long. When nothing more was to be hoped for from the side of the empire, the storm broke out from the side of the laity. Knights and peasants, who had been thrust on one side by the course of events, resorted to violence.

In the majority of the German territories, the nobility had already been obliged to adjust themselves to the Sovereign Government. It was otherwise with the knights of the empire, who were still settled in great numbers in the scattered States of the south and west. They ruled their little territory like princes, and acknowledged no master but the emperor. But they were forbidden to have any say in the Imperial Government; everywhere they were conscious of being restrained by the authority of the princes. The universal discontent found a spokesman in Franz von Sickingen, who had made a name for himself in private warfare against towns and princes, and as a captain of the mercenaries in the service of the emperor and of France.

Luther's attacks on Church property had been greeted with enthusiasm in the circle of Sickingen's friends, to which Hutten belonged; and it was against the lords spiritual that the first steps were to be taken. But Sickingen's attack upon Trèves was unsuccessful. The Landgrave of Hesse and the Elector Palatine came to the help of the archbishop, who was a seasoned warrior. The princely victors found the lord of the castle at the point of death, amidst the ruins of Landstuhl.

The rising of the knights of the empire was a sequel to the history of chivalry: the Peasants' War was a turning-point in the history of the German people. Even before the time of Luther, the peasants had risen here and there in their thousands. Religious motives, and those which were concerned with the social life of the Church, had already played an essential part in these movements (p. 192). Their demands did not in any way come short of those which were made later. But the movement had never before covered so wide a field. The fact that indignation had become so widespread may in part be ascribed to the effect of time, which in that period of universal ferment was quite different from what it had formerly been. But there is no doubt that Luther's words worked along with it, for the peasants translated his teaching on Christian liberty into earthly conditions, and felt their own oppression to be contrary to God's will.

The conspiracy began in the upper part of the Black Forest, upon Swabian territory, which had been prepared by former risings. The peasants of the Abbot of St. Blasius were among the first. A former foot soldier took over the command. The inhabitants of Waldshut were in dread of an attack on the part of the Archduke Ferdinand, because of their adherence to the new teaching; it was not long before they took part in the confederacy. They were joined by foot soldiers from Switzerland. In the district of Allgäu the peasants rose against the Abbot of Kempten, who had 'evilly entreated, weakened, and overpowered them' by 'captivity dungeons, prisons, loading with chains and heavy fines.' In the spring of 1527, the country from Ulm to the Lake of Constance was in uproar. A meeting of peasants at Memmingen founded the 'Christian Alliance.' Luther, Zwingli, and others were to be entrusted with the ordering of its religious affairs. Its secular demands were comprised in twelve articles. No revolution ever expressed itself in more modest language. 'Firstly, it is our humble prayer and desire that we may henceforth have power and authority for a whole congregation to choose and elect its own priest.' The peasants are willing to give the rightful tithe of grain, 'gladly, yet as it is fitting'; for the priest, for the needy, and for the defence of the country. 'Not that we desire to be quite free, and to have no more authority over us: God does not so teach us'—but serfdom shall be put an end to: hunting and fishing permitted: with free firing. And so it goes on, repeating their 'Christian offer' of an amicable arrangement again and again to the conclusion. No castle

Religious War

had yet gone up on flames. No murder had been committed. Yet, though the words sounded so restrained, they concealed revolution with them. It occurred to none of the princes to grasp the outstretched hand. Thereupon it was clenched and dealt its blow. Castles and monasteries sank into ashes.

While in Swabia, Alsace, and the Alpine districts the rising was chiefly confined to the peasants; in Franconia the towns, with the knights and the gentry, were drawn into the whirlpool. It began in Rothenburg—craftsmen and discontented folk overthrew the council of patricians, and opened the gates to the peasants. Heilbronn and other towns, including even Würzburg and Bamberg, joined in. Götz von Berlichingen and Florian Geyer became the most noted of the knightly leaders. The Knight of the Iron Hand took his departure when the period of his enforced engagement had come to an end. Florian appears repeatedly as mediator for the peasants; he was probably a 'degenerate offshoot of the nobility'—certainly not the commanding personality that Hauptmann represents him in his drama. But it is undeniable that the Frankish leaders had an eye upon the greater implications of the rising. The 'Reformation' of Weigant, the magistrate of Mayence, is a scheme of astonishing boldness for the constitution of the empire. Three centuries and a half before Bismarck, Weigant took for his political object the creation of an economic and judicial union, the strengthening of the central power of the emperor, and the limitation of the power of the princes: he wished to employ Church property for the alleviation of feudal burdens. Yet it was in Franconia that it was least possible to control the lust for robbery and destruction amongst the mob. The murder of the Count of Helfenstein and his fellow captives was, however, an isolated act, and was later thrown into the shade by the cruelties of the victors.

The rising also affected many of the towns in Thuringia. Mulhouse was the centre: and here Thomas Münzer, the iconoclast of Wittenberg, seized the leadership. Years previously the lower class of citizens had overthrown the council, and it was Münzer who had stirred up the agitation. He returned from the Black Forest in the first weeks of the year 1525, and now the movement spread rapidly over the whole north-west of Thuringia. While, in other places, the

The Principality

leaders, at least, clung to an accommodation, in one form or another, with existing circumstances, Münzer's greatest anxiety was lest these 'foolish men should consent to a false treaty, because they do not yet recognize the wrong.' He was working for a complete revolution in ecclesiastical and political conditions: 'Let not the blood grow cold on your sword'—this was the gospel of deeds which he preached to the miners of Mansfeld—'it is impossible, while they live, that you should be free from the fear of man.' It is uncertain how far the masses agreed with him: in any case, it does not appear from the events that in Thuringia they followed any separate aim.

When May came, Germany was on fire from the Alps to Westphalia. Nearly two thousand monasteries and castles are said to have fallen victim to the rage of the populace. But the same circumstance which helped the movement in its triumphant progress, excluded the possibility of any real success: the powers against whom they were fighting consisted of so many scattered States lacking any political centre that it was impossible to come to grips with them. The failure of the leaders grew ever more evident. In south Germany they consented to be restrained by negotiations: at Würzburg they did not succeed in dissuading the masses from the fruitless storming of the fortress of Marienberg: the Thuringians remained inactive near Frankenhausen. When the princes had recovered from their fright and acted together, their mercenaries won an easy victory over the loosely organized bands. By the beginning of June the insurgents had been scattered at almost every point: and then followed mutilations, burning, and tortures of every kind; a vengeance which exceeded in cruelty everything which the peasants could have deserved. Almost impossible payments for 'restitution' were demanded and rendered.

It cannot be proved that the burdens of the peasants everywhere in the revolting districts were permanently increased. Yet the results of the rising were disastrous enough: the unfortunate issue of the war cast the majority of the German nation back into dependence and torpor: excluded them from a share in intellectual and political life; and not only deepened the gulf between the classes, but fixed it for all time.

The Peasants' War left a deep scar upon the history of the Reformation. The masses everywhere had believed that their desire for 'divine justice' would be confirmed by Luther's teaching. Shortly before the outbreak of war he had called the nobles of the Imperial Government 'mad and drunken princes': he had described resistance to the rule of the bishops with 'body, goods, and honour' as a conflict with the Devil's Government, and had threatened the lay princes in these words: 'The world is no longer what it once was, when you could hunt and drive the people like game. If you will continue to draw the sword, have a care lest one come and bid you sheathe it, and not in God's name.'

Who could and would understand that such words were wrung from the deepest agony of heart, and that no one could be more violently averse to revolution by force than Luther himself? To him dependence in secular matters was as much the will of God as liberty in religious matters. At the height of the conflict, he travelled at the risk of his life from village to village in Thuringia, exhorting to quiet. When that was of no avail, he wrote in a wild fury: 'Against the pillaging and murdering troops of peasants.' A world of hope and trust had been shattered for him, but also for the peasants. What did it avail that when the war was over he urged humanity upon the bloodthirsty victors? In the eyes of the common man, the leader had become the betrayer. And Luther saw no other possibility of saving his lifework than the closest alliance with authority. Hitherto the building up of the evangelical Church from within had seemed conceivable on the basis of free congregations: now Luther put the organization and guidance of the Church into the hands of sovereign and urban authority.

So the territorial churches came into being. In place of the bishops, the princes as emergency bishops undertook the management of external business: they ordered the presentation of livings through the consistory courts, which were staffed by government officials, both clerical and lay. As an equivalent for its confiscation of Church property the State took over many of the tasks which had formerly been discharged by the Church, particularly the instruction in the upper and lower schools; the residue of Church property found its way into the princes' coffers. It was in the nature of the new order that the Church should be connected more and more closely with the State: it led in the end to the princes ruling their territorial Church as a State establishment. Even in the districts which remained

The Principality

Catholic, the princes undertook ecclesiastical reforms to a much greater extent on the part of the State, with State powers of compulsion, with the result that here too there was a notable increase in sovereign authority. Now, of necessity, political points of view came to the front: a war of religious convictions became a political war, in which the religious interest continually lost ground. The dispute about the faith ended in the establishment of absolute sovereignty.

Luther was not a man of political strife. That he left to his friends, that he might devote himself to the other tasks which met him in overwhelming numbers. His gospel, which was the fruit of most intimate personal experience, now for the first time became the actual basis of a 'doctrine': the spirit which moved within him was confined in words, till, in the end, it hardened into a creed. Under the burden of work, and the strain of defending himself from the bitterest attacks, his temper became still more irritable with the years, and his manner yet harsher. Even his contemporaries were sometimes terrified by his fierce outbursts.

At a critical moment he stepped once again into the centre of the stage. The confusion of the peasant rising had not prejudiced the spread of the Reformation. Already the estates of the realm, which were favourable to Luther, were strong enough to obtain a resolution from the Imperial Diet, which could be interpreted as a legal basis for the founding of the territorial churches.

Church organization in the Electorate of Saxony became a pattern for Hesse, Brunswick-Lüneburg, Auspach, and many imperial cities. The Grand Master of the German Order, who was a Hohenzollern, transformed his country into an hereditary dukedom, under Polish sovereignty: Denmark and Sweden adhered to the new teaching. Zwingli's Reformation was gaining ground in Switzerland. During his studies he had breathed the free air of Humanism. He had therefore never taken scholastic knowledge for the rule of his mental life, nor needed, like Luther, to free himself from it by a hard struggle. He had indeed to wrestle for his own knowledge of salvation: yet, in place of personal assurance, he took work for others as the central point of thought and experience. As priest at the great Cathedral of Zurich, he won over the guilds and the council, step by step, to his ideas, which from the beginning included social and political

222

reforms, such as opposition to military service under foreign Governments: the reorganization of the state of pauperism, the abolition of serfdom, and many others. God's word was to become the actual rule of conduct in secular life, and the State to have the ordering of Church matters also. So a State Church came into being, which was narrow and intolerant, and yet was supported by the independent government of a free people. The close connection of Church and State accomplished by Zwingli, resulted in Zurich encountering the strongest opposition from its own neighbours. Then, when the imminent return of the emperor threatened the Reformation with destruction, not only in Switzerland, but throughout Germany, Zwingli envisaged deliverance in a great alliance between the reformed Powers, which should include even the foreign enemies of the Hapsburgs, Venice and France.

On Luther's side, Philip of Hesse was revolving similar thoughts. With the exception of the doctrine of the Holy Communion, the doctrinal differences were trifling between the two reformers. If unity could be attained on this point, nothing seemed to stand in the way of the intended alliance. The future of Protestantism hung upon Luther.

Luther came unwillingly. A whole world divided him from Zwingli, the humanist and politician. The efforts put forth by the Swiss in the conference on religion at Marburg, to prove to him the error of his doctrine of the sacrament, did not succeed in convincing him, nor could Zwingli's tears move him: for he did not wish to be persuaded. It was even more impossible for Zwingli to yield, without being false to himself. The attempt at agreement came to nothing.

What Zwingli feared seemed to become fact. In the first war against Francis I, Charles V had won back Milan through the victory of his German foot soldiers at Pavia in 1525. His pretensions grew with his success: not until he had promised to give back Burgundy did the imprisoned French king regain his freedom. But in the act of swearing, he made up his mind to break the engagement which had been thus extorted from him. The pope allied himself with him. While the new teaching was spreading unhindered in Germany, German and Spanish soldiers in the pay of the emperor, marched plundering through the Eternal City. Charles was obliged by the conditions of peace to leave Burgundy to the French king: yet he came to an understanding with the pope, and received the imperial crown from the pope's hand as the last of the German emperors. Now he had a free hand to strike at the Reformation.

Before he appeared in Germany, a resolution of the Diet (the second Diet of Spire in 1529) ordered the Edict of Worms to be carried out. The States, whose sympathies were with Luther, protested: at that time, nothing but Luther's veto prevented the signing of an armed alliance between the 'Protestants.' They were to answer for their opinions before the emperor at the Diet of Augsburg (1530). The theologians had the first word. In the endeavour to minimize the existing differences, Melanchthon's 'Augsburg Confession' reached the extreme limits of what was possible for Protestantism: on the opposite side also, earnest efforts at reconciliation were being made. Agreement was reached in oral discussion upon the majority of the dogmas; but the service and organization of the Church presented unsurmountable difficulties. The resolution taken in the last decisive session of the Diet ordered again, and much more peremptorily, the carrying out of the Edict of Worms. The Protestants had not waited for the decision: they united for armed defence in the Smalkaldic League on the soil of Hesse. A warlike encounter seemed inevitable, when the emperor was robbed of his freedom of action by fresh complications in foreign politics.

Years before this, Hungary had already been subdued by the Turks. When the Hapsburg Ferdinand succeeded to the throne after the death of the King of Hungary, protracted fighting took place between the Hapsburgs and their new neighbours for the possession of the country. The first Turkish attack upon Vienna was frustrated in 1529: but a new assault soon threatened. This compelled the emperor to come to an understanding with the Protestants. In 1532, the Religious Peace of Nuremberg referred the decision to a general council. In the sequel the emperor, who had become entangled in foreign wars, was absent from Germany for more than ten years. In the first place, he attempted to break the Turkish command of the Mediterranean, which was specially coveted by the Spaniards. Then war broke out again on the subject of Milan, and Francis I did not shrink from concluding an alliance with the enemy of Christendom. The alliance was not of long duration: but the war against both enemies lingered on without decisive

Religious War

military events, and forced the emperor repeatedly to purchase by concessions the help of the Protestants. In this way he succeeded in making them fight the Turks as well as the French: they realized too late that they had been fighting against their own cause. Charles broke off in the midst of an advance upon Paris. While he restored the property to that State which had been agreed upon fifteen years earlier, Francis I bound himself to support the emperor at any time with 10,000 foot soldiers: the Protestants were not mentioned in the treaty, but they were understood. The pope promised considerable financial support. A truce was concluded with the Turks, by which they gained Ofen in 1545.

Meanwhile, Protestantism had spread over almost the whole of northern Germany, and in southern Germany also. There were also many adherents of the new doctrine in Austria, Bavaria, and the three ecclesiastical electorates, which were the only considerable States to remain Catholic. But the inward impetus had weakened: the jealousy of the princes came into play with disastrous effect: instead of bringing their powerful aid to the common cause, they began to quarrel in a very scandalous manner amongst themselves. Philip of Hesse, their most capable man, lay under the stigma of bigamy. It is true that to prevent a worse scandal, his rightful wife and the Protestant theologians had conditionally given their consent to his second marriage: even Luther was weak enough to yield to the Landgrave's wish. But the disgrace and the fear of legal consequences remained; and Philip found it advisable to approach the emperor.

Charles V had waited five-and-twenty years: now he was to strike a blow at princely autocracy through the Protestants. After the Protestants had rejected the council convened by the pope at Trent, the emperor succeeded in sowing dissension amongst his opponents. When war broke out, the Smalkaldic League alone opposed him, while Maurice of Saxony and other princes were actually on his side. In the beginning, the Allies were from a military point of view much more than a match for him. But they did not prevent the emperor from bringing up his Italian and Dutch troops. While the armies were still facing each other at the Danube, Maurice attacked the Electorate of Saxony, forced rather than persuaded to this course by the fact

The Principality

that the emperor had promised him the land and electoral dignity of his cousin. John Frederick hastened to Saxony, and in a short time the army of the Smalkaldic League was completely disbanded. South Germany lay at the emperor's feet. His victory at Mühlberg on the Elbe in 1547 brought the Saxon elector into his power, and the Landgrave of Hesse submitted and was likewise made prisoner. At the 'Armed Diet' at Augsburg, the victor dictated the course to be followed in religious matters 'until the decision of the General Council,' i.e. of the Council convened by the pope.

But his victory had made him incapable of rightly estimating the forces against him. Not a few of the princes, together with the city of Magdeburg, refused to obey the imperial decree: others submitted, but were either unwilling or unable to master the unanimous opposition of the people to its execution. There was unrest even among the Catholic princes.

Charles met them in a domineering fashion, ignored the obligations which he had undertaken at his election, and kept the princes of Saxony and Hesse in most unprincely captivity. Here was ground enough to alarm German 'Liberty.' Maurice of Saxony saw an opportunity for redeeming his treachery in the eyes at least of his fellow believers: of shaking off the imperial tutelage, and consolidating his newly won position. Through unremitting effort he accomplished a union of the Protestant princes of north Germany: there was no doubt of the neutrality of the Catholic estates of the realm. The French king gave money, and was granted in return the rights of 'Imperial Vicegerent' over Metz, Toul, and Verdun. The Protestant princes excused this step by the fact that these cities 'were not of German speech': and, at the same time, they explicitly upheld the 'Right of the Empire.' But this did not alter the fact, which was recognized even by their contemporaries, that they were guilty of unexampled treachery towards the Fatherland.

The emperor was warned: he considered himself safe. Yet when the hosts of the Allies advanced unexpectedly upon Innsbruck, he was forced to flee over the Brenner. At Passau, in 1552, Ferdinand concluded a treaty with the victors, which at least put an end to the state of war. The emperor protested: little by little he regained his *moral*.

Religious War

His first act was to oppose the spread of the French in Lorraine. But his assault upon Metz was a failure. Now at last he was broken; he quitted the empire never to enter it again.

The Religious Peace of Augsburg in 1555 acknowledged the Lutherans, though not the Reformed Church, to have equal rights with the Catholics. It was the right of the sovereign to determine the creed of his vassals: any who refused to submit should be free to depart unhindered. In the imperial cities alone, Lutherans like Catholics were to be left to enjoy their own religion.

The gain of the princes was not in doubt. In addition to their former power, they were given authority over the conscience, while the Lutherans won besides the acknowledgment of their right of disposal over Church property. But in the religious sphere the result was uncertain. The members of the Reformed Church, who were already numerous in south Germany, were still excluded from the Peace: the individual provisions could satisfy neither Lutheran nor Catholic. Lutherans in particular were opposed to the demand that a clerical prince should resign his throne on changing his religion. The agreement therefore was not really a peace, but a truce.

Long before the crisis arose in Germany, Lutheran doctrine had gained the ascendancy in the countries adjoining it on the north, and had penetrated those in the east. But in the west of Europe, the ideas of the Reformation were spreading almost exclusively in the form given to them by Calvin. To the work of reform the Frenchman brought his habit of resolute thinking, which did not shrink from any consequence, and his readiness to sacrifice individual peculiarities to the common cause. Thus he lifted the work of Zwingli out of the narrow limits of the territorial Church, to a position of world-wide importance. He saw the essence of the Church neither in the preaching of the word, nor in salvation through the mediation of the sacraments: for him the Church was the visible fellowship of God's elect, whose duty it was to prove themselves the elect in one faith, one obedience, one discipline, and in social and political activity directed towards a common end. Calvinism was harshly opposed to the temptations of worldly pleasure, and treated those who were otherwise minded with merciless severity. But this stern discipline

227

became the training school of an energetic, devoted race
of men. As the Calvinist pursued temporal success from
religious motives—for was not mundane prosperity the
proof of divine election?—he felt constrained to sacrifice
wealth and life itself for the sake of the Highest. While
Luther retained much of the old Church, Calvin broke
completely with tradition. Lutherism recommended passive
obedience: Calvinism trained men to resist to the death.
In the end, the Lutheran Church bound itself to the State:
the Calvinist sternly rejected the authority of the State
over the Church, even in places where it became the State
Church, as in Geneva, Scotland, and Holland. At times it
formed a State within the State, and was always a resolute
opponent of absolute power. To its individual structure of
legality, Calvinism owes its profound influence and its
world-wide dissemination over France, the Netherlands,
Scotland, England, and North America.

Meanwhile, unexpected powers of renewal and revival
had been aroused within the old Church. The Council of
Trent, from 1545 to 1563, dealt with questions which had
been pressed into the foreground by the Reformation. By
the uniform establishment of Church doctrine, it put an
end to all hesitation as to what was to be reckoned Catholic.
In spite of the opposition of the Spanish bishops, it
strengthened the position of the pope: it removed a great
number of abuses, tightened the bonds of Church discipline,
and cared for the education of capable priests. Thus it laid
the foundations upon which, in its further developments,
the Catholic Church has been built up. The Jesuits, together
with many other newly formed orders, worked in close
connection with the more distinguished popes for the
restoration of the Catholic faith. In the 'Fellowship of
Jesus' the former Spanish officer, Ignatius Loyola, brought
the pope a small but rapidly growing band of chosen
warriors. Bound to unconditional obedience, even to the
sacrifice of their own intelligent conviction—though not of
their conscience—they found their highest aim in overcoming unbelief, whether among the heathen or among the
heretics, or in the Church itself, and in confirming the
position of the Papacy.

Thus inwardly strengthened, the Catholic Church, on the
way to the re-establishment of its authority, had its first
encounter with Reformed Protestantism of the Calvinistic

Religious War

type. It was indeed the wide dissemination of Protestant ideas outside the boundaries of Germany which had brought the Catholic powers to a full recognition of the danger, and to a close alliance amongst themselves. In the first half of the century the relations between the States were still in great measure determined by political considerations: two Catholic powers had struggled together for the possession of Italy; the emperor was repeatedly at variance with the pope; and the French king had even been in league with the unbelievers. All this was changed after the middle of the sixteenth century. Community of religious conviction united fellow believers from different countries; creed became the determining factor even in the policy of rulers: the fight for religion came to the foreground of events. This change characterizes the second period in the great fight for the faith.

It filled the second half of the sixteenth century, the period of Philip II of Spain, and had the west of Europe for its stage. The northern portion of the Netherlands struggled from under the yoke of Spanish Catholicism, and founded a powerful State, sustained by the spirit of Calvinism, which in spite of its small extent was numbered for a whole century amongst the Great Powers of the world. Catholicism retained the upper hand in France: yet in a religious war lasting thirty years the Huguenots fought for equal rights as subjects, and maintained them for three generations. The Anglican Church arose during the reign of the English Elizabeth: and the English attained their unity of faith by the forcible deprivation of the rights of the Catholics. The head of the Catholic Mary Stuart fell beneath the axe; the Spanish Armada was broken in pieces on the coasts of the island kingdom. In the west of Europe also it was no longer possible to conquer Protestantism. But the Kingdom of Spain, the champion of Catholicism, declined from its proud elevation.

After Lutheranism and Calvinism had held their ground on separate theatres, the final decision fell out on German soil, where adherents of both creeds lived side by side in great numbers. The Thirty Years' War forms the last act in the Religious War of Europe. It struck a heavy blow at Germany's prosperity, but before that date the upward trend of the German people had been brought to a standstill.

Commerce both by sea and land still offered a broad basis

for living. But while others were gaining riches and power along the new roads of world trade, the Germans had to be satisfied with what was left over: and even of this, every now and then, a fragment crumbled away. Bruges and Antwerp had been the postern gates of German trade: Amsterdam's trading supremacy meant the cutting off of Rhenish commerce from the sea. Dutch trade began to make its way up the Rhine: and English trade penetrated into the interior of Germany by way of Hamburg. Elizabeth closed the Steelyard, and drove the Germans out of the country. If German trade had already to suffer severely from the effects of these conditions, the suspension of payment on the part of the Spanish and French crowns confirmed the ruin of the leading firms of south Germany. The House of Fugger is said to have lost eight million gulden to the Hapsburgs: in Augsburg one great house collapsed after the other. All business centres, it is true, were not hit by the disaster. Frankfort flourished as a depôt for Dutch trade: Hamburg as a port of lading for the English: and the fairs at Leipzig were scarcely inferior to those of the city on the Main. But, as a whole, there was a decided decline in German trade.

Industry felt the inevitable reaction. The craftsmen of Augsburg and Nuremberg had still no lack of orders: it was from them that the kings of France, England, and Spain obtained their splendid arms and equipment. Certain branches of arts and crafts, such as mechanics and the art of the goldsmith, did not reach their height before the seventeenth century. Yet the old endeavour to make sure of one's 'living' was universally becoming more pronounced. The guilds employed paltry tricks to make it difficult for the rising generation to set up as masters: the stocking-knitters of Nuremberg would only admit a man to their company if he promised to marry the widow or daughter of a master. It was not a rare thing for a bitter quarrel to develop over the work belonging legally to each guild, while those outside the guilds were persecuted with fury. Vigorous life was suppressed by an obstinate adherence to the letter of the guild law: what had once been a benefit became a plague: and neither the counsels of the estates of the realm nor the occasional intervention of the territorial princes relieved the situation. At the same time there was no falling off in the taste for coarse pleasure: indeed, it seems

as though certain national failings had never been so clearly
in evidence as during the period of strife between the old
and the new: a period which still as a whole was outwardly
so much at ease, and inwardly so deeply moved. The tales
told by contemporaries of drunkenness and gluttony, of
tasteless finery, of bad behaviour even amongst the upper
and the highest classes sound at times incredible. Yet the
red and fleshy faces, the bloated bodies, the overweighted
decoration on many of the portraits, the many sumptuary
laws and other ordinances, leave no room for doubt. More
significantly, the name of a scholar of that period is
responsible for the coining of the word 'beastly' (*unflätig*).
The spread of the passion for gambling may be inferred
from the fact that an author, who was widely read at that
time, was able to enumerate about five hundred society
games. The frequenting of bagnios and brothels, which had
increased unchecked in earlier centuries, was restricted:
but primitive ferocity broke out in other ways: in the
increase of torture in legal inquiries and executions, in the
trials for witchcraft, which grew with the force and speed
of an avalanche, and in the excesses of the hordes of
mercenaries. But we of the present day should beware of
joining in the sentence of condemnation which was pronounced by the age of enlightenment. The recognition of
how little many of the conditions of our own day answer
the most modest requirements of reason and humanity,
should preserve us from self-praise, and condemnation of the
past. Still more pernicious is the effect of the attempt to
accentuate the dark features of individual classes or creeds,
in order to furnish weapons for the political quarrel of the
day. Instead of disputing about the less or more of past
error, we should rather take pains to understand the causes
which produced the past, so that we may gain skill and
strength from this insight to shape our own future.

The decline affected the intellectual sphere earlier than
the economic. A period of exhaustion followed upon the
wealth of creative work, and the power which was still
available was for the most part enlisted in the service of
the contending religious parties. The theologian was by far
the most important man in the intellectual life of the day.
Literary and personal feuds raged most fiercely upon the
Protestant side; the various forms of Protestant thought
were more violently opposed to each other than to the old

231

The Principality

Church. This disunion made it easier for Catholicism to regain its lost ground. The Jesuits won widespread influence as preachers and pastors, and as teachers in the higher schools and universities, especially amongst the princes and the cultivated youth.

As the German Protestants had no scholar of the rank of Hugo Grotius, the Dutch professor of jurisprudence; and as the Catholics could produce nothing to compare with the ravishing eloquence of a Bossuet; so contemporary German art has no name which can be mentioned together with Rembrandt or Rubens. In the development of the native style of building, German architects had already achieved creations whose cheerful spaciousness is reminiscent of the Renaissance. So when Italian influences were brought to bear, either directly, as in the south (Bavaria) and east (in Silesia, Electoral Saxony, and Mecklenburg), or through the medium of the Netherlands, as in the Palatinate and in Danzig—the German masters, as a rule, did not allow themselves to be diverted from their own course. In many buildings, it is true, the Renaissance style is clearly to be recognized, as in the Otto-Heinrich's building in the Castle of Heidelberg, in the council houses and many private houses of Augsburg and Nuremberg. Yet for the most part German architects adhered to their customary ground-plan, as well as to their accentuation of the perpendicular axis, as may be seen, for example, in their gables; and the German delight in multiformity produced such a mass of decorative forms, such a gay irregularity of projections and turrets, that one is fully justified in speaking of a German Renaissance. But the emphasis is on the adjective.

There were few tasks set to the architecture of this period in that province where it had hitherto accomplished its best work; the disappearing Catholic communities required no new churches, and the Protestants established themselves in those which they had taken over from them. A substitute was offered in the commissions given by rich citizens, and in the building of castles for the princes, which were being erected at that period in considerable numbers. A building like the Old Castle in Stuttgart, which was finished in 1578, with its gardens and greenhouses, its racecourse, shooting gallery, and ballroom, is evidence of the change in the mode of life amongst the princes, as are also the Court festivals which grew more and more sumptuous, the art collections, and the other costly hobbies of the sovereigns, who as early as the sixteenth century were conforming in many respects to the brilliant example of the French kings. Many German territories were becoming familiar with the reverse side of the princely passion for ostentation, through the heavy burden of taxes and the squandering of State property. Yet a prince like Maximilian of Bavaria (about 1600) was capable of uniting the erection and the magnificent furnishing of his residence, with a far-seeing and economical administration.

Maximilian, like his friend Ferdinand of Styria, had grown up in the school of the Jesuits. While the successors of Ferdinand I upon the imperial throne left matters in the empire to take their own course, the counter-movement against the Reformation found its strongest support in these two princes. The measures taken by Maximilian against Donauwörth shocked the Protestants at last out of their quarrelsome inactivity. Because of their repeated interruptions of the Procession of the Host, the population, who were almost entirely Protestant, were placed under the ban of the empire. Maximilian came to put it into effect, and made use of his errand to incorporate the imperial city within his sovereignty, and to compel the inhabitants to return to Catholicism, thus violating the Religious Peace of Augsburg. His measures aroused the keenest apprehensions, far beyond the imperial cities which were immediately threatened.

In 1608, under the leadership of the Elector Palatine, the Protestants of south Germany concluded a defensive league; in course of time this 'Union' was joined by many other estates of the empire. In the following year a Catholic counter-alliance was formed, the 'Liga,' with Maximilian of Bavaria at its head.

Upon this the clash seemed to follow immediately. After 1609, France and the Netherlands were at once involved in the quarrel over the hereditary rights in Jülich-Cleeve, a quarrel in which Spain and the pope joined in at a later date. When the murder of Henry IV destroyed the prospect of French help against the emperor, the heirs immediately concerned sought support for their secular ambitions amongst the armed leagues which had been founded from religious motives. They did not find a change of creed too

233

The Principality

heavy a price to pay. Wolfgang Wilhelm of Pfalz-Neuburg seceded to Catholicism, and gained thereby the help of the 'Liga,' together with the hand of the Bavarian duke's sister: John Sigismund of Brandenburg became a Calvinist in order to bind the Union and the Netherlands firmly to his cause. The matter never came to a decision by arms. Yet all the motives which were later to characterize the Thirty Years' War can be traced in the events of these years. The armed leagues owed their existence to the growing acuteness of religious antagonism: the resistance of the estates of the realm to the emperor's supremacy was shown in his exclusion from the 'Liga': the change of religion undertaken by the hereditary princes was an example of the interweaving of religious and political motives: finally, the intervention of foreign Powers gave warning of the struggle for supremacy between the House of Hapsburg and France, which was to prolong the war in so disastrous a way.

The first act of the bloody drama was already unfolding itself, in the linking up of political with religious considerations: the Bohemians rose, because they believed their representative rights to be threatened, together with their religious freedom. It was not long before the conflagration was raging round the walls of the residence at Vienna. Ferdinand II (p. 233) stood firm, and so saved his crown.

In 1619 he was elected emperor, and allied himself with the pope, Spain, and the League: even the Lutheran Elector of Saxony joined the alliance, out of hatred for the Elector Palatine, who was a Calvinist. The Bohemians, on the other hand, had to fight their battle alone. Frederick V of the Palatinate, whom they had raised to be king, met with no assistance either from the English king, his father-in-law, nor from the Union of which he was the head: the Netherlands also hung back.

Tilly's victory at the White Mountain, near Prague, decided the future character of the Hapsburg inheritance: solidly Catholic regions were governed henceforth by an absolute monarchy. The immediate result of the battle was the conquest of the Palatinate: the Bohemian War became a German war. The advance of Spanish troops of the League towards the frontiers of Lower Saxony was a challenge to foreign intervention. The Danish king, Christian IV, joined with the Lower Saxon group to oppose the emperor. By right of his dukedom of Holstein, he was a prince of the realm, and was striving to acquire the bishoprics of Bremen and Verdun. England and Holland gave him their support. Thus the German War grew to be a European war.

Tilly's army of the League was now joined for the first time by a strong imperial army, under command of Wallenstein. When a few years had passed, the two generals had driven the Danish king from the mainland: north Germany, all but a few remnants, was in the emperor's hands. The Court of Vienna and its generals were busied with great plans: the Danes, Swedes, and Dutch were to be chased from the sea, and the sea power of Germany restored. But while the realization of these hopes was postponed to the far future, by Wallenstein's defeat at Stralsund, the possibility of dealing a decisive blow at the Protestants seemed to be within reach. By the Edict of Restitution of 1629, the emperor decreed that all property, including two archbishoprics and ten bishoprics, which had been seized by the Protestants since the Treaty of Passau (p. 226), should be restored. But the very princes who urged the emperor to this step, deprived him at the same time of the means to carry it out. Wallenstein's victories had raised the imperial authority too high: 'German liberty' felt itself gravely threatened. The opposition of the princes found a spokesman in Maximilian of Bavaria: the Diet of Princes, held at Regensburg in 1630, compelled the emperor to dismiss his victorious general and to reduce his army.

The growth of the emperor's power aroused opposition also amongst his neighbours. Incited by Richelieu, who supported him with large sums of money, Gustavus Adolphus of Sweden entered the war. The establishment of the emperor on the coast would have meant the collapse of his Baltic Sea policy, which had begun auspiciously with the conquest of two Baltic provinces. At the same time he was moved by the desire to help his German fellow believers, who were in the greatest jeopardy. As a matter of fact, it needed the fall of Magdeburg to incline the Brandenburg prince and the Elector of Saxony to Swedish alliance. But when that had taken place, the King of Sweden defeated the army of the League at Breitenfeld and Rain, and continued his triumphant march as far as Munich. His authority extended from the Baltic to the Alps: his most enthusiastic adherents looked upon him as the future Roman king, and he himself seems to have considered the same idea.

The Principality

Once again Wallenstein saved the emperor. The Swedish king met his death at Lützen in 1632. But instead of following up his success with an annihilating blow at the Swedish army, Wallenstein followed his own plans, which aimed at a reconciliation with the Protestants, and common action against Sweden.

Being threatened again with dismissal, he resolved to ally himself with the Swedish army. When in 1636 Wallenstein the outlaw fell under the steel of the assassin, the Spanish ambassador could applaud the deed as 'a great mercy which God has shown to the House of Austria.'

Wallenstein's idea was so far realized by the Peace of Prague, which was made in the following year, that the Protestants who signed the treaty—first the Electorate of Saxony, and later Brandenburg, Mecklenburg, and some of the other States of the empire—promised to co-operate for the expulsion of the Swedes. Yet the peace offered them very many less favourable conditions than Wallenstein had projected, and by no means included all the Protestant States.

The renewed ascendancy of the imperial arms caused Richelieu to exert all his power to conquer Alsace, whose acquisition he had already had in view when he sided with Gustavus Adolphus. He sent French armies to Germany, and renewed the alliance with Sweden; at the same time he assembled many allies to fight against Spain. Now Catholic France was at war with the Catholic House of Hapsburg, while the troops of the German Protestant princes were fighting against Protestant Sweden. The war, which had begun as a war of religion, became a struggle between Hapsburg and France and Sweden for the supremacy of Europe. For thirteen more terrible years the war fury stalked through the sorely tried German land. With every year, the soldiers grew more brutal and the sufferings of the population more intense. Despairing peasants abandoned their villages, and hid themselves in inaccessible thickets of thorn: entire districts became a desert. Famine and devastating diseases reduced the tormented people: dark superstition gained the mastery of their terrified hearts.

And then at last the day came when the bells rang out with the incredible message: there was to be peace again in Germany. But peace brought heavy burdens for the future to add to the terrible sacrifices of the past. The cession of large territories to Sweden (Pomerania with Stettin and Rügen, the Archbishopric of Bremen and the Bishopric of Verden), and to France of Metz, Toul, Verdun, together with Hapsburg possessions and sovereign rights in Alsace, the detachment of the Netherlands and of Switzerland, meant a loss of territory amounting to about a fifth of the present empire, with the trade supremacy of foreigners over the districts at the mouths of the great rivers. In consequence of the French advance towards the Rhine, the opposition between the Hapsburgs and the French became a 'hereditary quarrel' between the neighbour nations. The peace guarantee of France and Sweden was equivalent to a supervision of German policy by foreign Governments. The fact that France stood sponsor to the most disastrous provision of the peace showed in what manner the foreign Powers would bring their constitutionally guaranteed influence to bear. By its proposals, the German princes were assured of sovereignty, together with the right to form alliances amongst themselves and with foreign Powers: the proviso that such alliances should not be directed against emperor or empire was of little moment.

Two hundred and seventy years later, foreign Powers achieved the mutilation, the gagging, and the supervision of Germany in a similar way. But while the Treaty of Versailles laid economic burdens upon our people which were incomparably heavier, national unity stood firm against all temptation and attack. In the Peace of Westphalia, the last vestiges of political structure were destroyed, because the ambition of the princes was working in concert with that of the foreign Powers.

Yet this terrible Peace did disclose one ray of light; it confirmed the Religious Peace of Augsburg, and extended it to the Reformed Churches. This had not the same significance as religious toleration: for the mischievous axiom, 'Who owns the land, owns the creed,' was still in force. But the equalization of creeds prepared the ground for the development of more tolerant ideas. The age of religious wars had come to an end.

SECOND PART

SOVEREIGNS AND STATES

In Germany the battle for the faith had begun and ended. Economic life had been practically wiped out in many places in Germany through the Great War: intellectual life paralysed, and the Imperial Constitution thrown into disorder. For years to come, the German people had not the strength to take an active share in the political and intellectual life of the world. This was an irreparable loss. For the foundations of modern Europe were laid in the century and a half during which Germany was thus excluded.

This evolution was accomplished by such an exertion of national forces as had never been put forth in earlier times. Absolute monarchy became the predominant form of government. It was supported by a staff of officials working under strict supervision, and by a strong standing army: it was founded upon a flourishing political economy, and its objects were supremacy with the aggrandizement of territory.

In forming the guiding principles of foreign politics, purely personal elements, such as the interest of the ruling house, ambition, and religious views, still, as in former times, played an important part. Yet with growing insight into the importance of political economy, foreign policy also began to be more consciously adapted to the service of national economic security. Colonial possessions, overseas trading companies, powerful mercantile and fighting fleets became the means through which the States bordering the Atlantic Ocean dominated the world market. As the activity of the State increased, its governors became dependent in a peculiar degree upon the help of capital, which they already found indispensable for the encouragement of native industry and the supplies of the army. For this reason the most flourishing period of absolute monarchy coincides with a mighty uprising of capitalism, which was not, however, confined to the States which were thus governed. Even the two chief States, England and Holland, in which monarchy had not been victorious, were the leading representatives of the capitalist spirit in the seventeenth and eighteenth centuries. From the Bourse at

238

Sovereigns and States

Amsterdam the traffic in shares and State papers extended as far as London and Paris; it was only half a century later that a German stock exchange was founded in Vienna in 1771.

These world-embracing struggles for power and property showed that a higher value was being set upon temporal concerns. The religious conflict had ended in a draw, and all the creeds were living on side by side in the leading States. After Luther's appeal to revelation had destroyed the unity of the religious life, the question whether human nature is not based upon a common factor, uniting mankind beyond the barriers of creeds and nationalities, was forced upon the attention by the misery of the religious wars and the pressure of the ecclesiastical powers.

The answer had long ago been discovered by the philosophers. Working within the range of ideas known to the Italian Renaissance, Galileo, who died in 1642, had attained a conception of the world founded on pure reason, which relied upon mathematical reasoning and natural science. His younger contemporary, Descartes, had transferred the mathematical method of reasoning to the mental sciences. Starting with the question: What is certain? he found the fixed point in the self-consciousness of the thinking *ego*, and on this foundation, in strictly logical sequence, he built up his edifice of thought. Bacon, the contemporary of Shakespeare, laid stress on the value of experience, as opposed to the trustworthiness of pure thought, for the progress of the mental sciences. At first, it is true, the boldest of these thinkers produced little effect in the world: Galileo became involved in a lawsuit with the Roman Inquisition: Descartes found a second home in Holland. Here too Spinoza found a quiet refuge to develop his doctrine: material and spiritual happenings are not of a different nature, but two aspects of the same process: in all, the same eternal Godhead reveals himself. But if the number of disciples who drank in the new ideas was small at first, yet what was happening then was of endless importance: for the first time since the distant days of the Greeks, a conception of the world had originated on European soil which recognized no other command than that of reason, and no other aim than the investigation of truth.

Gradually, the middle class, as it grew more powerful, began to turn its attention to the wisdom of the philosophers.

The Principality

In reason, they saw a gift of nature, common to all men at all times, which will rescue mankind from their disunion. From her they firmly believed they could draw those principles which should set men free from traditional judgments and prejudices in religion, morality, law, and political science, and help to make the eternally valid truths supreme in all departments of life. The desire of great achievement united with belief in the goodness of human nature, to lead men towards the daylight of the Enlightenment. From England, where Locke, in addition to his teaching on the 'Human Understanding,' was giving a clearer definition to the ideas of morality and the State, and Newton was laying the basis of modern natural science, the ideas of the Enlightenment travelled to France. Here, about the middle of the eighteenth century, under the pressure of religious and political illiberality, some philosophers drew the extreme conclusions of radical thinking: man has no other possibility of perception, but material apprehension; the moral law, like the idea of the supersensual, is a cheat invented by the powerful and the hypocrites: he is a fool who makes it his guide! At the same time, Voltaire and Rousseau gave that brilliant form to the attacks upon Church, State, and Society which winged them for their triumphal progress across the Continent.

All the States named here had reaped rich booty from the collapse of the Spanish world-power, under Philip the Second's successors (p. 229). Foremost were the Dutch. In addition to their command of the Baltic trade, which even at that time was looked upon as the source of all European commercial wealth, they had expanded into the Asiatic seas and settled on the American coast. During half a century the Dutch East India Company gained an average profit of 95 per cent. In the strength of their capital and the number of their trading ships, the Dutch were for a long time greatly superior to all other nations, not excepting the English, who were handicapped by the war between the first Stuarts and the Parliament.

But scarcely had this struggle ended with the overthrow of absolute monarchy, when the English Republic struck the first blow against the lucrative carrying trade of the Dutch: the Navigation Act of 1651 provided that overseas goods must henceforth be brought to England on none but English ships. The Merchant Republic had no man of equal

Sovereigns and States

standing to pit against the dictator Cromwell, who held in his grasp the national forces of England. The English kept the upper hand, and gained further advantages in later passages-at-arms: but after the alliance of the later Stuarts with France, a truly national policy did not again become possible until 1688, when William III, the hereditary Stadholder of the Netherlands, was called to the English throne. He united the efforts of the Sea Powers, and those of France's opponents on the Continent, in the war against Louis XIV: who was striving, in addition to supremacy on land, for a strong position at sea.

It is usual to contrast Louis' egoistical absolutism with the 'enlightened despotism,' which subordinates itself to the good of the State: the ostentatious Court life of the French king, and the vanity which he displayed in his search for fame, with the hardworking simplicity of Frederick II and Joseph II. Yet the distinction is not so clear as it might appear. There are many of the French ruler's expressions which correspond to the beautiful phrase of the 'first Servant of the State.' And in many respects the actions of the Prussian king fell as far short of the demands of the ideal as Louis' government was superior to the axiom 'L'État c'est moi.'—It is easier to form a judgment of the methods of government from a comparison of results: Louis left behind him a State which was heading straight for the Revolution, while Prussia's position as a Great Power can be traced back to Frederick. Yet it should be taken into consideration that the consequences which were so fatal to France were obviously not the fault of the system, but of an overstraining of the system, and became apparent only towards the end of a reign covering more than half a century. Up till that time the French people had borne the burdens imposed upon them, not only willingly, but with enthusiasm. Power and glory were the aim of the subjects, no less than of their king; and Louis was past-master in the art of shaping the State, that it might become serviceable in this endeavour.

In no other country did political economy make such rapid strides. Faithful to the principles of 'mercantilism,' Colbert, by means of protective duties, joined to the encouragement of home-production, succeeded in an astonishingly short time in raising the status of industry. Silk-weavers from Italy—cloth-weavers from Holland—

The Principality

iron-workers from Sweden—were all invited to the country. Before long the French people had no need to go abroad for their silk, cloth, and iron. Internal trade was facilitated by the construction of roads and canals, as well as by the abolition of the greater part of the inland duties: while a powerful impetus was given to maritime trade by the creation of a fleet of merchant ships and the growth of colonial possessions. The rapid accumulation of national wealth gave rise to unexampled magnificence in Court life, and to a great increase in armaments. In the first years of his reign, Louis had thirty warships at his disposal, as compared with two hundred, twenty years later. Before the end of his life the army had been increased fourfold.

When the war against the encirclement of Spain had come to a successful conclusion in 1659, Louis set himself the goal of founding his supremacy upon the conquest of the districts round the mouths of the Scheldt, the Maas, and the Rhine.

In consequence of the intervention of the English and Dutch, his first war of aggression brought him only a small gain; through the second, which he waged against Holland, from 1672 to 1679, he succeeded, in spite of the defection of his Allies, the English king, and some of the German princes, in acquiring the independent county of Burgundy and Freiburg. The attack made by Louis upon the Upper Rhine, in pursuance of Richelieu's Rhine policy, was the most successful: the provinces of Alsace with Strasburg came under French rule for nearly two hundred years. In the third war of aggression, 1688–1697, which took its name from the Palatine inheritance, Louis was already opposed by a strong European coalition, inspired by the fiery soul of William III of England. After a ten years' struggle on all the frontiers of the country, the king was obliged to give way. Nevertheless he risked a war for the succession of Spain. But this war, which was to raise France to the position of a leading world-power, was waged against a powerful body of opponents; it overtaxed the strength of the nation, and became the decisive factor in the decline of the French paramountcy set up by Richelieu, Mazarin, and Louis himself. At the same time, France's ally, Sweden, lost her status as a Great Power in the northern war.

When the great wars came to an end, about the turn of the seventeenth century, the outlines of the division of

Sovereigns and States

power had been sketched in, which were to determine the course of European history up to the present time. Spain had become still smaller: France had lost her commanding paramountcy: Sweden was no longer reckoned amongst the Great Powers: Holland kept her importance only as a sloop of the proud frigate of England. England's command of the sea, growing out of the decline of all these States, was guaranteed by the 'Balance of Power' which had developed on land, in place of the French paramountcy: the rising States of the north-east, Russia and Prussia, took their place beside the old Powers of France and Austria.

Whilst the nationally self-contained peoples were re-making the face of Europe, and establishing their claim in the New World, the German people, without a body politic, had first to build up their life again upon the confused ruins of the old. It is difficult to judge of the extent of the desolation left by war, famine, and pestilence: the loss was not everywhere so great as in Wurtemberg, the Palatinate, and Thuringia. Until the progress of in-dividual research produces a more or less complete picture, one must be content with a reckoning, made some decades earlier, which computes the decline of the population at about a half, and the reduction in the number of cattle at a fifth. In any case, no nation in modern history has been overtaken by the like destruction. The arable land suffered most severely. Yet the towns, which had escaped being laid waste, had to bear the burden of debt, the loss of inhabitants, and the paralysis of economic life. The peasants bowed unresistingly to the will of their overlords; towns and estates had to submit to the reigning princes.

Many of them had been able to add to their lands in the Peace of Westphalia; amongst these were Brandenburg (p. 253), Bavaria, which acquired the Upper Palatinate, and Saxony, to which was added Lusatia: they all benefited by this extension of their sovereign rights.

The imperial authority was so closely connected with the Reichstag, and the Reichstag was so hampered in its activities by the unwieldiness of the process of passing resolutions—it was soon to sit at Regensburg as a perpetual Congress of Delegates—and by the multiplicity of con-tending efforts, that the empire at best seemed to be a Union of States, and might in Pufendorf's fierce phrase be looked upon as a 'monstrosity.' After the princes had been released from almost all obligations towards the emperor, most of them succeeded in the next decades in completely establishing their authority over their estates. A standing army and a staff of officials, bound to the personal service of the prince, supported his absolute authority. It is true that the sovereigns in return had to make a considerable concession to the nobility; they were granted freedom from taxes and the retention of their feudal rights over the peasants. This was a very important matter, especially for the east. For here the peasant was set under the power of law and police which belonged to his feudal lord: he had to render him unlimited service, and was bound to the soil: even if his lord deprived him of his land, he remained under obligation to service. As no change took place in these conditions, it was not too difficult for the nobility to agree to the loss of their political rights.

Nevertheless, serious complications arose here and there. The wars of the Elector of Brandenburg with the States of Cleve and Prussia are well known: less familiar are his agreements with the electors of Bavaria and Cologne, in order 'by common measures to enforce *every* demand, which one of the allies may make upon his subjects, for the ensuring of the present or future defence of the country, and the state of peace and quiet.' It goes without saying that every foreigner to whom the subjects looked for help was to be fought. On the other hand, many princes called in foreign assistance in the wars with their States; thus the Elector of Mayence led French auxiliary troops against Erfurt; and Charles Leopold of Mecklenburg-Schwerin led some thousands of Russians against the nobility of his country and against the empire. It is true that there were special reasons for this. The ecclesiastical princes were almost powerless against their cathedral chapter, and in Mecklenburg the nobility formed such a compact body that the constitution of the estates remained there in full force till 1918. In the same way the estates maintained their 'good old right' in Wurtemberg till far into the nineteenth century, and also, though with less significance, because of their less centralized structure—in Saxony, Hesse, and the Welf countries. Yet as a rule absolutism triumphed without any great difficulties—even in the non-sovereign territories. How well the councillors of the imperial cities adapted themselves to the new era we learn

Sovereigns and States

from a proclamation of the Hamburg council: 'Even though a superior authority be godless, tyrannical, and miserly, nevertheless it does not become the subjects to revolt and resist it; but they should rather acknowledge the same to be a punishment from the Almighty, which the subjects have brought about through their sin.

Absolutism brought a certain degree of order into the economic and political confusion and disagreement in the individual districts: it created a number of larger and more compact States, and so prepared the way for a united Germany: also its services in the encouragement of science and art should not be underestimated. But it is impossible to follow a certain school of historians, and stamp the founders of the power of Brandenburg-Prussia as conscious champions of national unity. The famous appeal of the Great Elector: 'Remember that thou art a German,' was no less the result of political calculation, than was that proclamation of Frederick the Great which permitted him to enter upon the second Silesian War with 80,000 men, 'auxiliaries of the Emperor' (p. 263). As a matter of fact, the Hohenzollern rulers troubled little about emperor and empire, if their interest or that of their house lay on the other side. The Great Elector allied himself with Louis XIV, and so made it possible for him to take Strasburg; Frederick the Great, in alliance with the same power, seized upon Silesia: at the critical moment his successor broke away from the coalition against the Western neighbour, in order to acquire land in the East. It is, of course, even more absurd to pillory these men as betrayers of the Fatherland: if this accusation were justified, it would have to be extended to cover a number of our most enlightened spirits, whom we honour as heroes of our spiritual history. But there is no justification for it. Where no fatherland exists, even in idea, relationship to it cannot serve as the basis of criticism. Like all their peers, the Hohenzollerns were guided by their dynastic ambition; it was not part of their plan that their success should advantage the entire German nation.

In one's judgment of absolute monarchy, however, it would not be right to limit oneself to Prussia, and leave altogether out of account the many smaller and smallest domains. In 1786, the year of Frederick the Great's death, the total number of German States, including the 1,500

The Principality

Knights of the Empire, is said to have corresponded exactly to the number of years which had passed since the beginning of the Christian era. The misery we are considering was much older than absolute monarchy, but was encouraged by the partitioning of the princely inheritances. Even such an excellent prince as Ernest the Pious of Gotha, who died in 1675, provided for each of his seven surviving sons with portions of his domain; the Great Elector made similar arrangements in favour of his younger sons, which were, it is true, upset by his successor. Thuringia remained the classic land of divided inheritances: about 1700 it maintained no less than twenty-seven princely households. In places where the right of primogeniture was strictly enforced, it occurred not because the State as such was held to be indivisible, but because an effort was being made to maintain unweakened the power of the dynasty.

If it proved at all possible, a ruler would try to make the fortune of his house along the lines of European high politics. The House of Wittelsbach was not satisfied with supplying the ecclesiastical principalities of Cologne, Liège, Hildesheim, Münster, and Paderborn, from the end of the fifteenth till past the middle of the eighteenth century, almost without exception, with princes of their race: they were unremitting in their efforts to gain a crown, either in the Netherlands, Sicily, Sardinia, or no matter where. After long and vain endeavour a Wittelsbach succeeded at last, for a few years, in wearing the sacred crown of the empire (p. 216). In 1697 Augustus the Strong of Saxony gave enormous sums for the Polish crown and went over to Catholicism, without however resigning the presidency of the evangelical Union of Princes. While Saxony and Bavaria had to pay a heavy price for their lords' ambition, the Welf countries, at least, were spared such experience when the Welfs rose to be electoral princes and in 1714 ascended the English throne. The gain of the Prussian crown signified an advance for Brandenburg, because the successors of the splendour-loving Frederick III thought it their duty to develop the forces of the country in such a way that it could with honour subsist as a kingdom.

It was not possible for the great majority of the princes to set their aims so high: the development of royal magnificence had to provide them with a substitute. All that was required for the ostentatious maintenance of a Court, the passion for building and collecting, the playing with soldiers and with Government officers, and all the other fancies of the all-powerful lord, had to be squeezed out of the subjects. A further source of income was offered by the conclusion of treaties, through which the prince, in return for handsome subsidies, put his troops at the disposal of any belligerent State. In course of time this developed into a lucrative traffic in soldiers. When Landgrave Frederick II of Hesse-Cassel hired his regiments to the English for the war against the United States, he was naturally slow in yielding to the request of his estates, and allowing the proceeds to be used for the good of the country. Other German princes made a worse use of this lucrative kind of subsidy: in the Seven Years' War the Prince of Schwarzburg-Sondershausen, after he had already furnished his contingent to the imperial army, succeeded in hiring a regiment to Frederick the Great. Great fortunes were also expected from the trade connections overseas. Such hopes were bound up with India and the South Sea; Persia and Abyssinia were explored, and a treaty concluded in regard to a colony in Guyana. The colonial plans of the Great Elector alone were carried out: but every ducat which even he had coined out of African gold was to cost him two good German ducats.

But the eternal lack of ready money had this one advantage, that it constrained many of the princes to come to the help of the economic life of their own country. So that the princely passion for cutting a great figure was not without its useful consequences, if only in the economic sphere. Immediately after the Great War the princes in many districts gave cattle, seed, and timber to the peasants for the rebuilding and furnishing of their devastated homesteads; at a later date they encouraged the cultivation of new market produce (the potato came to Germany at the end of the seventh century). Following the example of the great Colbert, new life was infused into native industries, and new industries introduced into the country.

The Huguenots who had been driven out by Louis XIV were made welcome in many States. In Hesse-Cassel they founded thirty colonies. About the year 1700, together with Waldenses, exiles from Bohemia, and other foreign sects, they formed one-fourth of the population of Magdeburg. Nothing but direct action on the part of the princes made it possible to set aside those obsolete privileges of the guilds, and those prerogatives of individual towns, which stood in the way of the unification of economic life. Karl Ludwig of the Palatinate, one of the most distinguished princes of his time, was the most advanced in this respect. In 1652 he granted complete freedom of trade and commerce to the newly founded city of Mannheim, and absolved it from all taxes. In the country districts of Thuringia an active home industry was developed, with the support of the prince.

In the great Prussian State, however, the economic cleavage between town and country was still present in all its rigour. In Westphalia, as late as the year 1800, an announcement was made from the pulpits that peasants requiring wheaten rolls and beer for their merry-makings must procure them in the town.

In any case, one must not set too high a value upon the economic achievement of absolute monarchy. The commercial principle of protection could only partially be adapted to the circumstances of Germany, where even in a comparatively large country such as Prussia there was so much 'foreign' and so little 'home' trade: this was shown in the coffee smuggling at the time of Frederick the Great. But in places where customs restrictions were in force, they made economic life more difficult, rather than fostering it, as was the case in France, which already formed a centralized economic department. The absolutism of the leading princes produced social equalization, when it set 'prince, nobleman, and peasant' on the same level.

Yet this was by no means the case in all the countries of Germany: absolute government for the most part accentuated class distinctions rather than softening them. Even the great King of Prussia was unable to improve the lot of the feudal peasants: only once did he nominate a commoner to be minister, and after the conclusion of peace he discharged almost all the middle-class officers whom he had been obliged to appoint during the Seven Years' War. The excessive making of regulations, which was customary in Prussia since Frederick William I, prevented free economic activity, and with it the reshaping of political opinion. The government of the State became an affair of the rulers, in which the subject had no voice: an alien matter, regarded with awe.

Sovereigns and States

If, as is generally the case, one looks upon absolutism as a strict but necessary discipline, which the German people had to undergo, one cannot overlook the fact that a high premium was charged for it, which has not yet been fully paid: the acuteness of social differences, the grafting of servility upon the German character, indifference to the life of the State, passionate advocacy of the 'concerns' of the individual mother-lands—much of what stands to-day in the way of national life and influence—if it did not arise during the period of the principality, was cultivated to a high degree at that time.

During the long and stormy period between the Peace of Westphalia and the Congress of Vienna, the fate of Germany was determined by the ambition of the princes, working in concert or in opposition. The two strongest of the single States were able with success to oppose the Swedes and the Turks, but great slices of imperial territory were sacrificed to attacks from the west, and without the co-operation of other European Powers it would have been impossible to check the French advance under Napoleon, which reached and crossed the Elbe.

The ground was prepared for the French king's success by the efforts of the German princes to hinder the House of Hapsburg from becoming too powerful. France indeed could not prevent a Hapsburger, Leopold I, from receiving the imperial crown after the death of Ferdinand III in 1658. But in the same year several of the German princes, led by the Elector of Mayence, concluded a Rhine league with the French king, which was said to intend nothing but mutual assistance in preserving the rights and possessions which had been seized in the Peace of Westphalia; but its point was obviously directed against the Kaiser. When Louis advanced against Holland in 1672, the Elector of Cologne and the Bishop of Münster had bound themselves to give active support to his invasion, and a considerable number of the other princes had pledged themselves to neutrality. Only the Elector of Brandenburg came at once to the help of the Dutch. Their resistance and the intervention of Spain revolutionized the situation; emperor and empire declared war, the German confederates fell apart, the Brandenburger, who meanwhile had concluded peace, again entered the lists. In the Peace of Nymwegen in 1678, the costs of the long war had to be paid by Spain through the loss of the independent country of Burgundy, and by the empire through the loss of Freiburg.

Now the French king no longer thought it necessary to wear the mask of a defender of 'German Liberty'; the Brandenburger had concluded a treaty with him; he was in any case secure of Cologne and Saxony. On the flimsiest of pretexts, and in time of peace, he caused the towns and villages of Alsace, which were still independent, to be occupied by France. His behaviour in the matter of the 'Reunions,' which was characterized on the German side as 'Robbery, veiled by preparatory legal decrees,' was condemned with scarcely less severity by leading French historians. In an attempt to make pretensions appear to be rights, his commissioners went back to the time before Charlemagne: while on the ground of a charter of the year 1075, the country of Saarbrücken was declared an appurtenance of the territory transferred in 1648. The Strasburgers found themselves besieged by an army, whose strength was greater than the number of their citizens: so the most flourishing city of south-west Germany was lost: a city which—in the phrase of a contemporary prince—signifies in German hands a lasting guarantee of peace, but in the possession of France an ever-open door to war. Indignation at the outrage ran through the empire: the emperor was resolved upon war; then Louis succeeded in directing the sultan's invasion towards Vienna. A truce recognized the French rule over Alsace for the next twenty years.

Louis felt the security of his conquest threatened by the rapid success of the imperial arms against the Turks. A new attack against the western territories of the empire was to bring him its final confirmation, and to bestow the electoral crown of Cologne upon his willing servant the Bishop of Strasburg, William Egon of Fürstenberg. With this in view, he advanced a claim upon the Palatine inheritance of his sister-in-law, Elizabeth Charlotte, in her name, but much against her will. But through the unanimous resistance of the German princes, and the intervention of William III of Holland and England, the military demonstration which he had expected developed into a wearisome war. A terrible laying waste of the country signalized the French retreat, beginning near the Swiss frontier, and extending northwards beyond the Eifel, first on the right and then on the left bank of the Rhine: Heidelberg, Mannheim, Spire, and Worms, with hundreds of villages and small towns, were devoted to a destruction, which cannot be explained by military necessity. The war ended in 1697 with the Peace of Ryswyk, which obliged Louis to restore at least the reunited districts outside Alsace. His star was in decline.

Nevertheless he found German allies again for his War of the Spanish Succession—the electors of Bavaria and Cologne, both of whom belonged to the House of Wittelsbach. Thus south Germany became one of the theatres of this 'world war'; the victory at Höchstedt compelled the French to retreat across the Rhine in that district also, and surrendered Bavaria to an occupation by imperial troops. For long years the German armies fought on the Rhine, in the Spanish Netherlands, and in Italy. When, after a struggle fraught with heavy loss, peace was at last declared at Rastatt, in 1714, the emperor received the Spanish Netherlands, Milan, and Naples, while the empire not only went empty away, but suffered the additional loss of Landau to France.

The shock to French paramountcy in the War of the Palatinate had already had fatal consequences for France's ally in the north. In the northern war Denmark, Saxony with Poland, and Russia, united to destroy Sweden's position in the Baltic. Saxony fell for some years into the hands of Charles XII, the victorious king of Sweden. Afterwards, when he yielded to the Russian arms, north Germany became the theatre of the Russo-Swedish conflict in which Prussia and Hanover joined with England also took part. Yet this sacrifice at least was not in vain; on the collapse of Sweden as a Great Power, Hanover acquired Bremen and Verden, while Prussia gained western Pomerania as far as the river Peene (Peace of Stockholm, 1719). The territories at the mouths of the Weser, the Elbe, and the Oder came again into the hands of German princes; the pressure of Sweden was lifted from Germany.

Because of the difference in the relative situations of the Powers in Europe and in the empire, it happened that the great wars of the end of the seventeenth and beginning of the eighteenth century exercised an exactly contrary effect: while in Europe they set up a certain 'balance of the Powers,' in the empire they allowed those which were later to become its leaders to rise out of the more or less

The Principality

uniform mass of States. They were not all gainers by their intervention in the high politics of Europe. As the ambitious plans of the Bavarian elector Max Emmanuel came to naught (p. 251), the Polish kingdom of Augustus the Strong signified nothing but sacrifice for Saxony. On the other hand, Hanover gained possession of the mouths of the Weser and the Elbe, and as the mother-country of the English Georges, it acquired greater influence in the empire, though only under the shadow of English authority. The advantage which accrued to Austria and Prussia was of very different significance.

With the exception of Bohemia and Silesia, the emperor's crown lands had suffered comparatively little from the Thirty Years' War. As a purely Catholic State under absolute government (p. 234) Austria entered the greatest period of her history. It opened in 1683 with the Turkish attack upon Vienna, the heroic defence of the city, and the victory of the relieving army. Now the emperor was faced by the choice either of seizing the 'reunited territories' from the French king, or Hungary from the Turks. In the age of the principality, it was almost a matter of course that he should decide for the aggrandizement of his house. In a few years the emperor's troops, together with those of the empire, supported by volunteers from every principality, had achieved such great success that the Viennese Court felt strong enough to resume the war in the west also (p. 251). The means possessed by the State was not indeed adequate to wage war in strength on two fronts. Yet in the year of the Peace of Ryswyk, Prince Eugene won his victory at Zenta, which gave almost the whole of Hungary to the House of Hapsburg. The area of the State of Austria was almost doubled by the acquisition of this country; she was permanently secured against the enemy in the east, and took her place amongst the Great Powers. The Government was able to engage with full vigour in the War of the Spanish Succession, and, in spite of a distressing lack of money, Prince Eugene led the imperial arms once more from victory to victory. The Spanish Netherlands and considerable possessions in Italy rewarded the sacrifice. And once again, by the victory of Belgrade in 1717, he extended the dominion of the Hapsburgs far towards the east, over a great part of Serbia and Rumania, as far as the river Aluta.

Sovereigns and States

Then counter-blows began to fall. The War of the Polish Succession ended in the iniquitous speculation in territories, through which, in the sequel, Lorraine fell to France (1766), and Duke Francis of Lorraine, the husband of Maria Theresa, the emperor's daughter, received Tuscany in exchange. A new Turkish war resulted in the loss of the great acquisitions south of the Danube. The far-seeing trading projects, by which Charles VI hoped to draw profit from the possession of the harbours on the North Sea, the Adriatic, and the Mediterranean proved to be impracticable. No really serious attempt was made to bring crown lands which differed from each other most widely in race and language into subjection to a strict centralized government. To these troubles was added anxiety about the succession of Charles VI. The Pragmatic Sanction, which nominated his daughter Maria Theresa as heiress, was indeed acknowledged by almost every Power; but the opponents of the Hapsburgs were lying in wait round about. No one could guess that Prussia would prove the most dangerous.

Until after the time of the Reformation, the Hohenzollern State was not essentially different from other principalities of the same size. The leadership of the North German Protestants fell to Saxony, which was larger and more advanced economically. At the beginning of the seventeenth century two important gains came by inheritance to the Electoral House: Cleve, Mark, and Ravensburg (p. 234) and the dukedom of Prussia, where the Hohenzollern line founded by Albert of Brandenburg (p. 222) had become extinct. In this way it had won a footing in the farthest west of the empire and in the east, outside its frontier. But these far-flung possessions, wedged in between neighbours who were hungry for power, could only be held if the princes succeeded in connecting their territories together by new acquisitions, and firmly uniting them internally: otherwise they must relapse sooner or later into their former unimportance. This decline seemed to be setting in during the severe testing-time of the Thirty Years' War. Prince and estates were equally to blame that the Mark of Brandenburg suffered most painfully under both the contending parties.

Matters improved when Frederick William came to the throne in 1640. Yet even he sought support, now on one hand and now on another, and at first with little success. The gains which he won at last, thanks to French mediation, in the Peace of Westphalia, were not very considerable: eastern Pomerania, together with Minden, Halberstadt, and reversion of Magdeburg, as a substitute for the eagerly desired western Pomerania. It was much more vital for the future of Brandenburg that the young prince, profiting by the experiences of the war and of the peace negotiations, should have formed the resolve to make his Government secure and influential through a strong standing army. The idea was typical of the period: but it was of special significance for the principality of Brandenburg, which was more in danger than others because of its wide area and its lack of internal cohesion, and it was carried out by the Hohenzollerns with a determination which was shown by no other royal dynasty. To this may be traced the success of their effort, as well as the one-sided character of their idea of the State.

It is true that the elector Frederick William, like others of his princely peers, did a great deal to assist agriculture and to develop commerce and industry after French and Dutch models. In addition to what has already been referred to (p. 246) one should mention the construction of the Frederick-William Canal, which opened up a new way to the sea for eastern trade through Berlin and Hamburg, across Brandenburg, thus dispensing with the Swedish harbour of Stettin. But the crucial point was the understanding between the elector and the States, which made it possible for him to create an army, maintained by the States, yet subject only to his authority.

This understanding followed a very different course in the separate territories of the electorate, and was arrived at most smoothly in the Mark of Brandenburg. There, in return for the ratification of their rights over the peasants (p. 244) and of their privileged position in relation to the citizens (which included a veto upon the acquisition of the goods of the nobility by the citizen class, etc.), the nobility agreed to a sum which sufficed at a pinch for several thousand men. It is true that the estates granted the money originally for a few years only: but as a matter of fact, it was sufficient to procure them their discharge; no general diet was ever again summoned in the Mark of Brandenburg. The estates of Cleve made the most success-

Sovereigns and States

ful resistance: they retained the right of sanctioning taxes, which, however, taken separately, was of slight importance. Nowhere did the elector do away with the estate constitutions: but he never rested till they had been universally deprived of their political importance for the State.

A new system of taxation was connected with the decline of the estates. Out of regard for the opposition of the nobility of the Mark of Brandenburg, a direct tax only was levied in the rural districts, to which the peasants alone were liable. For the towns, the 'excise' was introduced, which was essentially a tax upon articles of consumption, and soon proved to be a veritable gold mine. An electoral staff of officials was appointed to administer these taxes, in addition to the older estate employees. These were in particular the electoral commissioners, 'war' commissioners in the towns, district commissioners in the rural districts. They were grouped under a head office in Berlin, and gradually took over a large share of the work of the estate organizations. They vindicated the idea of a United State, more particularly as the prince preferred to appoint officials to these posts who were strangers to the country.

The elector expended not less than two-thirds of the entire revenue upon the army. But even this was not sufficient: he had to resort to bargaining for subsidies to make up the required sum.

He was further driven to seek support from the stronger Powers, because he recognized that the great States, with which Brandenburg had to do in the west and east, could throw a very different weight into the scales than his little country, even at the utmost stretch of her powers. The elector was a willing exponent of the art of making a virtue of necessity, of seizing his own advantage out of the rapid alterations in the political situation by a quick change of alliances. It is true that the others were no less expert and unscrupulous, and thus his see-saw policy brought him complete success in one instance only. That was in the war with Sweden and Poland, which was waged by Charles X in order to complete Sweden's supremacy in the Baltic. At that time the elector was able first to play Sweden against Poland, and then Poland against Sweden, and in this way he obtained in 1660 the sovereign possession of Prussia.

The Principality

But from the powerful country of France, the elector was unable, either as friend or foe, to extort the gains of land for which he was striving. It was only with hesitation that he entered the Rhine League (p. 249), and, during Louis XIV's attack upon Holland, anxiety for his Rhenish property drove him to adopt the defensive. In the end Louis set Sweden upon him. In the battle of Fehrbellin in 1675, the young army of Brandenburg, fighting without allies, for the first and only time in the whole reign of Frederick William won a victory over the dreaded Swedish army: the sequel was the expulsion of the Swedes from Pomerania and Prussia. But because neither the Netherlands, nor, as was to be expected, the emperor, would agree to the aggrandizement of Brandenburg, and because Louis XIV would not abandon his Swedish ally, the elector had to relinquish all his conquests at the conclusion of peace in 1679. He then attempted, with the help of a French alliance, to gain at the least western Pomerania. In return for a considerable yearly subsidy he pledged himself not only to work for the French king at the next emperor's election, but before long he promised to give his armed support also, without investigation into the justice of the case. If the case should arise, this would imply the defence of French rule in Alsace: for Strasburg fell a few months after the conclusion of the treaty. In return the elector succeeded again and again in raising the amount of the French subsidies: but in the end the French king refused his help in the war which he had planned against Sweden. When, with the support of Brandenburg, he had achieved the provisional recognition of the 'Reunited' territories, Louis even gave a decided no to the unfortunate beggar. The alliance had cost the empire Alsace, yet had not brought the elector anything approaching what he had hoped from it. Soon after the Revocation of the Edict of Nantes by the French king in 1685, Austrian subsidies began to flow into Berlin.

Schlüter's fine equestrian statue was intended to commemorate not the statesman, but the conqueror of Sweden. Yet it has a wider significance for later generations: it represents the man who laid the foundation of the greatness of Brandenburg-Prussia by caring for his country, by confirming the power of the principality, and by creating a standing army.

Sovereigns and States

His two immediate successors did not pursue the intricate paths of their predecessor, but held almost exclusively by Austria. From her, Frederick III received his subsidies, which he was the less able to dispense with, since he was as fond of ostentation as his Saxon neighbour, Augustus the Strong. But what the industrial State of Saxony was able to bear without serious injury, threw the Prussian finances into disorder. When the value of the Prussian Alliance was enhanced by the approach of the War of the Spanish Succession, the emperor agreed that the elector, 'on account of his dukedom of Prussia, should have himself proclaimed and crowned as a king.' This took place at Königsberg in 1701 with the greatest pomp, and had as its chief result that the son and grandson of the first Prussian king made it their one object to bring the as yet inadequate reality into accord with the brilliant appearance.

When Frederick William I (1713–1740) ascended the throne, the War of the Spanish Succession had just come to an end: thus the army was set free for the northern war, which concerned Prussia much more nearly. The young king allied himself with Sweden's opponents, and in this way he won a considerable portion of west Pomerania with Stettin (p. 251). But the projects, which had made this possession so desirable to the Great Elector, did not appeal to him. He was a man of practical work: but to this he gave himself so whole-heartedly, with all the strength of his passionate nature, that he impressed the stamp of his personality more deeply upon his State than any other of the Prussian kings.

It is with justice that Frederick William I lives on as the 'Soldier King' in the memory of his people—he was a soldier in body and soul, and the growth and training of his army was even more manifestly the central point of his doing and thinking than it had been with his grandfather, whose efforts had covered a wider range. He increased the army of barely 40,000 to more than 80,000 men. Thus his country, which held the thirteenth place in number of population, became the fourth military power on the Continent: wealthy France, which had five times as many inhabitants as poor Prussia, was satisfied with less than double the number of soldiers. Moreover, there were no better troops than the Prussian: when the king's infantry came under fire at Mollwitz some months after his death, their 'drill' alone brought victory to his son, who had already quitted the field. It is true that 'Prussian drill' was as notorious for flogging and punishment, as the violent methods of the Prussian recruiting sergeants at home and abroad. Young men fled in troops over the frontiers, officials lamented the falling off in taxes. 'Whoever hands over such a Prussian recruiting sergeant, dead or alive,' decreed their neighbours of Hanover, 'shall receive fifty thalers out of the war chest.' For this reason the king had recourse to a measure, which possessed the additional recommendation of relieving the State treasury. Definite districts were allotted to the various regiments, out of which they could yearly take by force a part of their military substitutes. The 'Canton Regulation' was indeed founded on the principle of universal military service, but because of the exemption of all men in better positions, it weighed only upon the peasant and lower middle classes.

The State authorities also became imbued with the spirit of militarism. As early as the first decade of his reign the king simplified the government by setting up a supreme authority, the 'General Directorate,' to which all the provincial authorities, i.e. the Offices of War and Domains, were subordinated. With his own hand, in the quiet hunting lodge of Schönebeck in the Schorfheide, he drew up the comprehensive instructions and the new Supreme Authority, of which he considered himself the president, set on foot the work of training, which in a very short time ousted the old routine, and made the Prussian official what he has remained to this day. In face of a staff of officials centrally governed and functioning with unexampled punctuality and sense of duty, the estates were placed more and more at a disadvantage: the king's absolute government became an accomplished fact.

Yet absolute monarchy, unlimited save for the separate position of the nobles, must remain no more than a deceptive appearance, unless it could succeed in maintaining the military and official services out of the current revenue. The king's grandfather, who was fertile in plans, had made the advancement of trade his special object; to his grandson, who held less ambitious views, it seemed more important first to strengthen the foundations by the revival of production. The 're-establishment' of east Prussia, where the king settled 12,000 of the Lutherans who had been driven out by the archbishop of Salzburg, was as truly his work as the rise of the native cloth industry. The work was undertaken with painful conscientiousness: in the new survey of east Prussia it was shown that 35,000 hides had not been reckoned in the previous assessment. Those who resisted became acquainted with the heavy hand of the master and his officials: the royal tax commissioner destroyed the last vestiges of urban self-government. The refractory were threatened with thrashing, or even with the gallows. But—the work went on. The king was able to increase his army and fill his war chest, without having recourse to foreign subsidies like his predecessors!

There was certainly little to spare for cultural objects, even for the national schools, which were always nearer to the king's heart than, for example, the universities. In another connection also, the supremacy of the military point of view was brought to bear, in a way which did not at all accord with his wishes. He would gladly have helped the peasants, but what he gave to them he must take from the nobility. Now Frederick William I was not by any means well inclined to the 'Junkers,' but he needed them to fill the officers' posts. So the nobility kept their prerogatives, by virtue of which their landed property formed a kind of State within the State. Life became easier to the peasants on the royal domains alone: yet even here, in spite of all decrees, the abolition of serfdom was not accomplished.

It was a recurring source of depression to the king, that the citizens did not exhibit that passion for work which was a necessity of his own life. But was this surprising in a State where the presidents of the War and Domains Offices were enjoined 'to punish in their body' those citizens in whom their exhortations to work had not borne fruit: where every lease amounting to more than one hundred thalers a year, and even the question whether a grave-digger might also act as night-watchman, must be submitted to the king for his personal decision? That ceaseless urging by the higher powers, that intervention of the State at every turn, was bound to stifle every tendency to more freedom of action. At the same time the king himself was not always able to carry his point with his officials, as he would have wished, and this too was the result of the nature of his State *régime*: many an office was bestowed upon the man 'who gives the most,' in return for a subscription to the recruiting fund.

The fact that this king, who had a keen appreciation of his own position, who commanded the best-governed State and one of the most powerful armies in Europe, should, in spite of all his forcible words, have swallowed every 'affront' which was offered him by other Powers, may be explained in great measure by his consideration for the army. The army was the vital nerve of the State: he dared not endanger it. In his last years he was forced to recognize that the emperor had never seriously meant his promise that the Hohenzollern should succeed to the Dukedom of Berg. Then indeed he spoke of revenge, and turned to France: but it is not likely that this new *rapprochement* would have had any result in actions if Frederick William had remained longer alive.

It is common knowledge that his Court was the antithesis of a Court of the Muses. A step had been taken in this direction under the first king of Prussia: but even at that time Berlin was not a 'northern Athens,' as Frederick the Great asserted.

It is true that Schlüter, the foremost master of his time, was in the king's service: he co-operated in the construction of the arsenal at Berlin, directed for many years the rebuilding of the castle 'in an old-fashioned, powerful baroque style,' which about 1700 was unknown in any other country, and in the statue of the Great Elector he created the most artistically important equestrian statue since the Renaissance. Yet he was obliged to give way before his enemies. In Prussia, as in other north German countries, learning flourished more than architecture and the plastic arts. It showed that tendency to develop one-sidedly in an intellectual direction, which is inherent in the nature of Protestantism. Thomasius was the chief teacher at the new University of Halle: the advanced spirit of this Academy is shown in the fact that he was one of the first to give his lectures in the German instead of the Latin tongue. Thomasius was one of the foremost representatives of German Enlightenment: and with his master, Pufendorf, who was employed as Court Historian to the King, was one of the founders of the German School of Natural Law. Like other representatives of the Enlightenment, the School of Natural Law derived the State from a covenant, but they saw in this origin a reasonable proof of the necessity of princely absolutism, as well as a summons to the prince to use his power in the interests of enlightened reason. The enlightened despotism of Frederick the Great and his period grew out of this conception.

Artists played a much more important rôle at other German Courts. Theirs was the task of raising the prince and the society at Court, above everyday commonplace into the world of brilliant appearance, which was the breath of their own life. Moreover, the vigorous vitality of the restored Catholic Church showed itself in the endeavour to influence the masses through richly varied and ostentatious buildings. Monasteries and bishoprics vied with the lords spiritual and temporal. All these patrons had no lack of money, and so it happened that at the end of the seventeenth century and during the eighteenth, at a time of the greatest national poverty, building was more actively carried on in Germany than ever before, saving at the period of the Late Gothic, when the wealthy citizen was decorating his town and his home. Not only was their character impressed at that time upon the older residences, such for example as Vienna, Salzburg, Dresden, and Würzburg, and upon the new princely foundations, like Mannheim and Karlsruhe, but the architectural appearance of whole districts, especially in Bavaria and Austria, underwent a uniform revolution. Italy and France provided the examples: but the enormous scale on which the work was accomplished would have been impossible without the co-operation of many German patrons, just as the characteristics of the development on German soil would have been impossible without the presence of gifted artists. The misery of war, oppression, and poverty had indeed succeeded in paralysing the soul of Germany, but not in breaking it. Out of mysterious depths rose courage and strength for new creation; and while the artists adopted the acquisitions of more fortunate neighbours, they made them the vehicle of the artistic aspirations of Germany. In architecture and music the German spirit first discovered the possibility of lofty creation: the first works of Lessing and Herder were published only a few years after the death of Balthasar Neumann and Johann Sebastian Bach.

According to a French author of the period, the endeavour of absolute monarchy was not towards the reasonable but towards the extraordinary. If the Renaissance may be described as an alliance of beauty with reason, in the baroque the extraordinary, a desire for the most exaggerated expression, took the place of the reasonable; it burst the fetters of form, and compelled every part of the building to conform to its passionate play of fancy. The Residence at Würzburg, which is essentially the work of Balthasar Neumann (about 1740), may be reckoned the most magnificent of baroque castles. Five courts are enclosed by the mighty main building; the central, or Court of Honour, opens towards the town, while the back frontage gives upon the park, which is laid out in terraces. The splendid staircase leads up from the richly articulated semi-darkness into a clear open space, facing the glory of the life of Olympus, which the master-hand of Tiepolo has called forth by enchantment upon the vaulted ceiling. Everywhere, even in the central building, where the plastic decoration of the architraves and mouldings is at its richest, reigns the spirit of noble proportion; the rococo is already perceptible in the decoration of the interior, lightening the heavy pompous forms of the baroque, and refining them into a delicate charm. The Abbey Church of the Fourteen Saints, which was also built by Neumann, produces a much more lively impression. A number of oval interior spaces were here introduced into a rectangular outer building, so that there was need for an unusually delicate construction of vaults and arches, and architecture, plastic art, and painting are harmonized into a most effective unity. In north Germany the Saxon capital possesses some of the most beautiful baroque buildings Pöppelmann, a native of Saxony, constructed the famous '*Zwinger*' —'a tilting ground turned to stone': the pillars of the west pavilion provide an example of the richest magnificence in their grouping, their diagonal arrangement, and their plastic decoration. As a rule, the Austrian masters, Fischer von Erlach and Hildebrand, preferred simpler forms. Thanks to the pleasure which the Court, the high nobility, and the rich middle class took in building, they were set such multifarious tasks as fell to the masters in no other country.

With the death of Frederick William I the barriers were broken down which had divided his Spartan State from the cheerful brilliance around it. Frederick II heads the list of

Sovereigns and States

the philosophic rulers in the century of Enlightenment, and he was the most important amongst them. In the first years of his reign he had already provided a home 'for Apollo and the Muses' in the Opera House at Berlin: and the Prussian Academy, which his grandfather had founded, awoke to new life. Frederick himself contended repeatedly for the poet's laurels, and still declared in his later years that he would gladly exchange his fame as a warrior for the glory which decked the name of a Racine. Yet it was not his fate to write *Athalie*: he lives in history as the hero of the Seven Years' War.

Frederick, as he himself said, was driven into the war with Austria, partly by youthful ambition, but chiefly by the resolve to put an end to the anomalous position of Prussia, which was more like an electorate than a kingdom. Long ago the Great Elector had recommended his successor, when the House of Hapsburg should become extinct, to vindicate the legal claim of Brandenburg to part of Silesia. Frederick relied neither upon his very dubious right nor upon the force of attraction exerted by his offer of alliance with Maria Theresa, but attempted in the winter of 1740-41 to present the occupation of Silesia to the Austrian Court as an accomplished fact. But he had underestimated the character of the young queen. She accepted battle, although now both Bavaria and Saxony had also taken up arms under the powerful protection of France (The War of Austrian Succession, 1741-48). England was forced by France's attitude to adopt the Austrian side. Before long the Great Powers were directing the game, and their conflicting views on world policy were being brought to an issue once more on German soil.

Frederick himself found support in the French alliance: in return he had to bind himself to help the elector Charles Albert of Bavaria to the imperial crown. At first success was with the allies. At Mollwitz (p. 257) the Prussian army conquered the Austrians. The scion of the House of Wittelsbach was crowned emperor in Frankfort. Once more the Prussians were victorious at Chotusitz.

In 1742 Maria Theresa, acting on English advice, gave Silesia with the county of Glatz to Prussia, hoping in this way to rid herself of her most dangerous opponent. The calculation proved correct. Bavaria was shortly afterwards in Austrian hands, the French army was thrown back

263

across the Rhine by an Anglo-German army: Saxony changed to the other side. Once more Frederick entered the war, proclaiming his desire to give back 'to Germany her freedom, to the emperor his dignity, and to Europe her peace': but actually in order to ensure for himself the permanent possession of Silesia. But fortune did not favour him.

His invasion of Bohemia miscarried: in 1745, after the death of Charles Albert, Bavaria made peace with Hapsburg, and the French turned their forces exclusively against the Austrian Netherlands. Only a military decision could still save the Prussian king. Therefore he allowed Prince Charles of Lorraine to enter Silesia. Frederick's unexpected attack near Hohenfriedberg brought him a brilliant victory, but the Austrians and Saxons continued the war. The allies did not yield until the old Dessauer, threatened with his master's displeasure, dared a battle with Saxony and was victorious at Kesselsdorf. By the Peace of Dresden, in 1745, Frederick retained Silesia and acknowledged Francis I of Lorraine and Tuscany as emperor. Once more it was England which compelled the Court of Vienna to resign Silesia, in order that the Austrians might carry on the war in the southern Netherlands with greater effect. When at last the war between the Great Powers came to an end, the cession of Silesia to Prussia had to be included in the general Peace, in spite of the opposition of the Austrian Government.

The third Silesian war, finally, was occasioned and decided by the changes in the European situation. New wars broke out between the French and the English at the Mississippi and the Ohio: in India the English were threatened with the rise of a French Colonial Empire: the impending reckoning between the two colonial powers necessarily involved the English Hanover in sympathy. The experiences of the last war stood in the way of a renewed *rapprochement* between Austria and England: for this reason the former allies struck out fresh paths. After the Peace of Dresden, Maria Theresa had formed an alliance with Russia to defend herself against a third attack on the part of Frederick: it was the aim of Prince Kaunitz to draw France also into this alliance. His endeavours, which signified a breach in the traditional policy against France, were based on the conviction 'that Prussia must be overthrown if the most serene Princely House is to stand.' Frederick himself helped to bring about the fulfilment of the almost impossible desires of Austria. When the English turned to him, he pledged himself to defend Hanover, as he feared the intervention of Austria and Russia, and the consequent threat to Prussia if France should invade Germany. But instead of preventing war on the Continent, his alliance with England became the very occasion of the closing of the ranks of his opponents; France saw herself impelled to take Austria's side, Russia grasped the chance of seizing east Prussia, Saxony was only waiting for a favourable moment to join in. England alone of the more important States was on Frederick's side. Without her subsidies, it would scarcely have been possible for him to carry on the war for so long, and after the first years the Anglo-German army approved itself as a flank defence against France: on the other hand, England withdrew from her pledge of relieving him of Russia, and ceased payment at the moment when she had attained her war aims. Frederick could complain with justice of perfidious Albion; but the French had the same right to reproach him with his manner of dealing in the two first Silesian wars.

Frederick's invasion of Saxony brought the rich and strategically important country into his possession in 1756. After his incursion into Bohemia in 1757, and the victory at Prague, only the relieving army, which was advancing upon Prague, stood between him and the Austrian capital. Yet Daun came off victorious at Kolin. Frederick was obliged to evacuate Bohemia, and now disappointments came thick and fast. East Prussia was occupied by the Russians, Hanover by the French: a second French army joined the imperial army in the region of the Saale: the Austrians were victorious at Breslau. But before the year was ended, Frederick had scattered the western enemy at Rossbach, and won back Silesia by the victory at Leuthen. Once again he was able to carry the war into the enemy's country. But in 1758 he was obliged to retire from Moravia, in order to ward off the Russian advance at Zorndorf: after his heavy losses in this battle, the defeat which Daun inflicted upon him at Hochkirch was doubly hard to bear. Under the pressure of the growing danger, in grief for the death of his mother, of his favourite sister, and of his friends, he lost the gay optimism of former years: it was

then that he became 'Old Fritz'—thin, bent, tormented by
illness, but sustained by the one thought: to conquer or
perish with his army. Russians and Austrians effected their
union, unchecked. Their victory at Kunersdorf in 1759
threw the way open for them to the Prussian capital: it
seemed nothing less than a 'miracle' to the king that they
did not take it.

In 1760, Silesia was won back for a short time by the
Battle of Liegnitz, and Saxony by the victory at Torgau.
After that the king dared not risk another battle. During
1761 he held out in the entrenched camp at Bunzelwitz,
till the bulk of the Russian army retired northwards. His
embarrassment was raised to the highest pitch by the
cessation of the English payments: and only from the
Turks could he now hope for deliverance. It came, but
from a different source, and more decisively than he expected. Upon the change of Russian rulers in 1762, peace
followed between France and England, the French ceding
to the English Canada and all the territories east of the
Mississippi. America was conquered for England on the
German battlefields, and the foundation laid for her position
as the first maritime and mercantile Power. In 1763 Maria
Theresa was obliged to subscribe to the Peace of Hubertus-
burg. Frederick had held his ground, because for seven long
years he had known how to conquer and to be conquered:
ever and again he had found a way out in a desperate
situation, and had burnt up every softer emotion in his
soul with the ardent desire to conquer or to die. Prussia
came out of the struggle a Great Power.

More was destroyed by the war than had been built up
by the work of ten years of peace. The wounds of war must
be healed, and the powers of the State developed in such
a way that it should be able to bear the burden incumbent
upon it as a Great Power; to this end Frederick devoted
his unparalleled powers of work. His father also had not
taken life easily. But in his case work was a necessity,
without which his full-blooded nature was unable to exist,
and he believed it his vocation to make his subjects happy:
he had a family upon whom he could vent his good and
bad humour: he had friends, even intimates: he valued the
pleasures of the hunt and of the table. His son's health
left much to be desired: he faced men and what they call
happiness with scepticism, even with contempt; he was

infinitely lonely. The days had long been left behind in which he had opened his heart to his friends, and made music in festive circles: the day would come when the question of his digestion would be more important than the problems of philosophy. Only the 'secret instinct,' which had driven him into the war for Silesia, summoned him to work: and he worked as though he had faith and love and hope.

In the 'New Creation' which he now took in hand, he kept entirely within the lines of mercantilism: yet wider conditions and enhanced means enabled him to take far more comprehensive measures than his father. By assisting those who had suffered in country or town, the nobility receiving the lion's share in the benefit, it was possible in a comparatively short time to make good the devastation of war. The encouragement of immigrants helped on the 'peopling' of the country: many of them were settled in the swampy districts of the Oder, Warthe, and Netze; with what success the king carried on the work of settlement is proved by the fact that, according to estimate, at the end of his reign every sixth inhabitant of Prussia had been an immigrant or descended from immigrants. Besides the linen industry of the Mark of Brandenburg, the linen weaving of Silesia and the Silesian mines, which had been neglected under Austrian rule, were specially favoured by the commercial policy of protective duties, which was supplemented by the completion of the Prussian network of canals. The king also was bent, in the spirit of Colbert, on the cultivation of new industries: this was a labour which cost in the beginning much money and vexation. But through Frederick the great aim of the mercantile system was attained, when the balance of trade became active. In the last years of his reign, the total of import and export increased so much as to amount to about $4\frac{1}{2}$ marks per head of the population, almost exactly the same amount as in France, whose industry was much older. Prussia had taken the great step from an agricultural State to an industrial. The State revenue rose in proportion; it was possible to increase the army in the field by nearly 200,000 men. The absolute State had reached the summit of its capabilities of achievement.

But for this king his honour lay not simply in being an absolute monarch, but an enlightened prince. This signified

The Principality

for his subjects the abolition of torture—which took effect in the first days of Frederick's reign—an administration of justice which was independent and free from partisanship: religious tolerance and freedom of the Press. If there were considerable deductions to be made from all this, the fact remained that the Prussian monarchy impressed a French critic as 'more nearly successful than any other in reaping such a fine harvest.'

Yet this firmly constructed State collapsed within two decades of Frederick's death. Why? Was it only because it came into conflict with a new age too powerful for it?

That may explain the defeat at Jena and Auerstedt; but it does not offer a sufficient explanation for the dissolution of the State throughout its whole extent. If the ideas of the new age had been at work, the citizens would certainly have been able to vindicate their rights in the State. Nothing of the kind took place. It is more correct to say that Frederick's ingenious edifice collapsed of itself: it fell in pieces because there was no longer anyone with his superhuman force of will to hold together the cracks in its foundation. It is conceivable that this was not accomplished without tugging and pushing; but one realizes also that while they gave all due honour to Frederick, the man and the hero, the Prussians as a whole did not enjoy their life as much as might have been expected: and even that the Prussian State exercised no force of attraction upon less-well-governed subjects. On his visit to Berlin, Goethe, who from his youth up cherished the conqueror's image in his heart, heard 'his own rascals grumbling about the great man'; and when Frederick died 'everything was as still as death, but no one was sad.' Without great force and pressure from above, the Prussian State could never have risen to the height which it attained under Frederick the Great. But the limitations of this kind of government must have been most strongly perceptible at the highest point of its development, and not least to him who forced his people to that high level, who lived through it all, and inspired it all. To this fact are due certain strange contradictions between desire and accomplishment, between word and deed.

The peaceful citizen was to notice nothing when the nation was at war; such was the king's will. Yet what a picture of desolation and misery does he himself draw in his description of the situation after the Peace of Hubertus-

Sovereigns and States

burg! He called himself a King of the Poor, and from the depths of his heart he abominated 'that kind of slavery where the nobleman treats the bondsmen like cattle.' But what did he attain with all his exertions? The 'inhuman ill-treatment' of the peasants by the lords of the manor was technically forbidden, and in fact restricted. The prohibition of socage (p. 244) was very important for the State since it ensured permanently a sufficient number of peasants who paid taxes and were liable to military service: yet no adequate protection was offered to the individual: for it was still possible for the lord of the manor to drive from his farm a peasant who was out of favour, if he found someone to fill his place. It was only to the peasants on his own domains that the king was able to render any real help: but the Government was well aware that only the greatest industry could enable even them to make a living, and then only if they escaped ill-luck. In addition to the consideration shown to the nobility, the strain put upon the State funds, in order to meet military expenses, was fatally apparent in the department of public education. One's judgment of the king's education policy will vary widely, according to whether one takes into account his own wishes, or what was actually accomplished. Wretched provision was still made for the care of the poor, and it was the poorer classes who were most heavily burdened by the great increase in the excise; the fact that this ran altogether counter to Frederick's intention made the burden no lighter.

There were similar anomalies in other departments. Like his father, Frederick did all that lay in his power to put new life into the industrial activities of his subjects: but his territories in Rhenish Westphalia, where industrial life flourished without royal intervention, were described by himself as 'those from which one can draw the least profit.' They did not adapt themselves to a *régime*, whose axiom was 'amongst us everything is done by the king,' and on this very account that they were later to prove so great an inspiration to the Baron von Stein.

The same rule of conduct explains the king's occasional intervention in the law courts: yet his extraordinary harshness towards conscientious, deserving officials was in strong contrast to his care for an independent administration of justice. If everything was done by the king, the officials could do no more than carry out the royal desires:

in point of fact, Frederick's Cabinet Government reduced even the highest officials, the ministers, with whom his father was accustomed to work in concert, into the tools of his will. He paid little attention to the necessary simplification of the greatly increased labours of administration. Yet instead of complaining that his 'old perukes' were lacking in penetration, the king might have found the reason for their failure in his personal government, which, in spite of all his ability, was no longer suitable to the circumstances of his greatly enlarged State. Even the army, whose increase and development was the aim of all his measures, prepared him a bitter disappointment in his last years: in the War of the Bavarian Succession the losses through desertion were greater than they had ever been in the Seven Years' War. In addition to outward circumstances this was chiefly due to a change in the method of procuring soldier substitutes, which the king had introduced for the benefit of the heads of companies. To relieve this situation would have required a sharp inroad into the privileges of the nobility, who had won a claim to special favour with their 4,000 dead in the great war, and it had been granted to them. In addition to their older rights (pp. 243 ff.) and generous support after the war, they had experienced a radical alleviation by the removal of the excise; they were given the office of *Landrat*, the administrative head of a district: they filled almost without exception the posts of the officers and highest officials: in short, their privileged position was re-established by Frederick the Great.

The opposite was the case in Austria. Maria Theresa, who as a monarch was scarcely inferior to her great opponent, and superior to him in the warmth of her human personality, exerted herself with success to treat as a whole the various powers of her empire. In this she had to recover much which had already been accomplished in Prussia. Yet in a social respect she went considerably farther: nobility and clergy were obliged to give up all claim to exemption from taxes on their estates: the manorial peasant was efficiently protected in his property and in his terms of service. This was possible in Austria, because the mistress of the wide empire commanded quite other resources than the Prussian kings, who were much more dependent upon their alliance with their lesser nobility.

Sovereigns and States

On the other hand, peculiar difficulties arose out of the great area of the State, with its multiplicity of nationalities, of language, and of historical ties. In this respect also the empress frequently won success by her prudent measures, so that she may be considered the founder of the centralized monarchy of Austria. Yet it was precisely on this point that the inconsiderate encroachment of her son, Joseph II, aroused the most passionate resistance.

Joseph II tried to act on the lines of 'What is expedient for the present day,' and to create a middle-class society, possessed of equal rights. This idea was quite in character with the 'Enlightenment,' and almost in the spirit of the French Revolution. But the path which Joseph struck out was that of an absolute monarch: good must only come to his peoples from above: all must submit themselves to the Central Government at Vienna: there was no thought of linking up with the connections and conditions which had grown up from below.

The work of the 'crowned Friend of Man,' which had been conceived on such generous lines, was soon shattered through his complete neglect of the accomplished facts of history. By his Edict of Toleration, his measures against the monasteries, his marriage law, founded upon the idea of a civil-law contract, he made the Church his enemy, and antagonized the nobility by the conversion of serfdom into a much softened relationship of dependence. The fight was hottest in the Netherlands and in Hungary, where a national public spirit had already grown up. Joseph had to give way before this opposition. Neither the deliberate strengthening of the feudal system, which was accomplished in Prussia by Frederick II, nor the Austrian attempt, to transform society into a mass as far as possible of one mould, under a strong kingship, could save absolute monarchy from collapse. Not until the State had been founded upon the free and spontaneous activity of its citizens did it succeed in overcoming Napoleon.

Many of the princes in the smaller German territories acted like those in Prussia and Austria. After the middle of the eighteenth century, it was considered at the princely Courts to be no longer in keeping with the spirit of the age if a ruler did not work for the good of his subjects. Here and there, more even was attained on a smaller scale than in the larger States, where it was natural that the weight of tradition should be more strongly felt. Thus, for example, the serfdom of the peasants was abolished in Baden by Charles Frederick, much earlier than in Prussia, and the right of self-government given to the communities in town and country. This advance will be elsewhere referred to, together with the exceptions to the rule, by which a doubly painful impression was now produced.

The antagonism between Prussia and Austria played a further decisive part in the course of political events in Germany. After the two States had fought out their quarrel within the area of the great conflict of the Western Powers, their relations with the East began to acquire a growing importance. The Russian empress, Catherine the Second, had succeeded in getting one of her favourites elected to the throne of Poland. When Polish 'patriots' appealed to the help of Turkey, war broke out between Turkey and Russia, in which Austria was on the point of taking part. As the King of Prussia was very anxious 'to save Europe from a universal war,' he proposed the partition of Poland as a way out of the difficulty. To this solution Maria Theresa, after violent opposition, at last gave her consent. By this means Prussia became possessed of west Prussia, exclusive of Danzig and Thorn—and of Ermland with the Netze district (1772).

Even at that period, when men lived under the rule of Cabinet politics, and were accustomed to the bartering of territories, they were shocked by the spectacle of the partition of Poland, which was carried out almost to the extinction of the kingdom. Nevertheless, this was not a case where a people possessed of a conscious national life were falling victim to the rapacity of the Great Powers. Only at the time of the Partition did the national sentiment of Poland grow strong enough to become an active force. Frederick defended himself against the reproaches of his contemporaries by the necessity of avoiding a universal war. Through his devoted care for the newly acquired districts, which were redeemed from the deepest misery by Prussian rule, he has justified his action at the bar of history.

The efforts of Joseph II to strengthen his position in Germany by the linking up of Bavaria to Austria produced new dangers. In Bavaria the electoral line of Wittelsbach had become extinct: the legal heir, Charles Theodore,

Sovereigns and States

Elector of the Palatinate, showed himself inclined to the proposals of exchange which were made by Austria. But the Prussian king put his troops in motion, and in this way frustrated Joseph's project (the War of Bavarian Succession, 1778). To counter a renewed attempt, Frederick made use of the jealous care of the princes for their 'Liberty' to incite them to form, 1785, the League of German Princes, whose purpose was to maintain 'every member of the empire in his possessions, and the entire empire in the Constitution based upon the Peace of Westphalia.' It is a strange spectacle to see this Protestant prince appealing for help for the defence of the Church territories—the conqueror of Silesia for the preservation of the empire's Constitution! His method of dealing must be judged as an expedient of Prussian politics, not as a national act.

Frederick died in the following year, and a few years later the first waves of the French Revolution were beating against the frontiers of the empire. The great king left the world with the conviction that 'the fashion of revolutions was over'; his successor hailed the change because, as he believed, it finally put an end to the possibility of a Franco-Austrian union. With its eyes shut, absolute monarchy went into the fight for its existence.

THIRD PART

FATHERLAND

THERE was nothing new and unheard of in the active principles of the French Revolution. The ideas of the rights of man, in particular the conception of the sovereignty of the people, had been coined by Calvinism in the seventeenth century, and victoriously defended against the absolute monarchy of the Stuarts. In the war of the English colonies against the Motherland, these very ideas had just given fresh proof of their power to create a State. Yet an attempt had never before been made, to reconstruct from these foundations a solid national unity maintained throughout the storms of centuries, and fusing together the government and the cultured classes, according to the demands of the intellectual leaders.

The essence of these proceedings escaped the penetration of German contemporaries. Since their outlook was bounded by the horizon of cabinet politics, the courts took account at first only of the change in the former European grouping. And those who longed to escape from the constraint of the absolute monarchy were fascinated by the 'glory of the new sun.' The outbreak of the Revolution appeared to them like the free action of human reason, the dawn of a day which would realize their own dreams of freedom and self-determination. They failed to recognize that events in France were continuing the development of a national State, and endowing it with new powers which had hitherto been inimical to it. The rulers of the absolute monarchy looked with the outer eye—their subjects with the inner: the former grasped the political form only—the others only the formative force of humanity. It was inevitable that understanding should be lacking for the mutual interplay of the two forces—the very singular feature of the French Revolution, and the most fertile in consequences—because as yet there was no bridge in Germany spanning the gulf between the State and the man. Only in a time of the severest testing, when first political, and then intellectual, life was in danger of being enslaved and wiped out, did the forces of the sundered spheres flow together into one stream: the Fatherland, which the French created for

themselves through the Revolution, became a living power to the Germans at the time of their subjugation.

In the intellectual sphere, as well as in the political, the new form was developed in conflict with the Western neighbour: but the reaction set in even more powerfully, and led to a reshaping of the German character which was incomparably loftier and purer.

In the decades after the great war, French influence grew, indeed, to such an extent, that about 1700 the German character appeared to be submerged for a long time to come. The domestic economy of Germany became subservient to the powerful neighbour, as had already happened, to a great extent, with the policy of the German princes. 'What the German scratcheth out of the earth with bitter sweat'—so an author wrote at the end of the seventeenth century—'he giveth by millions to the French and the Dutch, in exchange for rags and painted cobwebs. We sell yarn and wool for 1,000 imperial thalers; for 100,000 thalers the foreigner sendeth us back cloths and materials, which are made from this very wool and yarn.' The French model affected social and intellectual life, chiefly through the Courts and the nobility. The same princely Government which had created its political and economic organization after the pattern of French absolutism: which kept the peasants in dull subjection, and the citizens in petty restraint, and in which there was no room for the cultivation and employment of public spirit: this Government was foremost in adopting foreign manners and ideas. Once more, French Court culture became the guiding influence, and affected much wider circles than had been the case in the Middle Ages. But the courtier who was considered the flower of culture, was lacking in just that best quality which men looked for in the age of chivalry from the man at Court: a striving after the ideal. No Wolfram von Eschenbach wrote for this society: their poets were applauded, when they conducted prince and princess through a medley of thrilling adventures to a happy union, and were careful to cater for the man who was intent on the affairs of Court and government, no less than for the sentimental and the lasciviously inquisitive. There was no lack of keener stimulus, nor of 'political,' that is to say, worldly-wise, direction in the art 'of making one's fortune.' Never has more barren worldly wisdom

The Principality

been praised as the aim of human endeavour. An essential element in successful *Konduite* was the capacity of 'sustaining one's *état*,' the emphasis upon external honour, and with it the strict separation from the citizen class.

What was right for the 'perfect cavalier' seemed reasonable to the scholar. His fortune was dependent in no small measure upon his capacity for flattery. When one sees a Leibnitz excel along these lines, one will not pass too harsh a judgment upon a lesser spirit who addresses his sovereign in these words: 'If God were not God, who should with greater reason be God than your Serene Highness?' The worthy in question was—a theologian! Servility of this kind was counterbalanced by the overweening pride shown by scholars towards the unlearned. The same process went on through the ranks of the middle classes. To a far greater extent than property and culture, one's relations with the Court, and, closely connected with them, one's cultivation of the French language and customs, gave the measure of one's social importance. A man who could pass this test might shrug his shoulders over those who had failed: and even the poorest could look down upon the soldiers and the peasants.

This state of things had been maintained for a long time against a powerful attack. Until the end of his life the great King of Prussia remained devoted to French culture. When, as Goethe related in *Werther*, the count, out of consideration for his noble guests, showed his friend, the middle-class secretary of a legation, the door, it was no poetic invention, but a passage taken from the life of the departing eighteenth century. Duke Charles Eugene of Wurtemberg ground down his subjects, to provide the funds to maintain his Court in a magnificence unequalled in Europe: he quarrelled most bitterly with his estates, and at the same time, out of petty revenge, allowed the prominent jurist Moser, and later, after his publicly acclaimed conversion from despotism, the poet Schubart, to languish for years in a prison cell. Yet this tyrant was praised in a speech at the university, as the most loving father, the best and wisest and most just prince. Schiller, as is well known, had a different opinion of this most loving father. But Schiller knew also the effect of the favour of the nobility upon the simple citizen: the mother

Fatherland

heart of Frau Miller swells with pride over her Louise's love affair with the president's son.

How was such distortion possible? Is it not a fact that both earlier and later the Germans adopted a great deal from their French neighbours which enriched and ennobled their character? Was it impossible at other times to reconcile their nature with the strict manners of the Court? The explanation lies in the circumstances of that period. The poverty-stricken and oppressed generations, who had the task of clearing away the heaps of ruin left by the great war, did not possess the adaptability which would enable them to absorb what was foreign and of a finer stamp, in such a way as to make it one with their own nature. They rushed to lay hold of it, but only succeeded in grasping the external, which they exaggerated with miserable pedantry. A thirst for titles and a rage for compliments, unnatural expressions of sentiment, and other similar features of social life about 1700, were most repugnant to the French, who aimed above all things at the golden mean.

Yet this French influence, at once so powerful and so penetrating, produced an effect which was not only destructive, but constructive. Even before the Thirty Years' War, native discipline had no longer been able to restrain the excesses of a race who were eager to drink their fill of life (p. 231 ff.): and even this discipline was completely relaxed during the generation of the war. Then French manners stepped in as a substitute. Under their influence the ancient passion for drinking was actually restrained to a considerable extent. Coffee-drinking and smoking made it possible to enjoy a less rough kind of sociability, in which woman began by degrees to play a more important rôle. In the intellectual sphere, the fashionable ideal of the man of the world implied a renunciation of the blind fury of compilation which was typical of the scholar of the period, and at the same time a rejection of the idea of culture which was still strongly coloured by theology. The man of the rising generation wished to be a 'galant homme and no pedant.' In the academies for young noblemen which were founded about 1700, the youth of the upper classes were educated in much closer relationship to life than had been the case in the scholars' schools of the older kind; and the new universities, of which, after Halle,

Göttingen was the most notable (p. 260), owed their great
access of students to the like attitude.

These efforts were in keeping with the objects of the
best men of the time. The same Thomasius, who was one
of the first to employ the German language in the lecture
room, was most eager in his recommendation of French
culture. Leibnitz also had the idea of employing French
culture to fertilize the culture of Germany. He was the
first of the German thinkers to quarrel with the accepted
contemporary philosophy. For Leibnitz, the body as such
is not a reality. More correctly the 'unities' (monads) are
the true reality. They are, without exception, of a spiritual
nature, akin to the human soul. They ascend in stages
from the lower forms of organic life, live according to their
own laws, and in their countless multiplicity they compose
the universe. After Leibnitz had given expression for the
first time in philosophical language to a view of life which
was exclusively German—it was not till about 1730 that
Wolff arranged his ideas into a scholastic system—idealism
and individualism remained the basic features of German
philosophy.

But before Kant had given their clearest definition to
the characteristics of German thought, new forces had
flowed into intellectual life out of the depths of the German
soul itself. With its renunciation of the quarrels of the
theologians, pietism combined a resolute rejection of the
superficiality of the fashionable ideal of culture, and a
concentration upon the living power of the spiritual life,
which, even in the worst times, had been embodied in
Church songs. Dogmatic rigidity was broken down, and
place was made for a spiritualized Christianity, through
the principle of the practice of Christian love, even towards
the adherents of other creeds. Pietism found its eloquent
exponent in Klopstock, and the German people after long
years of stammering found the first of their poets to achieve
greatness. J. S. Bach, the leader of the choir in St. Thomas'
Church at Leipzig and the father of German music, composed
melodies inspired by pietistic devotion. Protestantism displayed pietistic features wherever, through the development of
intellectual leaders, it became a living force. Long after tendencies to pietism amongst the upper class had had to yield
to the advance of the 'Enlightenment,' pietism still dominated the intellectual life of the humbler classes of the nation.

Fatherland

Pietism prepared the ground for the Enlightenment, through its critical attitude towards the Church of tradition, and through the practice of piety in secular life. In the second quarter of the eighteenth century, it became the dominant power in Germany also, and the process of assimilation proved that the power of transforming the intellectual riches of other countries was once more active. Characteristically, Thomasius (p. 260) had already allied himself with those who derived from the idea of the State covenant, not the doctrine of the liberty of the people, but the intellectual justification of absolute monarchy. In agreement with this conservative attitude, the German 'Enlighteners' in the sphere of religion followed neither the English freethinkers, nor the French sceptics and atheists, but almost without exception attempted to reconcile the truths of the faith with reason. In general, the intellectual side of the Enlightenment in Germany was not nearly so strongly developed as was the case in other lands. As faith in progress acquired an almost religious character, gentle ingenuousness went hand in hand with cool intelligence. It was during the century of Enlightenment that the brightly lighted Christmas tree came into the German middle-class home, and the ancient fairy tales, in addition to receiving an instructive moral, underwent a most obvious transformation: the glory of the Royal Court shines upon prince and princess: the hunter well knows how to manage his gun. It is this union of ingenuousness and rationalism which explains the great popularity of the new mental alignment. After some initial resistance, the Church was also thrown open to the spirit of the times, and although the Catholic clergy were naturally more inclined to hang back, Bavaria and Austria again came more closely in touch with the literary life of north Germany. The Enlightenment created the first community of educated people, outside all barriers of creed, locality, and class: thus founding an empire of the spirit, in which every man of good will possessed the right of citizenship. It is this, above all, which constituted its great national importance.

Even if the bond of union remained purely intellectual in character, the citizens of this empire were conscious of being not alone a thinking, but also an acting community. For their faith in the power of reason to liberate man from 'the inferiority for which he was himself to blame,' pro-

The Principality

duced in them all the resolution to set to work to transform life, that the rising generation might grow up into a more reasonable world. As in the age of Humanism (p. 198) the educative side of the task was cultivated in Germany with peculiar zeal. In Hamburg, under English influence, there appeared the first of the *Moral Weeklies*, which at that time, chiefly through Gottsched's agency, became an intellectual power. It combated unnaturalness barren of ideas: superstition, fashionable superficiality, and class prejudices: it sought its public also among the humblest people, craftsmen and peasants. 'Naturalness and good sense' were its guiding stars, and the goal was inward and outward transformation.

The cultivation of the German language and its literature took a place of honour amongst the tasks of the Enlightenment, corresponding to their importance in national culture. As early as the seventeenth century, an enlightened thinker had described the effect of his dramas upon the spectator with the words, 'He thinks he is licking sugar, but swallows medicine with it into his very soul.' By weekly journals, German clubs, and the extensive correspondence which bound the intellectual leaders to their disciples, the conditions were created in which the work for German language and literature which had never been completely interrupted, could be promoted with a prospect of success. A beginning had been made by Opitz about the commencement of the great war: the language societies in which princes and scholars united, had continued his work: Gottsched and his circle carried it still farther. Imitation of the French model was still looked upon as the path to the goal: Lessing was the first to recognize that it could lead no farther. Yet though there was a total lack of poetic accomplishment, these students learned at least to avoid ingenious involutions, and the baroque overloading of the phrase, and to write clearly and simply: and that was no small matter.

Lessing gave shape to all that was healthy and virile in the Enlightenment. His combative and highly strung nature found its most appropriate field in polemical and dramatic writing. His unique combination of artistic sensibility and most keen intelligence made him capable of recognizing the fruitlessness, even the senselessness, of copying the French models. His fight against the un-

Fatherland

German constraint of rules finally cleared the way for the development of a national drama, after a master of lyrical poetry had already arisen in Klopstock, and an inspirer of the novel in Wieland. In *Minna von Barnhelm*, Lessing for the first time placed men and women upon the stage who really felt like Germans. With *Emilia Galotti*, he went to the root of the evils which the Enlightenment, however hard it exerted itself to overcome class prejudices, had hitherto passed over in silence: 'Guastalla' actually stood for the next little German residence. 'Nathan the Wise' soared to the heights of noble humanity, far above the honest, yet restricted efforts of enlightened tolerance.

All through his life Lessing had fought against the substitution of 'feminine delicacy for manly virtue.' But the heart's demands could not be suppressed, and while Lessing in quiet Wolfenbüttel was composing the works of his last years, *Sturm und Drang* (storm and violence) were raging over the land of Germany. There was a turning back from the work of the intellect, to revelations of the life of the soul, and sentiment was set free to rise above the plain of practical utility. This phenomenon, which announced the end of the Enlightenment, was common to the mental life of all the European peoples: French and English efforts in the same direction had a powerful influence upon German development. But while Rousseau was not without political aims, the German movement set itself solely against the restrictions of personal liberty, and produced within these limits a truly revolutionary effect. Young Goethe's Götz, beleaguered in his castle, raises a cheer for freedom in the face of the forces of law and order which are pressing hard upon him. More stormily still in the *Robbers* young Schiller sings the praise of freedom: she 'hatches colossi and monsters,' while the 'ink-slinging century' smothers all individual growth. Again, the particular theme of the social differences between the classes can be clearly heard already in Goethe's *Werther*: and in the third of Schiller's youthful dramas *Kabale und Liebe* (Cabal and Love) it becomes the cardinal point of the action. All these works are inspired by passionate feeling: the period of great German poetry had come. On his search for the road to free humanity, young Herder had brought this high, though still rather colourless, ideal more within the German grasp: Germany was the one nation which, on the strength of the originality of its talents, was called to show the way to human freedom: humane culture was German culture. Therefore the papers, which Herder and Goethe published in Strasburg, on German nature and German art, told of Shakespeare, the giant spirit of Germanic stock, and of Erwin, who built the cathedral under the prompting 'of his strong, rich, German soul.'

Yet the way to national culture had scarcely been trodden before it was again forsaken. At the moment when the possibility had dawned of an art belonging in the strictest sense to the Fatherland, the poets and thinkers reached out beyond the national frontiers to the ideals of a fair humanity which embraced the whole world. In the same way, at the period when the German State was in process of formation, the Saxon kings had snatched at the imperial crown which implied the world-power. But it is to these bold endeavours after a more than national goal that mankind owes two of the mightiest creations of the European race: first the earthly empire of the Middle Ages, and then the ideal kingdom of humanity.

In its aspirations after humane culture the new mental alignment had much in common with the Enlightenment: but its grasp of the problem was much more profound. Former generations had trusted unconditionally to the power of reason: in opposition to their uncritical faith, Kant proved that the understanding was unable to penetrate through the world of 'appearances' into the nature of the 'thing in itself.' Therewith the decisive blow was dealt to the Enlightenment, and at the same time the limits of the province of certain knowledge were marked out for the future. What the intellect lost in breadth of action, it gained in importance for the spheres which were left to it: the philosopher recognized in intellect the most individual and active faculty, through which, from the surrounding world of appearance, man fashions his image of the world.

Yet, according to Kant, it is neither thought nor action which decides the worth of a man, but will alone. In will we possess the power to follow the command of the moral law, and resist the allurements of the material. Since the moral law is not deducible from experience, it proves the existence of a moral world order, raised above the material world. It is man's unending task to conform himself to

this higher world, in will and deed. While the men of
the *Sturm und Drang* had abandoned themselves to their
feelings, Kant called for the control of desire. The men
of the Enlightenment had connected morality with considerations of expediency: for him the one thing necessary
was the agreement of the will with the teachings of a supersensual world, which was far removed from human objects
of striving.

Goethe and Schiller gave artistic form to the high ideal
of a fair human culture, which the Königsberg philosopher
had brought within men's comprehension with such extraordinary clarity. While Kant freed the ethical will from
the bonds of utilitarianism, they liberated art from the
dross of moral purpose, thus raising artistic creation to
a position of complete liberty and of the highest dignity.
Schiller demanded that the artist should follow the inspirations of his inner self alone: therefore he must recognize
his chief task in the raising of his inner self to the greatest
height of human nobility. From this creed flowed a prodi-
gious multiplicity of artistic work. Goethe's psychological
dramas are in accord with it, as well as Schiller's plays,
in which 'the great objects of mankind' are contended
for: the topical romance of *Wilhelm Meister*, and Schiller's
philosophical poems: the classicism of *Iphigenia* and the
romantic in *Faust*. But the work of the poets of Weimar
owed its unique character to the effort to create anew in
the German nature the perfect balance of the Greek ideal
of beauty. German art became classic, in the special sense
that it assimilated its standards to the creations of the
antique spirit. Before long the return to antiquity was to
meet with opposition; yet even its opponents had to soar
into the rarified air breathed by the great writers.

At no period was art more philosophic, and philosophy
more akin to art. In Kant's principal works on aesthetics,
the poets of Weimar read a description of the proceedings
of artistic work, which gave, to their astonishment, a true
picture of their own creative methods. Goethe pursued
extensive nature studies; Schiller developed a rich vein
as a writer on philosophic subjects. In this strange interpenetration of art and science lay the possibility of most
fruitful discoveries. The philosophic poet undertook to
overcome the antagonism between inclination and duty,
which Kant had accepted as unalterable. Inclination springs

The Principality

from the slave world of appearance, duty from the free world of pure morality. Between these worlds there lies a third: that of beauty. In it 'the troubled stream of grief murmurs no more,' it reconciles, it makes up the quarrel. So 'aesthetic education' became for Schiller the way to the liberation of the individual and of mankind. The philosopher of art was already forming the idea that the way to freedom of citizenship must lead through moral freedom, and the poet embodied it in the *Jungfrau von Orleans* and in *Tell*. Herder bridged the gulf between moral idea and political reality, with a different order of reasoning. While his fellow idealists cared for nothing but the development of the individual personality, he had early penetrated the nature and significance of the national character. Where the Enlightenment had seen little more than motionless phantoms, he saw colour and movement: he viewed the history of mankind as the mutual interaction of national unities modified in many ways, both external and internal: as an endless process of growth. In addition to his keen sense of national character, which produced the *Ideas towards a Philosophy of the History of Mankind*, he was already conscious that the fine flower of national individuality must pine without political freedom. Therefore Herder exhorted his readers to 'noble pride,' not to allow themselves to be disposed of by others, but to be masters of their own fate, as other nations have been from the beginning: to be Germans, on their own well-defended soil.

Through the cultivation of the national characteristics, Romanticism, in particular, came at a later date to have an influence upon political history. It began in the last years of the eighteenth century, not as a counter-movement, but as the continuation and completion of the classical striving after Humanism. Friedrich and August Wilhelm Schlegel, its founders, worked with the great men of Weimar upon their journal, and were most eagerly and successfully employed in spreading the understanding of Goethe's art and Schiller's aesthetics. They borrowed even the name of their efforts from *Wilhelm Meister*, which they considered the novel of novels. Then, under the influence of Fichte's philosophy, they gradually struck out new paths. The creative *ego* was called upon to form the world out of itself. The more personal and individual the artist,

284

Fatherland

the higher stands his work. As man's individuality is revealed far more in sentiment than in thought, the life of feeling, and even the half-conscious presentiment, desire, and dream, become the favourite subjects of artistic creation. Expression, not beauty, is the goal; not classical antiquity, but the Germanic and romanesque Middle Ages breathe the spirit of true, romantic art. There is nothing essential in form: it can be neglected, it is even deliberately destroyed: for in the possibility of destruction the limitless mastery of the creative *ego* is most clearly revealed.

It is in keeping with this philosophic attitude that the romantic poets and thinkers should have left only a few finished works, but exercised a deep and wide influence as inspirers and pioneers. They made their influence felt in every department of life, for the fully developed *ego* must revolutionize not only art, but life throughout its whole compass, including the life of women. To them Schleiermacher appealed: 'Covet a man's training, a man's art, wisdom, and honour.' Romantic sentiment and thought laid the basis for the evolution of poetry and philosophy, painting and music, the study of the German language and comparative philology, jurisprudence, and the writing of history, and bore fruit even down to our own times. We owe to romanticism in particular the definite advance towards world-literature. By the beginning of the nine-teenth century, A. W. Schlegel had practically finished his translation of Shakespeare; Calderon and Cervantes, Dante and Ariosto followed in quick succession. To the Romantics we also owe the revival of the older German style and art, especially of the old national wealth of popular songs and folk stories, fairy tales and sagas. It was upon these treasures that the poets of the War of Liberation nourished their ideas of the German character, and thus the work of the Romantics was not without effect in the war with Napoleon. Now and again the idea that civilization and the State cannot exist permanently apart from each other, fought its way to recognition amongst the Romantics. It sounds like an anticipation of Stein's reasoning, when Novalis defines the object of the State 'to make men absolutely powerful and not absolutely weak. The State does not relieve man of any work, but rather adds to his work in an infinite degree: but not without adding in an infinite degree to his strength.'

The Principality

But even this deep insight was not transmuted into the will to set up the imaginary State on earth. Classicists, the men of the *Sturm und Drang* and of the Enlightenment, resembled the Romantics in this: that while they wrestled with the most difficult problems of humanity, the State in which they lived seldom became the subject of their meditation. Whenever it did come to pass, the idea carried them to such heights, that they lost sight of the actual. Never did a spark fly from political reality to enflame to their work: and the same is true of their scattered disciples.

It is one of the most important facts of modern German history, that an economically powerful middle class should have grown up within the framework of the principality, and become the pillar of German culture. The absolute State deserves much of the credit for the growth of the national community, through its encouragement of trade and commerce. Frederick William I was the first to relax the outworn organization of the guilds; other regulations followed, some of them conceived in a still more liberal spirit, and before the century came to an end a uniform system had been set up in the majority of the States, which did away with the senseless difficulties attending the establishment of a master craftsman, and placed the number of journeymen at the discretion of those who carried on the trade. The business activities of the middle man (p. 182) were legally regulated in the same progressive way: the wool manufacture in Brandenburg and Saxony, the stocking weaving in Thuringia, the Silesian linen industry, and others. Thus the employer class in Germany was gradually enabled to conform to the French and English methods of doing business.

This was, of course, a matter of individual enterprise, since at that period the manufactures which played the most important part in the national economy were not in any sense called into being by the Governments. One need only think of Saxony and the Rhine territories of Prussia. In the main, the State tended to secure regularity and order, while it gave effect at the same time to social points of view. What the middle classes achieved was in great part due to themselves. And even before the middle of the century this achievement had already become considerable: modest comfort returned to the middle-class home, till it was driven out by the armies of Napoleon.

286

Fatherland

During this period of slow improvement, the towns began to flourish, and remained for a long time the centre of economic life; and not until the rise of modern industry did a change come over the picture. As the entrance port for English and French trade, and as the seaport of Berlin, Hamburg developed into the most important coast town of the northern continent. Lübeck, Danzig, and Königsberg came again into prominence through the Baltic trade of Europe. The extraordinary growth of the Prussian capital was due to its trading situation, and its rapid industrial development. Breslau, the old centre of the trade of east Germany, gained a new impetus after its incorporation in the great Prussian economic area: like Breslau, Magdeburg and Halle enjoyed the benefit of their situation upon important waterways. Leipzig made great strides as the centre of a highly developed industrial country; its progress was helped by the fact that, in consequence of the increasing difficulties of foreign trade, the Low German and High German halves of the Pan-German economic area (p. 186) gradually drew more closely together. It is true that Frankfort was unable to maintain its position, after Dutch trade had advanced still farther southwards: Mannheim became a dangerous rival to the city on the Main.

The effect of business life upon the intellectual attitude was most clearly perceptible in the large towns. Trade and commerce were freed from their fetters: competition grew: intercourse was carried on a little more rapidly: compared with the seventeenth century, there was a considerable improvement in the conveyance of persons and letters. A man had to stick more closely to business, but he could prosper if he took a correct view of distant matters, and had a firm grip of the near. He had, moreover, sufficient leisure, and through the increasing comfort of his circumstances he could be sure of satisfying his newly awakened intellectual needs. Beside the great contractors and the great merchants, who quickly succumbed to the outward habits of the ruling classes of society, there was growing up a large middle class with intellectual pretensions: the higher ranks were continually reinforced from this middle class. Many a time a family would continue to rise throughout some generations. A blacksmith's son took to tailoring, by a fortunate marriage he became the owner of a large

The Principality

inn, and gradually attained a respectable income and a cosmopolitan outlook: the grandson studied, travelled, and chose his wife from the patricians of the imperial city in which he lived: this great-grandson became a minister in Weimar and Germany's greatest poet. In most cases the road was much shorter: Winckelmann, Fichte, and others of the greatest men sprang from simple craftsmen's families. The intellectual and social needs of this middle class resulted in numerous citizens' unions and the rise of the 'lodges.' A feeling for the needs of the community called forth cultural institutions of the most varied kind: such, for instance, as the first German opera house founded in Hamburg as early as the seventeenth century, and followed almost a century later by a German national theatre, which, however, collapsed in a very short time. Other places were less ambitious: but almost all the cities mentioned above meet us again in the history of literature and of the mental sciences. The number of bookshops was growing: there were more than fifty in Leipzig, about the year 1800. The citizens occupied themselves with the care of the poor, and with questions of education. The external aspect of the towns was changed also: wide avenues replaced the fortifications, which had already been broken down here and there, and the country houses of the well-to-do multiplied before the gates.

It is true that work for the public good played a subordinate rôle in the life of this community. They sought chiefly for inward culture, to raise them above the triviality of the daily round. The rigid and apparently unalterable government was part of this daily round, allowing no space for the cultivation of individuality. Now and again the great name of Fatherland sounded in men's ears: 'the Fatherland produces it out of its abundance'—so ran the Rhine wine song of Matthias Claudius. But there came no echo. Men lived in a State, not a Fatherland, no matter how officious estates might misuse the noble word when they set up a monument to a still-loving prince. Men felt the Kingdom of the Spirit to be their Fatherland. There every man could be a citizen, a brother amongst brothers: 'We embrace you, O ye Millions!' Count Stollberg used the fraternal *Du* in his intercourse with J. H. Voss, the son of a serf. A poet merited such distinction: who could have shown the way better than he, into the secret Fatherland?

288

Fatherland

At a card table, so friend informs friend, one of the ladies draws an almanack from her pocket and begins to read Bürger's *Leonore* aloud; the cards are put aside. Men and women rise from the other card tables, and group themselves around the reader. Music was the only rival to poetry: the music of a Glück, a Haydn, or a Mozart. German opera houses were founded in Berlin in 1771, and in Vienna in 1778: the theatre at Mannheim was of European importance. When Beethoven was composing, the ground rumbled already under the tread of Napoleon's armies.

Nourished on the works of the greatest minds, the middle-class ideal of life was strong enough in a few places to win over the nobility and the Court. Intellectual effort and work for the public good succeeded in bridging the gulf. Leopold Frederick Francis of Anhalt-Dessau, Ernest II of Sachsen-Altenburg, Francis von Fürstenberg, vicar-general of Münster, and many others, range themselves at the side of Charles Augustus of Weimar; the 'Bourgeoisization' of the Prussian Court under Frederick William III is common knowledge. The 'mildest and most amiable' lord of Wurtemberg stood by no means alone: and even in the year before the death of Frederick the Great, the subjects of a Rhenish prince were admonished as follows: 'Subjects must demean themselves like servants, because the sovereign is their master, and has power as well over our life as over our goods.'

But because the political sense was lacking, neither the disturbing dramas of Schiller's youth could engender political action, nor the political events in Germany arouse the right interest. In spite of Goethe's famous words, even the heroic life of Frederick II found an astonishingly faint echo in poetry. Veneration and disappointment strove for the mastery in Klopstock; but his judgment was determined far more by cultural than by political points of view. The writer of *Minna von Barnhelm* looked upon patriotism as an heroic weakness. Herder likened Frederick's victories to those of Pyrrhus, and as a young man he gave impartial consideration to the possibility that his home in east Prussia might reach its highest development under Russian rule. But serious political considerations did not come to the front before the outbreak of the French Revolution. Amongst the youth of Germany, voices were loud against

The Principality

the existing State, which degraded men into machines. Drawing upon the ideas of classical Humanism, Wilhelm von Humboldt demanded that the State should limit its sphere of action to the safeguarding of life and property: somewhat later Arndt drew upon romantic sentiment for the image of a national State.

But how could such discussions become fruitful when every effort from below to attain political power was lacking? So slight was the connection with political reality that even the most cultured accepted with indifference the collapse of the empire. The question of who owned the left or right bank of the Rhine, did not disturb Goethe's mother 'either sleeping or eating.' It may seem like a symbolic phenomenon to us of a later generation, that at the moment at the turn of the century, when the flower of German poetry had fully opened, the independent political existence of the Germans not only in fact, but also in form, should have come to an end.

The opponents who faced each other in the revolutionary wars were very unequally matched. On the one side was a people, for whom the old order was breaking up in wild confusion, while as yet there was no indication of whither their way would tend: the army was disintegrated, and there was a total lack of money, and of the sinews of war. On the other side stood the great consolidated German States, with the best-disciplined armies and their finances in tolerable order: behind them the moral support, soon to be joined by the political, of almost all the old Powers. Yet the French rulers dared to declare war upon Austria, and as early as 1792 the Austro-Prussian campaign in France revealed the actual proportion of strength. In the Argonnes, at Valmy, the enemy at last made a stand against the advancing Prussians. Desultory firing went on throughout the day: but the order to attack, which was expected by the troops, did not come. In a short time, the military and political situation had so changed that the Prussians were forced to begin the retreat. A few years later the Prussian commander-in-chief, Duke Ferdinand of Brunswick, was staying in Nauheim: the view of the Johannis Mountain reminded him of the Heights of Valmy. 'Do you see the mountain there? Do you know what is behind it? Well—at that time I did not know either!' The French leaders knew that the enemy lay behind the

Fatherland

Argonnes and the Ardennes—and yet they advanced. Custine occupied Spire, Worms, and Mayence, and Dumouriez, Belgium. A few months later war was declared upon England, Holland, and Spain. The French armies were at first forced to give way before a great European coalition (the first Coalition War, 1793–1797). But in the course of years, the weakness of the one side and the strength of the other became more and more apparent.

From the beginning, the alliance between Prussia and Austria rested on an insecure foundation. Both were expecting further acquisitions of Polish territory. A long time previously Austria had already ousted her rival from the favour of Russia, and, in conjunction with the Tsarina, had begun a war against the Turks. When the allies met with unexpected difficulties, Frederick William II made as if he would attack Austria, and decide the question of supremacy. But with his slackness and love of pleasure, he was not the man to carry on the policy of Frederick the Great. An agreement with Austria followed immediately upon the threat of war, which applied also to France, in relation to whom Austria had much to lose, and Prussia scarcely anything to gain. Yet here, as there, the treaty was half-heartedly entered into. The Prussian king soon broke free from it again, in order to be able to throw his whole strength into the Polish question. As a matter of fact, in the second and third Partitions of Poland, he gained extensive Polish territories in addition to Danzig and Thorn. Yet they signified a burden rather than a gain for the State. In 1795 the Peace of Basle put an end to the state of war with France: Prussia consented to the cession of the left bank of the Rhine, in return for the assurance of compensation on the right of the river. If the peace had been followed by a closer alliance with France, it might have been the point of departure for a bold Frederickian policy: as it was, it remained a half-measure, fatal for the empire as for Prussia, and the imperial ambassador to the Reichstag could be sure of universal agreement when he stated that the king had subscribed to his shame in the instrument of peace.

While the coalition of its opponents was being broken up, France was striving unwaveringly towards the goal which the Revolution had inherited from the kingdom: the possession of the left bank of the Rhine. After the

The Principality

first defeats, the Convention brought in universal conscription. France became one broad armed camp. These troops which were in arms for their Fatherland could safely be left to fight in relaxed lines, without fear of their deserting the flag. The leaders were not obliged anxiously to avoid losses: for there was no lack of reinforcements, at any rate in the beginning. The superiority of the new method of warfare was soon shown in the renewed advance of the French.

The inspired strategy of Napoleon brought about a decision in northern Italy. Threatened by his advance upon Vienna, the Austrian Government consented in 1797 to the cession of the Netherlands, and of the left bank of the Rhine. England carried on the war: Austria was beaten, not conquered. The offensive launched by the second Coalition (1798–1801), in which at the outset Russia also took part, placed the results of the first war in doubt. Yet when Napoleon had returned from his unsuccessful Egyptian enterprise, the French arms were victorious at Marengo and Hohenlinden. In the Peace of Lunéville in 1801, the left bank of the Rhine was formally ceded. A committee of the Reichstag negotiated with the conqueror the matter of compensation for those German princes who suffered territorial losses. But the princes themselves thronged to him 'who held the scales in his hand.' In 1803 the enactment of the Reichstag's Commission was obliged to ratify their unworthy bargaining. Under the name of compensation, Prussia, Hesse-Darmstadt, and the south German States acquired extensive Church lands and many imperial cities. The ecclesiastical principalities, in which the emperor had found his chief prop and stay, disappeared with the exception of that of the Electoral High Chancellor of Mayence. With them the imperial throne lost its support in the empire, while Napoleon created for himself a retinue of considerable secondary States, through which he held Austria as well as northern Germany in check. Thus the power of the conqueror was strengthened by these revolutionary proceedings: but it was also important, for the future union of Germany as a nation, that by far the greater number of the single States should have disappeared.

Napoleon had in all essentials attained the objective of the Bourbons, which the Revolution in turn had made its own. After the emperor Francis I had adopted the

Fatherland

imperial title for the land which he inherited, the victor had himself crowned Emperor of the French, in 1804, and later King of Italy. His empire was to represent the continuation of the dominion which Charlemagne had founded. Yet the idea of world dominion aroused opposition, in forms which, unlike those of the period of the mediaeval empire, needed no long process of time for their development. England, which next to France was the most firmly united national State, was the standard-bearer in this war. Napoleon could only meet the English command of the seas with the massed strength of the European States. For Germany this meant the change from dependence to foreign rule: it was the work of a few years.

In alliance with England and Russia, Austria once again tried her fortunes in battle: Napoleon's strategy triumphed over far superior numbers in the 'Battle of the Three Emperors' at Austerlitz in 1805. By the loss of his entire south German possessions, including the Tyrol, the emperor had to resign even the authority which he had exercised up to that time as sovereign of the Rhenish territories. In addition to their promotion in rank, the south German secondary States acquired considerable gains of territory, not only from the surrendered Austrian districts, but also from the addition of numerous small domains, whose owners—princes, lords, or cities—had up till then been immediately dependent upon the emperor. Thereupon a number of south and west German States declared their complete independence of the emperor (their sovereignty): seceded from the political body of the empire, and in 1806 formed the Confederation of the Rhine: its 'Protector' was Napoleon. The emperor Francis II proclaimed the dissolution of the empire: with this the political bond was broken, which had bound the Germans together in good and ill fortune, since the beginning of German History.

Scarcely a quarter of a year later Napoleon entered Berlin. He had continued to show himself very accommodating in the negotiations regarding compensation (p. 292). At that time in the bishoprics of Münster, Paderborn, Hildesheim, in Eichsfeld and Erfurt, Prussia received five times as much as she had lost on the left bank of the Rhine. Napoleon's object was to gain the north German State to be France's ally. From the other side Russia was suing for an alliance. Yet Frederick William III attempted to remain neutral. The situation became more acute through the outbreak of the war of 1805. In order to force a decision, Napoleon ordered a division of troops to march through Prussian territory. Thereupon the king put his army in readiness, bound himself to armed interposition in favour of the Allies, and forwarded his demands to the Emperor of the French. After the decision had been given at Austerlitz, Napoleon pressed the delegate to accept an alliance, together with the possession of the English Hanover. The king did, indeed, disarm, but did not show himself at all compliant: and thus the tension grew. Encircled by Napoleon's armies, on bad terms with England, Frederick William in the end ordered fresh preparations for war, and sent the emperor a demand, with a time limit, for the evacuation of Germany by French troops. Napoleon replied by advancing his troops farther down the Saale. Again and again Prussia had let slip the suitable moment for intervention. Now she was reaping the fruit of the policy of the Peace of Basle: almost without allies she faced the conqueror, whose strength meantime had enormously increased. On the 14th of October 1806, at Jena and Auerstedt, the Prussians succumbed to the superior leadership and strategy of their opponents: their retreat became a wild flight. Without an attempt at defence, most of the fortresses went over to the enemy. Kolberg, Graudenz, and some Silesian fortresses made a successful resistance, and Danzig held out for a long time: but such loyalty to duty was of rare occurrence. The Government collapsed with the collapse of the army. Officials delivered up the money chests to the victor. Ministers took the oath of allegiance, without waiting for the king's authorization.

On the other side of the Weichsel, Napoleon encountered the Russians, and after his arms had once again decided the day, the two emperors came to an agreement in July 1807, in the Peace of Tilsit. Russia guaranteed her help in the war against England, by taking part in the Continental blockade: she was to hold up all traffic between the Continent and the island kingdom, and thus bring compulsion to bear upon England. In return, Napoleon abandoned Finland to the Tsar, though it had been up till then in the possession of Sweden, and allowed Prussia to remain an independent State: this was more advantageous for Russia than France's immediate neighbourhood. Nevertheless Prussia lost the half of her territory. All her possessions west of the Elbe were joined with Hesse-Cassel, Brunswick, and a part of Hanover to make the kingdom of Westphalia: the former Polish territories from the second and third Partitions came to the King of Saxony under the title of the Grand-Duchy of Warsaw. Danzig became a free port, under French occupation. Nothing definite was at first settled about the amount of war indemnity. When, in the following year, Napoleon needed his troops in Spain, he decreased the garrison which had to be maintained by the country, yet engaged Prussia not to raise the strength of her army to more than 42,000 men, and to make very considerable payments. In barely two years, sums of money and valuables to the amount of far over a milliard were squeezed out of the poor country.

Meantime Napoleon was labouring to exclude England altogether from the Continent. The Spaniards showed the world of what a brave nation was capable in the fight for its freedom. Even the emperor's victories could not break their resistance: and while his best troops were engaged in Spain, Austria struck yet another blow (1809). Count Stadion had been at work here, though without undue ardour, to promote the rising: what would happen to the Danube monarchy if Bohemia, Croatia, and Hungary were to become conscious of their national strength? Nevertheless, in addition to the troops of the line, a militia was called up which was quickly manned with volunteers. Enthusiasm ran high: the most beautiful songs which Austria contributed to the War of Liberation were made at that time. 'Germans! work along with us for your salvation!' cried the commander-in-chief, the Archduke Charles, to the 'German nation.' Such words bore witness to a remarkable change, which was evident also in north Germany in the bold enterprise of Major von Schill, Colonel von Doernberg, and the young Duke of Brunswick. But the time was not yet ripe for the People's Rising. Napoleon, indeed, lost the name of Invincible on the day of Aspern, but his success at Wagram made the Court of Vienna willing to make peace. Austria lost all her possessions on the Adriatic coast, together with Salzburg and the Inn district. The Tyrolese carried on their heroic struggle for some months longer: but their fidelity to an emperor who was making them a sacrifice, and their love for their home-

The Principality

land, had to yield at last to the superior force of Franco-Bavaria.

When Napoleon had suppressed the Austrian rising, his power might be considered to be re-established. Following the papal territories, Holland with the entire North Sea coast of Germany and a strip on the Baltic, were incorporated in the French Empire, which now extended from Lübeck to Rome. Actually, however, Napoleon was compelled to this extension of the immediate sphere of his sovereign authority, by the very fact that his idea of world power could no longer be reconciled with the claims of the dependent countries. His own brother Louis had rejected the Dutch crown, because he did not wish to share the blame of the ruin of Holland's internal economy through the Continental blockade. The national war in Spain was still being carried on, with English support: and the Tsar with growing clearness, and chiefly on economic grounds, refused to carry out the wishes of his ally. But it would not have been possible for the campaign in Russia to become the beginning of the end, if Prussia had not meanwhile undergone a profound change.

The rule of the foreigner was not equally felt as a hardship in all the German countries, nor in every class. As the States of the Confederation of the Rhine became assimilated to the French model, a new chapter began in their political life. The administration was simplified, inroads were made upon the privileged position of the nobility, hereditary vassalage was done away with. Men of the new spirit like Savigny, the jurist, and the philosophers Schelling and Hegel, found the scene of their labours in Bavaria. In this sudden change lay one of the chief reasons for the veneration of Napoleon, which still lingered for a long time amongst the cultured classes. In addition, of course, to the universal consequences of the Continental blockade, the demands which the emperor made upon the military and economic resources of the countries allied to him, became fatally apparent in course of time. From the first the burdens were very much heavier in Prussia. And a feeling of solidarity had grown up in Prussia, which was painfully affected by the parcelling out of the country. Even beyond the black and white frontier-posts, the collapse of the proud State produced a far deeper effect than the dissolution of the empire: out of this experience grew

Fatherland

the knowledge, that Germany could not exist as a civilized nation, if her political independence were destroyed. Many looked for the rehabilitation, no longer of Austria, which in the course of her history had grown ever farther away from Germany, but of the State of Prussia, which had extended its dominion more and more inwards towards Old Germany.

So it came about that on Prussian soil the intellectual world was fused with the world of political reality: from the union of the cultural and political halves of the nation resulted the idea of the German National State.

The intermingling of two worlds became apparent in the fact that the men who accomplished the revival of Prussia were chiefly non-Prussians or 'foreigners': Stein and Hardenberg, Scharnhorst and Gneisenau, Arndt and Niebuhr. The inward development is perhaps most clearly seen in Fichte. The founder of romantic philosophy began as a citizen of the world. The experience of Prussia's collapse changed him into a German belonging to Prussia. In Berlin he delivered his 'Addresses to the German Nation'; the liberation of Germany must begin with Prussia. But Fichte did not in any way stoop to a nationalism strictly limited by the national idea. Prussia must liberate Germany, but Germany must liberate the world: his aim was always freedom and not dominion. His proud, yet modest words on the value of the German character flow from a lofty conception of the task of mankind, and a strong conviction of European solidarity.

The work of Freiherr von Stein was determined by similar ideas. Out of veneration for 'the one and only Frederick,' this scion of an old race, subject immediately to the emperor's government, entered the Prussian administration, and had been serving it in the last place as a minister in the General Directorate, for more than a quarter of a century, when disaster fell upon Prussia. At that time the Governor of Berlin so far forgot his duty as to allow the weapons in the armoury to fall into the hands of the enemy. Stein, on the other hand, rescued all his treasury chests. It was to his energy that the king owed his ability to carry on the war, and to continue to pay the salaries of his officials. Scarcely three months later, he reproached his faithful servant, in a most ungracious letter, with being one of those 'whose manner of dealing

has a most harmful effect upon the cohesion of the whole.'
He believed he had spoken his mind 'in good German.'
In any case, Stein took it to heart, asked for and received
his dismissal. He had demanded that the king's cabinet
councils, which had 'all power and no responsibility,' should
disappear: this was felt by the king, and with justice, to
be an interference with his traditional rights. Was he to
meet with rebellion in his own house, after Napoleon had
driven him into the farthest corner? There was still a
way out. The baron had to go. But in the end he conquered
them both, the King of Prussia and the Emperor of the
French.

In the quiet of his castle at Nassau, he thought over
suitable means of reviving the body politic of Frederick
the Great. The Prussian State had been built from above
downwards: he too had thought to help matters by a
reformation in the highest posts. But the fault lay in the
substructure. For this reason alone the State had collapsed
so helplessly, because for form's sake it had excluded the
new forces which were welling up from the native soil of
the nation. If one could succeed in employing them for
the State, it would become a living entity, as indestructible
as life itself: and a field of virile activity would be thrown
open to those whom their exclusion from political
co-operation had forced aside into the world of pure
thought.

'To bind everyone to the State by conviction, sympathy,
and co-operation in the affairs of the nation, to give the
forces of the nation free play and direct them towards the
common good'—that was the path which Stein struck out.
Stein built from below upwards. The population in town
and country must learn through self-government to cultivate a public spirit; district councils and provincial diets
should be set up on the basis of municipal self-government,
and 'Imperial Diets' vindicate the idea of self-government
under the heads of the State administration. Stein could
not have thought so penetratingly and clearly without the
example in the West; and French influence may be traced
in many details of his plan. But he was revolted by the
purely reasonable and unhistorical character of the Revolution. His sentiment and thought were based upon the
results of historical development. He wished to liberate
the life forces of the past, which were languishing under

Fatherland

the police government of the present, so that they might give shape to the future. For the foundation of his work, therefore, he made use of his experiences with the estate representations, which he had gathered during his time of office as President of the Board and President-General in Westphalia. The fruit of English influences was seen more particularly in the superstructure.

Only a man who was in sympathy with German idealism could have had so keen a sense of organic development. The fact that Stein looked upon co-operation in the Government as a moral duty, is further evidence of the close connection between the two spheres of thought: to him the State was a moral power, whose fate was determined by the moral worth of its citizens, and, as was the case with Fichte, his idea of the State aimed at the idea of the organization of mankind. 'I have only one Fatherland, its name is Germany.' It was an iron word—yet it was a link in an iron chain. As Stein worked for Prussia in order to free Germany, so must Germany arise, not for her own sake, but to serve, in her own way, the Commonwealth of Europe. Far beyond the nineteenth century, which narrowed and restricted the national idea, German idealism can point the present the way into the future, along such lines of thought. The form which Stein gave to his work was naturally conditioned by his time: to him the 'owners' in town and country represented the sole support of the national community: in their 'Diets' he saw the best form of national representation. The form must grow old: the spirit remained alive.

It was Napoleon (certainly not moved by pure benevolence) who recommended the king to recall Stein. Both men agreed to ignore what kept them apart. Finally, an intercepted letter enlightened the French with regard to Stein's ultimate purpose. Nobles and officials, his bitter enemies, now left no stone unturned to effect his removal: not a finger was raised for him at Court. So Stein went for the second time. Napoleon's ban of outlawry drove him from the land of his choice. Yet in a single year (1807–1808) he had laid a new foundation for the Prussian State; its subjects might now become its citizens.

The subject might be bound, the citizen of the State must be free. Therefore Stein's first law gave that liberty to all peasants which was already enjoyed by the majority of the peasants on the royal domains. At the same time, another of the barriers separating the classes in the old State was broken down: henceforth peasant and citizen might acquire the landed property of the nobles, and the nobleman might carry on a citizen's trade. Thus the ground was levelled on which the citizen State was to be built up. Stein was, indeed, able to roof in only a small part of the building, but it was the most important part. His law regulating municipal government realized the idea of self-government for the citizen communities. Inside the towns, the graduated rights of citizenship gave place to a system of equal rights for the community: town deputies, chosen from this community, had to look after the interests of the entire body of citizens. Stein's last measure was the reconstitution of the highest State authorities. The ministers no longer had to administer a division of the country, but one definite department throughout the whole State (Ressort Minister). A president-in-chief stood at the head of a province, and had the oversight of the presidents of the provincial governments.

Hardenberg carried on the work of reform, chiefly by substituting freedom of trade for guild control, and by including the nobles amongst the taxpayers: the Jews were also put on a legal equality with the other citizens. Yet Hardenberg, the man of reason, lacked Stein's gift of linking up his reforms with the actual present, and his perseverance in carrying out his intentions. Hence the opposition, which Stein had already encountered, increased to such a degree that reform was brought to a standstill.

On the other hand, Stein's spirit was actively present in the reconstitution of the army. For this Scharnhorst was responsible, a man who as Arndt says: 'had raised himself from the lowest rank and learnt obedience as he rose, even obedience to poverty. Slim, and even gaunt, he stepped or rather slouched along, unlike a soldier, usually with a forward stoop.' Does it not read like a description of Moltke? At the side of the thinker Scharnhorst, stood Gneisenau the fiery spirit, Boyen the warm-hearted, and many others: all united in the endeavour to create a national army. There were difficulties, both external and internal, to be overcome. In consequence of the treaty with France, universal conscription could not be carried out till after the declaration of war:

meanwhile Scharnhorst had recourse to an ingenious system of increasing the army, without technically running counter to Napoleon's prohibition. By the abolition of recruiting and of corporal punishment, as well as by the participation of the middle class in the filling of officers' posts, army and middle class were drawn closer together. But that was not sufficient. Contempt for the soldiery was so deep-rooted amongst the citizens, that they invariably rose to their feet when a soldier sat down at the same inn table. For this reason when war broke out *chasseurs* divisions,' which drilled and fought by themselves, were formed for the well-to-do and refined. The idea of a national army was more clearly in evidence in the Militia (*Landwehr*), who were allowed to choose their own inferior officers. But the order of general levy of the people (*Landsturm*), which was afterwards altered, affords the deepest insight into the minds of the men who were rebuilding Prussia. If the army is compelled to retreat in its own country, then the homeland must be systematically laid waste, and the population remove elsewhere: towns and castles must be held by the troops till the last possible moment, and then devoted to destruction. So completely had men departed from the Frederickian conception of the citizen, who was to notice nothing, when the nation went to war. Like Government and citizens, army and people were welded together in a common destiny. The word of the poets hallowed the alliance between spirit and State, which came into being with these ordinances: Kleist, whose hatred of Napoleon had given rise to the verses *Germania to her Children*, and to the wildest scenes in his drama *Hermannsschlacht*, conducted his Prince of Homburg through good fortune and self-humiliation to moral action. And even while Jahn, 'the father of gymnastics,' steeled the limbs of the young men, he had a moral object in view.

But the plans which the energetic formulated, and the inspired already saw at work, were no more than poetry, or an airy nothing, for the king of the Prussian State. It was not given him to have a perception of spiritual forces. He saw only the 'actual' political conditions: Prussia enslaved, Austria overthrown, Russia insecure, and he yielded to Napoleon, when he demanded an alliance in order 'to conquer London in Moscow.' All his life he

The Principality

privately disliked old Yorck, who at that time, by arrangement with Russia, preserved his corps for the Fatherland.

In these difficult years, Gneisenau and others looked abroad for their field of action, despairing of Prussia, and full of hatred towards the irresolute princes. Stein had long recognized as an error the idea that Germany must be saved through Germany. He, and those who held his views, hoped for the fall of Napoleon by means of Russia and England, even though the German royal families might disappear in the process, and Germany's fate depend once more upon strangers.

Once again Stein gave the impetus towards a decision: he brought the Tsar to the point of resolving to continue the war for the liberation of Europe. Russian troops advanced into east Prussia. Stein took over its administration. Under his leadership, the province took the important step from 'blind obedience' to a national rising. The estates organized a militia, and armed it out of their own funds. Thus, to quote a saying of Boyen, the spirit which animated the Prussian people was manifest to friend and foe. But the king clung to the 'actual.' He too realized that it was necessary to take up arms: he gave the needful orders from Breslau. Were they to be turned against Russia, or against France? Volunteers and gifts streamed in, the generals gave their orders and asked no questions. The flood was rising. Would it submerge the throne? At last the king trusted himself to the waves: then followed in rapid succession the alliance with Russia, the declaration of war, the appeal 'To my People.'

Everyone knew that a hard struggle lay ahead. Napoleon had attained numerical superiority by a new levy. Saxony fell to him. But his victories at Grossgörschen and Bautzen were bought with such a heavy sacrifice, that he could not make up his mind to crush the beaten enemy. The truce brought a revulsion: Austria and Sweden took part in the hostilities, and arrangements for subsidies were made with England. In the autumn campaign, they were able to encircle the emperor with three armies. The French offensive against Berlin was shattered at Grossbeeren and Dennewitz, and Napoleon's advance upon Silesia at the Battle of Katzbach. Even his victory at Dresden lost its significance, by the defeat at Kulm and Nollendorf of the marshal who was sent in pursuit of the retreating army.

Fatherland

Then the ring was drawn closer. Blücher's march to the right—Gneisenau planned the movement, and Yorck at Wartenburg won the Elbe crossing—obliged Napoleon to retreat from his position at Dresden. At the Battle of Leipzig his command of Germany was broken.

The allied troops were able to penetrate France in greatly superior force. Austria's peace overtures delayed the invasion, and, together with the unsuitable measures taken by the Austrian commander of the main body of the army, retarded the advance upon Paris. Once again Blücher's march to the right brought about a decision. His victory at Laon prepared the way for the general attack upon Paris, which Napoleon was no longer able to hold in check by a threat to the Allies' communications in the rear. On the 31st March, 1814, the Allies entered the enemy capital. The Prussian corps, which had done most of the work, were excluded by their king from the military ceremony. 'Look badly—dirty fellows!' It was a fit prelude to what came after.

The princes owed the victory to a national rising. Yet it was not the peoples' wishes, but the Governments' striving after power, which determined the reconstruction of Europe. A new war almost broke out in the course of the Vienna Congress. Napoleon thought to make use of the dissensions between Russia and Prussia on the one hand, and between England and Austria on the other, to win back his mastery. Once more Prussian troops shed their blood at Ligny in 1815, and English and German troops at Waterloo. In the second Peace of Paris, Landau and Saarbrücken, outside the frontiers of 1792, were given back to Germany, but Alsace was still withheld. The diplomats had their hands full with the *arrondissement* and contiguity of their States—or, in plain English, with their rounding off and coherent formation. In addition to the Swedish portion of western Pomerania, Prussia received the northern half of Saxony, with large districts in Westphalia and the Rhineland. Thus the defence of the western frontier country fell to the north German State. Austria, on the other hand, renounced altogether her position on the Rhine, extended her dominion in Italy, and henceforth developed still more definitely into a 'Danube State.' The bulk of Poland was united to Russia, under one head: in this way the Russian Empire extended its influence far towards the West. England gained valuable colonial possessions, and also, after the overthrow of her troublesome enemy on the Continent, had no longer a rival to fear at sea.

The same forces which had prescribed the partition of Germany, determined the shaping of her Constitution. The efforts of the foreign allies to perpetuate Germany's divisions were backed by the princes, who refused to sacrifice the smallest fraction of their sovereignty. Thus instead of a united empire, the 'German Confederation' came into being. As though the passing of resolutions had not been sufficiently formal already—important resolutions requiring the unanimous consent of the deputies at the Confederation Diet—the Confederation was now thrown completely upon the good will of its members for the carrying out of its decrees. Only if the resolution were promulgated as a law of the land by the sovereign of the Confederation, was it binding upon the subjects: only if each member of the Confederation called up his troops, did the Confederation army assemble. In addition, the princes possessed the right of embassy and alliance. Their sovereignty could not have been more admirably safeguarded. The Confederation was already dependent upon the foreign, through the fact that the kings of the Netherlands, Denmark, and England belonged to it as lords of German soil. Yet as a matter of caution, the constitution of the Confederation was placed under the guarantee of the European Powers. And this Confederation was to ensure the internal and external security of Germany!

The work of the Congress of Vienna was a mockery of the experiences through which the peoples and their rulers had just passed. The absolute State tore up the covenant with the spirit, which had been hallowed by so great a sacrifice of life.

FOURTH BOOK

THE CITIZENS AND THEIR EMPIRE
From 1800 to the Present Day

PREFACE TO THE FOURTH BOOK

WHEN Napoleon's empire fell into ruins, it liberated the forces of the peoples of middle and southern Europe. Freedom for the citizen and unity for the nation, were the objects for which they strove henceforth, in their conflict with sovereign authority and foreign rule. After the South American States had thrown off the government of Spain about the year 1820, Greece won her independence —and was followed in 1831 by Belgium. In 1848 the fight for the Constitution in France gave the signal for the German Revolution. It did actually produce a constitutional limitation of the sovereign power in Prussia, and for a time also in Austria, but not the unity which was desired.

The alliance between the various Governments, which was intended to ensure the partition of power established in the Napoleonic period, had been dissolved during the storms of these decades. This enabled France to rise once again to a position of importance. Napoleon III helped the Italians to attain their national unity, which was accomplished in 1861, and in 1866, in the hope of gaining territory, he permitted the struggle between Prussia and Austria. In the war with France, Bismarck created the German Empire in 1871 in the form of a States Union under the leadership of Prussia. With this, a provisional conclusion was reached in the reshaping of Europe upon the basis of nationality. Bismarck's policy of alliances ensured the permanency of his creation, and the peace of the world.

Within the States men were still working for freedom. The middle classes, who were the first to feel the benefit of the advance in technical science, were still the supporters of the movement. Meantime, the evolution of capitalism was producing fresh tension, which transformed the conditions within and between the States. While the fourth estate, as well as the middle class, were pressing their demands, domestic economy was becoming more and more the decisive factor in the relations between the Powers. About the turn of the century, preparations were being made for new alliances between the Great Powers: it was no longer Germany, but England, the greatest colonial Power, which turned the scale. The tension between the great allied Powers gave way in the World War.

The Citizens and their Empire

In the reconstruction of Europe after the war, a great number of new national States were created by the victors; in this process the geographical and historical conditions of the peoples were so disregarded, that the peace of the Continent is to the highest degree endangered. On the other hand, the experiences of the war have strengthened the idea of the community of nations. Conditions within the States have in part developed in a sense contrary to the idea of national freedom; to-day, the East is governed by one class, and southern Europe by one man. But when the German people abolished sovereign power, they removed the greatest obstacles to the further centralization of the empire, and placed the authority of the State in the hands of its citizens. On this foundation they hope to build up a new national community, and to make it respected amongst the nations.

FIRST PART

TOWARDS FREEDOM AND UNITY

STEIN and Scharnhorst had laboured for a German Fatherland, and for it the soldiers of the 'Holy War' had gone
to their death. The experiences of the Vienna Congress
were not needed to open men's eyes to the fact that the
great German Fatherland could be founded only upon the
common responsibility of every member of the nation. He
who looked for one complete Germany, must strive for the
liberty of its citizens: he who hearkened to the 'enticing
silver tones' of Western freedom, and did not wish to be
bound within any narrower sphere, realized the necessity
of confining the free play of forces within a wide but rigid
circle; the man of liberal sympathies must demand a strong
national unity. Thus, from the first day, national and
liberal aspirations worked hand in hand.

The Germans had waged a war of liberation, but not
a war of freedom: the work of the diplomats in Vienna
left no doubt on this score. Nevertheless, the Governments
were forced to make some concessions to the spirit of the
age. In the Prussian law of 1814 relating to military service,
universal liability to service, together with the militia, were
preserved by Boyen for modern times; in universal liability
to service, Prussia alone of the European States maintained 'the most democratic of all institutions,' which,
one must admit, was not fated to develop on democratic
lines. Then, when the return of Napoleon called for new
sacrifices, the Prussian king brought himself to promise
to summon 'without loss of time' a commission, whose
task was to create a representation of the people, and to
devise a charter of the Constitution. On the other hand,
a professor of Berlin University dared, only a few weeks
after Waterloo, to publish a paper, which arraigned Freiherr
von Stein and other heroes of the great age as seducers
of the people. Gneisenau gave in his resignation no later
than the following year. But Hardenberg and even Boyen
retained their leading posts: Arndt was given a professorship at Bonn. Jahn exercised his gymnasts in greater
numbers than ever on the Hasenheide near Berlin. Charles
Augustus of Weimar was the first German prince to give

The Citizens and their Empire

his little country a constitution in 1816: the princes of south Germany followed suit: they saw rightly that a national representation of the people was the best means of welding together the territories which they had gained a few years before, with their old possessions.

Surely Lützow's *chasseurs*, who had returned to their lecture rooms, would there cultivate 'the young green crops' in their own fashion? At the universities the clubs formed by students from the various countries of Germany presented an image of her disintegration, but now the individualism of the separate countries was to be merged in a higher unity. The German Students' Association, formed in Jena in 1815, was the fruit of this endeavour. The students chose 'Honour, Liberty, and Fatherland' for their motto, and for colours the black and red of the uniform worn by Lützow's *chasseurs*, with gold facings. Thus the colours black, red, and gold came into German history: a few years later they were already looked upon as the old colours of the empire. In 1817, some hundreds of students from the whole of Germany united at the Wartburg festival to commemorate the tercentenary of the Reformation, and the fourth anniversary of the Battle of Leipzig. They celebrated German unity: they spoke of the tasks which lay before the student: they went to church with the militia, and in the evening a few unpopular papers, including the work of the libellous Berlin professor, were cast into a bonfire, together with a corset such as was worn by the Uhlans, a pigtail, and a corporal's cane. This was not to be misunderstood. Two years later a student named Sand murdered the well-known writer Kotzebue, who passed among the students for a Russian spy. His deed was intended to throw open the path of German liberty, but it only provided the Governments with an excuse for harsh laws, which aimed at putting an end to the unwelcome movement.

Here and there the Governments had met the wish for a constitution, as had been provided for in the Act of Confederation. But this Act recognized no German nation, much less a German unity. Those who strove for them, were attacking not only the basic law of the Confederation, but the foundation of sovereignty. One must support the other. The foreign Governments also, which had in a sense been made guarantors of the German situation, could wish

Towards Freedom and Unity

for nothing better than the maintenance of existing conditions. As early as 1815, the Tsar, Alexander I, with the Emperor of Austria and the Prussian King, had founded the Holy Alliance. In it, the rulers, calling God to witness, had sworn to look upon themselves 'as fathers of families in relation to their subjects.' As fathers of families? Then the rod was never far away, to bring undutiful subjects to reason in case of need. Every Government in Europe could sign this treaty, and did sign it: though England, indeed, held aloof. But the vain Tsar was not the man able permanently to lay down the law for the Continent. In his stead, the leader of Austrian politics was for a generation the oracle of all who were perturbed by the Liberal movement.

Metternich was far too wise a man to believe that he had nothing to do but to stifle the forces of agitation. But it seemed to him that a satisfactory conclusion could only be reached if these were firmly united with the forces of conservatism. Throughout two decades, a storm of subversion had raged over Europe: all Governments must now agree in the effort to strengthen the powers of conservatism. In any case, the Austrian State seemed to be best served by maintaining the existing order; to comply with the national desires of the peoples united in it would have meant the end of the Danube monarchy. But Metternich did not think only, perhaps he did not even think first, of Austria; he thought of Europe. The European balance of the five Great Powers had been restored: France in the west, Russia in the east, of the Continent; between them central Europe, in the form of a confederation, to which sufficient stability was ensured through the cohesion of Austria and Prussia. The second step must also be successful through the united efforts of the Great Powers: the restoration of a balance of estates within the States. No one who held this view could look upon the State as a living entity. As a matter of fact, Metternich, like Frederick the Great and Joseph II, was much more inclined to regard the State as an ingenious machine. But he had adopted from the world of thought of the eighteenth century, not only its intellectual sophistry, but also the sentiment of European solidarity, which at the period of national movements was thrust more and more into the background.

It is a fact that his sentiment of solidarity applied only

to the political powers, and not to the peoples: indeed, it was to do battle with the Liberal aspirations that he had summoned the Governments. It was no wonder that the majority readily answered the call. Then followed conferences between ministers, resolutions of the Diet of the German Confederation against 'revolutionary intrigues': dissolution of the Students' Association: prohibition of their colours: supervision of the universities: censorship of the Press and of publications: the institution of a central commission of investigation at Mayence. Then began one of the most mournful chapters in German history: the persecution of men of liberal and national sympathies, who were branded as demagogues or seducers of the people. The Commission of Mayence as the conclusion of its inquiries established 'not actually certain deeds,' but 'attempts, preparations, and introductions.' This sufficed, however, to condemn a doctor to fifteen years' imprisonment, a teacher to nineteen, and very many others to severe penalties.

Jahn was arrested at his child's sick-bed, and put in prison. It was in vain that his examination revealed the invalidity of the accusation. He was carried from fortress to fortress, and finally 'permitted' to take up his abode in little places, where he was cut off from intercourse with young men and from interchange of ideas. There he became a quiet man.

Arndt did, indeed, retain his professorship, but was not allowed to give any lectures. Görres fled before the persecution, and buried himself in the manuscripts of the Strasburg library. William von Humboldt, Boyen, and Grolman followed Gneisenau's example and resigned their posts.

The Prussian Government would scarcely have shown itself so zealous, if it had simply been following Metternich's orders. The reason lay deeper. After the hurricane of war was past, the nobles were once more advancing the pretensions which they derived from their union with the Crown. It was, indeed, impossible to repeal Stein's law for the liberation of the peasants: but limits were set to its effects. It was small gain to the peasant of a landed proprietor to be allowed to give up his situation. What he needed was freedom from forced service, and the free ownership of land. Hardenberg had tried in vain to solve the difficult problem. Now it was decided—to the satisfaction of the lord of the manor. Only the occupants of the larger peasant holdings, and they only by special request, and not by virtue of a general order, were given free possession, if they surrendered from a third to a half of their ground to the lord of the manor. It was easy for the lord to make up for what he lost by this regulation. By the surrender of the land, he added to the property which was his without restriction: after the peasants were no longer protected by the prohibition of the sale of their farms, the lord could add to his possessions, by purchase, as much peasant land as he liked; thus there was no adequate protection for the peasants, and unless a new agreement were entered into, he even retained the services of the small peasants, in addition to the right of jurisdiction and the power of police. On this basis, it was possible later on to develop landed property on a large scale to great economic advantage.

There was now no more question of giving the country communities self-government, as Stein understood it, than there was of the Constitution promised by the word of the king.

In 1823 provincial diets were organized, of course with a strong preponderance of landowners, and without publicity of discussion; they were to represent the various estates, divided up according to districts. It was Stein himself who had recommended the restoration of the estates: yet his plan was completely distorted by the omission of its crowning measure, i.e. the setting-up of a parliament representing the estates of the whole kingdom. Hardenberg also proposed to develop national diets from the provincial diets. But this was negatived by Frederick William III. As a matter of fact, a Government in league with the nobility, whose first object was the defence of monarchical authority against the attacks of public opinion, could promote no development which made the monarchy dependent upon national representation.

And the reaction upon the German question had to be taken into account. There was no need for the Governments to be agitated, if hard words were spoken against the Confederation in the parliaments of southern Germany. On the other hand, if a national representation should gain influence in Prussia, then the weights which maintained

The Citizens and their Empire

the balance of the Confederation would be disturbed. So the Government had good reason for its attitude. But it was fatal for Germany's future, that the old dissension between south and north was nourished by the aversion of the South German Liberals for the absolute government of Prussia.

Perhaps these disillusionments were not needed to check the impetus of the War of Liberation. Economic anxieties were weighing upon the entire population. Because the war debts were a painful burden upon the husbandry of the States, there was no means of alleviating the paralysis of economic life, which set in immediately after the war. It is true that a succession of good harvests followed upon two years of famine; but England and other States, which during the years of the restriction of sea trade had extended the area of land which they held under cultivation, now closed their markets to the importation of foodstuffs. The prices of agricultural produce soon fell so low that many farmers were obliged to give up their farms. By far the greater part of the population—in Prussia, four-fifths— still lived by agriculture; hence the agrarian crisis had a devastating effect upon trade and commerce. Added to this, the English manufacturers, who had accumulated reserves during the Continental blockade, now, when peace was concluded, threw their goods upon the market at ruinously low prices. Under these circumstances, only a few of those industries were able to maintain themselves, which at the time of the blockade had in some degree assimilated their methods of trade to those of England. The many customs barriers, the variations in the standard of the different German·States, and the lack of means of communication, contributed further to check the spirit of enterprise.

Oppressed by economic anxieties, excluded in large districts of Germany from all participation in the life of the State, supervised with suspicion by the Governments, the German citizen sank back into the narrow round of Philistine existence. If this failed to satisfy him, he sought consolation in the realm of the spirit. For a third genera- tion, the whole force of German genius was confined within the limits of scholarly and artistic creation. If their ideas no longer took quite so lofty a flight as in the days of classic Humanism and early Romanticism, yet the fullness of their aspiration, and the growing share taken in it by men of culture, might make amends for this shortcoming.

For the last time, the character of the age found fixed forms in the style of the *Biedermeier*: rectilineal and somewhat stiff, sparing of decorative accessories, yet comfortable and pleasing, it suited the plain condition of the time.

Three of the greatest men from the great years of German idealism, brought their life-work to an end in this changed world. Goethe completed his *Faust*, the 'chief business' of his old age, Beethoven created the *Ninth Symphony*, and Hegel, the last system of German philosophy. As Hegel's work acted as a link between the systems of Fichte and Schelling, the period as a whole owed its character to the fact that the seed of Romanticism was now bearing its full fruit. Uhland in his ballads glorified the virtues of olden times. The murmur of the German forest sounds through Eichendorff's verses. The harshness of the Westphalian soil forms a background to the works of Annette von Droste-Hulshoff: Mörike's poems reflect the charm of the Swabian hill country. As late as the middle of the century, Scheffel in *Ekkehart* sketched a colourful picture of the early Middle Ages in Germany. The painter, Peter Cornelius, under Dürer's influence, produced Biblical and old-German designs. Alfred Rethel chose his subjects from German history, and in the year of Revolution he, like Holbein, drew a Dance of Death. Moritz von Schwind became the painter of the German fairy tale. Ludwig Richter in his drawings immortalized the landscapes of Germany, and the life of her people and children. Spitzweg delineated the contemplative country town. At the same time, popular sentiment found expression in the work of the musicians: Weber, Schubert, and Schumann belong to the first half of the century. Attempts to revive the Gothic in architecture and sculpture were only of short duration, but the forms of classic art continued to exercise an influence long after the Wars of Liberation. In Berlin, the work of Schinkel can be seen in the museum; of Schadow, in the statues of Zieten and Blücher, and of Rauch, in the marble statue of Queen Louisa. Under the art-loving king, Lewis I, the neo-classic buildings of Klenze gave Munich its character.

The idea of evolution, which Romanticism had raised to a place of honour, proved extraordinarily fruitful in the

The Citizens and their Empire

sciences. The research into the origin of language, under-taken by Jacob Grimm, of poetry by Uhland and Gervinus, and of law by Savigny, pointed the way in other depart-ments. And Leopold von Ranke was already liberating the science of history from the tyranny of the purely philo-sophical point of view. Himself penetrating with an artist's insight, into the sources of growth, he was able in a masterly fashion to point historical research the way to a lofty goal; 'to recognize how it has really been.' The mind of the nation could find edification in the picture drawn by Raumer in the 'twenties, of the greatness of Germany at the time of the Hohenstaufen. Yet Roman-ticism, with its leaning towards the social and intellectual conditions of the Middle Ages, did not conduce to the growth of a Liberal sentiment. Many historians, teachers of public law, and philosophers owed the intellectual weapons which they employed in the war against the dreaded Revolution to their absorption in the past. Once more State and Church drew most closely together. While the mental sciences were in this position, they could scarcely any longer be expected to bring about a decision in the political war. Hegel had taught that all which is, is reasonable. Yet not only the champions of the existing order, but also the founder of social democracy in Germany borrowed his weapons from Hegel's system. The motives, which roused the sluggish stream of life to a more rapid flow, grew out of the cares and pains of every day.

In spite of economic pressure, the population of Germany increased by a fifth, during the fifteen years following the conclusion of peace. Many Governments could find no other expedient than that of putting obstacles in the way of marriage; yet the Prussian authorities succeeded in offering the possibility of work even to the population which had thus increased. In the higher ranks of Prussian officials, the proud tradition of Frederick's time blended with the classical and romantic culture which was fostered at the universities. In these circles the idea of German unity, together with the Liberal demands, were met as a rule with decided refusal. They desired to work for Prussia, on the lines of a glorious tradition, and to the best of their ability, without submitting to the tutelage of the people's representatives. The Prussian officials were of one mind in their lofty conception of their office, whether they were

Towards Freedom and Unity

living in the ideas of the Enlightenment like Schoen, who was a Kant scholar and Stein's fellow worker, and became the High-President of East and West Prussia: or whether, like Vincke, the indefatigable High-President of Westphalia, they had received their actual impulse from the political and economic conditions of England.

The work of the Finance Ministry was opening the way to decisive reforms. In 1818 the Prussian customs law repealed the internal duties, and transformed Prussia into a Customs Union, whose intercourse with foreign countries was no longer regulated by prohibition of import and export, but by the height of the tariff. Partly from considerations of principle, partly out of regard for the ruling party of landed proprietors and for the foreigner (England and Russia), the duties as a whole were on a very small scale, allowing Prussia to pass for a free-trade country. Although at the time and frequently afterwards, this regulation was contested on many points, especially by the industrial producers, yet the law fulfilled the expectations of its authors. Because the custom-houses in the interior were disused, and only the frontiers required watching, considerable sums were saved to the State. At the same time the import duties on colonial wares and other highly taxed products brought in a good revenue. But, above all, the revenue from the tax levied for carrying on a trade rose considerably after a few years: and gave indisputable proof of an increase in native production, at least with regard to the goods most in demand.

In the levying of transit duties, the financial politicians of Prussia had furnished themselves with a tool whereby they could compel other German States to come to terms with them. Here they met with much opposition. Contractors in south Germany feared the competition of certain more highly developed Prussian industries. The princes trembled for their independence: the South German Liberals detested the connection with a State governed by absolute monarchy. This opposition was welcomed in England. In later years, when negotiations in Carlsruhe came to nothing, the English ambassador made so little secret of his satisfaction that he invited all the mandatories of the Governments to his hotel for the evening: the gentlemen had sufficient tact to decline unanimously. After several of the small States, whose territory was encircled by that of

Prussia, had allied themselves with their powerful neighbour, south Germany and then central Germany attempted separate unions. It was in vain. The end came in 1835, with the German Customs Union under Prussia's leadership, from which certain only of the North German States, including Hanover and the Hanse towns, still held aloof. The advantages were obvious; the entire Customs Union had fewer frontier miles to watch than Prussia, after the proclamation of her customs law, while production for the German home market was visibly increasing.

When business had become in some degree attuned to the new conditions, the construction of railways was taken in hand. Before long, so much railway plant was being imported from England, that the imports of the Customs Union exceeded the exports. New stimulus was given to trade and production by the railway traffic, through the speeding-up and cheapening of the exchange of goods: the rise of wholesale business, of large-scale industry, and of banking, first became possible through the increasing conveyance of goods in bulk over long distances. It is true that German trade at that time was still immensely behind the English. Manual labour predominated, and even in the factories, steam power was at first employed on a very small scale. The change came about slowly. When Saxony, the home of the spinning industry, entered the Customs Union, scarcely more than 6 per cent. of her spindles were worked by steam, and these only in case of the failure of water power. Ten years later, the English were still producing twenty times as much yarn as the Germans, reckoned per head of the population. In 1835, the year of the first German railway, Frederick Krupp set up the first steam engine in his factory, which employed at that time some sixty workmen: ten years later, the number of employees had not yet been doubled.

This progress was much too slow for a hothead, like the Swabian Frederick List. In a memorial to the Diet of the German Confederation, fifteen years before the Customs Union was set up, he had demanded the abolition of all internal dues: he was supported by some thousands of south and central German manufacturers and merchants. But the time was not yet ripe. List's activities, in the Chamber of Wurtemberg, soon landed him in the State prison on the Asperg. When he was allowed to choose

Towards Freedom and Unity

whether he would serve his time or emigrate, he decided to go to America. After a few years, he returned and was employed as American Consul in Leipzig: his work as 'the unpaid advocate of Germany' was more important. He strove indefatigably to develop the economic unity, which in all essentials had been already attained, into a unity of traffic, by the creation of a connected net of railroads. The national industry fostered by these means was to be developed by protective tariffs, till it was able to enter into free competition with the English industry. Liberty was the beginning and the end of his thinking: but even his object was to be attained through State compulsion. The very title of his chief work is indicative: he called it *The National System of Political Economy*. His ideas first began to be realized when Imperial Unity, the political object for which he had striven along the lines of domestic economy, had been attained. His life was broken on the opposition of his contemporaries. But he bequeathed to posterity the courageous resolve 'to believe in a great national future, and in this faith to march forwards.'

While industrial evolution was long hampered by the fact that science, in spite of ingenious but isolated discoveries, had not yet come systematically to its assistance, the Hanoverian Thaer had already founded a science of agriculture. In the 'thirties, when ground-rent rose through the revival of all branches of business, it began to pay the great landed proprietors to improve their management. The general endeavour was to enhance the yield of the ground by the rotation of crops, and by continuous stall-feeding to improve the results of cattle-breeding: artificial manure came into use through the researches of Liebig, a Hesse chemist. At the same time the cultivation of sugar-beet opened a promising branch of industry for certain districts. The improvements were gradually adopted by the smaller agriculturists, especially in districts such as Hanover, where peasants' property had to a greater extent been already rounded off by State action, such as the joining together, and the dividing up, of the common ground.

Judged by the standards of the present day, the economic progress was small enough: but it showed the beginning of an advance, which continued almost without interruption till after the foundation of the empire, and at the same time the commencement of the social reconstruction,

The Citizens and their Empire

which accompanied this advance. Many little lives in country and town were torn up by the roots, through the dissolution of the old economic conditions. From these classes was recruited the army of workmen, which the manufacturers took into their employ. This frequently took place under the most unfavourable conditions: but at that time the development of proletarian class consciousness was not yet possible. The employers raised themselves from the mass of the middle classes, less by the increase of their numbers, than by the growth of their trade. With them the consciousness of economic advancement was most directly translated into political demands: it was these classes, therefore, which provided prominent leaders for the political agitation of the "forties."

There were other signs which pointed to the awakening of the sense of actuality, which was steadily to gain strength in the following decades. The beginnings of a great work of Christian charity arose out of a deepened insight into social needs. Wichern began the work of the Home Mission with the founding of the Rough House (*Rauhes Haus*) in Hamburg: at that time also Pastor Fliedner laid the foundations of the Deaconess Institutes. The work of the Roman Catholic Kolping for the Workmen's Associations followed somewhat later. Such activities could not, indeed, prevent the alienation from Church dogma, which was spreading amongst the cultured classes, from penetrating to the masses. Fresh attempts were made, under the influence of the idea of evolution, to give religious conceptions a reasonable explanation. Beginning with D. F. Strauss, whose *Life of Jesus* was published in 1835, materialism developed through Bauer and Feuerbach in sharp antithesis to Christian teaching, and philosophic idealism. It looks upon faith solely as an embodiment of man's desires, and sees nothing actual in life beyond what can be grasped by the senses. If religious ideas were no longer understood as the visions of the individual man, but as the embodiment of the economic aspirations of society, then that step had been taken towards religious materialism which Karl Marx introduced into his system.

In political life the trend to actuality, which was becoming evident in every department, was expressed in the attempt to transform Liberal thoughts into deeds. At the same time that the persecution of demagogues was begun

Towards Freedom and Unity

in Germany, the risings against the restored royal houses in Italy and Spain were suppressed by the Governments of the Holy Alliance. But the revolt of the Greeks against Turkish rule (1821–1829) actually broke up the structure of the Alliance. No one knew better than Metternich and the Tsar that this movement was calculated to stir up the 'Liberal conflagration,' yet it would have been unthinkable to help Turkey against her Christian subjects. After a long struggle the Greeks gained their independence. In the end the allied Powers had the disappointment of knowing that Liberal aspirations were victorious in one of the countries of the Alliance. In July 1830 the rule of the restored Bourbons was overthrown: Louis Philippe of Orleans, a cousin of the exiled king, took over the government.

In sympathy with the movements abroad, everything that was labouring in Germany for the same ideals drew closer together. Because the Governments put obstacles in the way of working for the cause of the Fatherland, the pent-up national feeling found relief in a boundless enthusiasm for Greek liberty:

> Up then, from slavery's chains,
> From dungeons dank and bare,
> On wings of liberty
> Up, into life's free air!

In such verses Wilhelm Müller embodied the spirit of the Greek War of Liberation: but they might equally well have been sung to the Germans, and the Governments had good reason for suppressing such 'Greek Songs.' Then when news came of the battle for freedom in Paris, it gave rise to greater unrest. The storm broke out in several States of northern Germany, which had revived with some alterations the mediaeval system of estates. Saxony, Hanover, the Electorate of Hesse, and Brunswick were obliged to establish Constitutions: at the same time the Duke of Brunswick was expelled from the country, and the Elector of Hesse, who was only slightly better than he, forced to make over the government to his son. Prussia as a whole was spared. But in south Germany, the Liberal leaders began to work with vigour for a reorganization of Germany. In this connection, the idea was already being expressed that the unity of Germany could only be attained under Prussia's leadership. But men laboured first, to secure the freedom of the subject in the individual States, in order to prepare the way for German unity. In this struggle for liberty, they were conscious of their kinship with the Poles, as they had formerly felt akin to the Greeks, and, indeed, to the oppressed throughout the whole world. While thirty-four princely coat-of-arms, the tokens of 'separation, restraint, and oppression' were still set up in Germany, men's thoughts flew to the day 'when a German Fatherland shall arise which will embrace all its citizens with the same love and the same protection, when noble Germania will bring to all the warring nations the law of peace for which she herself has prayed.'

At the Festival of Hambach in 1832, the democrat Siebenpfeiffer, a native of Baden, spoke of such dreams to tens of thousands, who had decked themselves with the black, red, and gold colours. 'Hail to the nation which breaks its chains, and takes with us the oath of the covenant of freedom! Hail to the Fatherland! to the self-government of the people; to the confederation of the nations!' Another speaker attacked the French hankerings after the left bank of the Rhine: but he too, ended with a cheer for the United Republics of Germany and a confederated republican Europe.

It did not need the disorder provoked by a few dozen students, in their storming of the main guard at Frankfort, to set in motion the Diet of the German Confederation. The pressure of persecution fell even more heavily than before upon the German countries.

But there was no return of the graveyard peace of the 'twenties. For a time, the poets of Young Germany directed their attack against 'all unnaturalness and oppression.' All their writings were prohibited by the Confederation Diet. Yet it was not so easy to silence Boerne and Heine, who continued to write in Paris: and events in Germany were even more successful in shaking up the drowsy subjects, and making them occupy themselves with politics. A conflict between Church and State broke out in Prussia over the question of mixed marriages. In the same year of 1837, when this quarrel reached its height with the imprisonment of the Archbishop of Cologne, events in Hanover aroused excitement in still wider circles. The connection between England and Hanover was broken with the death of William IV: in England his niece Victoria

Towards Freedom and Unity

succeeded him, and in Hanover, following the law of German Succession, Duke Ernest August of Cumberland. His first act of administration was the repeal of the Constitution of 1833. Seven Göttingen professors entered a protest, amongst them Weber the physicist, who in conjunction with Gauss had made the first electric telegraph, the brothers Grimm, and the historians Dahlmann and Gervinus. All were relieved of their offices, and some banished from the country. Though the Prussian Minister for the Interior might declare that 'it was not becoming for subjects to judge the actions of the Head of the State by the measure of their restricted understanding,' his pedantic words could only heighten the respect which was felt for the seven just men. Their action, as Dahlmann said, poured the fresh life-blood of united patriotic conviction into the veins.

Singers, gymnasts and riflemen, scholars of natural sciences and of languages, came together to discuss the affairs of their common Fatherland, in addition to those of their association and profession. The assemblies of the Liberal deputies of south Germany, in which politicians from north Germany also took part, were of immediate political importance. Nothing of all this became known in public. Yet the doings of the Chamber and other political events were now followed with the same passionate sympathy by the educated classes, which they had formerly given to a new play or a new book. The universal excitement found expression in the songs of the poets. Never again has political passion in Germany borne such noble fruit as in the poetry of the 'forties. Beside Hoffmann von Fallersleben, a young generation was growing up who could express their bitter anger over the illiberality, national dismemberment, and social misery of the present no less powerfully, than their longing for a brighter future. Dingelstedt poured scorn upon the splendour of the princes, while Herwegh declared hate to be the sacred duty of the living, the hate which breaks fetters:

> Germans! trust the men who see,
> Iron will our present be,
> Clashing steel our future part:
> Now Black Death is all our earning,
> Fairy Gold to dust returning:
> And our Red, a bleeding heart.

The Citizens and their Empire

With his *Confession of Faith*, Freiligrath took his place in the ranks of the patriotic army. Not all that flowed at that time from their hearts' desire, has preserved its power and freshness throughout the decades: but it was with justice that these men boasted: 'We sow the seeds of future deeds.'

For the first time for many years, the danger and misery of one was again felt to be the danger and misery of all. Internal difficulties had arisen for the French Government through the failure of their plans in the East. In order to overcome them, the French Ministry in the year 1840 seemed inclined to venture an advance upon the Rhine. Then indignation flamed up throughout Germany. The Rhine song of the Rhinelander Nicholas Becker was sung everywhere: Max Schneckenburger, a citizen of Wurtemberg, composed *Die Wacht am Rhein* (The Watch on the Rhine), and somewhat later a native of Thuringia wrote the melody for the song. When a conflagration laid a great part of Hamburg in ashes, public spirit made itself felt once more with unsuspected force: the flow of gifts from every district of Germany seemed like a promise of better days for the Fatherland.

> And so let us, hand in hand,
> Heart in heart entwine:
> Native town and native land
> Be our common sign,
> So may Hamburg's fiery blaze
> Be the dawn of freedom's days.

In the midst of these events, in the year 1841, appeared Hoffmann von Fallersleben's *Song of Germany*. Thus it was not only in a vision of distant days that the poet saw Germany fraternally united for offence and defence: but the vision had yet to become an everyday reality. And the exile was bitterly to experience in his own person, how great was still the lack of justice and liberty.

In these years of growing political agitation, Frederick William IV (1840–1861) succeeded his father in the government. He also was known to cherish the vision of a united empire. Very soon it became common knowledge that he was opening the prison doors for the unfortunate victims of political oppression, and was nobly doing honour to many of the suspected. Yet it was in vain that the

Towards Freedom and Unity

Coronation Diet in Königsberg urged the fulfilment of the royal promise of 1815. In vain did the old High-President von Schoen give warning in a memorial: 'If we do not use the time we have, and avail ourselves of the good which is in it, and help it to develop, then time will bring its own punishment.' The king was, indeed, disposed to re-organize the inadequate representation of the estates: but he would not have a representation of the people, in the true sense of the word. He looked upon it with horror as a fruit of the revolution, a fashionable equalizing process. A multiplicity of life, a manifold gradation of rights and duties, were inseparably bound up with his conceptions of a healthy State.

But the age was no longer capable of comprehending his romantic tastes, however ingeniously and eloquently he might present them. The years went by and increased the tension. In 1847 the king at last saw himself obliged to summon the diets of all the provinces to Berlin, as a United Diet. The State had to take up a loan for the construction of the Eastern Railway, and needed the consent of the national representatives. The king spoke, as usual, with emphatic eloquence, but he left no room for doubt. 'Never will I consent that a written paper should intrude like a second Providence between our Lord God in Heaven and this country, to govern us through its paragraphs.' It was possible to understand this as mockery of the desire for a Constitution. As a matter of fact, it arose only from lack of understanding, yet this was of such a kind that any agreement seemed out of the question. The loan was refused: even the deputies from east Prussia voted against it, much as they desired the railroad. For the moment, the wishes of the majority of the diet remained likewise unfulfilled. After a few months the king gave way: at the last sitting of the committees of the diet he gave his consent to some of their most vital demands. But it was too late. Eleven days later the battle of the barricades broke out in the streets around the castle.

The change in living conditions had caused many kinds of distress and misery, amongst the middle and lower classes. Bad harvests increased the strain. At the time of the dissolution of the United Diet, wheat in northern Germany was costing on an average twice as much as had been the case a few years previously: two succeeding

The Citizens and their Empire

potato crops failed completely. After extreme misery had already driven the Silesian weavers to revolt, many thousands were destroyed by hunger-typhus: in administrative circles they spoke pityingly of 'the natural laws of domestic economy.' Social evils, hunger, political bitterness—this could not continue: such was the universal conviction, even in the most conservative circles.

Matters were not much better in other parts of Germany. But it was only amongst the South Germans that the sullen anger came to the surface: the people there had been schooled by three decades of parliamentary life, restricted though it frequently was. In the Second Chamber of Baden, in February 1848, Bassermann moved that a National Parliament of all Germany should be established beside the Confederation's Diet, even against the will of the Governments; somewhat later Heinrich von Gagern made the same demand in the Second Chamber of Hesse. But his voice was soon drowned by one more powerful. About the middle of the century the forces which Metternich had kept down throughout a generation, freed themselves in various parts of Europe. In 1847 the Swiss overthrew the *Sonderbund* (Separate League) of certain cantons, which had an aristocratic government and were supported by Austria. The Austrian possessions on the far side of the Alps were endangered by the Italian War of Liberation. At the same time, the working classes in England, and still more stormily in France, put forward independent claims for the first time: in 1848 the February Revolution overthrew the kingdom of Louis Philippe, and France became a republic. In a few days the movement had spread from France throughout the whole of Germany. The people's demands were made known through mass meetings, speeches, resolutions, and processions. The princes almost everywhere bowed to the storm, without making any serious resistance, and admitted into the Government men who were universally trusted, for the most part respected members of the Chambers. They were known as 'March Ministers.' The black, red, and gold flag was hoisted on the palace of the Confederation Diet at Frankfort. Three days later, on the 13th of March, Metternich had to flee from Vienna.

Events in Vienna had their effect upon Berlin. A royal patent of the 18th of March promised all that one could wish—a Constitution for Prussia, a national representation beside the Diet of the Confederation, and much else. But no one had confidence any longer in the vacillating and hesitating king: after the sanguinary encounters of the previous days, the masses faced the military with hate in their hearts. When the soldiers had to clear the palace square, two guns went off. Barricades rose, as if by magic: the battle began. By midnight the victory of the troops was no longer in doubt: but on the next morning they were withdrawn from the city. What share the king, his ministers, and the general in command had in this measure cannot be satisfactorily explained. Hours of humiliation now followed for the monarch. 'We all lay on our stomachs,' he said afterwards, in the picturesque Berlin idiom with which he was familiar. Yet even in this uncomfortable situation he could give free rein to his impulsiveness. Making the round of the streets of the capital, he announced: 'From this day forward, Prussia is merged in Germany.'

Words, words, words. If the sovereign people were really to compel the princely powers to their will, to overcome the spirit of particularism, and lead back their Austrian brothers into the great Fatherland, it would only be possible—if then—when they were fighting for the democratic republic, whose strongest support was found in the ranks of the workmen. On the other hand, the cause of the middle classes would have been extraordinarily hampered by a close alliance with the 'Fourth Estate.' It would have been infinitely difficult to bring the still undefined demands of the workmen and small handicraftsmen into accord with the Liberal aims, whose outlines had already been fixed with some clearness. And the triumph of the movement had been too rapid: it was thought that the goal had been reached, and that there would be no more need of the workmen's fists, which had done so much to bring about the result in Vienna, Berlin, and elsewhere. To-day, we can see that this was a grave, perhaps even the fatal, error. A Socialist movement, with much more far-reaching demands, split off from the middle-class movement. Their wild utterances had scarcely any other result than to drive the more moderate into the arms of the old authorities. This already became evident in April during the insurrection which was attempted in Baden, by Hecker, Struve, and Herwegh. The leaders of the left in the Frankfort preliminary parliament were amongst those who were most decidedly opposed to such plans: Frederick Engels also had strongly advised against this playing at revolution.

In May, the delegates chosen by the entire German nation, in universal and equal suffrage met in the old imperial city of Frankfort on the Main. Their task was to create the free and united German State. They must decide how to deal with the alien minorities in their own country, as well as with the Germans in Austria. Many kinds of social aspirations also pressed for notice: for masters and craftsmen from all over Germany had met at the same time to deliberate in the city on the Main. Never before had the like demand been made upon the men of Germany, and not till the present day has any German Parliament again been faced by so gigantic a task. What the delegates of the German nation were expected to accomplish in a few months, was only achieved, at least in the essential points, step by step, throughout many decades, amidst the most violent convulsions of the national structure. One should keep this in mind, in judging of their work.

In any case, the German people had done their best to ensure success. Germany's most enlightened spirits belonged to the Assembly: the sunset light of the classical and romantic period broods over their utterances. Yet the title 'Parliament of Professors' is not the correct one: lawyers and Government officials were far more strongly represented than the members of any other profession. The assembly numbered only four craftsmen, and no working men: but it may be doubted whether even a far stronger representation of this class would have given another turn to affairs. The great majority of the German people were inclined to reconcile the new order with the rule of the princes. Immediately after the sanguinary battles of the barricades, the attempt had been made in Berlin to proclaim the Republic: universal indignation nipped it in the bud.

Something similar happened later, in June, in Vienna. Here one of the barricades was even decorated with the portrait of the emperor, and christened the 'Kaiser Barricade.' The rising, as was said at the time, 'came to a stand before the throne.' This fact was also apparent in the attitude of the people's representatives. They owed the

Towards Freedom and Unity

quiet dignity of their first step to the skill of their President, Heinrich von Gagern. Without consulting the Governments, and on the strength of the mandate they had received from the people, they set up a provisional central authority. But in the election of the Austrian Archduke John to be 'Vice-regent of the Empire,' one could again detect the wish to resume relations with the princes: the man whom they elected devoted himself only too eagerly to this part of his task.

A still greater danger lay in the fact that the central authority, the vice-regent of the empire, and the imperial ministers lacked the machinery to carry out their resolutions. Even the German Confederation had made shift without its own officials, without confederate police or military: but its very example showed how necessary it was to create these organizations for the empire. If they failed in this, then the central authority, as one of the delegates said, would remain 'an inverted Peter Schlemihl, whose body and not his shadow had been stolen by the Devil, leaving only a shadow behind.' To perform this task, it was necessary to be clear upon the outlines of the future Constitution. But before they attacked the question of the Empire's Constitution, they let the months slip by in which it might perhaps have been possible to compel the Governments to accept the new order. If we believe that an understanding with the princes could ever have led to the desired end, then we must recognize this delay to have been the fatal mistake. The men of Paul's Church thought otherwise. After their overwhelming initial successes, they had so firm a belief in the power of the revolutionary idea that they underestimated the difficulties with the princes. To them it seemed much more difficult to create a Constitution before parties had been formed, and before opinions had been settled on questions, some of which were very complicated; and it was to become evident in the later proceedings how completely justified they were in this opinion. The best method of clearing their views seemed to them to be the discussion of the fundamental rights of the citizen. It must be added that the long oppression exercised by the police State had had a profound effect upon the mind of the deputies, including many of those on the conservative side: the majority of the deputies, especially on the left side of the house, felt it to be their first, though not their chief task, to prevent for ever the recurrence of such a state of affairs. Thus practical respects, and considerations of principle, pointed the same road: they resolved to ensure liberty before they turned to the question of unity.

While the assembly was discussing—only too thoroughly—the fundamental rights of the German people, the spirit of particularism in the population made common cause with the antagonism of the princes, to attack the work of Paul's Church.

The mere summoning of a Prussian National Assembly at the beginning of May 1848, was bound to call in question the work of the Frankfort Assembly. The relationship between the two parliaments rendered the task of each more difficult, especially as the Berlin delegates came more and more under the control of the man-in-the-street. It came to such a point that the Berlin democrats tried to influence the soldiers, though as a rule with small success, to refuse the oath to the vice-regent of the empire, which was required by the provisional central authority. This was grist to the mill of the Conservative Old-Prussians. In an unfortunate moment, the delegates of Paul's Church came to the king, to declare their wishes in the matter of Schleswig-Holstein. As the royal house of Denmark was about to become extinct, the question arose of the succession in the Elbe dukedoms, where the right of male inheritance was in force. The Danes had attempted to decide the question by incorporating Schleswig into their State. Yet a division of the dukedoms contravened the Charter of 1460 (p. 163): in March 1848 the population had taken up arms, and Frederick William IV had supported them in the name of the German Confederation. But when complications threatened with other Powers, he had retired from the field. His retreat was felt on both right and left of Paul's Church to be a disgrace to Germany. But as he held to his resolution, the assembly in the end could not well refuse their assent. The result was a wild rising of the Frankfort masses in September. Robert Blum, and other delegates of the Left, attempted, at the peril of their lives, to put a stop to this madness. Two members of the Right fell victims to the rage of the people. Through these events, the National Assembly at Frankfort lost much in esteem, not only with the Governments, but with the masses.

Towards Freedom and Unity

These first heavy blows were soon followed by others. At the beginning of the summer, it looked as if the Austrian State were about to dissolve into a number of national States. Hungary had been the first to break loose: an insurrection was raging in Lombardy: an all-Slav Congress was sitting at Prague: Illyria and Serbia summoned similar assemblies, and the Germans were expecting their incorporation within the empire. The Empire's Diet, which had to devise a constitution, was faced with an impossible task. Yet in autumn the picture had changed. In the capital, workmen and visionaries had taken the place of the citizen soldiers; the army remained true to their oath and won victory after victory. Vienna fell on the 1st of November. Robert Blum, who had been sent there by the United Left of the Frankfort Assembly, was shot by martial law. It might be a moot point whether the fighter on the barricades was protected by his immunity as a deputy; there was as little doubt of the political significance of the sentence, as of the resolve of the Schwarzenberg ministry, to allow Austria to continue to exist only as a joint empire. A few days after the taking of Vienna, the Prussian king formed a new ministry. Count Brandenburg, uncle of Frederick William IV, who was the ministerial president, was able to transfer the National Assembly of Berlin to Brandenburg, a little city on the Havel, and a little later, to dissolve it, without arousing any opposition. In the beginning of December, the Government proclaimed a constitution on their own authority: it was not by any means as bad as its name—*Oktroyierte Verfassung*, the Constitution imposed by authority—but followed closely the plan sketched out by Waldeck, the democratic leader.

Towards the end of the year of revolution, the single-State Governments had again closed their ranks. This fact had to be reckoned with, if the Constitution framed by the Assembly in the Paulskirche was ever to come into being. Their dream of a Greater Germany, which would include their Austrian kinsmen, must be wrecked by the refusal of the Government of Vienna; only a Lesser Germany now seemed to be attainable, with the Prussian king at its head as hereditary emperor. This small union could be expanded into a greater, if ever Austria should agree to enter it.

This solution of the German question was devised by

The Citizens and their Empire

Heinrich von Gagern, and won the concurrence of the advocates of the 'Little Germany.' Thus they went a long way towards meeting the democratic demands in order to gain a majority. Accordingly the empire's Constitution of March 1849 was founded on the idea of unity, and of government by the people; it was centralizing and democratic. The rights of single States were greatly restricted, to enhance the central authority: the rights of the empire swallowed up the rights of the country.

Central authority was shared between the Kaiser, who convened the Cabinet of the Empire, and the Reichstag. The Reichstag was made up of a States House, formed of representatives from the various Governments, and from the Parliaments of the single States, and a Second Chamber (*Volkshaus*), chosen by ballot, which was at once universal, equal, direct, and secret. The ministers were responsible to the Reichstag, which thus kept all the affairs of the empire under its own control. The Kaiser was entitled to object to the resolutions of the Reichstag, but his objection could only postpone and was powerless to repeal them.

After the Schwartzenberg Ministry had formed the Austrian territories into a centralized empire, the Greater Germans had no choice but to make common cause with the partisans of a Little Germany. At the end of March the King of Prussia was chosen Emperor of the Germans. After a few weeks of hesitation, he finally refused the offer. It was not difficult to understand his refusal. With his conviction of the divine right of kings, how could he consent to wear a crown by right of the people, and declare war upon Austria to please them? But his refusal meant the end of the dream of a united Germany.

In a few weeks Paul's Church was deserted. A small body remained true to the black, red, and gold flag. About one hundred delegates fought on in Stuttgart for the acceptance by the Governments of the Constitution of the Empire, until the Ministry of Wurtemberg put an end to their deliberations. The word spoken by one of these stalwarts came true seventy years later: 'They may conquer in Germany with their bayonets: but, by God, the German nation will not forget, and next time she will make a clean sweep!'

After the monarchy had become impossible as the head of the empire, the republican movement was revived once

Towards Freedom and Unity

more. Risings occurred in many Prussian towns: in Dresden men like Semper, the architect attached to the Court, Richard Wagner, the leader of the Court orchestra, and Theodore Mommsen, the university professor, fought on the barricades. The revolt in the Palatinate and in Baden had the most far-reaching effect, yet here too peace was restored with the help of Prussian weapons.

That the satyric play might not be wanting at the end of the tragedy, the Prussian king now took in hand to unite Germany in his own fashion, i.e. through an alliance with the princes. Saxony and Hanover did not absolutely refuse: a Union Parliament even met in Erfurt in the following year. But immediately afterwards the Confederation Diet assembled again in Frankfort on Austria's instigation. When Schwarzenberg took the matter seriously, and found the support of Russia, Frederick William gave way all along the line at the Treaty of Olmütz in 1850. Never before had a Prussian king had to submit to such a humiliation.

A short time previously, the law had been passed by which even the small peasants obtained land as their free property, discharging their obligations towards the lord of the manor by the help of the State banks. This was fortunate: for immediately afterwards political darkness descended once more over Prussia and Germany. The Prussian Constitution, originally liberal, had already been so altered as to give additional strength to the power of the throne. The graduated three-class franchise deprived the mass of the property-less and of the middle class of their rights, in favour of a small number who were privileged because of their property. In case the House of Deputies itself should put difficulties in the way of the Government, it possessed a reliable support in the House of Lords, for the First Chamber was formed on the basis of royal mandate. The powers of magistracy and police belonging to landed proprietors, had been taken away by the Revolution: they were restored in the 'fifties. An egregious police government suppressed all free movement. But the real rulers were the Conservatives, who created the *Kreuz Zeitung* as their party organ: their will was law with the king, the administration, and the chambers. Even the minister-president foresaw the worst consequences from their domination. 'Our progress,' he explained to

333

the king in a memorial, 'is only ostensible, while our decline is quite obvious: the deceptions encountered at the head of the Government, the dishonesty and arbitrariness of the lower officials, are likely before long to lead Prussia to the fate of Poland.' The Elbe dukedoms were handed over to Danish rule by the united European Powers, though with the condition that they should not be incorporated into the Danish State, but only connected with it through a personal union (London Protocol 1852). In the same year the little German fleet, which had been created by the Imperial Ministry, was put to the hammer.

But yet the work of Paul's Church was not in vain. The great questions of liberty and unity had been thought out, and definite shape given to their possible solutions. This work set a standard for Bismarck, and still more for the men of the Weimar Constitution. Much has been realized by the legislation of our own day, which at that time was demanded in vain by the leaders of the left. They were the champions of imperial unity and democracy. Ever and again they pointed out the necessity of including within the duties of the State the ordering of social conditions: demands were already brought forward from their ranks that the workers should enjoy full liberty to form unions: they urged the 'sacred' right to work, and the right of the workless to support. Even less than their contemporaries, whom they had far outstripped, did posterity give them the honour which is their due: how could it have been otherwise in an age which was entirely dominated by the idea of force?

SECOND PART

BISMARCK'S EMPIRE

WHILE the German Governments were turning back into pre-revolutionary paths, the alliance of the three Eastern Powers was dissolved, through which Metternich had directed the fortunes of the Continent. The rearrangement of inter-State relations heralded a new Europe. The revolution in the West had strengthened the power of Russia: the moment seemed favourable for her to risk an attack upon the Dardanelles. But 'the Sick Man on the Bosphorus' found helpers. England discerned a threat to her command of the Mediterranean, and France to her Eastern plans, which had been first pursued by Philippe the Citizen King.

In the Crimean War of 1854–56 Russia was beaten by the Allies. Yet Russian anger was directed less against them than against Austria. Only a few years earlier the Government of Russia had rendered armed assistance to the Danubian monarchy for the suppression of the Hungarian Revolution, and now Austria had left her completely in the lurch. Since then the two Eastern Powers faced each other as enemies, and the Russians made advances to the French.

The Russian defeat left the way open for France to rise. The February Revolution of the year 1848 had created the Second Republic, which was not, however, of long duration. In the very year of the revolution, struggling with economic difficulties, rendered uneasy by the pretensions of the working class, and tempted by the magic of his name, the majority of the French nation chose the nephew of the great Napoleon to be President of the Republic. From this vantage-ground he made his way in 1852 to the throne of the empire. The army and the masses supported his government; he hoped to gain the successes which his people expected from him by bringing into play the forces of France—not, however, like his uncle, by fighting European coalitions, but by adapting himself to the contemporary forces which were making history, through the encouragement of democratic and national efforts in other countries. A few years, therefore, after the Crimean War

335

he allied himself with the Italians in their struggle for unity, which found its military support in Victor Emmannuel II, the King of Sardinia, and its Bismarck in his minister Cavour. In 1859, French arms were victorious over Austrian at Magenta and Solferino. At this moment Prussia mobilized, and in order to avoid her intervention, the adversaries came to an understanding. Lombardy fell to the King of Sardinia, who gave Savoy and Nice in exchange to the French emperor. Two years later, Victor Emmanuel proclaimed himself King of Italy.

These events gave a different aspect to the German question. The breach between Austria and Russia was favourable to a Little-German solution. But it was also to be expected that Napoleon would likewise urge his policy of intervention in the case of the Eastern neighbour. For here was the prospect of a gain which lay infinitely closer to the heart of the French people: the control of the left bank of the Rhine. There was a man in Germany who was determined ruthlessly to make use of the favourable elements in the European situation, and was not afraid to face its disadvantages. But at that very time he was deliberately 'put into cold storage on the Neva': immediately before the outbreak of the Franco-Austrian War, Bismarck was obliged to exchange his post as ambassador to the Diet of the Confederation at Frankfort for that of ambassador in Petersburg. In the Court of Berlin, as throughout Germany, national hopes had been revived by events in Italy; yet no one thought it possible to realize them otherwise than by the way of union with the old Imperial Power of Austria.

The two decades between the revolution and the founding of the empire were a period of rapid development in economic life; only once, towards the end of the 'fifties, a painful setback interrupted its progress. Smelting works and forges sprang up one after another in the coal districts on the Lower Rhine, in Westphalia, around Aix, on the Saar, in Saxony, and in Silesia. In the year 1850, Alfred Krupp employed barely 250 workmen and employees, and in 1873 the number had already grown to 16,000. Berlin constantly attracted fresh industries: locomotives were manufactured by Borsig, guns by Ludwig Löwe, telegraphic plant by Siemens. Towards the middle of the century, when the Prussian State required a greater number of locomotives, Borsig was able to furnish it with all but two, which were manufactured in another German workshop. Twenty years after the opening of the first German railroad, Germany had become independent of the foreigner in the department of the railways. A similar advance was made in other branches of industry: in the production of cotton and woollen goods, and of chemical products. A new chapter began in maritime trade with the founding of the Hapag and of the North German Lloyd. The more rapid circulating of capital was seen in the extension of already existing banks, and the rise of new. (Diskonto-Gesellschaft and Darmstädter Bank—the Discounting Company and the Bank of Darmstadt).

There was a change in intellectual life, corresponding to the economic advance. The philosophic outlook common to earlier decades was relegated more and more decisively to the background, and its place supplied by keen observation and research into actuality. It was at that time that the natural sciences attained to paramount importance for the understanding of the world as a whole, and for the shaping of life. When Robert Mayer discovered the law of the conservation of energy, a firm foundation was won for all later research into the forces of Nature. Closer co-operation between science, technics, and practice brought about a revolution in the working methods of many departments. What the discoveries of the ingenious Werner Siemens were for electrical engineering in its infancy, the agricultural chemistry of Justus Liebig was for agriculture. Artists, too, increasingly recognized that their task was to gain command of reality along their own lines. Gottfried Keller, Gustav Freytag, Storm, and Fontane headed the long list of German novelists of the realist school. Hebbel's dramas cleared the way for realism upon the stage. Adolf Menzel, the master of realistic painting, took his place beside Feuerbach, who painted mankind ennobled by a classic idealism, and beside Böcklin, whose pictures of the teeming life of southern nature had a fabulous beauty of colouring. Adolf Menzel wished neither to proclaim the sublime, nor to delight in the moods of a susceptible mind: the objects of the world of appearance had attracted him solely for their picturesque effect. So no object came amiss to him in the daily round—the corner of a room with the door opening upon a balcony, the Berlin–Potsdam railway,

The Citizens and their Empire

a Berlin market in winter. Perhaps the very simplicity of these objects shows most clearly what close observation, what manifold means of expression, this artist had at his command. Thirty years before the French masters of the open-air and impressionist schools, he ventured to set on canvas the changing play of light and the movement of larger masses. In his *Iron Rollers* he conquered a field for art which till then had been scarcely cultivated: the representation of modern industrial labour. The same fidelity with which he held fast to present-day impressions he employed to portray the great King of Prussia and his period; since then he lives on in the memory of posterity as Menzel saw him.

The feeling for actuality and the national pride, which gave its character to the work of the Prussian master, were also at work in the political evolution, which was once more in a state of flux towards the end of the 'fifties. A 'New Era' began for Prussia when Frederick William IV lost his reason, and in 1858 his brother William finally accepted the regency. He made an end of the evil police régime, reconstructed the ministry on liberal lines, and proclaimed that 'Prussia must make moral conquests in Germany,' not indeed without the qualification that 'Prussia is prepared to defend the right in every place.' What the Prince Regent meant by this was yet to become clear. What the people expected was shown by the victory of the Liberals in the election to the House of Deputies. Soon afterwards the Italian war broke out. The Prince Regent believed that the hour was already come when he, with the sword of Prussia, would be able to 'throw a heavy weight into the scales'—meaning, of course, the scales of Austria. Yet his offer of alliance aroused little enthusiasm at the Court of Vienna.

Negotiations were broken off when the Prussian Government demanded the chief command of the non-Austrian troops of the army of the German Confederation; and when, after the French victories, the Prince Regent mobilized the army, the Austrian Government preferred to sacrifice Lombardy. This was a snub for Prussia. Yet it was at that very time that the German National League (Deutscher Nationalverein) began to work openly for the unity of Germany, under Prussian leadership. Not only men who had already stood for a Prussian Empire in the Frankfort

Parliament, but former republicans also, were amongst
the founders of the League. Would the Prussian Government grasp the proffered hand? Or was the national
enthusiasm which was apparent at the celebration of the
centenary of Schiller's birth, and again and again at the
society festivals of gymnasts, singers, and marksmen, to
remain without fruit?

The following years gave the answer to this question.
When the Prussian army was set on a peace footing,
recruits were immediately enlisted by order of the Prince
Regent, so that the peace strength became considerably
higher than before. Then the newly appointed War Minister,
von Roon, moved in Parliament the grant of the costs of
the increase which had already been introduced into the
army. In spite of strong misgivings, the House of Deputies
sanctioned the Bill, though not in its entirety, and with
the important limitation that the money was granted only
temporarily. Of the 322 deputies present, 315 voted in this
sense. They wished to avoid a breach. The costs were
granted once again in the following year. But little by
little the controversy came to a head.

It could not be denied that the composition of the army
was no longer suited to the altered conditions. The enlist-
ment of recruits had been so far from keeping pace with
the growth of the population, that during the 'forties more
than half of those who were liable remained free from
military service, while many thousands of fathers of
families, up to the age of thirty-nine, were called up for
training and mobilization. This was not only at variance
with the idea of universal liability to service, but it lowered
the standard of the troops. Hence a rejuvenation of the
army was not to be avoided, either on social or on military
grounds. But there was a wide divergence of opinion upon
the best way to undertake it.

The majority of the deputies demanded the reintro-
duction of the two years' service, which had already been
in force for two decades, when it was raised in the 'fifties,
and fixed finally at three years. In other points the
structure of the army was to be retained. But this was
the very thing which the Prince Regent wished to alter.
His intention was so to reinforce the troops of the line by
admitting a greater number of recruits under a three years'
service that in time of mobilization the militia could be

dispensed with, and it would only be necessary to call up a few classes of those who had been last discharged. The essential question, therefore, was whether the militia should be retained as before, or be separated from the regular army. If they were separated, then the king, in his disposal of the troops, would no longer be obliged to consider the feelings of the older men who were liable to service: the army would become the tool of the war-lord, in which he could place implicit confidence.

In the other case, he remained as before at the mercy of those political tendencies which predominated amongst the wide classes of the electors. The fight for the reform of the army was thus nothing else than a struggle for authority in the State. If—as Bismarck assured the king when he was called to office—it was not altogether a question of 'the rule of the King or the supremacy of Parliament,' yet a decision would have to be arrived at on one or the other side.

It had been possible to come to an understanding in the matter of details, but there was no yielding upon the fundamental question of policy. The militia stood for the embodiment of the union of people and State, which had approved itself in the Wars of Liberation; and for the very reason that the military efficiency of the army must in any case be enhanced, the majority of the deputies refused to place unconditionally in the hands of the Government a weapon which had been thus strengthened. On the other hand, the military, as Roon expressed it, wished 'to be master at least in their own house'; that could only be possible if the militia were separated from the army and the three years' service retained. Even the Prince Regent admitted that two years' service was sufficient for purely military training. Yet not till the third year did the soldier acquire a 'feeling for his profession,' i.e. he became an unconditionally docile tool. So intimately was the endeavour after such a reconstruction of the army bound up in the personality of the Prince Regent, that it was impossible for him to retreat without sacrificing his *ego*. His army reform was not only the result of military considerations, but also the expression of a political conviction. Like his brother, he detested the revolution and everything connected with democracy. But the experiences of his stay in England during the year of revolution, and the influence of his consort Augusta, the cultured daughter of Charles Augustus of Weimar, had the effect of making his attitude less unyielding than that of his brother. He could come to terms with the Constitution, when he saw that the people would not consent to part with it. But in his opinion, ascendency over the national representatives must be preserved to the Government. This safeguard had been neglected, and must now be secured through the reform of the army.

In the autumn of the year 1861 the prospect of arriving at an understanding tended more and more to disappear. At that time the German Progressive Party split off from the Liberals. As the name indicated, they worked with the object of subordinating Prussia's foreign policy to her national cause: with this in view, the ministers were to be responsible to the national deputies. From this time forward, the German National League worked on the same lines. The fact that the king at his coronation in Königsberg laid stress on his divine right was not likely to improve the atmosphere. A few weeks later the Progressive Party, for the first time, stood as candidates at the election, and gained at one blow almost a third of the deputies' seats. The king took up the challenge. He replaced his Liberal ministers by Conservatives, and sent home the deputies. The answer was a still more decisive victory for the Left: the costs of army reform were refused by 308 votes to 11. Now William I was at his wits' end. Should he abdicate, or should he seek help from the man whose realist politics, unhampered by any bias to either side, were equally antagonistic to his political views and his private character? On the same day that the Government was defeated in the House of Deputies the king received Bismarck in the castle at Babelsberg.

Prussia's position was most severely shaken. Instead of leading the country out of the humiliations of Olmütz and bringing it internal peace, the policy of the 'New Era' had come to a deadlock. In the war between France and Austria it had not succeeded in 'defending the right,' but only in putting a keener edge upon the enmity of Austria and making an enemy of France. Immediately afterwards the struggle for power in the State began to rage with such violence that the monarch was at the point of abdicating in favour of his son, whose liberal opinions were well

The Citizens and their Empire

known. Such a State was incapable of making any 'moral conquests': neither from Austria nor from Prussia did men look for the solution of the German question.

A few years later, peace had been established between the Throne and the Parliament. Germany, united under Prussia's leadership by Bismarck, rose to be the Power which turned the scale upon the Continent, and was preparing to enter the lists of the great nations for the mastery of the world. At the same time, after a bitter struggle, the border-line between political and ecclesiastical authority was newly defined, and an attempt was made to co-ordinate the Fourth Estate, which had awakened to full consciousness of its own will, within the body politic. The most far-reaching decisions, in foreign and domestic politics, in political economy, and in social and cultural life, such as could slowly come to maturity amongst the more favoured nations, were crowded into the small space of a few years. Bismarck evaded no decisions. Shaping and rejecting, attracting and repelling, he went his own way, and compelled the German people, and even for a considerable part of the way the other European peoples, to follow the same road. The world changed when he began to work, and changed when his work came to an end. More deeply than any German statesman, he impressed the stamp of his character upon his age.

This man was very German in his overmastering will and his joy in battle; very German were the strength of his feelings, his intimate union with the life of nature, and the character of his religious sentiment: the practical clearsightedness with which he looked upon the world was an inheritance from Lower Saxony. In this scion of an old Brandenburg family lived the aristocrat's consciousness of mastery, which brought no right understanding to bear upon the life and aspirations of the middle classes. In former times the family of Bismarck had been a source of trouble to the Prussian rulers, until they made their covenant with the throne and sealed it with their blood in the great Frederick's battles. Otto von Bismarck also took the first opportunity of entering the lists in defence of the authority of the Prussian throne: to it he devoted his life-work. Yet from the beginning the unique strain of individuality was no less apparent, dividing him from his peers and even from his period. His master-will was too

Bismarck's Empire

strongly developed for him to adapt himself like others to the career of an officer or a Government official. Where it was his place to command, no other opinion could be heard; he held all who contradicted him to be stupid or bad or both, and treated them accordingly. Bismarck was a good hater, and for that reason few men have been better hated. Even his connection with the Hohenzollerns—'a Swabian family, no better than my own'—was only in the long run tolerable to him because he believed it to form a part of the divine world order. And this God, whom he had found, after a wild youth, at the same time that he found his dearly loved wife, was a God of the Puritan type, the Leader of the Chosen People, a stern Judge, who could be approached not through membership with the Church, but through strong faith inspiring the individual. In political matters it could be seen more clearly, even with alarming clearness, how greatly this man diverged from the viewpoint of his world. King, Court, and nobles could imagine the future of the State only as allied with the conservative forces. Bismarck was prepared to ally himself with Napoleon III to-day, and with the work of the Paul's Church to-morrow, if in either he could foresee any advantage for Prussia. His grasp of the German problem showed how completely he had freed himself from the bias towards one side or another, which was a feature of 'sentimental politics.' We know of no contemporary statesman who had imagined any other solution than what might come through the leadership and co-operation of Austria; yet Bismarck, during his employment as ambassador to the Diet of the Confederation, had arrived at the conviction that the path through blood and iron alone could lead to the goal.

His views were known to the king. Up to that time they had made him afraid of a closer connection with Bismarck. But he needed him and was obliged to stifle his misgivings. Bismarck, too, had need of the king, in order to go his own way. This mutual need brought the two men together, and kept them side by side through times of bitter conflict and depression. The statesman subordinated himself to the king; the king submitted to the superior insight and the titanic will of his counsellor, who was almost two decades younger than himself; and yet he remained the master.

Only step by step would Bismarck be able to win over the king to his plans; he knew this and acted accordingly.

The Citizens and their Empire

Thus the conversation under the trees of the park at Babelsberg led to a close understanding. A few days later Bismarck, as Minister-President, declared in the Committee of Receipts and Expenditure set up by the Chamber of Deputies: 'Germany looks not to Prussia's liberalism, but to her force.' These words sounded the *leit-motif* with which the ear was now to become familiar through constant repetition in every conceivable variation: away with 'moral conquests'—the State is Force, or it ceases to be! He who would not hearken must be made to feel. Officials who held other opinions were punished by hundreds with transference to another post; officers of the militia received their discharge; contractors who held independent views were threatened with the withdrawal of Government orders. The masses were cowed into submission by police evictions and press laws which contravened the Constitution. A few years later they had learnt to worship Force alone of all the good gods of the State: the people chose the cuirassier's top-boots from their hero's wardrobe and set them up as a symbol of the Bismarckian régime. Yet, to the honour of the German citizen, it must be said that the change was not a light matter to them all. Voices were raised in the keenest opposition. When the Government declared that after the rejection of the Army Bill they would be obliged to administer the State finances on a different basis from that provided by the Constitution, the deputies entered a formal protest against Bismarck for breach of the Constitution. Yet their appeal to law did not move him; for him, constitutional questions were questions of force. After a few months he dissolved the Chamber. In spite of the exercise of powerful official influence, the newly elected members brought only a very small reinforcement to the Right. The conflict continued to rage with undiminished fierceness, and before long fresh fuel was added through Bismarck's foreign policy.

At that time, in addition to the fight for the Constitution, another question was agitating men's minds, far outside the boundaries of Prussia. In 1863, under pressure from the Nationalist party, the Danish Government had at last decreed the incorporation of Schleswig in the State of Denmark. In the general opinion there could be only one answer to this breach of the London Protocol (p. 334): the Elbe duchies must be set free from their connection

344

Bismarck's Empire

with Denmark, and become independent under the rightful heir, the hereditary Prince of Augustenberg. The Austrian Government showed itself disposed to act on these lines, and at the same time took a step forward in the national question of the reform of the Confederation. A Diet of Princes, held in 1863 at Frankfort under the emperor's presidency, was about to resolve upon a change in the Constitution, which went so far as to provide for a species of popular representation in the Confederation. Many looked upon Austria's proceedings as a national gesture; they could not know that she aimed at clearing the Prussian enemy from the field, already weakened, as he was, by the struggle over the Constitution. While the black, red, and gold standard still floated hopefully over the palace of the Federal Diet, the Prussian king was travelling in all secrecy through Frankfort. Bismarck, under threat of resignation, had carried his point that the king should keep away from the Assembly. Beside him, the Prince of Augustenberg alone was absent. But nothing could be accomplished without Prussia. This experience moved the Court of Vienna to a *rapprochement* with the Prussian Government. It was not long before Bismarck forced the Court of Vienna to resign itself to his guidance in the Danish question.

The European situation was not unfavourable to Bismarck's plans. He had newly placed the Russian emperor under an obligation during the Polish rising of 1863. Napoleon could not well oppose the national demand, and was, moreover, out of temper with England. Opposition was to be feared from England alone, but it was not likely to lead to armed intervention on the side of Denmark. So long as the two German great Powers demanded nothing but the observance of the London Protocol, England found no ground for interference. Austrian policy went no farther than this demand. Bismarck, on the other hand, intended to annex the duchies to Prussia, and it is probable that he also already envisaged the possibility of bringing the quarrel with Austria to a head in connection with this question. When the Danes rejected the demand of the two German Powers, 50,000 Prussians and 20,000 Austrians advanced into Schleswig, on the 1st of February 1864. If old Wrangel, whom King William had unfortunately placed in supreme command, had exactly followed Moltke's

The Citizens and their Empire

plan of campaign, the much weaker Danish troops would have been cut off from the islands, and the war probably ended in a few days. It fell out otherwise. Months passed before a decisive success had been obtained, through the storming of the Düppel redoubt by Prussian troops. In the negotiations which followed, the English stiffened the backs of the Danish Government; it is possible, too, that Bismarck was partly to blame for their unyielding attitude. Summer had come before the occupation of the island of Alsen by the Prussians at last broke their resistance. In autumn, Denmark ceded the Elbe duchies to the Allied Powers.

For the Austrians, the joint command of the duchies was nothing but a burden. For this reason, and in accordance with the whole of public opinion, they were not long in demanding the appointment of the Prince of Augustenberg.

Yet 'a new duchy, with a vote in the Diet of the Confederation, and the inevitable function of fearing Prussia and making common cause with her enemies,' could only be acceptable to Bismarck if Prussia's supremacy were assured by suitable measures. But Austria could not endure a Prussian vassal State in the north. In the end, by the Treaty of Gastein, 1865, they agreed upon a division of control, by which Austria undertook the administration of Holstein and Prussia of Schleswig. No more was heard of the rights of the Prince of Augustenberg; in the shortest possible space of time Bismarck had manœuvred his opponent out of his strong position. But the treaty could 'only plaster up the flaws in the building'; matters were moving towards a crisis.

The attitude of Russia and England in the event of a quarrel between Prussia and Austria differed little from that which they had taken up towards the intervention of the German great Powers in the Danish question. On the other hand, the intervention of the French emperor would certainly have to be reckoned with on this occasion (p. 335). The imminent conflict was a stroke of good fortune in Napoleon's eyes, which he intended to turn to account in more than one connection. It was to serve to obtain Venice at last for the Italian people, and so induce them to give up all claim to Rome. If the pope were indebted to the French emperor for the maintenance of his secular govern-

346

Bismarck's Empire

ment, then a most valuable ally would be gained against the internal enemies of the empire. Moreover, it was Napoleon's intention to advance into the Rhineland in the course of the war, and to sell his support dearly. Hence he was more than willing to mediate an alliance between Prussia and Italy, but refused to tie his hands by making claims upon specific German provinces.

He expressed himself in this sense to Bismarck, who visited him at Biarritz a few weeks after the Treaty of Gastein. Thereupon, trusting to the fighting strength of the Prussian army and his own superior statesmanship, Bismarck made up his mind to risk a war. After prolonged effort he succeeded in winning over the king to the idea of the alliance; the settlement with Italy, in the spring of 1866, hastened the *dénouement*.

For Austria had not remained in ignorance of the negotiations, and was most gravely disquieted by them. Bismarck, too, was forced to act, because the Italians had limited their obligation to three months.

On the very day after the signing of the treaty, he moved in the Diet of the Confederation the summoning of a National Assembly on the basis of universal, equal, and direct franchise. Thus he gave world-wide publicity to the fact that the coming war had no other purpose than the reconstitution of Germany. The return to the 'revolutionary' franchise included in the Imperial Constitution of 1849 was a warning to foreigners 'not to stick their fingers in our national pie.' At the same time Bismarck hoped to be able successfully to play off a German parliament, originating universal and equal suffrage, against the Prussian House of Deputies. For the Prussian delegates, who gave him so much trouble, had been elected by the three class suffrage, i.e. for the most part from the propertied middle class. After the experiences which he had had in the year of revolution with his Schönhausen peasants, he certainly seemed justified in expecting more loyalty from the 'lower classes.' At that time it was not known what intentions he was pursuing with the grant of universal suffrage; his contemporaries felt as if the devil had mounted the pulpit to read the Gospel. There was reason enough to distrust the Junker's alliance with the revolution.

The only result which Bismarck's proposal produced in

The Citizens and their Empire

the Diet of the Confederation was that the Central States bound themselves still more closely to Austria. This reacted upon King William, who in any case failed to understand how an alliance with the revolutionary forces at home and abroad, and a war against the conservative Austria with which the Prussian dynasty had lived in friendship for many decades, could strengthen the power of the throne. His king's opposition gave Bismarck more trouble than anything else. He paid little attention to the storm of public opinion, but he admitted to himself that he would never survive a defeat. 'In a case of necessity there is no room for doubt; I am fighting now for my head and for my life.' In these words he summed up the emotions which swayed him in these critical days.

The diplomatic battle hastened to its climax. A Prussian scheme of constitution for the Confederation, which excluded Austria, was met by her in June 1866 with the proposal to mobilize the non-Prussian federal fighting forces. This meant war. For many weeks Prussian troops had been prepared for war, but owing to his recollection of the long friendship with Austria, it was late before the king could be induced to agree to Moltke's plans of attack. Only by the most rapid action could lost time be in any degree made up. Saxony, the Electorate of Hesse, and Hanover were occupied almost without resistance. In Hanover, through the action of their leader in taking the law into his own hands, the Prussian troops suffered a defeat, which, nevertheless, was almost immediately atoned for. In the Main district they succeeded first in preventing the superior power of the enemy from effecting a junction, and then in pressing him back. The Italians were beaten by the Austrians at Custozza; yet the Emperor Francis Joseph resigned Venice to Napoleon, in order to obtain his intervention. That happened on the day when news reached Vienna of the decision in the chief theatre of war. The Prussian troops had penetrated the passes of Bohemia in three army columns; the fiercest fighting fell to the army of the Crown Prince, which marched farthest to the east. The Austrians, and the Saxons who had joined them, were threatened with encirclement; they retreated to the little fortress of Königgrätz. In the early morning of the 3rd of July, two Prussian armies attacked from the west and south-west. Although the Prussian needle-gun caused heavy losses amongst their opponents, who still fought in close formation, the offensive was brought to a standstill under the devastating fire of the Austrian artillery. In the early hours of the afternoon the Crown Prince's army arrived from the north-east upon the field of battle. This decided the victory; yet the Austrians succeeded by a retreat in evading the encirclement which had been planned by Moltke. Austria was beaten, but not annihilated. The king's military advisers insisted that the war should be carried on till Vienna was taken. Bismarck opposed this intention with all his might. Immediately after the battle, Napoleon, through the French ambassador, had offered his services as mediator.

Bismarck did not dare to reject them, but endeavoured as quickly as possible to come to an understanding with Austria. If for no other reason, he was obliged to propose mild peace conditions; but he was thinking also of the future.

He hoped to compensate Prussia by the extension of her rule in northern Germany, against which neither Austria nor Napoleon had any objection to raise. But it was infinitely difficult to win the king over to this idea. He was conscious of being the leader of a victorious army, and intended to renounce neither the further advance, nor the 'punishment' of Austria and her allies in the shape of loss of territory; yet it would never have entered his mind to dethrone one of them. In the twentieth chapter of *Thoughts and Recollections* Bismarck has described his conflict with the king, which was finally decided in his favour through the intervention of the Crown Prince. Austria agreed that Prussia should reshape the political conditions of Germany, and paid a trifling war indemnity; no more was asked of her (the Peace of Prague, 1866). Their separation from the great German Fatherland meant the beginning of a difficult time for the Germans in Austria. The centralized monarchy, in which they had occupied the leading place, was transformed in 1867 into the dual monarchy of Austria-Hungary; in both halves of the empire the other peoples resisted German nationality, and the Government yielded to them.

The State of Prussia was extraordinarily aggrandized and strengthened by the incorporation of Hanover, the Electorate of Hesse, Nassau, the free city of Frankfort, and the Elbe duchies. The founding of the North German Confederation turned the whole of northern Germany into a Greater Prussia. Its economic association with the south German States was given a new form in a Customs Federal Council and a Customs Parliament, which represented an extension of the Federal Council and Parliament of the North German Confederation. The alliance between north and south was strengthened by secret military covenants for defence against a French attack, which were entered into at the conclusion of peace.

Bismarck's successes effected a revolution in the life of party politics, which was scarcely less marked. The very fact that he took seriously the solution of the German question had converted many of his opponents.

At the new elections, on the day of Königgrätz, the Forward Movement and its allies lost no less than 105 of their 253 seats; on the other hand, Bismarck's Conservative following was badly shaken by his revolutionary disregard for the rights of the princes. He had very little left to lose with his Conservative peers, when he actually persuaded the king to petition the House of Deputies for an additional grant to cover the State expenditure since 1863. This was a shattering blow for the Prussian Left. If they assented, they would be false to the policy which they had pursued for so many years. Yet it was impossible to avoid accepting the Government proposal; after Bismarck's brilliant successes the electors would not have consented to a rejection. This broke up the Progressive Party. A considerable part of their members went over to the National Liberal Party, which Rudolph von Benningsen had called into existence in his Hanoverian home. It stood for a foreign policy in the national, that is to say, in Bismarck's, sense, but in domestic politics, for the preservation and extension of the Liberal gains. Throughout a decade the National Liberals, together with the Free Conservatives, who agreed with Bismarck from their Conservative standpoint, formed his strongest political support.

Bismarck ordered the relations with the federated States in such a way that they retained the entire internal administration, including that of ecclesiastical and educational affairs, and almost all the legislative authority and the administration of justice; only economic affairs, posts and telegraphs, he assigned to the Confederation. The preservation of Prussian individuality was ensured by this settlement, and the later entrance of the southern States into the Confederation was facilitated. In return, the military high command, the administration of the army, and the conduct of foreign policy fell to the Prussian king as President of the Confederation. The Federal Council shared with the Reichstag the legislative authority of the Confederation. The Federal Council was composed of the mandatories of the Allied Governments; the preponderance of Prussia was ensured not in form but in fact, so that the Prussian Crown need fear no infringement of its authority from this quarter. Again, this Federal Council acted as a restriction upon the Reichstag. The deputies had no possibility of calling to account the Federal Chancellor, who conducted the business of the Federal Council; even their wish for a daily allowance remained unfulfilled, and with good reason. During the time of conflict Bismarck had had the most unpleasant experience with the Government officials, the leaders of the Liberal opposition; he wanted to see business men in the Reichstag who would devote themselves to their business affairs and leave the conduct of politics to the Government. Such a Parliament, especially in its expanded form as a Customs Parliament, was capable of becoming a valuable support for him against the Prussian House of Deputies, as, if the case were reversed, the Government would be able to play off the one against the other.

It was true that the 'freest franchise in the world,' upon which the work of the Paul's Church was founded, had been incorporated by Bismarck in his creation, yet not as a sustaining force. The difference in his ideals from those of 1848 was perceptible in the choice of the mercantile flag for the Confederation. To his king, Bismarck justified the addition of the red to the colours of the Prussian flag, by referring to the colours of the Electorate of Brandenburg; to the citizens of Hamburg he derived it from the Hanseatic white and red. It is not easy to explain what it was that decided him; in any case he regarded the new colours as national colours from the beginning, and it was not long ere they became such, through the national experience of the Franco-German War.

The rapid conclusion of the preliminary peace had crossed Napoleon's plans. Ten days later, when he advanced certain claims upon German land—Rhenish Bavaria, Rhenish Hesse, and the Saar territory—Bismarck rejected them, and the emperor was not in a position to press his demand. Thereupon Napoleon came to an understanding with the Government of the Netherlands over the sale of Luxemburg; but Bismarck, who had to be consulted, because the country had belonged to the German Confederation and still lodged a Prussian garrison, refused his consent and caused Luxemburg to be declared a neutral State. It was not that he was averse to allowing the emperor to receive the coveted 'compensation'; but Luxemburg at that time was still counted as German land, and the German people would have looked upon its cession to France as a betrayal of the national cause. For Napoleon, the ill-success of his plans meant a considerable aggravation of the difficulties of his position, while, with the publication of the military treaties between Prussia and southern Germany, the French people lost their hopes of a protectorate of southern Germany. In the end, the emperor needed a success if he was to maintain his position; Prussia must be humbled before there could be any thought of gaining territory. Napoleon therefore approached those who had been vanquished in 1866. 'Revenge for Sadowa' (Königgrätz), which was the desire of the French people, became the leading idea of the imperial policy. In the spring of 1870 the Archduke Albert spent some weeks in Paris, in order to come to an understanding on military matters. It is improbable that the emperor was aiming at war; he was much more disposed to strive for his ends by the arts of diplomacy.

It may be said almost with certainty of Bismarck, that he did not wish to challenge France to war over the question of the Spanish succession. It is true that his conduct was not quite so innocent as he liked in his old age to represent it. If a Hohenzollern could be set on the throne of Spain, it would mean a much desired support in face of the opposition which France offered to the complete union of Germany. It was, moreover, impossible that Bismarck could doubt the irritation and excitement which his endeavours would arouse in the French nation. He, no less than Napoleon, must reckon with the possibility of war, and, as an extraordinary chance would have it, in the same February days when the Archduke was discussing the military co-operation of France and Austria, he began vigorously to take up the Spanish question.

The Spaniards had overthrown and banished their queen of the House of Bourbon. When other plans had failed, the provisional Government offered the crown to Prince Leopold of Hohenzollern-Sigmaringen; he sprang from a Catholic branch of the Royal House of Prussia, and had married the sister of the King of Portugal. The Hohenzollerns were not inclined to meddle with the affair, but Bismarck overruled their scruples, with the result that, in June 1870, the Prince at last declared his readiness to accept. The negotiations were concluded in all secrecy, and on 2nd July the Spanish Government informed the French ambassador of the coming election. This occasioned great indignation in France. Not to be outdone by the popular agitation, the Foreign Minister expressed the general opinion in the sharpest terms: he declared that the Government would not suffer a foreign Power to set one of its princes on the throne of Charles V (!) and would fulfil its duty without hesitation and without weakness. An appeal to the Foreign Office in Berlin met with no success; the Spanish affair, it was there explained, was a family matter for the Hohenzollerns, which concerned neither the North German Confederation nor the Prussian Government. As a matter of fact Bismarck had from the very beginning treated the question in this way. If the king had followed his wishes, he also would have referred the French to the Spanish Government and the Prince. But the king was too human, too little of a practical politician of Bismarck's stamp. When the French ambassador Benedetti went to see him at Ems, he entered into parley with him. It is true that he sharply rejected the provocative declaration of the French Minister-President and refused to forbid the Prince to accept the crown; but secretly he made his authority felt in Sigmaringen, with the result that the Prince, in the name of his son, withdrew his candidature for the Spanish throne: the father's intervention was explained by the fact that the Prince was at the moment on a tour in the mountains.

Instead of being satisfied with this success, the French Government advanced new demands, which had for their object the humiliation of Prussia. The first step was for Benedetti to require a declaration on the part of the king

The Citizens and their Empire

that he would never in the future permit a member of the House of Hohenzollern to accept the Spanish crown. On the morning of the 13th July, the ambassador discharged his commission on the Well Promenade. This was too much even for the king; he replied that he could not give such a declaration. Benedetti would not yield. In the end King William put an end to the conversation: 'It seems to me, Ambassador, that I have expressed myself clearly and unequivocally, and that I have nothing further to add.' Benedetti expected to have another audience, but he had to content himself with the adjutant, who went several times to and fro. Then came the news that the French Government had even demanded, in the second place, a royal letter of apology from the German ambassador in Paris. Now, indeed, the king had nothing further to add. Next morning he left Ems, as had been previously arranged, and had some friendly words to say to Benedetti at the station.

By this time Bismarck had already acted. If he had had any suspicion of such a turn of affairs, the summer quiet of Varzin would long since have become unendurable to him. Late in the afternoon of the 13th July he received in Berlin the despatch from Ems, which informed him of events up to the arrival of the demand for a letter of apology; the king left to his judgment the publication of the despatch and the manner of making it known.

In a few minutes he edited 'a concise version,' as he said later, 'by means of omissions, but without the addition or alteration of a single word,' which was immediately sent to the German representatives abroad and to the newspapers. The critical sentence now ran as follows: 'His Majesty thereupon refused to receive the French ambassador again, and informed him through the adjutant on duty that His Majesty had nothing further to communicate to the ambassador.' This was correct in itself, yet put in such a way as inevitably to produce the impression that the king had broken off relations with the ambassador. King William had only parried; Bismarck gave the counter-blow: he placed the choice before the French Government, which they had intended for the German—the choice between humiliation or war.

His redaction certainly did not do complete justice to the facts of the case, but to characterize Bismarck's

Bismarck's Empire

statement as a 'forgery' of the Ems despatch is to do it much less than justice. The statesman's task differs from that of the historian. Bismarck's redaction expressed the sense of the historic moment more correctly than the original despatch.

Popular passion was aroused in Germany by the importunity of the French demand, and in France by Bismarck's counter-stroke. 'My journey to Ems and back was like a triumphal procession,' wrote the king; 'I never dreamed of such a thing, nor thought it possible.' In the French Chamber heated debates silenced the voice of reason. Tears sprang from the emperor's eyes when he was asked to give the order of mobilization, but there was no retreat. The French troops were sent in all haste to the frontier, and not till then were they brought up to fighting strength and provided with arms. Yet the army administration was not equal to the task; instead of the advance which had been planned, there was no question of more than the defence of the frontier country. When the French declaration of war arrived on the 19th July, the Germans stood solid behind the Prussian king: the gulf between north and south had been bridged over. Moltke had assembled the German army within the narrow space between Luxemburg and the Palatinate, and in the Palatinate itself. With the same boldness which had led him in 1866 to leave the Rhineland undefended against a French attack, he now trusted that the long frontier of Baden would be sufficiently safeguarded by an advance on the flank. The smooth course of the mobilization, and the concentration of the troops, made it easier from the very beginning for the military command to oppose a numerical superiority to the enemy at the critical points. In addition to the leadership of a genius like Moltke, the habit of independent action which was common to officers and under-officers, together with the superior training of the troops, turned the scale in favour of the Germans; they had also the better artillery, while, on the other hand, the French had the better arms.

The III Army, which, under the command of the Crown Prince advanced farthest to the south, came first upon the enemy. On the 6th August, they gained a victory at Weissenburg and at Wörth over General MacMahon, who retreated as far as the Marne, in order to fit his army again for battle in the camp at Châlons. On the day of the Wörth battle, the I (Northern) Army, under Steinmetz attacked and beat the French at Spichern. This was contrary to Moltke's plan, since the II (Centre) Army under Prince Frederick Charles was still behind; it was now impossible to encircle General Bazaine east of Metz. He marched through the fortress, to join MacMahon at the Marne. But meantime the II Army had marched round Metz to the south of the fortress, and barred his way in the bloody battle of Vionville-Mars la Tour. At Gravelotte and St. Privat, troops of the I and II Armies co-operated, and threw Bazaine back upon Metz, which was being besieged. MacMahon now made up his mind to await the decision among the cannon of Paris; but he was forced by the Government's order to attempt the relief of Bazaine, and deployed towards the north, to march along the Belgian frontier. As soon as the military command had word of this movement, the III and the newly formed IV Army also wheeled northwards. At Sedan, Moltke's masterly plan of encirclement was so completely successful that, after the bravest resistance, the entire French army were forced into the fortress, and on the 2nd September were obliged to capitulate.

Napoleon had in vain courted a soldier's death.

Four weeks had sufficed for the conquest of the field army of imperial France; the struggle with the French Republic lasted nearly five months. The leaders of the German army were faced above all with the necessity of bringing the capital to surrender, as well as the great fortresses in the east, and to this end the armies which were advancing to their relief must be turned back.

Strasburg capitulated after a heavy bombardment, and Metz succumbed to hunger four weeks later on 27th October; 183,000 men were made prisoners of war. Altogether there fell not less than twenty-two fortresses. While the Germans were compelled to break up their forces in the fortress warfare, the provisional Government of the Republic had initiated the People's War. The population answered the call to the flag, if not with the enthusiasm of the national rising of the year 1783, yet with a devoted love for the fatherland, and the supply of munitions became a remunerative business for the English. But the numerical superiority of French armies, raised in rapid succession,

Bismarck's Empire

could not compensate for the better leadership and training of the German troops. In the battles round about Orleans at the beginning of December, and in the three days' battle at Le Mans, the army of the Loire was overthrown, at St. Quentin the northern army, and finally Bourbaki's army also. After the French advance upon Paris had been frustrated, Bourbaki had undertaken the task of breaking through the German communications with the east, and was attempting in the first place to relieve the besieged Belfort. In three days' fighting, a feeble force of militia from Baden beat back his attack at the Lisaine; then, with the arrival of reinforcements, his army was pressed back across the Swiss frontier.

Meantime the fate of Paris had been decided. At first there were only 150,000 men available to surround the city, which possessed more extensive fortifications than any other stronghold of that time. It is true that the fighting strength of the large garrison was so small, that only one of their sorties at the beginning of December seriously endangered the besiegers. Bismarck pressed for the bombardment of the city, because he feared an intervention by neutrals; under the pressure of this anxiety he thought it necessary to ascribe the opposition of the military to irrelevant motives, and still maintained this accusation in his *Thoughts and Recollections*. After Christmas, however, the bombardment was begun; yet it was to hunger, and not to the German artillery, that the French capital surrendered at the end of January 1871.

Military considerations preponderated, when the conditions of peace were drawn up. As early as the day of Sedan, Bismarck had made a declaration to the French bearers of the flag of truce, whose justice may be tested by the experience of centuries. 'In the possession of France, Strasburg'—so he said at that time—'is an ever-open sally-port upon south Germany. In the possession of Germany, on the other hand, Strasburg and Metz acquire a defensive character.' At the same time, he did not in any way underestimate the difficulties which the empire was bound to encounter through the linking up of Alsace-Lorraine, and was therefore no friend to its annexation. But he yielded to the demand of the military, and the German people realized the fulfilment of an ardent national wish, in the regaining of the districts which had been seized from them

357

two hundred years before: while the warning voices, which were not entirely lacking, were shouted down. In the peace of Frankfort, in May 1871, France resigned Alsace and German Lorraine as well as Metz, and bound herself to a war indemnity of five milliards of francs. The wealthy country raised the sum in much less time than had been expected, and in the autumn of 1873 the last German troops were withdrawn.

The most valuable and lasting result of the war was the political unity of Germany. While the German tribes were fighting shoulder to shoulder, the wish to give legal status to their union was naturally strengthened: the day of Sedan witnessed not only the conquest of the enemy but of the spirit of particularism. It is true that the final victory had not been won, either in the sphere of home politics or upon the battlefield. For Bismarck it was only a question of completing the work of 1866, by the entrance of the South German States into the North German Confederation. His chief supporter among the German princes was the Grand Duke Frederick I of Baden, King William's son-in-law. By his liberal legislation he had quickly and completely wiped out the memory of the years of revolution, which had been so cruel for Baden—it was at that time that Baden became the 'Little Pattern Country' of Germany—and he had early advocated the programme of the partisans of a 'Little Germany' along the lines proposed by the National League (p. 338). In 1866, under the pressure of national sentiment, he joined the other South German States; but after Bismarck's reconciliation with his Chamber of Deputies, feeling in Baden veered round, so that the minister Mathy was able to work successfully for Prussia. In order to give the French emperor no excuse for intervention, Bismarck refused at that time to consent to the entry of Baden into the North German Confederation, which was desired by her Chamber. Now, when the Prussian Government entered into preliminary discussions with the South German States, the Grand Duke smoothed the way for them, and was the first to announce his unconditional entrance into the North German Confederation. In spite of the enmity which its minister felt for Prussia, there was no fear of a refusal on the part of Hesse, which, with the territories to the south of the Main, was still outside the Confederation. Wurtemberg, of her own accord, had already made application before the discussions were taken in hand, but this eagerness was accompanied by the wish to ensure favourable conditions for herself, and the same desire led to serious difficulties on the side of Bavaria. The negotiations were broken off when they were nearing conclusion, a misfortune for which the Austrian Minister for Foreign Affairs was partly responsible. Subordination to Prussia, such as existed in the North German Confederation, was out of the question for Wurtemberg and Bavaria.

There was, however, a totally different way: the mould of the Confederation might be broken, and the empire built up on another basis. It would suffice to create a Ministry of the Empire, and make it responsible to the Reichstag; the representation of the whole German nation would thus be changed from a mere piece of decoration, into one of the supporting pillars of the imperial edifice, and the evolution through freedom to unity would receive a powerful impetus. Such plans were advocated by the German Crown Prince, and for a time also by the Grand Duke of Baden; but they were not to the taste either of Bismarck or of the other South German princes. The liberal character of the solution was particularly repugnant to the man who had saved the authority of the Prussian throne, and created the North German Confederation. How would he be able to grant to the empire what he withheld from his own country and the Confederation? The idea of unification or unitarism was particularly repugnant to the princes. Thus a third course only was possible: the form of the Confederation was retained, yet special rights (reservation rights) were granted to the Federal States of Bavaria and Wurtemberg. It is true that all the wishes of the Bavarian Government were not fulfilled; they had to resign all claim to the acquisition of the Palatinate of Baden, as well as of territory in Alsace, and to the alternation of the title of Emperor between Bavaria and Prussia which Lewis II had demanded only a few days before the proclamation of the emperor. But enough remained: their own administration of the army, their own posts and telegraphs, independent regulation of the beer duty, ambassadorial rights, and for Bavaria, in addition, the supreme command of the army in peace time, and other matters.

The Empire came into existence as a union of the Governments: 'H.M. the King of Prussia in the name of

359

The Citizens and their Empire

the North German Confederation, H.M. the King of Bavaria . . . make an everlasting covenant . . .' so ran the preamble to the Imperial Constitution. Instead of developing in the direction of unitarism, the North German Confederation, through the preservation of individual rights, had developed in the direction of a States union along federal lines. And even upon this basis it was hard enough for Bismarck to effect an understanding. In the case of Lewis II, he had to resort to a money payment amounting to 300,000 marks a year (£15,000) which, up to the death of the unfortunate king, was fetched in person from Berlin by Count Holnstein, his lord equerry, for which service he pocketed the royal messenger's fee of 10 per cent. Bismarck took the money from the *Welffund*, the property of the Welfs, the confiscated fortune of the dethroned King of Hanover. When one feels disposed to reproach the founder of the empire with having obtained too little at that time, one should remember the words spoken by him immediately after the conclusion of the Bavarian treaty: 'The newspapers will not be satisfied; and anyone who writes history in the usual way may find fault with our agreement. He may say, "The stupid fellow should have asked for more; if he had demanded, they must have given," and he may be correct about the *must*. But I was more concerned that the people should be genuinely satisfied. What is the good of a treaty founded on *must*?'

He had done his best to preserve the paramountcy of the Prussian Crown in the Confederation. A change to Prussia's disadvantage in the number of votes in the Federal Council was unavoidable, with the entrance of the southern States. It was therefore provided that fourteen votes should suffice to prevent any change in important questions; Prussia, however, possessed seventeen votes. Nevertheless, Prussian particularism found a voice in King William. It was hard for him to accept a title which thrust his dignity as King of Prussia into the background; and if he must be called Emperor, he wished to be called Emperor of Germany. At the proclamation of the emperor in the Hall of Mirrors at Versailles on the 18th January, 1871, the Grand Duke of Baden skilfully got over the difficulty by calling upon the princes, generals, and the army's deputations present with their colours to give three cheers for the 'Emperor William.'

Bismarck's Empire

But the agitations and conflicts of the past weeks were still reverberating: the emperor shook hands with the generals, and passed Bismarck by.

With the founding of the empire, a new State took its place in the political system of Europe, of very much greater importance than Russia, which had been defeated in the Crimean War, than Austria, which had been beaten in 1859 and 1866, or than France, which had just been overthrown; even England's traditional influence upon the Continent lost some of its weight. If it was already difficult for her neighbours to adapt themselves to the fact of this change, the circumstance that the empire was the result of three wars was bound to arouse misgivings for the future. Full of distrust, they expected that the hero of the policy of blood and iron would seize the first opportunity totally to destroy one of the vanquished, or to link on to the empire another of the neighbouring provinces inhabited by Germans; the fear had already been aroused at that time amongst the English that a strong German fleet of battleships would challenge their supremacy upon the sea. While still in process of formation, the young empire had been threatened by the possibility of a European coalition reminiscent of the work of Prince Kaunitz (p. 264), that is, of the coalition of the Powers against Frederick the Great and his war on two fronts. For, during the siege of Paris, Austria placed herself on the side of France, and the situation was saved only by the fact that Russia found it more to her advantage not to join her allies of the eighteenth century, but to obtain the withdrawal of the restrictions upon her fleet, which had been imposed on her by France, England, and Austria after the Crimean War. The fear of a recurrence of such threats—'the nightmare of the coalitions'—henceforth decided Bismarck's foreign policy.

There could be no doubt that France would enter into such an alliance. For it was naturally most difficult for the French nation to accept the redistribution of power in Germany's favour; the leading position which she had enjoyed for centuries had only been made possible through the weakness of her eastern neighbour. The annexation of Alsace-Lorraine brought her enmity to a head, and showed her an immediate object which was within her grasp. At bottom, however, the French Government were concerned

361

to destroy the unity of Germany, which was the basis of German power. Bismarck's exertions, therefore, were all directed towards the 'isolation' of France, partly through a policy of alliances, which robbed the French of the possibility of finding support amongst the other States, and partly by supporting their republican form of government. This made them, at least in the Tsar's eyes, appear incapable of entering into an alliance, and was also likely to prove less favourable than a monarchical government to an outbreak of hostilities.

After 1871, the policy of the Danube monarchy underwent a complete revolution. Count Andrassy, the first Hungarian to whom the emperor entrusted the guidance of foreign affairs, turned away once for all from Middle Europe, and sought his ends in the Balkans. Here he encountered the opposition of Russia, and thus found himself thrown upon a close alliance with Germany. Friendly relations had subsisted from of old between Russia and Germany, and by the events just mentioned, which happened at the time of the Franco-German War, the good understanding had been still further strengthened. Yet these very relations with Russia forced the Imperial Chancellor outside the circle of the politics of Europe, into the midst of the problems of world politics. Since the days of Peter the Great, Russian policy had been seeking an outlet, now in one path and now in another, to one of the oceans. After her defeat in the Crimean War, she had extended her Asiatic possessions beyond Turkestan and Bokhara as far as the Amu-darja river; but towards 1870 she turned back upon the Balkans, to make the Dardanelles, which were from of old the chief goal of Russian aspirations, ripe for an assault. And at that very time, Russian efforts after expansion were hallowed by the idea of gathering all Slavs together under the leadership of Russia. 'Panslavism' recognized a sacred mission in putting an end to the depravity of the civilization of western Europe, and building up a new world, in which the God-fearing, unspoilt, Slavonic race would lead and govern; taken in this connection, the aggrandizement of Russia seemed a God-given task, in which all Slavs must co-operate. Thus Panslavism became a danger to world-peace: for its aims could only be attained by the annihilation of Turkey and the dissolution of Austria-Hungary. English efforts after expansion were opposed to those of

Bismarck's Empire

Russia. In the East Indies, South Africa, and Australia the English had greatly extended their possessions, and after a period of indifference towards colonial questions, the extension and internal settlement of her colonies became in the 'seventies the aim of English policy: after Disraeli took the reins in 1874, Queen Victoria called herself 'Empress of India,' and England stretched out her hand towards the Suez Canal. Newly united Germany was still a stranger to this imperialism—this struggle for world-supremacy. She did not strive for an expansion of her European territory; she was 'saturated,' as Bismarck said, and felt only the first stirrings of economic and colonial ambition. But as the Russian menace to India and the Dardanelles was causing severe tension between Russia, England, and Austria, Bismarck must strive to hold the Powers apart, and thus preserve peace. Whether at bottom he would rather have decided for England or for Russia, is not quite clear, even to-day. But, in any case, he saw as little promise of a successful foreign policy for Germany in the connection with Russia, as he felt permanently bound to Austria by the Dual Alliance. Even the isolation of France was not intended by him to exclude the country permanently from the support of another Power, provided that such an alliance was calculated to insure the peace of Europe.

For this was the only object pursued by Bismarck's foreign policy: he needed peace, that he might, in peace and quietness, build up the empire. In course of time even his opponents were obliged to admit the sincerity of his endeavours, a fact which did not endear him to those who could only attain their desires by embroiling others in war. An extensive system of alliances served his end. Seeing that Austria as well as Russia looked for support from the empire, in 1872 he brought about an understanding between the monarchical and conservative Eastern Powers (Relation between the Three Emperors) which, like the Holy Alliance, was also intended to serve the ends of domestic policy. Yet the Russian partner soon proved himself a most irksome confederate. In the middle of the 'seventies, when the tension between France and Germany was growing more acute, the French Chamber had determined upon a considerable increase in her standing army; and a German newspaper had alarmed the public with the critical question: 'Is War in sight?' Thereupon Gortschakoff, the Russian chancellor, on the occasion of a visit to Berlin, felt it his duty to assure the world that 'Peace is now guaranteed' —because Russia had taken the side of France. Three years later the breach came. A revolt of Serbs and Montenegrins against Turkish rule stirred up Panslavist passion—Russia declared war on Turkey after, at Bismarck's instigation, she had resigned Bosnia and Herzegovina to the Danube monarchy. After severe fighting, the Russo-Turkish War (1877–78) ended with a complete victory for Russia. But both Austria and England raised a protest against the conditions of the peace of St. Stefano, by which Turkey-in-Europe was almost wiped out, and the Russians obtained large stretches of territory in Asia. To prevent a world war, Bismarck declared his readiness to mediate. Under his presidency, the conditions of the Near East were set in order at the Berlin Congress of 1878. Russia gained Batoum, which was important as the port of the petroleum district, together with Bessarabia (for which Rumania received the Dobrudscha in exchange), and became paramount in Bulgaria, which was declared a principality under Turkish rule. Servia, Montenegro, and Rumania gained their independence, and Austria-Hungary was granted rights of administration and occupation in Bosnia and Herzegovina, so that the Sultan's sovereignty over these territories became an empty form. Turkey ceded Cyprus to England. Bismarck had devoted all his diplomatic skill as 'an honourable broker' to the task of reconciling the conflicting Powers. On the Russian side, however, they had looked for the services, not of a broker, but, as Bismarck bitterly remarked, of a vassal. Russian ill-humour was so openly expressed that he looked about him for a safeguard. Under these circumstances he concluded in 1879 the Dual Alliance with Austria-Hungary: both Powers promised each other mutual help in case of a Russian attack, and benevolent neutrality in case of attack from another quarter. The Dual Alliance might be looked upon as the realization of the 'wider union' which had been planned in the Paul's Church, and it enjoyed extraordinary popularity. Yet, contrary to Bismarck's wish, it was not submitted to the national representatives for their approval, and remained therefore an alliance of Governments, not of nations.

When the excitement had died down in Russia, Bismarck

again took up the question of their relations. A treaty which was less comprehensive, but more definite, took the place of the vague understanding between the emperors. The three Governments guaranteed each other mutual neutrality, in case one of them were to become involved in a war with another Great Power; this put an end to the danger of a Franco-Russian alliance. But after a few years, it became evident that even a treaty of this kind was incompatible with the tension which existed between Russia and Austria. If Bismarck hoped to continue in any sense to exert a moderating influence upon their antagonism, he must content himself with binding the two Powers separately to Germany. On the basis of the Dual Alliance, he was sure of Austria; in 1887 he entered for three years into a new treaty with Russia, the so-called Reinsurance Treaty. Russian neutrality if Germany should be attacked by France; German neutrality in case of an attack by Austria upon Russia; favourable settlements for Russia in addition to the conditions of the Congress of Berlin—there was nothing remarkable in these conditions. But what followed was peculiar: if the Tsar should find it necessary, in defence of his rights on the Black Sea, to seize the Dardanelles, Germany bound herself not to simple neutrality alone, but also to moral and diplomatic support. Now Bismarck had bound himself in a treaty with Italy to guarantee Turkey in her possessions: the understanding between Italy, England, and Austria, of which mention has yet to be made, rested on the same basis. As Bismarck himself admitted, it was not easy to reconcile his assurance to Russia with these stipulations. Yet he accepted the fresh obligation in order to keep Russia apart from France, with which war seemed almost inevitable in this same year.

Bismarck succeeded in attaching even England, Russia's enemy, to his system of alliances. This was accomplished by way of Italy. The Italian Government asked for admission into the Austro-German Alliance, because in 1881 they felt themselves hampered in their efforts to expand, and even threatened in their property, by the settlement of France in Tunis. It is true there were serious points of difference between Italy and the Danube monarchy: for the Italians demanded not only the inclusion of their 'unredeemed' compatriots in the southern Tyrol, but also the control of the Adriatic coast, on which lay Austria's sea-ports, Trieste and Pola. The Triple Alliance of 1882 did at least prevent these quarrels from coming to a head, while at the same time Germany gained a further guarantee against France, on which Bismarck, it is true, set very little store. In case Italy should be attacked by France, the two other Powers were to come to her help. Italy accepted the same obligation towards Germany. In other cases, the signatories to the treaty were to preserve a benevolent neutrality. But if England should take the part of the aggressor, the treaty was not to apply. This had been expressly stipulated by Italy. England was naturally well disposed to the treaty, seeing that it counteracted the further expansion of France in the Mediterranean. Some time later, Bismarck even brought about an Anglo-Italian agreement, in which both States promised to support each other against the Franco-Russian efforts to expand in the Mediterranean and the Black Sea; in 1887 Austria entered into the agreement, and was thus protected against Russian expansion in the Near East.

If one adds the alliance formed in the year 1883 between Rumania, Austria, and Germany, which was chiefly intended to strengthen Rumania's position in regard to Russia, and was not expected by Bismarck to be of longer duration, then one has a view of the ingenious system, with its wide-spreading ramifications, through which the peace of Europe was at that time ensured. This system enabled its creator to pursue a 'backhand policy.' Even Russia and England, whose world-policy seemed to be irreconcilably opposed, found it difficult, because of the settlements which they had agreed to, or supported, to bring their quarrels to the point of hostilities, and if war should break out, Germany was in a position to turn the scale. It is true that in Bismarck's last years, the tension between the Powers was aggravated to such an extent that he was forced to follow such an intricate path as that of the Reinsurance Treaty; and the failure of the German-English and Anglo-German negotiations, which played once more an important rôle, particularly at the end of the 'eighties, pointed to the growing difficulties of the situation, in which Bismarck's successors were afterwards involved.

He knew how to overcome them: even at the eleventh hour he won a share for the German people in the overseas

Bismarck's Empire

world. It was against his will that he took up the task: for his first care was the safeguarding of Germany within the European State system. Yet he did not close his mind to the necessity of affording the protection of the empire to the mercantile undertakings, which had been called into life by German daring overseas. With this in view, the creator of the national empire on the Continent founded a second overseas economic empire, which posterity with all its efforts was not able materially to extend. From the year 1884 onwards, German South-West Africa, Togoland, Cameroon, German East Africa—whose annexation was chiefly due to Karl Peters—Kaiser-Wilhelmsland in New Guinea, the Bismarck Archipelago, and the Marschall Islands became German colonies.

The colonization of distant coasts bore witness to the prosperous development of German business life. Political unity had opened up a field to the spirit of enterprise which seemed to be unlimited. In 1878, 1,000 kilometres of railroad had been laid down in Prussia; by the end of 1872, 5,000 kilometres were in course of construction. At that time there was no lack of funds. So far as the French milliards, which were flowing in with a rapidity beyond all expectation, were not employed at once on great imperial tasks, they found their way to the private banks, and from thence they fructified business life. And the simple middle classes, who at the outbreak of war had without hesitation placed their lives at the service of the national idea, and their purses also, though in very inadequate measure, now in the period of bubble companies hazarded the last penny of their savings to obtain shares in the businesses which were springing up like mushrooms out of the ground. In the two years 1871 and 1872 more than 750 Prussian limited companies, not all of which, by any means, were free from objection, were added to those which, to the number of about 200, were already in existence.

The crash on the exchange in the year 1873 brought a terrible disillusionment; thousands of families lost their economic support, hosts of workmen had no bread to eat. Germany did not recover from the blow till towards the end of the decade, but then matters quickly took an upward trend, for the business life of Germany rested on a sound basis. In the year of the founding of the empire, the output of coal had risen to double the yield of 1860; in 1880, to

The Citizens and their Empire

four times; in 1890, to fully six times; and in 1914, to fifteen times the amount. Trade developed in a similar way.

All the abundance of energy and intellect, which became evident in the upward trend of business life in Germany, was placed by the middle class at Prince Bismarck's disposal for the building up of the empire. In the first Reichstag, the National Liberals held 119 out of 382 seats, fully double as many as the Centre, which was the next strongest party. Bismarck neither could nor would reject such an alliance. It was true that his Liberal allies were not allowed to prejudice the Conservative character of Old Prussia, particularly her powerful army under the command of the Prussian king. Under Bismarck's leadership, the Conservative powers in the 'sixties had beaten back the Liberal offensive, and thus made possible the rise of Prussia and the founding of the empire; they were now to be the determining factor in Prussia, and, by means of the Federal Council, in the empire also. For Prussia's voice was authoritative in the Federal Council, and the Federal Council was not only of decisive importance for the legislation—no law of the empire could be passed without its assent; it also possessed all the executive power. If the Reichstag disapproved of any measure of the Imperial Government, it could only appeal to the Imperial Chancellor, who bore the responsibility for those who held office in the empire—the States Secretaries subordinate to him; yet the Reichstag was unable to bring about his removal, since the dismissal as well as the appointment of the Imperial Chancellor was dependent upon the will of the emperor alone. As a last resort, the Parliament had in its power the refusal of the grant of the imperial revenue: but the experiences of the Prussian fight for the Constitution were a warning against the application of this extreme method.

Bismarck met every attempt to extend the rights of Parliament, with the most decided negative. Even at that date the deputies received no daily allowances, nor even their railway fares, but a pass only, which was restricted a few years later to the line of rail between Berlin and their domicile. How, then, could the desire for an Imperial Ministry which should be responsible to the Reichstag—above all, the desire for an Imperial Finance Minister—have met with success? The Reichstag had no influence whatever upon foreign politics: under threat of resignation

Bismarck's Empire

Bismarck won the further point, that the means needed under any circumstances for the required strengthening of the army were granted him for seven years, and on expiry of the time, a majority was again forthcoming for the same demand. Since the parliamentary right of assent was seriously impaired in this manner, its activities were limited to the economic and legal departments, which Bismarck had marked out for it from the beginning. Here the co-operation of the Liberals with the Imperial Chancellor had been extraordinarily fruitful: whether one calls to mind the uniform regulation of the coinage and of weights and measures, the setting up of the postal, telegraph, and telephone services, which were directed in an exemplary way by Heinrich von Stephan, a man who had risen from the humblest circumstances, the penal code of the empire, the constitution of the law courts in 1876, or the rules of court, and the preparatory work for the civilian code which became law in 1900. In addition, during the early years when Bismarck was at feud with the Conservatives, he permitted his Liberal allies to attack the seignorial rights of the great landowners. In 1872 the bye-laws of districts were formulated, which did away with the police authority and village administration of the eastern landowners; and these were followed some years later by the Provincial Order: these laws carried Stein's idea of self-government a stage farther, though not yet to its consummation.

The help of the Liberals was most valuable to the Imperial Chancellor in his fight with the Centre Party. The ecclesiastical dominions in Germany had fallen victims to the storms of the Napoleonic era; the victory of the national idea strengthened the powers of Liberal opposition and still further circumscribed the sphere of the Church. Catholic Austria broke away from Germany; Prussia, which was predominantly Protestant, took the lead in the new empire; during the Franco-German War the Italians put an end to the secular rule of the Pope, and Rome became the capital of United Italy. Yet tribulation only strengthened the inner force of the Church. The Prussian Centre Party was formed in 1870 with the object of defending the liberty of the Church, and maintaining the elementary schools, which were separated according to creed. At the election to the first Reichstag, the Bishop of Mainz, Freiherr von Ketteler, defined the task of that fraction of it: to provide that the Catholics, 'being neither led astray nor diminished even in the New Germany,' should be able to live in accordance with their faith, and not be dependent upon the caprice of a hostile majority. As the Prussian Government, after its defeat in the struggle over mixed marriages (p. 322), had admitted some articles into the Constitution which adequately ensured the ecclesiastical right of self-determination, the Centre moved the adoption of these articles into the Imperial Constitution. Although the proposal called for drastic alteration in the law of the empire, a conflict would not have arisen on that account: there was more in question. The Welfs, who denied the legality of the annexation of Hanover, joined the Centre Party; Windthorst, who had served the dethroned King of Hanover as his minister, was one of the founders of the Centre Party, and after a few years accepted its leadership. In the Polish territories where, thanks to Prussian administration, a strong peasant class and an ambitious middle class had grown up, the people looked upon the Catholic priests as the leaders of their national revolt against German rule, which was giving anxiety to the Imperial Chancellor. As early as the first election to the Reichstag, the Centre candidate easily defeated the Duke of Ratibor, who a few years before had himself attracted almost all the recorded votes. There was a further point at issue, which had arisen as a consequence of the Vatican Council of the year 1870. The Council had declared the Pope to be infallible, if he should promulgate a decision in matters of faith and morals; the German bishops bowed to the decree; yet there were many university professors and teachers of religion who did not submit, and the Centre demanded that the State should remove these insubordinates from their offices. Bismarck regarded the whole attitude of the party as 'a mobilization against the State,' and a serious threat to the empire, because of the support which it received from Catholics outside Germany, and from the papal chair, and he resolved to take the most severe measures in alliance with his Liberal following.

The main battle was fought in Prussia. In 1872 the elementary schools were withdrawn from the control of the priests and put under State control. The 'May Laws' of the following year gave the State authorities the right of prohibiting the appointment of priests, prescribed the education of priests in German high schools and German universities, and deprived the Pope of criminal jurisdiction over the clergy. By the Civil Registration Law, legal marriages and the registration of births and deaths, which till then had been part of the official duties of the clergy, were transferred to the Civil Service. In other German countries the struggle ran a much less bitter course. Yet Bismarck had the Federal Council upon his side: the imperial law forbidding the clergy to attack the State during divine service, arose out of a Bavarian motion. The expulsion of the Jesuits in 1872 was decreed by imperial law, and the Civil Registration Law adopted by the empire. The State endeavoured by fines, imprisonment, and banishment to break the opposition to these measures, of which the 'May Laws' in particular interfered most seriously with the internal law of the Church. In Prussia, with few exceptions, the bishops' seats and about a quarter of the livings were left desolate. But priests and laymen stood firm, and the oppressed party found unexpected support. It had been founded by men of Conservative leanings; now it became a party of the discontented masses; in 1878 it won more than 100 seats in the Reichstag, and maintained this number with slight variations for many years.

Bismarck found himself obliged to give way. When Leo XIII had ascended the papal chair, he opened negotiations with him, and gradually annulled the contentious laws. After the law against the Jesuits had lapsed during the World War, the Constitution of Weimar destroyed their remaining vestiges. The attempt of the State to transform at will the ecclesiastical law was defeated, equally with the attempt of the Church to alter the constitution of the empire to suit its wishes. State and Church must come to an understanding: this was the moral of the cultural war.

The year 1878 marked a turning-point in Bismarck's domestic, as well as his foreign, politics. After the Berlin Congress it was no longer possible to reckon as before upon the friendship of Russia: the Imperial Chancellor had to seek new means of ensuring peace, and found them in an extensively ramified system of alliances. In the same way the course of domestic politics had up till then been predominantly determined by questions whose roots lay deep in the past. In economic and legal life the consequences of German disunion were done away with. State and Church,

The Citizens and their Empire

which in earlier times had again and again opposed each other as enemies, marked out new boundaries for their spheres of action. The Conservative forces also adapted themselves to the new circumstances, though not at first without a severe struggle. The events of 1866 had already alienated the Conservatives from the Chancellor (p. 350); the cultural war deepened the enmity: a law like that of the State control of schools was an infringement of the authority of the Evangelical Church, no less than of the Catholic. An ugly campaign of calumny was started against Bismarck, and he never rested till he had thrown some of his Conservative opponents into the House of Correction. But in the end reason conquered on both sides: the Conservatives needed the Imperial Chancellor, even as he had need of them. And after Bismarck gave up the struggle with the Centre, that party also proved ready for peace and co-operation. On the other hand, the Government's retreat before this party put many of the Liberals out of humour. The Liberal confederate of the first years was no longer the same; new possibilities of alliance became apparent, and the Imperial Chancellor pressed them with much less success into his service, as he had done in the case of his foreign policy. With his new allies he faced the two tasks which were entirely concerned with the future, and gave its character to the last decade of his official life: the linking on of the fourth estate to the empire, which had been built up on a Conservative basis, and the creation of financial independence for the Imperial Government.

The decisive change was heralded by Bismarck's customs policy. For a long time German industry had had to contend with the competition of the English, and in an increasing degree with that of the Americans also; many new businesses had been launched during the period of bubble companies, and the purchasing power of the home market was crippled by the after-effects of the crash on the exchange. In the first place, big business demanded the change from free trade to protection, if only in order to shake off foreign competition, and it was joined by agriculture, which was beginning in the 'seventies to feel the competition of cheap foreign grain. This decided the Conservatives, a great part of the Centre, and those of the National Liberals who were interested in big business, to stand for protective tariffs. Bismarck hoped that this opportunity would allow him to obtain revenues from the new duties, which would insure greater independence for the Government in its relations to the Reichstag. Owing to party opposition he was only able to realize this intention in a very modest degree. Yet the measure of protective tariffs passed in 1878 had the effect desired by manufacturers and agriculturists, and became of great importance in domestic politics. The agriculturists, who in the 'sixties had still voted preponderantly Liberal, learnt from this time forward to look partly to the Conservatives and partly to the Centre to represent their class, and the Conservatives made a close alliance with the Imperial Government, which was fulfilling their economic wishes. In northern Germany the three ideas covered by the words rural, Conservative and loyal to the Government, came in time to have an almost identical meaning. Even the Centre began to pay more attention to the needs of its agricultural electors, but were preserved from the same one-sided attitude by the very varied composition of its electorate. The gain of these parties was the loss of the National Liberals. Part of them held so firmly by the doctrine of the free development of economic life, that they could not accustom themselves to such an interference on the part of the Government as was represented by protective tariffs. These men turned their back on party, and were later absorbed into the Progressives, who went to form the German Independent Liberal Party (Deutschfreisinnige Partei), who prided themselves on as resolute an opposition to the Government, as the remainder of the National Liberals upon unconditional obedience. The great age of the Liberal Party was over. It was on the majorities arising out of these conditions that Bismarck depended, when he went forward to meet his new tasks.

In consequence of the employment of steam-power, manual labour had been superseded to a large extent by machinery. When the processes of labour were divided up into the smallest possible fractions, the workers were robbed of their joy in their daily work: it became soulless, monotonous, and stupefying. But the misery of life continually drove new crowds into the manufacturing towns, calling nothing their own but their power to work. Employers utilized the great demand for work, to lower wages, to lengthen the working hours, and to replace the work of men by the cheaper labour of women and children. In Germany too the majority of industrial workers passed a dismal existence in hard drudgery, between the factory, the miserable dwelling, and the inn; through the fluctuations of trade they were exposed without defence to perpetually recurring loss of work, and were without provision for the days of illness and old age. Family, home, Fatherland, which for other classes represented the values of life, lost all meaning for them.

In this way the conditions were laid down for the growth of a proletarian class consciousness. Yet it was not till the 'sixties that a labour movement broke away from middle-class Liberalism to work for its own aims. Its leaders came from the middle class. Ferdinand Lassalle was inspired no less than they by the idea of national unity and greatness; like the Liberals he worked for universal suffrage. He looked forward by its help to seizing the paramount influence in the State for the working classes: the working men were to found 'co-operative societies,' in which the employer's profit would be excluded, and the full reward of their labour given to the workers. As a matter of fact, the 'Universal Union of German Working Men' founded in 1863, through which Lassalle hoped to realize his plan, did not grow to a membership of more than a few thousands. Yet the ground was prepared for the ideas which Karl Marx evolved in his London exile, and Liebknecht and Bebel promulgated amongst the German working class.

His studies in Berlin determined the course pursued by the Rhinelander Marx. Here he learnt to know and to master the philosophy of Hegel. Hegel's methods of reasoning set the standard for his own work: but it was also affected by the master's way of pressing actual phenomena into the service of his system of thought. At the same time, Marx became acquainted with the men who were building up the system of religious materialism (p. 320). A stay of several years in Paris and Brussels gradually matured his plan of superseding the ideas of the French Socialists, by a great expansion of the field of materialistic thought: it was not religious conceptions alone which Marx explained by social conditions, but all human thoughts and desires; while social conditions—in which were included political forms—were traced back by him to the methods of production belonging to the period in question. While thinking along these lines, he came into contact with Frederick Engels, the son of an Elberfeld manufacturer, who at that time was preparing his work on the position of the working classes in England. Community of views drew the men together, and laid the foundation of a lifelong partnership. With the self-sacrificing support of his friend, Marx was able later to accomplish his great work *Capital*, in which he laid the basis of his teaching.

In accordance with his materialistic conception of history, Marx looked upon the conflict between Capital and Labour as an evolution, which was working itself out with the unerring surety of a process of natural law. It was this view chiefly which distinguished him from earlier Socialist thinkers. As inevitably as the growth of great industries leads to the accumulation of capital in a few hands, and to the proletarization of the rest of mankind, will the 'dictatorship of the proletariat'—when at some future time its way is prepared by the union of all working men outside the frontiers of country—disappropriate the disappropriators, and communalize, that is to say, socialize, the means of production. To this day thinkers are divided into two camps: those who recognize that this development will follow with the inevitability of a natural phenomenon, and those who deny it. As we are here concerned with the historical point of view, our main object must be to discover whether his thought could arouse the forces which make history. In this the Marxian doctrine succeeded to an extraordinary degree. Marx was the first to bring into action the 'independent movement of the huge majority.' He was the first to lead the working masses into close union, and direct them towards political will and action. Even in the last decades, this fact exercised an influence not inferior in importance to that of the liberal and national ideas in the nineteenth century, and its final development is not yet within sight.

Under the influence of the Marxian teaching, Bebel and Liebknecht separated the Saxon and South German Workmen's Unions from the democratic National Party, and in 1869 founded in Eisenach the Social Democratic Labour Party. In 1875, after a series of violent quarrels, Lassalle's followers united with the Marxists at Gotha, to form the Socialist Labour Party of Germany. Two years

The Citizens and their Empire

later, the party were already sending twelve deputies to the Reichstag: half a million electors stood behind them. It was in a harsh and narrow-minded form that the social-democratic idea first made its appearance in political life. Even the middle-class Left was conscious of being threatened by a movement which proclaimed war upon Capital, upon the State governed by it, and upon the pillars of the State, the Army and the Church. Bismarck took up the challenge: the newly formed party must be smashed, but the working class must be incorporated into the structure of the empire. During the first years after the foundation of the empire, he had already exhausted every legal means for the persecution of social democracy. An attempt to assassinate the old emperor seemed to create the atmosphere which he required for the passing of an emergency measure 'against the attempts of social democracy which are dangerous to the commonwealth.' Yet the Reichstag rejected the motion. When the emperor was dangerously wounded by a second murderous attack, Bismarck dissolved the Reichstag, and in 1878 the newly elected house agreed to the law against the Socialists, which stood for twelve years. It prohibited all Socialist meetings and publications; those who resisted were severely punished. But each election gave fresh proof that men of Socialist views were holding closely together. In the middle of the 'eighties they sent twice as many delegates to the Reichstag as in the year before the Socialist law was passed. Under these circumstances the social legislation for sickness, accident, disablement, and old age insurance, which was enacted between 1883 and 1889, did not result in reconciling the working class to the existing State, the more that the State regarded its disbursements not as the fulfilment of a claim, but as a favour, and neglected to recommend insurance to the working men by securing them a considerable share of self-government. For this reason the social policy of a later date did not help to relieve social tension, to the extent that might have been possible if things had been managed differently.

For this legislation was a magnificent and beneficent work. Through it the German State stood confessed as the first to take up a task, about which, with the exception of some employers, only a few of the parties had till then concerned themselves, while the workmen had endeavoured to help themselves in their unions out of their own resources.

Bismarck's Empire

On the Catholic side, Bishop von Ketteler had taken the lead, gathering together a part of the Catholic workmen into social working-men's clubs, the precursors of the Christian trade unions. But the free trade unions formed on Marxist principles developed more strongly than either these or the Hirsch-Duncker unions: in the year 1928 they numbered approximately five million members.

Bismarck had to fight hard to extort the Socialist law from the parties, and almost all the legislative work of the last decade of his chancellorship was accomplished under the same unlucky star. Even the Reichstag, which had been elected while the impression of the attempt upon the emperor was still fresh, proved by no means docile: a few years later the Progressive Party won approximately 100 seats, and not till 1887 did the electoral alliance between Conservatives and National Liberals secure a safe majority for the Government. Bismarck obtained the assent of this Reichstag to a number of great legislative proposals: it passed a comprehensive law regarding military service, and the insurance against old age and disablement: a duty was placed upon brandy, and the duties on rye and wheat considerably increased. The two last laws filled the pockets of the great landed proprietors; the duty on brandy was called, not unjustly, a love-token for the agricultural land-owners. But Bismarck himself was nearing the goal, which he had pursued during these years with peculiar earnest-ness: the opening up of adequate sources of revenue for the Imperial Government. He had at least won so much for the empire by the protective tariff laws of the year 1878, as to be able to give back to the single States the 'food' con-tribution which they were under obligation to render. The Government had still to solve the problem of becoming more independent of the Reichstag. Again and again Bismarck returned to the attack. He made a new attempt, as he had already done in the 'seventies, to bring the railways into the possession of the empire: he had to content himself with purchasing the Prussian railways for Prussia. He tried a duty on tobacco, a tobacco monopoly, a brandy monopoly: the duty on brandy already men-tioned remained the sole fruit of all these efforts. At the same time he did not hesitate to use threats: he would remove the Parliament from Berlin, summon it only every two years instead of yearly, as was prescribed by the Constitution: he would let it 'grow rusty' while for the most part he performed the legislative work with the diets of the single States; he even tried to alarm the deputies by changing from a secret to a public ballot, and went so far as to discuss with an intimate the possibility of a new basis for the empire, in the form of a League of Princes to the exclusion of the Parliament. It was all in vain: the majority of the delegates had no inclination to reduce still farther the slight influence which they exercised upon the conduct of the empire, by resigning the right which they possessed to sanction taxes.

The fact that the founder of the empire had recourse to such threats, demonstrated more than any other circumstance the tension which had developed between the governors and the majority of the governed, after a few years of his leadership. The creature had revolted against its creator. Bismarck's sensitive nature suffered severely under the struggle, and in a speech in the Reichstag which has become famous he gave violent expression to his feelings. He set out the nature of the quarrel in an allegory, in which he represented the electors as seduced by party strife, the old hereditary enemy of Germany, to slay their own Fatherland; as in the Germanic Saga of the Gods, dark Loki pressed into the hand of the blind Hödur the arrow which slew the shining Sun God. To prevent the last extremity the Imperial Chancellor, like a valiant hero or saga, attacked the Dark One wherever he imagined he could be found: yet he did not strike the weapon from his hand. It did not and could not occur to him to grant sight to the blind elector, to give him an interest in the fortunes of the empire through really responsible co-operation. He did, indeed, suspect the power of the forces which were surging up out of the depths and demanding influence and authority; but how could the man who, by his own confession, felt himself to be first of all a royalist, and only secondarily a Prussian and a German, have been able to comprehend their nature and to connect their future with the future of his creation? His work is restricted by a fatal and tragic limitation.

For a while Bismarck was able to set his hopes upon the young heir to the throne, believing that he would carry on the fight at his side; but the prince changed rapidly under the influence of the Court circle, which was anti-Bismarck. The Emperor William died in the year 1888. He was followed to the grave a few months later by his son, the Emperor Frederick III, who showed manly self-command in bearing his incurable sufferings. The third generation came into power with William II (1888–1918). Bismarck's fall became certain when the young emperor turned against the main lines of his policy, and the Reichstag also withdrew its adherence. Under the influence of Count Waldersee, the General Chief of the Staff, the emperor had acquired the firm conviction that a war against Russia, with which Bismarck had only with difficulty kept the peace during the last few years (p. 366), was now imminent, and that for this reason, if for no other, the Russian policy which had been hitherto followed must now be abandoned. The fact that in the labour question William II took up an attitude opposed to that of Bismarck, led to direct conflict with the Chancellor. Bismarck wished to utilize the great strike of the year 1889 to give the decisive blow to social democracy; for a long time he had harboured the thought of depriving the social democratic electors of their vote. On the other hand, the emperor intervened personally to settle the strike, and resolved to introduce the Workmen's Protection Act: all parties were agreed upon its necessity, but the Imperial Chancellor rejected it, as before, in the most decided manner. And Bismarck not only clung to his point of view: he intended to put a still sharper edge upon his weapons. Hence he was not displeased that the Reichstag this time threw out the Socialist Bill (1890). The new election of February 1890 brought a considerable gain in seats to the Liberals and Social Democrats, the latter polling nearly $1\frac{1}{2}$ million votes, the greatest number obtained by any of the parties. If Bismarck was determined to demand from this Reichstag a more drastic Socialist Bill, and a great increase in the army, there could be no doubt that he was working for an open breach. And William II left no room for doubt that he would not follow him along these lines. Subordinate points at issue heightened the tension. Pressed by the emperor in March 1890, Bismarck at last gave in his resignation.

'To me has fallen the duty of the officer on guard upon the ship of State. The course remains the same. Full steam ahead.' These were the closing words of the communication

The Citizens and their Empire

which William II sent to one of the federal princes. . . . It was a nervous hand which seized the helm.

There was no lack of difficulties in the single States also. In the case of Prussia, for example, the growth of Polish influence in the eastern provinces presented a danger which there were no means adequate to meet. But conditions in the States were less involved than in the empire: it was not necessary first to familiarize oneself with them; fixed political traditions were in existence. This lightened the labour of legislation. In Prussia, under Bismarck, this work had come to a complete standstill; his departure left the way free for a number of important innovations. The Parish Act carried on the idea of self-government; Miquel's reform of taxation—a graduated income-tax in connection with a tax on property—gave effect to social points of view. In the social sphere also, imperial legislation took a considerable step forward. At first William II actively espoused the case of Workmen's Protection; the increase in the numbers of workmen and the growth of the Social Democratic Party worked later in the same direction. The Workmen's Protection Act, therefore, first came into being in 1890; the introduction of Sunday rest, the protection of women and children, with the regulating of working contracts, were some of its most important provisions. In the Imperial Insurance Act of 1911 the various social laws were assimilated one to another, the obligation of insurance substantially extended, and survivors' insurance added. The empire also intervened more intimately in the affairs of the industrial middle class, not only through the cultivation of craftsmen's boards and of the system of guilds, but through the extension of the obligation of insurance to the employee. Yet all personal relationship was lacking between the leaders of industry and the workmen's leaders, and not one of the great acts of legislation reconciled the master standpoint of the employers with the desire for power felt by the social democratic working class. Since the Government was neither willing to alienate the employers, nor able to venture upon open war with the masses, the leadership slipped gradually out of their hands.

Even in the first years of William II they had made substantial concessions to the Reichstag, in order to induce it to agree to the greatly increased expenditure upon military service. In 1892, under the Imperial Chancellor Caprivi, the period of military service was reduced to two years: and a few years later the Reichstag was given the right to pass the army estimates year by year. Yet not one of the parties was prepared to seize the reins. By means of the 'Farmers' Union,' the Conservatives gained the adherence of the smaller proprietors, where these proprietors did not associate themselves with the Centre: they had a firm hold at the same time of the House of Lords; on the basis of the three-class franchise, they dominated the Prussian House of Deputies; the National Liberals supported them in the Reichstag on questions of duties and customs. A change in the existing state of things would have created nothing but embarrassments and dangers. On the other side, Social Democracy could calmly await developments. Almost every election brought it a large increase in votes, so that, in the end, in the Reichstag of 1912, it won by far the largest number of seats. It is true that responsibility increased with the number of votes; was this mighty force always to be held in reserve for the critical moment, or to be introduced now, on the basis of existing conditions, and in the regular course of parliamentary work, to improve the lot of the working class? The 'Revisionists' decided on the second alternative, and their influence was steadily growing: in Baden, matters had already gone so far that the Social Democrats joined the Liberals of the Left, and voted for the Government estimates. But the Socialist deputies in the Reichstag persisted in their hostile attitude towards the State. In the sharp antithesis of Right and Left, the Centre became the 'pointer on the scales,' and with the exception of a few years (1907-9) the Government was dependent for a majority upon this party, whose Conservative nature ruled out any substantial alteration in existing conditions. Under these circumstances how could a far-seeing man, like the Liberal Frederick Naumann, have carried through his demand for a democratic empire? Party life had become torpid. It was only with difficulty that the Government could procure the most necessary funds to meet the ever-increasing expenses of the empire. About 1900 the single States were again obliged to raise contributions for the help of the empire; the National Debt grew to such an extent that, in spite of the raising of existing duties and the intro-duction of new by the 'great' Finance Reform of 1909, almost half the calculated increase was swallowed up by the payment of interest. And this happened at a time when the national wealth was growing on an average from six to seven milliards yearly, which in the years 1908–11 was actually exceeded.

After the height of culture attained at the beginning of the century, after the great political events which attended the founding of the empire, the German nation, from the middle of the 'nineties, experienced a period of economic and social growth so rapid and powerful as has scarcely fallen to the lot of any other people. Industry and commerce continued to draw fresh classes of the people into their service; during the twenty-five years which ended in 1907 the number of those employed in industry was almost doubled, and the number of those employed in trade more than doubled. Within approximately the same period, the population of the towns of over 20,000 inhabitants increased from barely a fifth to fully a third of the entire population. If the machine power at the service of production be reduced to units, each approximately equivalent to the work of one man, the sum-total of these units corresponded in the 'nineties to the number of workmen; on the other hand, on the eve of the Great War, in spite of the great increase in the population, the ratio was so altered, that the amount of machine power far more than doubled that of man power. Industry was harnessing the still unutilized forces of Nature, by employing electricity as an active force and a source of light, together with the gas-power machine and the Diesel motor. Stuffs also which hitherto had been almost disregarded, came to be valued for their potential profit. Carburets were obtained from coal-tar, and a great chemical industry was developed in connection with their manufacture. The importance of the rich German alkali fields was first appreciated, when alkali was turned to account for artificial manure. The production of iron yielded phosphorus in the form of Thomas slag, which was in demand for the same purpose; nitrogen was produced from the manufacture of coke and through other processes of production.

With the help of artificial manure, and of machine power, agriculture attained a considerably increased output of crops for food, although the number of those employed in it remained approximately the same. In potato growing Germany took by far the first place; almost as much beetroot sugar was produced as in the two immediately neighbouring countries, Russia and Austria-Hungary, taken together.

In the production of rye, oats, and barley, Germany held a respectable third place after Russia and the United States. And this was due less to protective tariffs than to the skill and industry of the farmer, as was proved by the fact that no other country could show so high a yield per acre. In spite of this progress, the agricultural yield was not sufficient to feed the growing population.

Finally, England's coal output was almost equalled, and her yield of pig-iron nearly doubled. The fierce competition at home and abroad made it necessary for industry to unify production. There were two ways in which this could be done. In particular the coal and iron industry united the various branches of production into powerful companies. A business such as Krupps included the mining of coal and ore: the manufacture of coke: foundries: the working-up of iron and steel into machines, cannon, and armour-plates: in addition to electric works, wharves, and transport by river and sea. On the other hand, a great number of related businesses were united into societies (syndicates, cartels, concerns): one such syndicate fixes prices, orders the share taken in production by the individual factories, and regulates wages according to a uniform rate. Similar giant undertakings were formed to obtain command of traffic.

Germany's network of railways and telegraphs grew till it exceeded those of all other European countries: the empire possessed the largest letter-post, and by far the greatest number of post offices in relation to the number of inhabitants. Goods traffic, with and between the foreign nations, was made possible by a strong mercantile marine, which, however, was still surpassed three or four times by that of England; no Continental port had a busier goods traffic than Hamburg. The Hamburg-American Line and the North German Lloyd developed into the greatest shipping companies in the world; they possessed the largest number of trading ships, the most powerful docks and cranes, with the largest and the best-equipped steamers for passenger traffic, the *Imperator* and the *Vaterland*. Every year, almost as many passengers were carried between Europe and New York by the German companies, as by the English and American companies taken together.

The Citizens and their Empire

The bulk of German products were consumed by the home market, but a considerable amount went abroad. In 1912 German foreign trade reached the high-water mark of 19·7 milliards, and was no longer so very far below the English, which stood at 22·9 milliards. Almost nine-tenths of the imports came under the head of food and luxuries, cattle and industrial raw material, and approximately two-thirds of the exports under the head of finished goods. The distinguishing mark of Germany's economic life, therefore, was the fact that raw products were imported and manufactured goods exported. A population which was increasing yearly by about 800,000 was able to support itself by the labour to which the above numbers bear witness. Emigration which, in the 'eighties, had reached the alarming total of 230,000, dropped to approximately the tenth part, and was surpassed by immigration; the land of emigrants had been turned into a place of immigration by the flourishing state of economic life. The consumption of more costly food and clothing increased with the share of the individual in the national income: in 1896 it was approximately 450 marks, and in 1913 approximately 650; and housing conditions also began to improve.

But with success the dangers increased which threatened its continuance. Even supposing that Germany should not be sympathetically involved in the warlike complications between other States, it was questionable whether the upward trend which set in at a period of universal economic prosperity would continue, and one could scarcely reckon seriously upon the other possibility. Germany was so closely connected with the other nations through the purchase of raw materials and the sale of her products, that every European conflict must have a disastrous effect upon her economic life. But Fate had ordained a much harder trial for the German nation than economic insecurity.

THIRD PART

COLLAPSE

THE share taken by the German nation in world trade increased more rapidly than that of other countries, while Germany's percentage rose from 10·3 per cent. in 1895 to 12·9 per cent. in 1912, England's percentage fell during the same period from 19·2 to 16·6. At the same time, however, the total for import, export, and transit reached a permanently higher level in all industrial countries; Germany came next to England, with her 18·8 milliards in 1904 and 28·6 milliards in 1913, and was immediately followed by the United States, and—at a considerable distance—by the non-German countries of the Continent. All over the globe men were employed in ever-increasing numbers in the production of goods; the factories hummed with work; lines of railway and lines of steamships girdled the world with a close network; incomes rose and wealth accumulated. In the course of this evolution, the individual departments of business became increasingly involved in the world economy. The textile industries of Europe were dependent for cotton upon the United States, Egypt, and India, and to a considerable degree upon Australia, South Africa, and South America for the supply of wool; and they were contending for the markets of the whole world. Capital followed along the roads opened up by trade or politics, with a prospect of high dividends in the countries whose business life was still undeveloped. Before the war, something like a tenth part of the national wealth of Germany was invested in foreign securities, in railways, bank, trading, or factory concerns, and in State loans; two-thirds of this huge sum fell to non-European countries. Business required the backing of the State, in order to maintain itself in foreign markets; and with the growing importance of relations with foreign countries it was no longer enough for the State to take a hand in the economic and social evolution at home, it must accompany industry, trade, and capital into distant parts, smooth the way for them, and protect their sphere of action. In proportion as the State borrowed from prosperous business the means to provide more and more powerful armaments, she made the endeavours of business her own, and placed her diplomatic and military powers at its service. World politics developed out of world economics; the Great Powers were transformed into World Powers, whose mutual relations were determined more and more by their share in world trade, the expansion of their colonial possessions, and the strength of their trading and battle fleets.

Until after the middle of the century, England and Russia alone gave practical proof of their status as World Powers. Their mutual opposition came to light in the 'thirties in the conflict over India and Constantinople; but since as a rule their spheres of expansion lay widely apart, they came only seldom to blows (p. 335).

The undisputed command of the seas provided the conditions for a Liberal trend in English politics. England stood firm by Free Trade, and gave the great colonies a certain measure of independence, while she did little towards the deliberate building up of her colonial empire. In the 'seventies and 'eighties Gladstone was still leading the British Empire along Liberal lines, though he was forced repeatedly to resign the reins of State to the Conservatives, who had Disraeli for their most prominent politician. When the United States, Germany, France, Japan, and Italy began to follow world politics, the Conservative idea was triumphant.

After that, the creation of a 'Greater Britain' became the aim of English politics, a world empire of such dimensions and such solidity that it would be politically and economically self-supporting. In this endeavour, imperialism, the modern effort after world-power, became most clearly apparent. Now, as in earlier times, Russian policy was dominated by the urge for territorial expansion, whose immediate object was an outlet to one of the oceans. The need of the economic and military support given by great colonial possessions, added to the recollection of her former predominancy, were the chief factors in France's advance in Asia and Africa. At the eleventh hour Bismarck had created a modest colonial empire for Germany; as there was no hope of increasing it substantially, his successors were obliged to turn their minds to keeping open other sources of raw material, and other markets for German industry. As matters stood, economic ends alone could be pursued by German imperialism.

If any one thing can be said with certainty of the many-

sided personality of William II, it is that he never wished
for war. Yet with the first independent step taken by
him in the sphere of foreign politics, begins the series of
self-deceptions which produced their own fatal effect and
played their part in exciting world opinion against Germany. Immediately after Bismarck's dismissal the Foreign
Office refused to renew the Reinsurance Treaty, although
the Russians were prepared greatly to reduce Germany's
obligations. Important reasons of a practical nature could
be assigned for this change; it was believed that the treaty
could not be justified in the eyes of Austria; it was feared
that a renewal would put it in the power of the Russians
'to determine the moment of the future European War.'
Caprivi, the new Imperial Chancellor, expressed himself
with military candour in conversation with Bismarck.
'A man like you can keep five balls in play at the same
time, while other people do well to limit themselves to one
or two balls.' The fact that the decision was influenced by
personal enmity towards Bismarck, on the part of the men
who were now in power, was indeed a serious matter; even
more serious was the Kaiser's assumption that the refusal
would produce no alteration in the relations between
Germany and Russia. A few months later the empire
received the island of Heligoland, which belonged to
England, in exchange for the cession of extensive territory
in East Africa; the Heligoland-Zanzibar Treaty strengthened the impression that Germany had taken her stand
on the side of England in the Anglo-Russian quarrel. At
this point the Russian Government ceased to repel the
approaches of France. The visit of the French fleet to
Cronstadt in 1891 brought about an *entente cordiale*
between the two nations, which found expression in the
following year in a military agreement. What Bismarck
succeeded in preventing during two decades, came to pass
barely two years after his departure: France found the
powerful ally who was able to threaten Germany from the
east. The German ambassador in St. Petersburg, Herr von
Schweinitz, felt himself to be 'an incarnate anachronism,' a
survival from past ages, as he pinned on the Russian Order
of St. Andrew beside the Black Eagle and the Order of
Stephen, in preparation for his ride to the parade ground,
where he would listen to the *Marseillaise*.

The breach with Russia, which was at all times violently

censured by Bismarck and his adherents, might have introduced a clearer if less ambitious policy, if the Imperial
Government had steadily continued along the path which
was now struck out. But self-deception darkened their
eyes. They had already begun to hope for a return to the
old footing with Russia. After William II had initiated the
correspondence which supplied his 'dearest Nicky' with
political advice, an opportunity arose of rendering a more
solid service to Russian politics. In the war between China
and Japan which took place in 1895, Japan had completely
vanquished her opponent, and was stretching out her hand
towards Manchuria. Germany, as well as France, joined
in the protest made by Russia, while England stood on one
side. The Japanese were obliged to give way; Germany
had succeeded in diverting Russia's attention towards
the Far East, and her relations to the Franco-Russian
Dual Alliance had been somewhat improved. But the
transitory success was bought by the lasting disaffection
of Japan, which up till then had been friendly to
Germany—a disaffection which was further aggravated
through the harsh attitude taken up by the German
representative at the time of the combined action of the
Three Powers.

Meanwhile the Government had made many attempts
to move the English to a formal adherence to the Triple
Alliance. But at that time England was not yet willing to
abandon her 'splendid isolation.' The German Government
believed that they might gain their end by means of a threat.
When the commissioner of the English colony of Rhodesia
invaded the Transvaal, William II at first meditated a
military interposition in favour of the wronged nation.
When he was with difficulty dissuaded by his advisers, he
congratulated Krüger, the President of the Boer Republic,
on having preserved the independence of his country
against outside attacks 'without appealing to the help of
friendly Governments.' The Kaiser's telegram had no
other result than that of offending the English, and causing
them to dissolve the loose bond which united them to the
Triple Alliance. Immediately after these events the English
Government gave notice of the Mediterranean Agreement,
which they had arrived at with Italy and Austria (p. 366).
In the course of a few years the policy of Germany had
driven Russia into the arms of France, irritated England

388

Collapse

and Japan, and exposed the allied country of Italy to the threats and solicitations of France.

Yet the foreign Powers were by no means free from disagreements, and towards the end of the 'nineties these led to open enmity. The first clash took place between France and England. Bismarck himself had encouraged France's colonial enterprises, in order to distract the French people from 'staring at the gap in the Vosges.' During the 'eighties and 'nineties the French possessions in Indo-China and West Africa (Senegambia and Algeria) had been considerably increased. After she had acquired Tunis in 1881, the whole of West Africa, with the exception of Morocco, Liberia, and the comparatively small English and German possessions on the Gulf of Guinea, was brought under the dominion of France, and in addition almost all the land between Cameroon and the Belgian Congo State, with the Island of Madagascar.

In order to extend the powerful West African empire beyond the Upper Nile, as far as the Red Sea, an expedition under Marchand penetrated into the Egyptian Sudan. At Fashoda it was brought to a halt by England, which since the occupation of Egypt in 1882 had become possessed of a great part of East Africa, and was striving to establish overland communication between the Cape and Cairo. In 1898, in face of England's warlike preparations, the French Government gave way. The 'gap in the Vosges' was of more importance to Delcassé, the Foreign Minister, than ambitious plans of colonization; but on the other hand hatred of England took the place with the French people of the spirit of revenge dating from the Franco-German War.

In addition, the antagonism between Russia and England became more acute towards the end of the century through Russia's garrisoning of the mountain rampart of India, and the course of events in the east. Japan's attack upon China had put an end to the political isolation of the Far East. After Korea had been brought under Japanese influence, the European World Powers came forward with their various claims, and in addition to economic concessions they extorted a number of important ports from the weak Chinese Government. In 1897 Germany obtained Kiao-chau. The national counter movement came to a head in the sanguinary Boxer Risings of the year 1900; the United States co-operated with the European Great Powers to suppress it. Russia had seized the opportunity to become possessed of the greater part of Manchuria, and from thence threatened the English situation in Eastern waters.

The dangers of 'splendid isolation' were even more directly felt by the English, when they encountered an unexpectedly obstinate resistance to their subjugation of the Boers (1899–1902). While leading English statesmen were seeking a *rapprochement* with Germany, the Franco-Russian Dual Alliance applied to the Imperial Government in the hope of gaining their support for intervention in the Boer War. German politics were given the opportunity of abandoning their isolation and attaching themselves to one of the Powers, which they had hitherto solicited in vain. Was Germany prepared to understand the needs of the hour—the eleventh hour as we now know it to have been?

In Bismarck's empire the Kaiser was the representative of Germany in her relations with other nations; it fell to him to declare war and conclude peace, to make treaties and other agreements with foreign States—and all on the responsibility of the Imperial Chancellor. But responsibility meant no more than an empty form in the case of a Reichstag which up to the last weeks of the World War was allowed an insight into foreign politics in exceptional cases only, and was shut out from all co-operation in this field, as well as in the appointment and dismissal of the Chancellor.

In reality it was the Kaiser alone who had the disposal of the fortunes of a nation of sixty millions. William II was quite aware of this fact. While it leads him in his book, *Ereignisse und Gestalten* (published in England under the title of *Comparative History*), to claim the credit for all the good which happened under his government, the imperial author does not seem to realize how ill this attitude accords with his invariable laying of the blame for neglect and failure upon the shoulders of others.

At times he was so keenly conscious of his responsibility that he grew to feel a peculiar relationship between himself and God, and once again the doctrine of the Divine Right of Kings was presented to the German people in the manner of Frederick William IV, and even in the same terms.

On the other hand, it was much more rarely that the Kaiser's feeling of responsibility gave him the force to act, in defiance of obstacles, upon his better judgment of the needs of the moment. In the opinion of Freiherr von Schoen, who was certainly a lenient judge, he lacked, as a rule, just the gift of a commander which would best have served him, 'the capacity for calmly balancing political considerations.'

In its place he was all the more richly endowed by nature with the desire to be looked upon as a leader and ruler.

Sudden inspirations, which never ceased to suggest themselves to his restless mind, had to supply the place of plan and vigour of action; boisterous words were used to distract the attention of the speaker, as well as of the hearers, from all shortcomings.

'As the Huns made a name for themselves a thousand years ago under the Emperor Attila, so, through you, may the name of German be of such force in China for a thousand years to come, that a Chinaman will never again dare so much as to look askance at a German.' (Address to the China troops before embarkation, 1900.)

Military instructions were on the same lines: 'I anticipate that when the troops march in, they will bag at least 500 people.' (To the General Command of the Garde du Corps during a strike demonstration.) No enemy of Germany, no opponent of the existing order of government, could have put more irritating words into the Kaiser's mouth. No less serious were the consequences of William II's aversion to everything which was calculated to encroach upon his sovereign rôle, and of his incapacity to endure any opposition, however well founded. There were remarkably fine men amongst the ambassadors to foreign Courts, especially in the first years of the Kaiser's reign, but because they were all dependent upon his favour, both they and his other councillors were afraid to show him affairs in their true light, and he made decisions of great consequence upon matters which he did not and could not rightly understand.

This failure of the highest officials and of the Kaiser's entourage clearly shows why the weaknesses of the royal personality were able to operate with such fatal effect. The appointment and dismissal of leading men at the pleasure of the prince suited a period in which cabinet politics decided the fate of the States; the preponderance of great landowners in the Prussian House of Deputies, as a result of the three-class franchise, suited the conditions of an agrarian State. But the three-class franchise was as little compatible with the development of industry and trade, as was the independent action of the Kaiser in the election of the Imperial Chancellor and of the Ministers with the age of world politics. For in consequence of the interpenetration of State and business, this age strengthened the authority of the Government to an extraordinary degree, and allowed an infinitely deeper and wider scope to its operations. If one recognizes the fault of the system, one will not refuse one's human sympathy to the men who, being dependent upon the favour of the ruler, frittered away their strength in the thankless double rôle of Imperial Chancellor and Prussian Minister-President. Their own view of their office throws light upon this fact, no less than upon the extreme diversity of their personalities.

To General Caprivi the Kaiser's will was equivalent to a military command. 'If the presentation of my practical point of view has no result, there is nothing left for me but to carry out the command and to go under. What does it matter? Man overboard!' Old Prince Hohenlohe believed he might look forward to a monument from posterity in reward for what he had prevented during his time of office. Prince Bülow, who was the only chancellor to bring the gifts of a statesman to his office, had for a time a somewhat firmer support in the majority created by himself in the Reichstag. William II was all the more circumspect in the choice of his successor. Herr von Bethmann-Hollweg finally formulated in philosophic terms the 'divinely ordained dependence' of the Germans as a whole, and of the Imperial Chancellor in particular. The fact that, up to the time of Bülow, Herr von Holstein, who had been promoted, exploited, and in the end feared by Bismarck, in his relatively subordinate position as Councillor to the Foreign Office gave directions to the ambassadors over the head of the Imperial Chancellor, is as much a part of this picture, as the silence of the men in the Kaiser's entourage who were rivals for their master's favour, though they cherished no illusions as to the dangers of his methods of government.

Bismarck, as Caprivi expressed it, had transferred the methods of unscrupulous foreign politics into home politics, had educated the official class to obsequiousness, and weaned the nation away from the idea of self-help. However far

Collapse

the leading men diverged from Bismarck's foreign politics, in domestic politics they left things as they were. Not until an English newspaper, the *Daily Telegraph*, reported a speech by the Kaiser, which with almost incredible indiscretion imperilled the relations between England and Germany, was the indignation aroused by the personal rule of the Kaiser expressed from all sides in the Reichstag. That was in the year 1908, when William II had already reigned for twenty years.

But the German nation had not descended to such a degree of materialism and militarism as is still largely believed and taught abroad. In the 'eighties and 'nineties, at the moment when the high tide of economic prosperity had set in, masters like Liebermann brought about the triumph of impressionism in Germany, the art of reproducing 'fragments of nature, seen through the sensitive and entirely individual eye of an artist.' Naturalism implied a similar expansion of vision and creation, through which the world of 'little people,' the city proletariat, was now introduced to the world of imagination. While the philosophy of Kant underwent a further development, Nietzsche's teaching was beginning to make its influence felt. He appears, to the biassed judgment, only as the prophet of the idea of Force, a kind of philosophic pendant to Bismarck. But it was a different matter which gained him the hearts of the young people: the fact that he opposed to the superficial pursuit of pleasure, characteristic of the period, the stern command to fix one's eyes upon work and not upon enjoyment, and that he took up arms, of course with the biassed vision of a prophet, against moral superficiality, pointing to a lofty goal: 'Man is not an end in himself, but a bridge, a passage, a cable, connecting animal and superman.' Towards the end of the century the works of the leading spirits, by their heightened subjectivity and their deepened spirituality, proclaimed that the day of naturalism was over; architects and handicraftsmen discovered new forms, born of that desire for objective simplicity which is perhaps the most valuable artistic heritage bequeathed by the pre-war years to those who are alive to-day.

Official Germany under the leadership of William II opposed an emphatic dissent to those who were preparing the way for the new spirit; the fact that the author of *The*

The Citizens and their Empire

Weavers was in Bülow's time an intimate of the Imperial Chancellor's palace, was a noteworthy exception to this rule.

In the bulk of the middle classes also there was little understanding of the new ideas. If it was in the nature of the mechanical age to set an ever-increasing value upon tangible success, economic progress played its part in bringing the intellectual into disrepute. While efforts to attain a higher standard of national education were influencing a wider circle, and the Socialist papers supplied their readers with very solid literature, the citizen was satisfied with attaining excellence in his own calling. Artistic questions appealed to him as little as political. The same lack of intelligence, which in the 'Wilhelmine era' accumulated senseless forms of decoration in buildings and furniture, led the mass of the middle class to applaud all too loudly the Kaiser's ostentation, his military displays, and his 'powerful' foreign policy.

'The ocean is indispensable for Germany's greatness, but the ocean also proves (!) that upon it and in distant parts beyond it no decision can any longer be reached without Germany and without the German Kaiser.' 'An empire not less authoritative than the Roman world empire of old time'—such words from the Kaiser were applauded. The Pan-German Alliance and the Fleet Union carried on their activities with great stir, while the mass of the working population stood grumblingly aside. William II could believe that he had his people behind him as he steered towards the future of Germany, which, as he said, lay upon the water.

When, in 1897, Bülow was appointed Secretary of State to the Foreign Office, he was obliged at the Kaiser's desire to undertake the duty of advocating the building of a powerful fleet. The Reichstag agreed to the building of the fleet, while at the same time a proposal to bring the land equipment up to full strength was defeated by the opposition of the majority. In the year 1914 the French, with a population of 39 millions, had brought the peace strength of their army, apart from the coloured troops, up to almost 800,000 men, thus outnumbering the 'militarist' Germans with their 65 millions. Some weeks before Bülow's acceptance of office, William had summoned Herr von Tirpitz to be Director of the Imperial Marine. He found in him the right man to carry out his plan. The new fleet became the work of Admiral von Tirpitz, which he advocated in the Reichstag and in public with the same skill and success which he was later to evince in opposition to the Imperial Government, when Bülow, from political considerations, endeavoured to curb his ardour.

The ascendancy of military leadership over political, which was to prove so fateful in the World War, was announced by the Admiralty's victory over the Imperial Chancellor. While the development of the High Seas Fleet was assured (Proposals for the Fleet, 1898–1900) the Imperial Government was working for the aggrandizement of the colonial possessions. After the acquisition of Kiaochau, a German squadron was despatched to the Philippines when the United States blockaded Manila during their war with Spain. In the following year, 1898, the empire, with the consent of America and England, was able to purchase some Spanish colonies—the Carolines and the Islands of Palawan, together with the Ladrones, excepting the island of Guahan, which fell to the United States. At the same time, the plans which Germany had pursued in Turkey since the 'eighties took more definite shape. If their primary object was merely to create new openings for German industry, trade, and capital, yet the undertakings also achieved political importance since they held out a prospect of rehabilitating the 'Sick Man' with German help. One result was Turkey's consent to the construction of a portion of the railway Konia–Bagdad–Basra in 1899, in which French as well as German capital was engaged. It is true that new dangers were created by Germany's advance. The Russian designs upon Constantinople, and the English plan of an overland route between India and Egypt, were threatened by the Turco-German friendship, while the French feared for their economic and political situation in Asia Minor. At the same time the Imperial Government, by its method of dealing, provided a welcome excuse for representing Germany as a disturber of the peace. If the appearance of the German warships before Manila had already given considerable annoyance to the Americans, Germany's situation was rendered more difficult in regard to Powers who were interested in the dismemberment of Turkey, from the fact that during his travels in Palestine William II had used exaggerated language to celebrate the Turco-German partnership. When the Russian Government proposed the discussion of universal disarmament, with the object of securing perpetual safety in their rear while they were engaged in east Asia, the German representatives to the first Peace Conference at The Hague in 1899 allowed themselves to be led into a blunt rejection of the Russian proposals, and when the Boxer Rising was being put down William II never rested till he had forced von Waldersee upon the other Powers as commander-in-chief.

Only few people in Germany suspected anything of the effects of this foreign policy upon world opinion. When the earth was being apportioned out, one felt justified in demanding 'a place in the sun,' and thought it possible to presume upon this right. Germany, like the others, was pursuing a policy of force, but, conscious of her young strength, she pursued it openly, instead of allying herself, as these others professed to do, with the great ideas of the right of nations and the peace of nations, while not for a moment losing sight of their imperialist aims. Proud of winning a victory, no matter how trivial, now here and now there, to-day at the expense of this Government and to-morrow of that, those who filled the vital offices in the State considered that the 'policy of the free hand' was worth more than a permanent understanding with one of the World Powers.

The result was that Germany, which at the beginning of the century had been frequently sought after, stood a few years later alone with her feeble Austrian ally, and in the end was forced to take up arms against a world of enemies. Even England, with her command of the sea, realized that she could not pursue her world policy if she persisted in her 'splendid isolation.' The statesmen who served as Minister of the Colonies for the Island Kingdom knocked first at the door of Germany. While in the field of world politics England disagreed on principle with the Powers of the Franco-Russian Dual Alliance, she would have been able to come to an understanding with her German cousin as each case arose. It is true that William II was in the habit of offending English susceptibilities, and only a short time before had roused public opinion against Germany with his telegram to Krüger; people were uncomfortably aware of the increasing economic rivalry between the two countries, and the German plans for the fleet were disturbing. But all this was still at the initial stage, and one could have tried to arrive at an understanding on these very points.

It has, indeed, never been known what effects and counter-effects were looked for by the English statesmen when in 1898, 1899, and 1901 they tried to come to an understanding by means of conversations with German ministers. They never reached the point of an official offer. The Imperial Government were in no hurry. Instead of exposing themselves to the risk of pulling other people's chestnuts out of the fire, they preferred to wait till the English situation had become more desperate, when they would have been able to demand a still more favourable offer, and an obligation binding in detail, entered into, if possible, with the consent of the English Parliament. They did not doubt that time was on the side of Germany: so strong was the belief in the unalterable character of the English opposition to France and Russia. In this case also the Imperial Government sought for an immediately tangible success, and underestimated the value of fundamental understanding. Shrinking from any sacrifice, it did no occur to them that others would be willing to sacrifice a great deal to arrive at agreement. The English gave them quite openly to understand that in case of a refusal they would be obliged to come to terms with their former opponents. Yet even if Bülow had taken these words as they were meant, would he have been in a position to carry through the reduction in the battleship programme—in opposition to the Kaiser and Tirpitz, to the Fleet Union, and to public opinion which took its colour from them? He would simply have been replaced by a more willing instrument.

During these years, the Imperial Government rejected with equal persistence all attempts at *rapprochement* which came from the other quarter. While England was engaged with the Boer War, Russia had proposed common action by the three Continental Powers, which would have been welcomed in France both by the Government and by public opinion; then, when the understanding between England and Japan threatened to put serious difficulties in the way of Russian advance in eastern Asia, Petersburg issued repeated invitations to common action. But just as the

The Citizens and their Empire

Imperial Government had reaped no advantage from England's distress, she did not make the collapse of Russia in the Russo-Japanese War (1904–5) an opportunity for falling upon France; at the same time Austria also took no steps to alter the situation in the Balkans to suit her wishes. Nothing is better calculated to disprove the talk of the desire for war on the part of the Central Powers, than their attitude during these critical years.

Germany has, indeed, had to pay heavily for the fact that none of the Powers which were attempting the reconstruction of the world from the imperialist standpoint, were able at that time to win over her Government to their side. After she had rejected England's overtures, the English Government took up a definite attitude towards the Franco-Russian Dual Alliance, drawing France to herself, and creating a dangerous enemy for Russia through the Anglo-Japanese Alliance of 1902. In 1904, soon after the beginning of the Russo-Japanese War, the *Entente Cordiale* came about between England and France: an understanding was arrived at upon all colonial questions, Egypt ceded to England, and almost the whole of Morocco to France. At this point the Imperial Government sprang to the defensive. With the object of breaking through the snare which was threatening her, she entered a protest against the 'peaceful penetration' of Morocco by the French, and at the same time made advances to her Russian neighbour. Yielding against his own conviction to the wish of the Imperial Chancellor, William II landed at Tangier in 1905, during a Mediterranean cruise; on his own initiative he induced the Tsar some months later, on board the *Polar Star*, to subscribe to a defensive alliance. But the intended treaty was soon wrecked through the opposition of the Russian Foreign Minister, and in the endeavour 'to ride France on the curb' (Holstein) Germany's policy only tightened the bond which up till then had but loosely united her opponents, and suffered a severe defeat in consequence. Not content with the dismissal of Delcassé, the Foreign Minister, and with the comprehensive offers made by the French, the Imperial Government insisted in 1906 on the summoning of a general Morocco Conference. With the support of the Foreign Minister of Austria-Hungary, they succeeded in securing recognition for the principle of the 'Open Door,' but it was left to the French

Collapse

Government little by little to close that door: and the fact that France, England, and Russia opposed a united front to the Central Powers, while Spain and Italy, which had been bound by treaty to France since 1902, appeared in their train, weighed much more heavily than the ostensible success. In 1907, the English Government came to an understanding with the Russians on the questions of Persia, Afghanistan, and Tibet, and with this vanished the last chance of a Continental alliance against England.

Taking a long view, and not shrinking from sacrifice, the English Government had completed their task—a task which was looked upon in Germany as 'encirclement.' A Triple Alliance of superior strength, with England at its head, was opposed to the alliance of Germany with Austria, in which Italy's part was scarcely now to be reckoned upon. It is certain that England's policy, in whose service King Edward VII travelled indefatigably through Europe, did not aim at war: but it created 'dangers to peace which were only too real,' as the Belgian ambassador in Berlin acknowledged already at that time. While the Central Powers clung to the point of obstinacy to the *status quo*, England's backing encouraged her allies to pursue ends which could only be attained through a European War: English policy in particular co-operated with the French to divert the Russian expansion towards the Balkans, while opposing a barrier to it in eastern Asia and at the Straits.

The growing pressure upon the Central Powers was associated with efforts to induce the Germans to reduce their programme of battleships. The standpoint of the English that their fleet must be 10 per cent. stronger than the two greatest Continental fleets taken together, was met by Admiral von Tirpitz with the endeavour to increase his fighting fleet to such an extent that an attack upon Germany would mean a hazardous enterprise even for the strongest sea-power. At the second Peace Conference at The Hague in 1907, the German representatives lodged a protest against universal disarmament, and also against compulsory arbitration, and thus, as was said by the Russian Foreign Minister, saved the Russians and French the trouble of 'providing a first-class funeral' for the English proposals. In the two following years, English statesmen, through individual pronouncements, effected a slight *rapprochement* on the side of Germany, but it was not enough to move them to the political agreements which Prince Bülow held in readiness. In England's unyielding attitude the Kaiser and Tirpitz saw a justification of their theory of 'risk,' and so perished the last attempt at mediation, undertaken by Lord Haldane, who was friendly to Germany.

While the prospects of an adjustment of the German-English quarrel grew more and more faint, the English Government scarcely allowed a year to pass without adding to their political alliances by conferences and military agreements. In one year, 1908, King Edward received the President of the French Republic, and shortly afterwards Delcassé had a meeting with the Tsar at Reval, and with the French-Minister President and the Russian Foreign Minister at Marienbad. Even before this, England had removed a great part of the Mediterranean Fleet to the North Sea, and later, in 1912, she undertook the defence of the coast of France on the north and west, and in 1914 she entered into negotiations with Russia in regard to the disposal of the two fleets. In discussions between England and Belgium at the time of the Morocco Conference, Belgium had been agreed upon as the English deploying ground in case of a German attack upon France, and when matters came to a head in the Balkans, Poincaré informed his Russian ally that France could count upon an English army of 100,000 men. One year later, in 1913, the French commander-in-chief inspected the fortresses in the west of Russia, and an English general the fortresses on the eastern frontier of France. The World Press controlled by the future Lord Northcliffe, provided for a united front of public opinion; every event of any importance was made to serve for the baiting of the Central Powers.

Under these circumstances the danger of war was brought nearer by every disagreement which arose between the two groups of Powers: and relying upon the increasing value set upon alliances, the weaker States on both sides began to act on their own initiative. The Austrian Government knew that Germany would not leave her in the lurch, lest she should lose her solitary ally. As she was conscious of being threatened by the endeavours after a Greater Serbia, as well as by the Turkish Revolution of 1908, she dared to pronounce the annexation of Bosnia and Herzegovina (p. 364).

Collapse

A European war was only averted because Germany, 'in Nibelungen faith,' stood beside her ally, while Russia had not yet recovered from her defeat in the Japanese War. The idea of the *Revanche* had been revived in France by the harsh proceedings of the German Government during the new Moroccan crisis of the year 1911; and by the unexpectedly ample support which she received from England. With the election of Poincaré, a native of Lorraine, to the presidency in the year 1913, a man came to the head of the republic whose whole policy was directed towards the regaining of Alsace-Lorraine. In the previous years, he had expressly given the Russian Government to understand that they could only reckon on French help if Germany also should become so involved in the Balkan troubles as to appear like the aggressive party. A Franco-Russian naval agreement, a loan of 500 million francs for the further construction of the stragetically important lines of railway, the introduction of the three years' military service in France, gave the required weight to this friendly warning. In London also, the Russian Foreign Minister learned that England would help with all her power—again if Germany were the aggressor.

At this period, Russian activity in Serbia and the other Slav Balkan States had already borne fruit. In autumn of 1912, Bulgaria, Serbia, Greece, and Montenegro made a united attack upon the Turks, and their armies advanced almost as far as Constantinople. Under pressure from the German Government, the Danube monarchy accepted without resistance the menacing change upon her frontier.

Once more the danger of a European war had blown over. But Poincaré had used the opportunity to impress once again upon the Russians: 'Russia must make the first move, that is to say, she must take military steps in reply to an attack by Austria upon Serbia: France will fly to her aid as soon as military intervention becomes apparent on the part of Germany.'

About the same time, the French ambassador succeeded in obtaining a declaration from Grey: in case France and England expected a threat to the common peace, they should immediately discuss the desirability of concerted action; if the case should arise, the plans of the General Staffs were to be passed, after which the Governments would have to decide to what extent they should be carried out. This was at the end of 1912. A year and a half later, in July 1914, the opportunity arose of putting the example to the proof. Meantime the Russian Foreign Minister himself had acknowledged his conviction that Russia's establishment upon the Dardanelles 'could hardly be obtained otherwise than by way of European complications.'

He had been led to this remark by the nomination of the German General Liman von Sanders to be Commander of the First Turkish Army Corps. The German Government held fast by the friendship of Turkey, even after the Turks in 1911 had lost Tripoli to Italy, one of the Powers of the Triple Alliance, and their European possessions, with the exception of a small remnant, to the Balkan States.

Just as little would the Imperial Government agree to barter the alliance with Austria-Hungary for a better understanding with Russia, although they were aware of the weakness of their confederate. The Imperial Government had no other allies; it was faced by a superior enemy Power. This was the final result, as far as foreign politics were concerned, of the peace years of the Wilhelmine era.

On the 28th June, 1914, the Austrian heir-apparent with his consort was murdered by Austrian Serbs in the capital of Bosnia. As the inquiry showed, the actors belonged to a Nationalist Association, which was working for the union of Bosnia and Herzegovina with Serbia, the Serbian Government not daring to oppose them; Serbian officers and officials had co-operated in the preparations for the murder, which threatened the continuance of the Danube monarchy. In order to make Serbia, which was Russia's most active and powerful ally in the Balkans, 'harmless for ever,' the Austrian Government prepared an extraordinarily sharp ultimatum for Belgrade. Almost four weeks went by in investigations and deliberations. During this time the Austrian statesmen were informed by the Imperial Chancellor, von Bethmann-Hollweg, that they must judge in Vienna what ought to be done in order to clear up their relations with Serbia: they need not doubt Germany's faith as an ally. Thus Germany delivered herself over, with bound hands, to Austrian leadership: even the wording of the ultimatum was learnt by the German Government when it was too late for any alteration. Again, Serbia could rely upon the help of Russia, and the Russian war-party were urged on by the certainty of French support.

Collapse

When the Serbian Government handed in their reply to the ultimatum, they foresaw its rejection by Austria; the order for Serbian mobilization had been given a few hours previously. The Austrian counter-move was followed by preparations for war throughout the whole of European Russia. Although England and Germany were endeavouring to keep the peace, Austria would not consent to be restrained from declaring war upon Serbia on the 28th July. This was followed in Russia, on the 30th, by an order for general mobilization—and thus the 'European complication' was created, which eighteen months previously had failed to materialize, and the sequel also developed in every respect as the French had foreseen at that time.

The German Government demanded from Russia the suspension of the warlike measures, which constituted a direct threat to Germany: when their demand remained unanswered, they declared war on the 1st August upon Russia, and two days later upon France. The invasion of neutral Belgium by German troops made it possible for the English Government to assume the rôle of defender of the small States: for the public knew nothing of their Anglo-Belgian agreements. The English declaration of war upon Germany followed on the 4th August. The Central Powers, who were not far from having exhausted their possibilities of military preparation, found themselves faced by an enormous military superiority and the indignation of public opinion throughout the world. In the fear of losing their last allies, the German Government had once again shown the helpless inflexibility which had robbed their foreign policy up to that time of any fruits, and it was an easy matter for her opponents to represent Germany to the whole world as the aggressor, who had been preparing for a long period to strike a sudden blow. The judgment of history has acquitted the German people of this crime: but all the burdens imposed upon them by their enemies since the time of the Armistice, have been based upon the hypothesis of the sole guilt of Germany for the war.

In time of danger, the German people were united more closely than had ever been the case in the course of the thousand years of their history. The Reichstag unanimously passed the War Credits: volunteers flocked to the flag by hundreds of thousands. The overwhelming advance in the West seemed to justify every confidence in the military leadership. In a few weeks four German armies had penetrated through Belgium and across the Marne. But then came the order of retreat, the extension of the lines as far as the sea-coast, and the stiffening of the frontlines. There was now no hope of rapid victory over the enemy in the West. The forward march of the millions of the Russian armies was watched with anxiety.

General von Moltke, the Chief of the General Staff, had adhered in essentials to the plan of Schlieffen, which in the case of a war on two fronts aimed first of all at gaining a victory by encirclement over the Western enemy. But instead of making the right wing, which was to carry out the encirclement, as strong as possible, General von Moltke engaged a great part of the Western army in the battles in Lorraine, and besides this, in the last days of August, he weakened the right wing still further by despatching two army corps to east Prussia, which was being gravely threatened. General Joffre, on the other hand, was opportunely reinforced also from the Lorraine front, and sent a new army in the rear of the German flank troops under General von Kluck, which had marched in pursuit eastwards past Paris. Von Kluck did, indeed, drive back the newly arrived enemy, but the troops at his disposal were not sufficient even to fill the gap which had occurred between the encircling armies and that of von Kluck. Inadequately informed in his distant Luxemburg headquarters, and hampered by severe illness, the General Chief of the Staff despatched one of his officers to the front, who on the 9th September gave orders for a general retreat. General von Moltke collapsed under the burden of the Battle of the Marne: the emperor replaced him by von Falkenhayn, the Minister of War.

Special difficulties arose in the Russian campaign on account of the huge extent of the Eastern area, and the numerical superiority of the enemy. Even if the whole fighting strength of Germany had been available for the East, the total of Germans and Austrians at the beginning of the war would only by a small number have exceeded that of the Russians and Serbs.

But this possibility, which was reckoned upon in Schlieffen's plan, vanished with the breaking of the German offensive in the West, and in May 1915 great bodies of Austrian troops were also engaged through the entry

Collapse

of Italy into the war. The more do the achievements of the German armies under Hindenburg and Ludendorff, and of the Austrians under Hötzendorff, call for admiration. As early as August 1914, Hindenburg had annihilated the Russian army of the Narew by an encirclement carried out on a huge scale: the advances upon Warsaw and Lotz, if they had no other result, frustrated the break-through planned by the Archduke Nicholas, and in the winter fighting on the Masurian Lakes, east Prussia was finally freed from the enemy. In time following, Hindenburg and Ludendorff continued their efforts to bring about a decision by means of heavy blows, delivered by great masses of troops.

Falkenhayn, on the other hand, held on principle to the trench-warfare, and tried to demoralize the enemy by a series of well-planned and isolated blows. Nevertheless, in the spring of 1915, he placed greater numbers of troops at disposal for the East, with the result that the Austro-German campaign at Gorlice at last brought about a perceptible relief: the Russian fortresses fell and Poland was occupied. The Austro-German front now ran northwards from the Rumanian frontier, nearly to Dünaburg, and from thence down the Dwina to the outskirts of Riga. Serbia was conquered after Bulgaria had joined the Central Powers, thus throwing open the overland route to Turkey. Under the leadership of General Liman von Sanders, the Turks succeeded in repelling the attacks upon the Dardanelles. Meantime the Western armies were holding their ground in heavy fighting at Ypres, at Arras, and in Champagne. Again and again the German troops had done great deeds, but neither in the East was the enemy vanquished.

Falkenhayn began the operations of the year 1916 with a surprise attack upon Verdun, through which he hoped, even in the least favourable event, to produce a considerable weakening of the fighting strength of France. But during the six months' struggle, it was the attacking armies which endured the heaviest sacrifice of life, and while the fight in the inferno of Verdun was still going on, the attempts to break through at the Somme were inaugurated by the English and French on the 1st July, and continued till November, with the employment of artillery and of aircraft on a scale never before known. Previous to this, General Brussilow, commanding an army of two and a half millions, had broken in the Austro-Hungarian front. Scarcely had his advance been checked by German troops, when Rumania joined the Multi-alliance, and occupied Siebenbürgen, which was undefended: at the same time the Italians conquered the hotly contested Gorz, on the Isonzo front. In this extremely threatening situation, William II conferred the High Command upon Hindenburg, making Ludendorff, the Quarter-Master-General, co-responsible.

When the year came to an end, the most pressing danger had been exorcised. The enemy in the West had gained nothing but small local successes, while the Central Powers had occupied by far the greater part of Rumania. But their military strength was strained to the utmost, and the homeland was suffering severely under the prolonged fighting.

Millions had lost their breadwinner, and hundreds of thousands the hope of their old age. Every day brought renewed fear for the fate of the men who were fighting, and still no end was to be seen. Hunger and deprivations of all kinds, the results of the English blockade, made the mental torture more acute. The Government, indeed, did all that was possible to control the necessaries of life and to apportion them rightly; but in spite of the measures taken by them and in spite of rising wages, the bulk of the workmen were unable to satisfy their hunger, and the more the State interfered in the business of agriculture, the more heavily the peasant class also felt the burden of the war. Anxiety for daily bread gave rise to the idea that the men in command and in possession, the speculators and war-profiteers, were to blame for the continuance of the war. Now the German nation had to suffer because they had not learnt to look upon the State as a concern of their own. The Wars of Liberation had been preceded by the rebirth of Prussia, and in the Franco-German War the German people had experienced the fulfilment of their desire for unity: on both occasions they had been faced by the Western enemy only, and the impetus of success had strengthened their will to victory. But this struggle was putting a far greater strain upon the strength of the masses: but what effect would it produce, after the homeland was protected from the invasion of the enemy?

Each of their opponents was aware beforehand of the prize for which his nation was contending. The Germans,

Collapse

who were fighting solely in their own defence, lacked from the outset every motive of this nature. Neither at the time of the conflict between Austria and Prussia, nor under Bismarck, had they ever learnt to reflect upon matters of foreign policy. Even during the war, all insight into foreign politics was denied to the people's representatives. While the English and French, whose Labour representatives were employed in the Government and in administrative posts, as a rule subordinated their party political quarrels at this time to the national needs, the war aims of Germany were shaped by party-political ambitions. Heavy industry desired the annexation of coal and iron districts in the north of France and in Belgium: the great landed proprietors of Prussia, the acquisition of land for colonization in the Russian border States: this determined the attitude of the Conservatives and National Liberals. In the same way, more or less in agreement with Conservative and Liberal wishes, the military circles called for annexation. The desire to free the western districts of Russia from the rule of the Tsar, determined the attitude taken by the Social Democrats. To the Victory Peace, acclaimed in particular by the Pan-German Societies, was opposed the 'Peace by agreement,' which abandoned all idea of annexation. In order to compel the 'Peace by agreement,' a minority of the Social Democrats, at first inconsiderable, refused the War Credits (December 1915), whereas the Majority-Socialists both before and after voted the costs of the war; the Independent Social Democratic Party developed by degrees out of the minority. As German troops were occupying large tracts of the enemy country, both war aims appeared to be attainable. If one only 'held on,' declared the champions of the Victory Peace, the enemy would agree in the end to the annexations, in order to recover their remaining territory; the possibility of bringing the war to an immediate end would look still more bright if the Government would offer the complete evacuation of the invaded territories. But as a matter of fact, Germany could as little hope for a general readiness to come to terms as she could hope for a victory over her united enemies: but at that time salvation would still have been possible, if the Government could have come first of all to an understanding with Russia.

It became of fatal import for Germany that the Imperial

Chancellor, von Bethmann-Hollweg, did not energetically pursue this idea by which he was at times attracted, and also made the handling of the question of war aims dependent upon the conditions of home politics. He exerted a soothing influence upon both sides, and thus for a long time maintained public peace between the parties. But as differences became more acute with the continuance of the war, his influence disappeared. The Kaiser, who in peace time had made so many public appearances, abandoned responsibility to the military and political leaders. There was not one amongst the parties which would have wished to take the reins. While affairs were in this condition, Ludendorff acquired decisive influence: since all economic and political matters were related to the military, the time came when nothing could happen even in these departments without his consent. Conscious of their responsibility, the deputies in the Reichstag, excepting the Independents and the revolutionary Socialist groups, avoided all public criticism of the steps taken by the army leaders.

Ludendorff's dictatorship meant that the last ounce of strength was to be put forth to win the Victory Peace. An understanding with Russia was made impossible by the proclamation of the Kingdom of Poland in November 1916: when Ludendorff decided upon unlimited U-boat warfare, he reckoned with the entry of America into the war.

Tirpitz had laid the main stress upon the construction of the battle fleet, and allowed the building of U-boats to take a second place: he believed, and may have had good reasons for believing, that they were not the decisive weapon in the command of the seas. As it was not thought desirable to risk the High Seas Fleet, it was not till the Battle of Jutland (May 1916) that it was able under Admiral von Scheer to prove its pre-eminence as a fighting force. But it was important for it to defend the home coasts: what would have happened if the German armies had had to fight on a northern front also? As for the English blockade, the U-boats alone were available to combat it, and success could only be looked for even from their employment if the captain of the boat launched the torpedo without first holding up the ship he had sighted. It was natural that neutrals should oppose this mode of attack: the United States, whose industry was realizing great profits

Collapse

through the supply of the armies of the Entente, threatened to go to war. Bethmann-Hollweg took measures accordingly, bringing about the dismissal of Admiral von Tirpitz in March 1916, and incited Wilson, the American President, to a peace overture. Ludendorff chose the open enmity of America: it is not certain whether, apart from this, Wilson would not sooner or later have resolved upon war. The Supreme Army Command were convinced that they could bring England to her knees, before America's entry could be appreciably felt: the Admiralty held out a prospect of certain success within six months. The Reichstag submitted, trusting to their calculations: only the Social Democrats entered a protest. On one and the same day the Imperial Chancellor handed in the German peace-conditions, which Wilson had asked for as a basis for his peace overture, and—the declaration of unrestricted U-boat warfare. The calculations were false, and the conviction of the Supreme Army Command was not justified.

Yet no one could wish for the Victory Peace without also desiring unrestricted U-boat warfare.

The Supreme Army Command for the year 1917 had stood merely upon the defensive. Without the withdrawal along the Somme front, and without the 'Hindenburg Programme,' which raised the supply of munitions to the highest point, the German armies could not have maintained themselves throughout the fighting of this year. Shortly before the opening of the offensive at Arras, on the Aisne, and in Champagne, in March 1917 the Russian Revolution broke out. But the war was still carried on against the new citizen rulers; the German East front was advanced by 150 kilometres, and not until the Bolsheviks came into power was there a suspension of hostilities in the East. During the peace negotiations, the Army Command again ordered an advance of the German troops as far as Finland, and into the Caucasus district, and even at the conclusion of peace (at Brest Litovsk, March 1918) they threatened the Russians with the mailed fist. On the other hand, the overthrow of Tsardom had a surprising effect in the sphere of home politics. Disaffection and anxiety suddenly found expression in clearly defined demands. All the parties, from the Independents to the Centre and the National Liberals, united to form a majority, with the

The Citizens and their Empire

object of altering the Imperial Constitution in such a way that the Imperial Chancellor and the leaders of the Government should be responsible to the Reichstag. But the Supreme Army Command was stronger than the Reichstag: nothing came of the desired reconstitution of the empire. Neither was the cause of peace served by the Peace Resolution, which was moved in the Reichstag (July 1917) by Erzberger, a deputy of the Centre. But it was most highly significant that a majority composed of Social Democrats, Progressives, and Centre should have come together, and remained together, during the debate upon the Peace Resolution: it was this majority, composed of workmen, with broad strata of the middle class, which took over the reins when the Supreme Army Command advised the cessation of fighting. The fact that the Kaiser was constrained to promise an equal franchise for Prussia also, proclaimed the birth of a new Germany. The political desires of the labouring masses in the great strikes of April 1917 and January 1918 were in all essentials covered by the demands of the majority in the Reichstag. The influence of events in Russia was most clearly to be traced in these mass movements: their leaders were drawn, not from the leaders of the Independents, but from those chosen by the workmen of the individual factories and from their Workmen's Councils. But the Spartacus Union, the extreme Left, which was at that time negligible in point of numbers, was alone in aiming at an alteration by force. Not till the Supreme Army Command itself declared the uselessness of further resistance, did the way become clear for the reconstitution of Germany. Up to that time Ludendorff's authority drew its strongest support from the patriotic sense of duty which was found amongst the party leaders and the masses. During the debates upon the Reichstag's Resolution, the Kaiser, at the desire of the Supreme Army Command, replaced the Imperial Chancellor von Bethmann-Hollweg by Michaelis, and again a few months later by Count Hertling. Hertling was a leader of the Centre, and pledged himself to act in the sense of the Reichstag majority: von Payer, a Progressive, was associated with him as Vice-Chancellor: but at that time, as before, Ludendorff determined the course of foreign policy. As late as June 1918, he removed von Kühlmann, the Secretary of State, from office, because he had declared

Collapse

in the Reichstag that the war could not be won with weapons alone.

When the Peace Resolution was passed by the Reichstag the prospects of success for the unrestricted U-boat warfare had already vanished. The captains and crews of the submarines had accomplished more than could have been expected of them, but the number of boats was not sufficient: the enemy perfected their means of defence, and replaced their lost ships with new. In the storms of the Flanders fighting, and in the struggle around Cambrai, where the English attacked with hundreds of tanks, the West front stood firm. But the strength of the brave armies had been exhausted in the terrible battles fought against a steadily growing superiority in troops and munitions: the supplies from home left much to be desired. At that time, the symptoms of disintegration, which were strikingly apparent upon the French side, were confined almost entirely to the great battleships, where peace-time routine, with its sharp division between officers and crew, was still carried out. Count Czernin, the Foreign Minister of Austria-Hungary, tried with impressive words to convince the Government that the Danube Monarchy could no longer be reckoned upon: as a matter of fact, the Emperor Charles, who had succeeded Francis Joseph in November 1916, was only waiting for the opportunity to save his throne by a separate peace. Also, the power of resistance on the Bulgarian and Turkish fronts was scarcely any longer to be counted upon. From their exact acquaintance with these circumstances, the leaders of the Entente formed the resolve to carry on the war to the bitter end. Time was on their side, more than ever before.

Every month brought reinforcements in troops and munitions from America, while the German submarines failed to sink a single one of the American transports. Under these circumstances, the Papal Peace Overture in autumn 1917 had little prospect of success. The opportunities for an understanding had been let slip: now that fighting was limited to the defensive, the balance of strength had altered more and more to Germany's disadvantage. If the Military Command were unwilling to surrender, there was nothing left them but to attempt to annihilate the Anglo-French armies before the Americans could intervene in force.

411

The Citizens and their Empire

Since the autumn of 1917, a great part of the Eastern armies had been transferred to the West. It is true that a strong force, far over a million, was required to occupy the great stretch of land in question; the mistaken Eastern policy was fatally in evidence even in the last great action of the war.

From March to July 1918, the German armies once more proved their heroic valour in the four months' battle in France. They advanced to the outskirts of Amiens, into the Forest of Compiègne, and as far as the Marne: but they did not succeed in breaking through. Thus vanished the last chance of a German victory. Yet in the vague hope that one of the Western Powers might still perhaps collapse, Ludendorff carried on the struggle. But a new offensive, eastward from Rheims, was brought to a stand, and when in July General Foch with strong American support, and in August the English, launched a counter-offensive against the front which had already been driven in in many places, the German troops retreated step by step from one position to another. In the middle of September the resistance of the Bulgarians and Turks collapsed. At the same time, the Government of Vienna made an overture for peace: five weeks later the Austro-Hungarian army was dispersed.

On the 29th September, acting under the impression of the Bulgarian collapse, and in sharp contrast to their previous attitude, the Supreme Army Command demanded the immediate cessation of the war, by a simultaneous request for an armistice, and for peace: they declared that every hour of delay meant danger. Ludendorff's confession that he had lost the war was tantamount to a renunciation of his authority as dictator. A change of Government was necessary, for reasons both of domestic and foreign politics. Prince Max of Baden offered himself on October 1st for the difficult post of Imperial Chancellor: Majority-Socialists, Centre, and Progressive Party formed his ministry. Without a fight, even without their own seeking, the Reichstag majority had become possessed of the power of government. It was not till four weeks later that this fact was constitutionally established. The Imperial Chancellor and his representatives were made responsible to the Reichstag: as a further limitation of the authority of the emperor, the same responsibility was laid upon the war ministers of the Single States, and the appointment of officers made dependent upon the counter-signature of the war ministers.

The new men were entering upon a terrible inheritance. The request for an armistice, made in such unseemly haste, was calculated to injure rather than improve the situation of Germany, and could not fail also to create internal difficulties for the Government. For this reason Prince Max hesitated.

Not until Hindenburg had given in writing his judgment upon the situation was the request for Peace, Mediation, and an Armistice sent to the American President. The interchange of notes was protracted for several weeks, till at last, in addition to the complete disarmament of Germany, Wilson, in words which it was impossible any longer to misunderstand, demanded the abdication of the Kaiser. Ludendorff hoped to be able to ward off the extremity by making a supreme effort and rousing the people to a war of desperation. Such ideas were rightly rejected by the Government. Thereupon Ludendorff asked for and obtained his discharge. General Groener took his place. In the end, Prince Max also yielded to the necessity of repeating the request for a truce, with a disclaimer of any reservation. On the 8th November Erzberger, the Secretary of State, as head of the German plenipotentiaries, received the conditions of truce from Marshal Foch in the Forest of Compiègne.

They not only made it impossible for the German people to carry on the war, but at the same time put into the hands of the Entente the means of compelling the empire to any peace, without further military action: these means included, in particular, the retention of the German prisoners of war, the continuance of the blockade, and the occupation of the Rhineland. But there was no choice left: even Hindenburg counselled acceptance. On the 11th November the plenipotentiaries affixed their signatures—two days after the fall of the monarchy.

The declaration of the Supreme Army Command on the 29th September had come as a complete surprise even to the chief military and political authorities: it had a devastating effect upon the masses, who had so long been deluded with hopes of victory. They were conscious of having been badly led: even, what was worse, of having been deceived. The desire became more and more widespread: to have

The Citizens and their Empire

done with the war at any price; away with any who would wish to prolong it! In this mood, the nation was not capable of grasping the significance of the political events. The carrying through of the equal franchise in Prussia—the transference of the political power to the Reichstag—the subordination of military to civil authority—all this made little impression. The new Government did nothing to make themselves conspicuous. After the first weeks of October, the Reichstag met only once again, and that for a few days, and neglected to explain to the nation why the war was still going on. What could be seen and felt was the activity of the Supreme Army Command: upon them fell the blame that there was still no peace. The longing for peace felt by the despairing masses beat like a rising tide against the military authority, and submerged the dynasties in which military authority was most visibly incorporated. In the light of Wilson's notes, the imperial throne must appear the chief actual stumbling-block to peace. The activity of the revolutionary groups operated from within outwards, working on the Russian model through functionaries and Workmen's Councils.

On this basis the revolutionary movement was evolved which seized upon the whole empire, and even penetrated the army. It is difficult to follow in detail the interweaving of the various threads. But the parliamentary committee, which after the war spent years of laborious work in examining the causes of the collapse, cleared up much which was obscure even in this respect, destroying the legend that the German army was stabbed with a dagger by the advocates of a peace by negotiation, and other legends of the same kind. According to the finding of this committee 'the German battle-front—both by land and water—accomplished all that lay in their power up to the last.' The same could not be said of the army behind the lines, nor of the High Seas Fleet. After the events of the summer of 1917, there is no proof of the existence either of a revolutionary association or of a union with some sort of political status amongst the crews of the battleships. Certainly in addition to the universal war weariness on board the great ships, there was a feeling of exasperation against the officers, which became more acute through the restraint of the life lived together at close quarters by 'gentlemen' and crews—a feeling which was not overcome,

Collapse

as in the case of the crews of the submarines, by warlike
action and danger encountered in common. The exasperation broke out when, in the last days of October, the
admirals of the Fleet ordered an advance into the Canal,
with the object of relieving the West front. The sailors
were dominated by the idea that after the request for Peace,
there was no sense in the sacrifice which was demanded
of them: the intended expedition even served as a proof
that the admirals of the Fleet were working against the
Imperial Government's endeavours for Peace: as a matter
of fact, the Admiralty had made no communication to the
political authorities, as indeed they were not required to
do by the letter of the law. Part of the crews of the third
and first squardons refused to obey: the expedition had to
be abandoned: six hundred men were arrested and sent on
shore. A few days later many thousands of sailors, soldiers,
and workmen made common cause with the prisoners:
they encountered no serious opposition. When Noske, the
Majority-Socialist who was despatched by the Government,
arrived in Kiel on the 5th November, he found the city
in the hands of the mutineers, and a universal lack of
command and leadership. What the Soldiers' Councils
demanded were alleviations of military service, some of
which were of a peculiar kind: they were entirely free from
political designs.

But during the revolution in Munich on the 7th November, the efforts of the Independents under Kurt Eisner
gained their ends, to the extent of overthrowing the
Wittelsbach dynasty: for the masses, the royal house
represented the connection with Berlin, and with it the
compulsion to continue the war, at a time when the population—after the collapse of the Austrian front—were
already conscious of being threatened by the enemy
offensive. The proceedings which took place in Berlin,
aimed a blow directly at the highest War Lord, who
figured in the Wilson notes as the chief obstacle to Peace.
To the last moment the Majority-Socialists did everything
possible to save the democratic monarchy, which lasted
only a few weeks in point of fact, and from the constitutional standpoint only a few days.

In this endeavour, under threat of resigning from the
Government, they demanded the abdication of William II
and the Crown Prince. If the Kaiser did not abdicate, so

The Citizens and their Empire

Ebert declared to the Imperial Chancellor on the very day of the Munich revolution, the Socialist Revolution was inevitable: 'But I do not desire it, indeed I hate it like sin.' At that time, even the Patriotic Party (*Vaterlandspartei*), which was extreme conservative, found no other solution than that of making the abdication of William II conditional upon a national vote. Yet, try as he would, Prince Max received no decisive word from the Belgian headquarters, whither the Kaiser had retired immediately after the ratification of the change in the Constitution: as he had evaded the Revolution by a flight from Berlin, so now he evaded it by a flight from Spa over the Dutch border.

Events in Berlin took their course under pressure from the masses. When the Independents and the determined revolutionaries summoned the workmen into the streets, they were joined by the Majority-Socialists, who would otherwise have been forced into the background. The Revolution was accomplished with much shooting and uproar, but without actual fighting. After the Majority-Socialists had announced their withdrawal from the Government, the Imperial Chancellor announced at midday the abdication of the Kaiser and the Crown Prince in order to anticipate their deposition. Half an hour earlier he had at last been informed from headquarters that William II was resolved to lay down the dignity of Kaiser, but not the royal crown of Prussia. Such a step could not for a moment be seriously considered: as to the Crown Prince, it had been impossible to get into communication with him. In the afternoon, Scheidemann, the Majority-Socialist, who a few hours previously had still been Secretary of State under the Kaiser, proclaimed the Republic from a window of the Reichstag building. Both the Socialist parties united to form the new 'Government of National Delegates.'

Prince Max had resigned the office of Imperial Chancellor to Ebert, the Majority-Socialist. He said as he took his departure: 'Herr Ebert, I lay the German Empire upon your heart.' Ebert replied: 'I have lost two sons for this empire.'

FOURTH PART

ON THE WAY TO CONSTITUTIONAL UNIFICATION

BEFORE the end came, four-and-twenty States, with 1,345 million inhabitants, had taken part in the war against the Central Powers and their allies: for this reason the effects of the war and of the terms of peace made themselves felt over the whole world. They meant for Europe a metamorphosis, with which no other event can be compared. Their most essential characteristic is the destruction of the State System of middle Europe, which was based upon a powerful Germany, and the formation of a number of new States in the eastern half of the Continent. Where a concession to national wishes seemed to threaten the success of the victors' plans, all formalities were cut short by their fiat. For the rest, they considered the principle of national self-determination, in so far as it could serve to enhance their own authority and that of their favourites, and to weaken their opponents. The performance of the task, which, even apart from this, would have been almost impossible, was on a par with the distortion of the principle. How little they succeeded in creating national States is shown by the example of Poland, of which almost the half is composed of non-Polish inhabitants. Conflicts with powerful national minorities occur in almost every one of the new State Systems: they meet with other difficulties through the inadequate consideration paid to the economic necessities of life. The other States suffer in sympathy with the unrest which ferments in the new creations. While the Peace Treaties raised the number of European States from twenty-six to thirty-four, they split up the power of the Continent, increased the old discords by adding new, and created a 'peaceless Europe.' In many cases nations and Governments look with deep distrust upon their neighbours, and the preparations for war are more alarming than ever.

But the same treaty which in its own fashion made the principle of national self-determination victorious in Europe, though not in the spirit, nor with the result, of reconciliation amongst the nations—contains in its first part the statutes of the League of Nations, which are intended to lead the nations back to co-operation, and to prevent the recurrence of the catastrophe of war. To no people can the idea of the reconciliation of the nations make a more intimate appeal than to the Germans who, from the Saxon emperors down to the founder of international social democracy, have produced and entertained so many world-embracing ideas. It was not by chance that Kant, Germany's greatest thinker, found the crown of his life's work in showing mankind a way 'To everlasting Peace'—nor that even the rebellion against the foreign rule of Napoleon was placed at the service of humanity by its spiritual leaders (p. 297). One of the after-effects of the war spirit was the impossibility of making the League of Nations become what its creator, the American President Wilson, had imagined it. Too long the victorious Powers degraded it into an instrument of revenge and despotism. For years Germany was excluded from it. During this period the League of Nations gave its decision against Germany in all cases connected with the Versailles Treaty. It has shown itself incapable up to the present of limiting armaments to any perceptible degree, and thus banishing the most serious threat to world peace, which is nowhere more painfully felt than in disarmed Germany, surrounded by powerfully armed neighbours. But not even these disappointments could destroy the deeply rooted idea of a true league of the peoples, which should put an end to the exaggerated national sentiment which springs from an obsolete habit of thought. Therefore Germany's entering into the League of Nations was hailed with glad hope by the overwhelming majority of the German people as the beginning of a new era, which was to unite all nations to work together under the sign of peace, and to realize higher values in life than had been possible in the past.

The victorious Powers had gained much by the war. England need no longer fear the competition of Germany, either on the market or on the paths of world politics: she was able to realize her colonial plans in ways she had never dreamed of. The tricolour floats again over Alsace-Lorraine: since Russia has lost her western territories and been cut off from the community of European nations, France's domination is uncontested upon the Continent. It is supported by close alliances with other States, especially in the east of Germany, and by a vast system of armaments, whose man-power is in great part recruited from the newly extended colonial empire. Italy has gained the Welsch and German Tyrol as far as the Brenner, and her position on the Mediterranean has been materially strengthened. The vanquished have to shoulder the costs of these changes: but the fact that Europe has lost her leading position in the world bears hardly upon the victors also. Even before the war, the North American Union had taken their first steps on the path of world politics, through their acquisition of Cuba and Porto Rico, of the Hawaiian and Philippine Islands, and through the construction of the Panama Canal. During the course of the war, the United States reduced their allies to financial dependence: they developed their trade in manufactured goods with unexampled rapidity, created a strong fleet, and conquered new markets—with the result that the centre of world trade and world politics is no longer to be found in Europe but in North America. Moreover, the experiences of the World War have awakened and strengthened the self-confidence of all the races which were subject to the European nations. The old colonial empires are still in existence; but there are many indications that they are tending towards reconstruction, even towards dissolution. Probably the nations which are still governed by Europeans will one day be united, like those in the east of Europe, where Russia has grouped the nationalities occupying the vast areas from the Peipus Lake and the mouth of the Dniester to the Behring Sea, into a system of States having equal rights. But if the many nations of the wide areas in the west and east of the Old World attain the solid union of which there are already indications, a dismembered Europe must lose the last vestige of its prestige and independence. It still seems possible to meet this danger by a union of the European peoples. It is certainly hard to find a formula for a European States Union, especially as an arrangement of this kind demands co-ordination within the whole, from the States which are now predominant; but the Union must be accomplished if the old Continent, to which the world owes so much, is not to fall into ruins.

In addition to the disillusionments which arose out of the lowering of the status of Europe in the world's estimation, the victorious Powers encountered others through the transformation of European conditions. The war had changed and destroyed the old economic frontiers, increased individual industries disproportionately, and created new ones in many places: this led to economic difficulties, which up to the present have not been overcome by any of the industrial States of Europe. In addition to the threat to her supremacy at sea, England had to suffer the predominance of France on the Continent, and saw her insular isolation endangered by the French air-fleet. These conditions explain many of the decisions arrived at in England's post-war policy, which have aroused a painful feeling in Germany. During the Versailles negotiations, France's statesmen had expected to be able in one form or another to carry through their designs upon the Rhine frontier: these hopes at least were destroyed by the opposition of England and America. After this, the French Government believed that in the manipulation of their Reparation demands they had found the means calculated to break up the structure of the empire, or at the very least to hold the fallen enemy on the ground for all time.

Immediately after Wilson's return, the United States turned their backs upon European affairs, and instead of signing the Versailles Treaty they made a separate peace with Germany, which includes neither the enforced confession of war-guilt, nor the arrangements for the reconstitution of Europe. At that time the English allies, burdened by their own anxieties, scarcely raised a serious protest against France's action. Thus the French Government was able to put into practice all those violent measures prompted by disappointment, distrust, and fear which have brought our nation to the verge of despair. Throughout long years German foreign policy was almost exclusively a Reparations policy, and the course of domestic policy also was actually determined by the state of the Reparations question. Not till the management of Reparations had been taken out of the power of French caprice, did the work of Germany's reconstruction meet with permanent success.

Independent Socialists and revolutionary groups had urged on the movement which led to the Revolution, but had proved incapable of directing it: the party leaders of the Majority-Socialists had not intervened till they saw their influence upon the crowd endangered. What was going to happen? Already the loosening of social and moral ties

On the Way to Constitutional Unification

had gone far enough to make the victory of Bolshevism possible even in Germany. But men of really revolutionary spirit formed only a small minority, and their leaders did not make up their minds to act until it was too late. The lack of purposeful leadership had a still more paralysing effect upon the Independents. The Majority-Socialists and the 'citizen classes' were also lacking in the dominant personalities by whom history is made.

In these circumstances the masses and the parties had no choice but to trust to the logic of facts. The manner in which they did it bears no bad testimony to the political instincts of the Germans: by an overpowering majority they united in the idea that after the collapse of the old States order, no other structure was possible save on the foundation of the people's will. The elections to the National Assembly, and the co-operation of the Majority-Socialists, the Centre, and the Democrats, were all dominated by this idea. The elections signified the first step into the future: but it was not easy for the Majority-Socialists in the Council of National Delegates to keep open the path which led to it.

In the summons to the National Delegates on the 12th November, 1918, the following passage occurred: 'The Government will maintain organized production, and in addition to the freedom and safety of the individual, will protect property against the attack of private persons.' Only a few days later, the employers joined with the leaders of the trade unions for the common regulation of their mutual relations: in this way the procedure was introduced which has come to seem a matter of course to us to-day. At the States Conference in the building of the Imperial Chancery on the 25th November, the adherents of the system of Workmen's Councils inveighed not only against this method of settling the relations with labour, but also against the project of a National Assembly. But Ebert, the president of this conference, proved himself equal to the occasion, and summed up the very contradictory views in a 'unanimous' resolution. In it was stated that 'All the German tribes pledge themselves to work resolutely for the unity of the empire: it is universally agreed to summon a National Assembly to grant a Constitution: until it meets, the Workmen's and Soldiers' Councils are the representatives of the people's will.' The meeting of the Central Council in Berlin on the 16th December showed that the

The Citizens and their Empire

Councils were in the hands of the Majority-Socialists; after stormy debates a strong majority decided for the National Assembly, against the system of Councils.

The triumph of the middle-class idea of a Constitution cleared up the situation, but it also produced conflict: the Spartacists under Liebknecht's leadership aroused the masses. The Government could count neither upon the Safety Guards (*Sicherheitswehr*) organized by the Chief of Police, who was an Independent, nor upon the troops belonging to the Military Governor of Berlin. As though this were not enough, the National Marine Division had taken up its quarters in the Castle, in the Royal Mews: their own leader called them 'an organized band of robbers.' Military action taken against the sailors produced no effect, beyond the secession of the three Independents from the Council of National Delegates: that is to say, from the temporary Government of the Empire; it was only after protracted negotiations that the marines vacated the buildings which they had occupied. Then, when the masses were summoned to overthrow the Ebert-Scheidemann Government, Berlin actually fell for some days into the hands of the revolutionaries. 'Vast masses of people surged along Unter den Linden, around the Reichstag building, and in the Tiergarten, thousands of whom were in possession of weapons. One single detachment of machine-gunners would have been enough to clear the Wilhelmstrasse in less than a minute, when the masses who were pressing behind would have occupied the Imperial Chancellery and all the Government buildings, almost without striking a blow' (Noske). The Government had recourse to negotiations, and meantime brought up trustworthy troops, whom they strengthened with fresh reinforcements drawn from Berlin itself and the neighbourhood. The rule of the revolutionaries collapsed with the entry of the military. A week afterwards, on 19th January, 1919, the elections to the National Assembly took place.

Nothing had been altered in the demands which formed the programme of the Socialist parties: the Communists, who had separated meantime from the Independents, took no part in the election campaign. The other parties accommodated themselves to the new era by a stronger adherence to the idea of the National State, which became evident even in their change of names. The German Democratic

On the Way to Constitutional Unification

Party entered the arena as a new organization. It united the Progressive National Party with a great part of the National Liberals, but only with a part; while the remainder held together as the German People's Party: this put an end to the possibility of forming a single Liberal-Democratic Party. The franchise law had considerably increased the number of voters; in addition to women, all men over twenty years of age were given the vote.

The Majority-Socialists won 163 seats out of 421, the Independents only 23, the Centre 91, the Democrats 75, the People's Party 22, and the German Nationalists 42. Behind the union of the Majority-Socialists, the Centre, and the Democrats, stood three-quarters of all the votes given. From these parties Ebert, the former National Delegate, formed the first Imperial Ministry, when, in pursuance of the law respecting the provisional authority of the State, he was elected President of the Empire in February 1919. There could be no question of the validity of this election, by which the will of the majority of the German nation handed the reins of empire to the man to whom, more than any other, that will was indebted for its realization.

Three years later the Reichstag by 314 votes to 76 changed the provisional election into a final one.

'I desire to act, and will act, as representative of the whole German nation, not as leader of a single party'—such was the solemn promise of the President of the Empire when he assumed his office: he filled it with sagacity and vigour, as a uniting and reconciling influence, till he was snatched away by a premature death.

Two chief ideas formed the basis of the draft for the Imperial Constitution submitted by Hugo Preuss, who was at that time Secretary of State: 'The German Republic must be founded upon the free right of self-determination of the German nation as a whole. The first and vital matter is not the existence of the Single States but the existence of this nation itself as a—Unity.' The democratic idea encountered no opposition: all the more violent were the attacks made, chiefly from the side of the Single States Governments, upon the unitary basis of his work. The second draft was drawn up with their co-operation. It restored the power of government to the Single States, provided for an Imperial Council representing the Single

The Citizens and their Empire

States in the legislation and administration of the empire, and made impossible the disintegration of Prussia by law of the empire or by the decree of individual provinces into several States of medium size. The second draft received its final shape in the debates of the Committee of the Constitution. All parties were represented in the Committee, according to their strength, and in that hour of trouble and urgency they co-operated in an objective and conciliatory spirit, as befitted the great work. Their faithful labour could indeed only smooth over the deeply rooted antagonisms, and not remove them: what Bismarck said of the Constitution of the Kaiser's empire after he left office was equally true of the Weimar Constitution. 'It is imperfect, but it was the utmost that we were able to accomplish.' Yet its imperfections do not spring from the narrow-mindedness either of a dogma, or of a pretension to authority; but from the multiplicity of German life, and its provisions everywhere leave room for further development. While the Imperial Constitution offers to every class of the nation the possibility of making its influence felt within the State by legal means, conformably with its importance in the nation as a whole, it ensures internal agreement, and fosters the growth of internal unity, which is our chief need. But in retrospect, as has been justly said, it is seen to have been the victory of the will to self-preservation, over the will to annihilation, which threatened from within and from without.

Although the Armistice had deprived the German people of all possibility of further fighting, the victorious Powers allowed the blockade to continue without mercy. Want was first actually experienced after the demobilization of the ten million belonging to the army, and the influx of Germans repatriated from abroad. There was a lack of food and clothing, of housing and employment: where work was to be found, it was frequently badly done. For the uncertainty of all conditions robbed daily toil of its meaning and value: the war-profiteers were succeeded by the usufructuaries of the Revolution and the inflation. In these circumstances political life was bound to run to waste. While in Goethe's city the National Assembly was labouring at the task of the Constitution behind barbed-wire barricades, political murders, mass strikes, and street fighting showed that the revolutionary unrest was

424

On the Way to Constitutional Unification

not yet allayed. Karl Liebknecht and Rosa Luxemburg, Eisner, the Bavarian Minister-President, and Neuring, the War Minister for Saxony, fell victim to assassins: following upon a Communist rising in Berlin came the short rule of the Council's Republic in Munich, sanguinary strikes in the coal and manufacturing districts of Rhenish-Westphalia and Saxe-Thuringia, and at midsummer the great railway strike. Even after the Imperial Government had gained complete command of the capital it was difficult, and in many cases impossible, for them to carry out their will, in opposition to the provincial and local authorities which had sprung up during the Revolution. The Workmen's and Soldiers' Councils, which at the Revolution had everywhere seized the executive power for themselves, showed small inclination to follow the orders from Berlin. The fact that public administration survived the collapse unimpaired was due principally to the Government officials, who worked on, even through the most difficult weeks, frequently hampered, sometimes supported, and seldom thrust aside by the Councils.

The men who were used by the Government to create order by force of arms, and to oppose the increasing disintegration of German territory, came from the ranks of the old soldiers. The army in the field had been unequally affected by the Revolution. Beside the divisions, which maintained their accustomed discipline during the retreat, and opposed a successful resistance to the attempts at disarmament made by the Councils at home, there were also not a few in the west, amongst whom the old order had given way. Shoulder-straps and cockades were torn off, and red flags and favours proclaimed the hope of a new age of brotherhood. Yet, under wise leadership, insubordination was still rare, and military cohesion was scarcely prejudiced through the Soldiers' Councils. Thus the ordered withdrawal of the great masses of troops across the Rhine in precipitate haste, under pressure from the enemy, was successfully carried out. It was the last great achievement of the old army, introduced by Hindenburg's declaration: 'I shall lead the army home again!' and ending with their reception by the people of the Rhineland, who waited days and weeks to offer their thanks and love to the field-grey troops. It was not, indeed, an easy matter for many of the returned soldiers to adapt themselves to the changed

425

political conditions and the economic distress, and amongst those who belonged to the Volunteer Societies, attachment to the old Government was allied with military *esprit de corps*, to become, as time went on, a source of trouble to the Government. The trials for secret murder during the last few years have thrown some light upon the outrages to which many 'traitors' fell victim. But without the Volunteer Associations it would not have been possible, even at the eleventh hour, to check the advance of the Poles in the Netzebruch district, and of the Soviet troops in Livland, close to the German frontier, nor to prevent the excesses of exasperated mobs.

When the victorious Powers laid the yoke of the Versailles Treaty upon the German nation, all attempts to attain internal peace seemed to be in vain. In addition to her colonies, Germany lost a territory of 70,000 square miles in extent, with seven million inhabitants: the Saar district and the Rhineland were occupied, together with the 'bridge-heads' of Cologne, Coblenz, and Mainz. The empire lost a seventh part of the entire agricultural area, principally districts which produced more than they could themselves consume, almost a third of the coal output, two-thirds of the zinc ore, and three-fourths of the iron ore; and in addition to the great blood-letting of the Armistice conditions and the destruction of her status as a power in world-trade, she was burdened with new deliveries of goods of huge amount, within long or short periods, and with a Reparation debt, whose amount was not finally fixed till a decade later. The treaty made the German people permanently defenceless, and robbed them of important sovereign rights: they were compelled to declare that they had forced the war upon the opposing States by their own offensive and that of their allies. The victors added moral infamy and open shame to the crippling, robbing, and gagging of the vanquished enemy. And all this after they had with slight variations subscribed to Wilson's Fourteen Points, which promised a peace of justice and reconciliation as the basis for the conclusion of peace.

What this treaty contained was not peace, but the continuation of the war in the political, financial, and even in the intellectual, spheres. The German Foreign Minister, Count Brockdorf-Rantzau, was justified in reproaching the statesmen at Versailles to their faces with the hatred which had dictated this peace. In spite of a clear recognition of the immediate consequences of refusal—prompt occupation of the principal ports and of the districts which yielded important supplies: wholesale devastation by the destructive means known to modern warfare: with a closer blockade of the remainder of Germany—he advised the refusal of signature. But we can as little share his expectation that the peoples of the Multi-alliance would not go all the way with their Governments, as we can share the hope of the Independent Socialists for a world revolution. Even if the attempt had been successful to rouse the weary and ruined German people to revolt, the French Nationalists would probably have accomplished their ends in the Rhineland, the Poles have seized upon still more territory, the English have been in no haste to evacuate the ports, and in Bavaria the efforts directed against the empire have gained the upper hand. The 'bitterly hard struggle between exasperated sentiment and cool deliberation' (Bauer) was decided, not according to the views of the political parties to which the responsible men belonged, but to their individual attitude. The fact that a majority was at last found for signature did at least preserve the unity of the German nation.

After the signing of the treaty, the blockade was succeeded by the burden of Reparation payments. The population of the Rhineland was handed over to the bitter fate of occupation, to the propaganda of French culture with its varying methods, and to the excesses of coloured troops. Upper Silesia was also occupied for two years, and the French delegate on the Voting Commission permitted cruel outrages on the part of the Poles towards the German inhabitants to pass without a word. The voting resulted in an almost two-thirds majority for Germany: but the Council of the League of Nations decreed a partition, which was a direct contravention of the Versailles Treaty. A similar caprice governed the voting proceedings in other districts. Under pressure from outside, internal political tension rose to the highest pitch. A 'national' Opposition, with partiality which it would be hard to outdo, threw all the blame for the distress upon the new Government and its men, and laboured to overthrow them. In March 1920 Kapp, the former leader of the Patriotic Party (*Vaterlandspartei*), struck the first blow in Berlin: the Government

427

buildings were occupied by troops of the marine brigade, who were due for demobilization. The enterprise collapsed pitiably after a few days. But, on the other hand, the Government had for weeks to fight for its life against the Communist rising in the Ruhr district. The last powerful onslaught of Bolshevism was repelled by the Reichswehr, the police, and the volunteers. But the unrest continued. In June 1920, the parties of the Weimar Coalition lost a hundred seats in the elections to the first Reichstag. The Independents gained nearly sixty: a few more were won by the German Nationals and the German People's Party together: the lost Centre seats passed to the Bavarian People's Party, which had made itself independent. The wavering of the will to unity, which had been upheld by the Weimar Assembly, was evident in the weakening of the Centre parties, and the strengthening of the right and left wings.

The French Government knew how to make even the German civil war serve their own ends. As a punishment for the employment of the Reichswehr in the Ruhr district, which was contrary to the Treaty of Versailles, they occupied Frankfort on the Main and other cities.

This was a prelude to what was to come. Up till the beginning of 1923, not less than twenty-seven conferences were occupied with the question of German payments. After the first had come and gone without result, a final sum of 286 milliard marks was arrived at, payable in forty-two years. In the London Conference of spring 1921, the Allied Powers reached a final settlement, rejected the German counter-proposal, and threatened the empire with measures of compulsion. Düsseldorf, Duisburg, and Ruhrort were in fact occupied as a 'sanction,' and a prospect was held out of the invasion of the Ruhr territory. Yielding to pressure, the Imperial Government finally signed the engagements which were far in excess of their capacity, and once more brought sore distress upon Germany. In order to meet the accepted payments, short-term foreign loans had to be taken up at high interest: the mark fell in a few months from sixty to three hundred to the dollar. All the efforts of the Imperial Government to obtain alleviation at further conferences came to nothing. Through its ill-success in this matter of Reparations, which gradually produced more and more severe derangement of economic

On the Way to Constitutional Unification

life, the ground was prepared for the political and private persecution of the leading men. After Erzberger, Rathenau, the Foreign Minister, fell in 1922 by the hand of an assassin. Youths between the ages of sixteen and twenty-one helped to carry out the murder. Rathenau had self-sacrificingly placed his stores of knowledge and great capabilities at the service of the Fatherland: others could not hope to accomplish what had been denied to his leadership.

In January 1923, after the French Government had pronounced a trivial delay in the deliveries of timber, and the shortage of a seventh in the coal delivery, to be 'intentional default,' French and Belgian troops advanced into the Ruhr, ostensibly for the security of 'productive pledges.' Poincaré expressly repudiated every idea of a military occupation, or an occupation of a political nature. Yet six months earlier he had publicly declared: 'We are going quite simply to undertake the permanent occupation of the left bank of the Rhine, and it does me good. It would be a grief to me if Germany paid. In that case, we should have to evacuate the Rhineland, and would be robbed of the fruits of our efforts to conquer the population on the bank of the frontier river, peaceably, but with our weapons in our hands.' Even the leaders of French industry took a hand in the game. The German coal and iron industry was to be made to submit to an alliance with the French, whose conditions France intended to prescribe. These aims were not attained by the invasion of the Ruhr. All classes and parties drew closely together, and met the armed invasion with unarmed resistance. The occupying Powers resorted to the severest measures to break this passive resistance; more than 100,000 people were expelled; thousands thrown into prison, and countless outrages offered to the defenceless. Neither violence and threats, nor the enticements of the Separatists paid with French money, brought about the desired result. Yet, after it had lasted nearly nine months, the struggle in the Ruhr had to be abandoned. The cost of maintaining the millions who would not work under French masters, and the injury done to business as a whole, and the exclusion of Germany from the world's capital markets, had caused the work of the banknote printing press to be speeded up to such a pitch that the mark sank to a billionth part of its value.

As soon as the danger of the invasion of the Ruhr became

imminent, party relations had to a certain extent tended to clarify themselves: the Independents united again with the Majority-Socialists, and the People's Party entered the Government. After the cessation of resistance had become inevitable, all parties, with the exception of the Communists and the German Nationalists, united under the leadership of Stresemann, of the People's Party, to form a Great Coalition Government. They announced the abandonment of the struggle in the Ruhr, and after that, in October 1923, they received full authorization from a large majority in the Reichstag. This voluntary renunciation of power was a memorable event in the young parliamentary life of Germany. In this way the Government was empowered to take the measures which marked the first steps of Germany's recovery from the deepest misery.

The Reichswehr marched into Saxony, to make an end of Zeigner's Socialist-Communist Government, which had set itself above the Imperial Constitution. But before order had been restored in Saxony and Thuringia, the attitude of the Bavarian Government was causing new difficulties. When the struggle became more acute, Hitler, the National Socialist, proclaimed a dictatorship in the Löwenbräu Cellar at Munich, of which he himself, with Ludendorff and von Kahr, the Bavarian General States Commissioner, were to take over the direction. Instead of beginning the march upon Berlin, Hitler's followers were scattered the very next day upon Kahr's instigation; but it required protracted negotiations and great patience on the part of the Imperial Government, to come to an agreement with the Bavarian Government. Meantime the Imperial Government succeeded in placing German values on a new basis by the creation of the Rentenmark, and in stabilizing the imperial exchequer by a ruthless restriction of expenditure and the tapping of all sources of revenue. Indeed, the 'Emergency Decrees' made so deep an inroad into economic and social life that strong opposition arose after a time amongst the people's representatives, and in May 1924 the dissolution of the Reichstag once more strengthened the extreme Right and Left. The Communist and National Socialist Parties, which for the first time took part in the election, won 62 and 32 seats: the German Nationalists increased the number of their delegates from 66 to 106: on the other hand, the reunited Social Democrats decreased from 194

430

to 100, while Democrats, Centre, and People's Party lost far more than was gained by the young Economic Union.

A decisive turn was given to foreign politics, also, in the months following the Ruhr conflict. Germany's will to self-preservation and rehabilitation did not fail to make an impression on the outside world. Moreover, when his undertaking proved unsuccessful and endangered the French currency, Poincaré found himself obliged to yield to the proposals for negotiation made by the Allied Powers: a few months later he was forced to make way for the Herriot Ministry, which was prepared to negotiate. On the basis of a report made by experts under the direction of the American Dawes, the London Agreement of 1924 regulated the scale of German payments. The Dawes Plan also laid heavy burdens upon the German people, which could not permanently be borne; while the Imperial Bank and the Imperial Railway, which was made self-supporting, were placed under foreign control, the autonomy of the empire in the departments of finance and traffic was considerably impaired. But German liability to pay was set free at last by the Dawes Plan from its political implications, and the method of sanctions, beloved by the French Government, was superseded by arbitration, while a loan was guaranteed to the empire for her immediate needs. Order and continuity took the place of insecurity and caprice; once more the German people saw a path stretching before them, steep and narrow though it might be.

After the provisional regulation of the Reparation engagements, German foreign policy could turn its attention to other ends. Although the French people possessed the strongest army in the world, and were, moreover, protected through their alliances with the States in the east of Germany, they thought it necessary to insist upon insurance against attack on the part of their disarmed neighbour. No French Government, however ready it might be to come to an understanding, was able to escape this demand, which had been raised to a legal claim by the Versailles Treaty. Even the Imperial Government had to reckon with it, if they wished to relieve the lot of the Rhinelanders. Following therefore upon earlier offers, which had been rejected, Stresemann, the Minister for Foreign Affairs, submitted new proposals to the Allied Powers, which instead of military precautions, provided for the insurance of peace by peaceful means. The exchange of views sustained by the spirit of reconciliation, and encouraged by the English Government, led in 1925 to the settlement of the Locarno Conference. It was decided by the 'Western Pact,' upon the security of England, Belgium, and Italy, that the frontiers of western Germany could not be altered through force of arms by any of the Powers concerned. Yet the statement of the League of Nations, that treaties which had become untenable might be subject to alteration, applies also to this agreement. In case of dispute, appeal was to be made to a neutral court of arbitration. The idea of a court of arbitration was further taken as a basis for the 'Eastern Pact' signed by Germany, Poland, and Czechoslovakia; but this treaty includes neither the definite recognition of frontiers nor the security of other Powers. By voluntarily renouncing the attempt to alter their frontiers by military action, and by recognizing the proceedings of the court of arbitration, the States which shared in the making of the treaty took an important step on the road which leads to the spiritual defeat of the Treaty of Versailles. When Düsseldorf, Duisburg, and Ruhrort had already been evacuated as a sequel to the London Agreement, and the troops withdrawn from the Ruhr territory, the new treaty led in 1926 to the evacuation of the Cologne zone, and a mitigation of the burden of the occupation in the territories where it was still maintained, together with the reception of Germany into the League of Nations. But there were no small difficulties still to be overcome. Exceptional provisions had to be made for Germany, because in case of common military action on the part of the States of the League of Nations she, as a disarmed Power, could not accept the same obligations as the others. After this question had been settled, it was necessary to repel the efforts of some of the States, which aimed at a transformation of the Council of the League of Nations when Germany entered the League. At the meeting held in August 1926, Germany was able to enter the League of Nations on an equal legal footing with the most privileged Powers. Thus was shown, actually if not formally, that the theory of Germany's sole war guiltiness has been dropped by her former enemies, and that the Treaty of Versailles has also been revised on this point. During the short period of her membership of the League

On the Way to Constitutional Unification

of Nations, the empire has already had frequent opportunities of working for the cause of peace.

After the acceptance of the London Agreement, the president of the empire dissolved the Reichstag, hoping to make the success which had been won in foreign politics bear fruit by increasing the number of the adherents of the Government amongst the deputies. By the election in December 1924, the National Socialists and the Communists were considerably weakened: the Social Democrats returned as the strongest party in the Reichstag with 130 delegates, a position which was still further strengthened at the next election. Next to them, the German Nationalists gained the most votes: but the Social Democrats won more than the Nationalists and all the remaining parties put together. Following the result of the election, ministers of the German National Party now also formed part of the Imperial Government. But since the party considered what had been accomplished by the foreign Powers through the Treaty of Locarno to be inadequate, they resumed their opposition to the Government after a few months, and did not again take part in it until after the entry of Germany into the League of Nations, when they were granted not less than four ministerial posts. The affairs of domestic politics, such as the dispute over the flags to be flown by German embassies abroad, the plebiscite concerning the indemnification of the former dynasties, the fight over the Imperial Education Bill, played their part in crippling the activities of this Reichstag and Government, so that in the end the intervention of the imperial president was required before even the most urgent legislative measures, including a great programme for the relief of distressed agriculture, could be carried through. In the new election of spring 1928, the number of German National delegates dropped from 111 to 78, but almost all the other non-Socialist parties also suffered losses. The fourth Reichstag of the republic took its character as much from the increased number of Social-Democratic and Communist seats—which rose from 131 to 152 and from 42 to 54—as from the great number of very small parties, which take their stand, not on any general view of politics, but on a purely economic platform.

To the Social Democrats, as by far the strongest party, fell the task of forming a Government. After protracted negotiations, Hermann Müller, the Imperial Chancellor, set up a ministry in which, at first, all the older parties, from the Social Democrats down to the German People's Party, were represented.

Although the rise of minute party groups has made it peculiarly difficult for the German nation to express her political will, there is yet a preponderance of facts pointing to a new stability in the life of domestic politics. Even after the sensational public activity of the parties of the Right had been considerably restricted, by the grouping of the convinced republicans out of various camps, under the 'Banner of the Empire' (*Reichsbanner*), the German National Party also undertook co-responsibility for the government, and, while accepting the four ministerial posts, they declared themselves not only in favour of the continuation of foreign policy along the lines which had been laid down, but also of the stabilization of the political order, thus standing for the prolongation of the law for the Defence of the Republic. The election of Field-Marshal von Hindenburg as successor to Ebert in the year 1925, and his conduct of the office, deprived the opponents of the Republican State of the last pretext for describing their movement as a 'national' one. The war of the future will be waged no longer for the existence, but for the inner meaning, of the republic.

With the stabilization of political conditions, both foreign and domestic, the conditions were laid down for the recovery of German business life. The war, followed by the provisions of the Versailles Treaty, had done it serious injury in almost every department. Export trade, upon which the empire had come to rely in great measure for the subsistence of her population before the war, had been reduced to its extremest limit, through the crippling of production, the confiscation of German business abroad, the destruction of the mercantile marine, and the protective measures taken by many countries. Although in consequence of the fall of the mark, German products were extraordinarily cheap for foreign purchasers, the value of export trade in 1922 was little more than a third of that before the war. It is true that in many departments of economic life the increasing inflation gave rise to increasing activity: but this apparent prosperity was paid for by the steady depreciation of the substance behind the business, that is,

434

the money invested in it. When a fixed standard was again established, German business was faced with the task of adapting itself to the new circumstances of production, sale, and competition. The total of bankruptcies for two years amounted to more than 30,000: businesses which had been founded during the inflation period were chiefly affected, but many old and respected firms were also involved.

The English coal strike had for a time a reviving effect, chiefly upon the coal and iron industry. The year 1927 brought a period of rapid expansion: for the first time the figures of the pre-war period were reached and exceeded: the numbers of unemployed, including those on short time, who were counted as completely out of work, were reduced to about a third of the figure of over two millions on the 1st November in the previous year. In 1928, in consequence of disagreements about wages, lack of capital, and growing burdens resulting from the Dawes Plan, a decline set in, which manifested itself in a great increase in the numbers of unemployed. Yet the export of manufactured goods exceeded even the favourable standard of the year 1927.

The development of the traffic industry is typical of the general revival. After the German railroads were taken over by the empire, their first working year closed with an adverse balance of 15 milliard paper marks, as contrasted with a surplus of about 1 milliard gold marks in 1913. Two years later, railway traffic again produced a small, clear profit: then the struggle in the Ruhr nipped the recovery in the bud. After the new monetary standard had been set up, a considerable profit was made, even in the first working year, by reducing all expenditure to a minimum: and since that date the Imperial Railway, notwithstanding the cost of continual improvements in its working methods, has borne a great part of the burden of Reparations, originally about twice as much as the empire and industry taken together. The injury done to ocean traffic was still more serious. While before the war it possessed steamers of over 50,000 tons, the Treaty of Versailles left it no ships over 1,600 tons: the largest which the North German Lloyd had at their service was a pleasure steamer of barely 800 tons. To-day the German mercantile marine once more holds the third place in the world, with approximately 4 million tons, in spite of the fact that other States have expended larger sums upon the extension and working of their mercantile marine: Hamburg, as before, is the busiest port on the Continent. In July 1929, the steamship *Bremen*, of the North German Lloyd, succeeded in winning the blue ribbon of the ocean. In the organization of a centralized air service, also, Germany is not surpassed by any country, although up till the year 1926 her development was most painfully hampered by the restrictive regulations of the Allied Powers. After Hermann Koehl with two companions had accomplished the first ocean crossing from east to west in his aeroplane, the *Bremen*, the world flight of the airship, *Graf Zeppelin*, under Eckener's captaincy, opened up new possibilities of world intercourse.

In addition to the load of duties and reparations, business life had also to bear the burdens imposed by the growth of social legislation. The hope of the nationalization of the great industries, which was at first shared by many, could only be realized in the most modest degree in the face of economic facts: the law passed in the year 1919 for the nationalization of electricity was a step on the way. Yet from the first moment, the Socialist parties had recognized it to be their duty to imbue the democratic State with the idea of social service. Social endeavours took a foremost place with the other parties also: for, in consequence of the severe testing time both during and after the war, the feeling of national solidarity had become a living power throughout the nation.

Thus it was possible further to amplify the insurance laws, in which the autocratic German State had shown the way before the war to all the other States. To-day, approximately 20 million male and female operatives and employees enjoy the benefit of the sick fund, while the invalid insurance covers almost as many. In 1925, the sick insurance was called upon to compensate approximately 230 million days of sickness: the payment of pensions under the accident insurance of 1927 benefited about 600,000 injured and 150,000 survivors; and under the invalid insurance, $1 \cdot 8$ million invalids, 235,000 widows, and 800,000 orphans under fifteen years of age. According to official calculation, the total contributions for the year 1927 to all these branches of insurance, including the allowance from Government, came to over $3 \cdot 5$ milliard marks.

On the Way to Constitutional Unification

While the development of the system of insurance was carrying out a work which had been begun long before the war, old laws were changed and new paths struck out in the department of workmen's protection: to this belongs the new regulation of working time, which takes as a basis the principle of the eight hours' day, and the law dealing with labour exchanges and unemployment benefit. But the peculiar characteristic of social legislation of the post-war period is that it extended its care far beyond the circle of the working class, and developed its organizations in extraordinarily varied forms. Youth is served by infant homes, play and sports grounds, children's homes, children's libraries, and holiday settlements. The poor and destitute are supported by the town's welfare centres. The community has also taken over the care of settlement and housing. An attempt was at least made through the settlement law to bring about an approximation to the endeavours of the land reformers: during the war they had demanded as 'The Thanks of the Fatherland' a law which was to make it possible for every German family to acquire a cottage with a garden, or a small peasant holding. This goal is still far distant. The system of compulsory rationing of dwellings, applied by official boards, involved an interference with private circumstances which could scarcely have been more drastic: but it would have been impossible by any other methods to combat the terrible need which existed, and to prepare the way for gradual reconstruction even in this department.

All this represents a great sum of achievement, testifying to the unbroken will to live of the German nation. But even without fixing one's attention upon the conditions of housing and settlement, one need not be afraid of taking too rosy a view.

Present conditions speak all too clearly. With the depreciation of the mark, a period of prosperity seemed to set in for agriculture. Since the purchasing power of their produce had increased, the farmers were able to free themselves from debt and improve their working methods. Only two years after the restoration of the gold standard, however, a new state of indebtedness had arisen as a result of the growing difference between industrial and agricultural products. In the succeeding period, under the pressure of duties, taxes, and social burdens, this debt increased in

437

many rural properties to such an extent that the total sum
at present, according to a computation by agricultural
experts, is approximately equal to the burden of the
pre-war period. In any case, the weight of debts presses
more heavily, since in place of the long-term loans of the
pre-war time, short-term loans have been largely introduced, for which a higher interest has to be paid. Industry
has also to bear a heavy burden through lack of capital,
through taxes, and through social obligations. While
Germany's exports are very great, her imports are much
greater: the total amount for four years (1924-1927) of
imports uncovered by exports is computed at more than
10 milliard marks. The agreeable and sometimes brilliant
exterior conceals much care and misery. From the point of
view of population, as it affects politics, we are faced with
the fact that we are a nation with no room to expand;
this embarrassment comes to light in the decline of the
birthrate, in the exaggerated value set upon qualifying
certificates, and other phenomena. Apart from the threats
to social policy which arise from the unsatisfactory condition of the nation's domestic economy, the fundamental
doubt will not be silenced, whether the way of social
legislation is altogether the right one, and whether it is a
desirable end to guarantee a secure life to a great majority
through the giving of office. A further question for the
future is bound up with the progressive dehumanizing of
labour, which is being hastened by the compulsory imitation
of American business methods.

In the political sphere, the old antagonisms have not
been softened as one would have wished, and new
antagonisms have arisen; the proceedings in the Reichstag
are followed on many sides with a lack of sympathy, which
is much less tolerable in democratic than in autocratic
government. Though it may be caused in part by the
growing materialization of legislative work, as for instance
the transference of the chief weight to the deliberations
of committees, and may in so far be a universal phenomenon
in the parliamentary life of to-day, yet the growing
torpidity of our party life, the frequent petty haggling for
party advantages, must bear the blame to a considerable
extent. But so long as no better means are discovered of
giving expression to the people's will, the democratic State
stands or falls by the freshness and vigour of its party

On the Way to Constitutional Unification

system, which must be supported by the interest of all the citizens of the State. Further, foreign politics are burdened by anxiety for the fulfilment of the obligations which have been accepted. When, in its fifth year, payments on the Dawes Plan had reached their full height, the universal need felt by the nations for the regulation of war debts, led to the attempt to solve the problem of Reparations by a final and comprehensive agreement. In the year 1929, the Young Plan came into existence, as the result of long and difficult labour on the part of the economic experts, with German collaboration. In contrast to the Dawes Plan, it fixed a time-limit for the German obligations, provided for a more gradual increase in the yearly instalments, did away with foreign controls together with the system of pledges, and gave the German Government the task of furnishing the payments in foreign values, on their own responsibility. In spite of these alleviations, it was a hard thing for the Imperial Government to resolve upon the acceptance of the Young Plan: for it bound Germany for thirty-seven years to yearly payments averaging about 2 milliard Reichsmarks, and to further payments for the following twenty-two years. In any case, such a burden for so long a period only appeared tolerable if Germany, when the plan took effect, were to recover full political and economic control over her entire territory. For this reason, at the Hague Conference of the year 1929, the Imperial Government was obliged to demand with all urgency the evacuation of the occupied territory. A decade after the conclusion of peace, when Germany had voluntarily given the securities demanded by France, and had been admitted as a member, with equal rights, into the League of Nations, the occupation, as Germany believed, had in any case lost every appearance of justification. But even after the evacuation had been carried out, the 'Organization of Peace' still offers many tasks. The discrepancy which exists between the universal efforts of the nations for the establishment of peace, and their actual achevement, must be present to the German people with peculiar clearness. Armaments continue to grow, although the Treaty of Versailles had in view a universal limitation of armaments for all nations, to be introduced by the disarming of Germany.

Reconstruction is not made an easy task for the German people, and even under favourable circumstances at home and abroad will demand the labour of generations. No one can tell whether the next few years will bring good or ill fortune. But we may perhaps believe that we have passed the hardest stretch of the road. In any case, the experiences of the first decade of the republic will not be lost upon us in our shaping of the future. It was the will to union rather than any other thing, which helped the recovery of economic life. The first years of distress produced not only the close bond of the unions of employers and merchants on the one hand, and of the associations of workmen on the other, but also the first steps in their fruitful co-operation, which finds expression in the tariff agreements, the system of adjusting disputes, and the formation of the Economic Council of the Empire (*Reichswirtschaftsrat*).

The same feeling of participation in a common destiny, which is the basis of the growth of social legislation, is taking effect in intellectual life. While research is bringing an open mind to the study of life in all its fullness, and aims at apprehending the growth and nature of mankind in Germany and in Europe, the knowledge that science itself is a social good is more deeply felt by its representatives.

It is remarkable that one of their demands should be: To bring 'Weimar and Jena into inner union with Leuna and Leverkusen'—that is to say, they aim at establishing a synthesis between German idealism and the technical achievements of modern times. With these words, a goal is set up towards which some of our best men are striving successfully. The struggle for intrinsic cultural unity, in spite of all the diversity of educational forces, dominates the work of the school: notwithstanding the widest divergency in detail, the same idea is the foundation of the organic structure of the entire system of education in Prussia, as well as of the clear shaping of individual types of formative forces in the department of the higher school.

In the political field, powerful majorities have repeatedly been welded together by the pressure of outward and inward distress. In regard to the outside world, the German people's will to unity has not been without result, and will not be so in the future. In spite of outward powerlessness, in spite of molestation from without and from within, the empire of 60 million inhabitants in the centre of Europe signifies a power in the life of the nations. At the period of

On the Way to Constitutional Unification

her bitterest distress it was impossible to prevent her from establishing neighbourly relations with the Soviet State. Under the conditions which obtained at that time, the Treaty of Rapallo of the year 1922 was of little value beyond a statement of principle; but the resumption of relations with Russia may prove of extraordinary importance for the future. Closely as we are bound to the Russian nation by the frequent similarity of our recent fortunes, we are bound more closely to Austria by the bond of blood, of speech, and the history of a thousand years. To-day the dictate of the Victor-Powers still prevents the union of the two nations, and here and there in the empire the voice of the blood is silenced by the reasonings of the brain. But even these reasonings will yield to necessity. Austria cannot rest till she has found an ally, whether in Bavaria, the Danube provinces, or the empire. The first would mean the disruption of the structure of the empire, the second the revival of the Slav-Romano-Germanic combination, from which Europe was delivered by the World War. These dangers can only be averted by the reunion with the empire of the Germans of the Danube, which will, in addition, strengthen and enrich German nationality in the north and south. No one can divine when the hour will strike. It is our part to wait for it, and to prepare the ground for its coming, as is already being done, for instance, by the co-operation of the kindred nations in important legislative measures.

The movement towards the unification of the forms and purposes of life is making itself felt in every department, with a force which has never before been known. It demands the sacrifice—frequently a painful one—of individual aims: it by no means excludes conflict: but it shapes the future out of sacrifice and conflict. Simplification is the law of life at the present time, and even political organization is subject to it.

The necessity of evolution will produce the constitutional unity, which the Germans in the course of their thousand years of history were unable to create. The introductory measures were taken under the impulsion of the distressful financial situation of the empire. In 1928, at the Conference of German States in Berlin, all the Governments expressed themselves unanimously to the effect that the regulation of the relations between Empire and States which was set up at Weimar, was in need of fundamental reform. The forms of this regulation are contested, as could scarcely be otherwise considering the individual character of the German countries, and the multiplicity of the German nature. Once again, through the failure of prominent leaders, the German nation is thrown on its own resources, to discover the appropriate means of solving the great problem which was beyond the genius of a Bismarck. The solution will probably be reached step by step, through a gradual evolution. We shall have to accustom ourselves to conceive of the unification of our State more as a process than as a transaction.

The constitutional unity might prove a dangerous boon if it came in the form of a gift: the constitutional unity, as a problem to be solved, sets free the forces which support the democratic State. He who advocates a State system of the most unified form possible, can render a service to the democratic idea. He who is active in the spirit of true democracy, is labouring to form the constitutional unity. The form creates life, only when it is filled with the spirit: the spirit alone is living. If the German people succeed in preserving and strengthening the spirit through which they reconstructed their State after the collapse, then they will create their own unity, and by it attain once more to freedom and greatness.

Then the word will be fulfilled in them, which was spoken at a time of distress and yet of hope, by one of the men of the Paul's Church:

The waters are climbing high—but the flower climbs higher!

APPENDIX

I

GERMAN TRIBES

ALEMANNI OR ALAMANNI.—A name which either signifies: All men, or is derived from the name of their sanctuary, the 'alah.' A German race of Suevic origin, occupying the region from the Main to the Danube, in the first part of the third century. Defeated by Clovis, 498.

CARLOVINGIANS OR CAROLINGIANS.—A royal house descended from the Frankish lords in Austrasia in the seventeenth century. It furnished a dynasty of French kings, German emperors and kings, and Italian sovereigns.

CATALAUNI.—An ancient people of Gaul whose name survives in the modern Châlons.

CHATTI.—One of the most powerful of the German inland tribes, of whom a part were ultimately merged in the Salic Franks.

DALEMINZEN.—A Slav tribe occupying both sides of the valley of Freiberg between Elbe and Chemnitz. They were conquered in 927 by Henry I, and became part of the Mark of Meissen.

FRANKS.—The name assumed in the third century by a confederation of German tribes, and divided in the fourth century into three groups:

Chatti.

Ripuarian Franks (dwelling near Cologne).

Salian Franks (along the lower Rhine).

The Merovingian monarchy of the Salian Franks was established under Clovis (481–511) and gave origin to the name France.

GERMANI.—An important Teutonic race inhabiting Central Europe at the beginning of the Christian era. Their chief tribes were the Alemanni, Franks, Saxons, Goths, besides the Burgundians, Frisians, Thuringians, and Longobards.

HEVELLER.—A tribe settled on the banks of the Havel, the most important tributary of the lower Elbe, which waters the Mark of Brandenburg. They were finally conquered by Albert the Bear in the twelfth century.

LOMBARDS, LONGOBARDI.—Members of the Germanic tribe, who about 568, under Alboin, conquered the part of northern Italy still called Lombardy. They founded the kingdom of that name, which was afterwards extended over a much larger territory, and was finally overthrown by Charlemagne, 774.

MARCOMANNI.—A German tribe, a branch of the Suevi, first mentioned by Caesar as part of the army of Ariovistus. In the second century they were defeated by Marcus Aurelius in the so-called Marcomannic War. They were in frequent conflict with the Romans, down to the fourth century, and in the sixth century they occupied Bavaria.

443

Appendix

SALII.—A division of the Franks, first mentioned in the fourth century, who were settled along the lower Rhine. In the fifth century, under Clovis, they overthrew the Roman power in Gaul, and founded the Merovingian Frankish monarchy.

SAXONS.—An important tribe, who towards the end of the third century formed a great tribal family between Ems and Elbe. The leading princely family of Germany is descended from the Saxons, as also was Bismarck.

SWABIANS.—Natives of an ancient duchy of Germany, corresponding roughly to Wurtemberg, Baden, and south-west Bavaria: one of the five great duchies of the early German kingdom, which endured from 517 to 1254. The Swabian House of Hohenzollern furnished a famous dynasty of German kings and emperors.

II

PRINCELY FAMILIES

ASCANII.—A noble family, whose name goes back to a castle near Aschersleben. Albert the Bear was invested with the Mark of Brandenburg in 1134, and his family reigned till 1319.

BABENBERG.—A princely family of Franconia, prominent in the ninth and tenth centuries, whose castle stood on the site of the modern Bamberg. The Austrian dynasty of Babenberg, which ruled from 974 to 1246, is supposed to be descended from this Franconian House.

HABSBURG OR HAPSBURG (orig. HABICHTSBURG, HAWK'S CASTLE).—A German princely family, which derived its name from the castle of Hapsburg on the banks of the Aar, and has furnished sovereigns to the Holy Roman Empire, Austria, and Spain.

HOHENSTAUFEN.—A princely family which furnished sovereigns to Germany and Sicily in the twelfth and thirteenth centuries. Conrad, the last of the line, was executed in 1268.

HOHENZOLLERN.—A German princely family, which ruled over Brandenburg from 1418. It has furnished the kings of Prussia since 1701, and the German emperors since 1871.

WELFS OR GUELPHS.—A famous princely house, from which are descended the Hanover and Brunswick lines. They take their name from Welf I, a contemporary of Charlemagne.

WETTIN.—A Saxon family taking its name from the ancestral castle on the Saale, thirty-two miles north-west of Leipzig.

WITTELSBACH.—The family name of the former electors of the Palatinate and Bavaria. The duchy of Bavaria was granted by Barbarossa to the ancestors of the dynasty, who reigned till 1918.

Appendix

III

GEOGRAPHICAL NOTES

ON PLACES NOT DESCRIBED IN THE TEXT, WITH
THE PAGE ON WHICH THEY ARE FIRST MENTIONED

See also Index of Names and Places

AMU DARJA OR OXUS, p. 362.—A ri verof central Asia, flowing
through Bokhara and Khiva to the Sea of Aral.

ASPERG, p. 318.—A hill near Stuttgart, well known in Germany for
the State prison situated upon it.

CATALAUNIAN FIELDS, p. 9.—A plain near Châlons-sur-Marne
famous for the victory (A.D. 451) of Aetius and the Gothic
King Theodoric over Attila.

CLUNY, p. 44.—A town in the department of Saône-et-Loire, France,
celebrated for its Benedictine abbey, where the reforms of the
cloister were originated in the tenth century.

DOBRUDJA OR DOBRUDSCHA, p. 364.—The south-eastern portion of
Rumania, between the Danube and the Black Sea; a marsh
and steppe region, traversed by the ancient wall of Trajan. It
was occupied temporarily by the Russians in 1828 and 1854, and
by the French in 1854, and was incorporated in Rumania in 1878.

EYDER, p. 43.—A river in Schleswig-Holstein, Prussia, which flows
into the North Sea about twenty-six miles north of the mouth
of the Elbe. It gave its name to a political party in Denmark in
1863 (die Eyder-dänische Partei) which pressed for the incorporation of Schleswig within the State of Denmark, with the
Eyder for its frontier.

HILDESHEIM, p. 54.—A city in Hanover, renowned for its mediaeval
and German Renaissance buildings, particularly the cathedral,
which dates from the eleventh century. It became the seat of a
bishopric in 822, and was one of the Hanseatic towns.

HIRSCHAU, p. 60.—A village in the Black Forest, in Wurtemberg, on
the river Nagold. Noted in the Middle Ages for its Benedictine
monastery. Built in the ninth century. In 1077, Abbot William introduced the reforms of Clunyin to Hirschau, and his 'Regulations of Hirschau' spread over the greater part of the German
monasteries.

MARBURG, p. 140.—A town in the province of Hesse-Nassau, Prussia,
famous for its mediaeval buildings, and the library of the
university, founded by Philip, Landgrave of Hesse, which contains 150,000 volumes. Marburg was the scene of the fruitless
conference held in October 1629, between Luther and Zwingli.

MASUREN, p. 134.—A region in the south of East Prussia, containing
over 3,000 lakes of varying dimensions. Its towns were founded
and fortified by the Teutonic Order, and it was the scene of
their final defeat at Tannenberg in 1410. Here also, in the
World War, Hindenburg and Ludendorff won their great
victory over the Russians in 1914.

Appendix

NETZE, p. 267.—A river in Posen and Brandenburg, affluent of the Warthe. It is about 200 miles long, and gives its name to the district through which it flows.

NEUSS, p. 163.—The ancient Novesium. A town in the Rhine province, Prussia, four miles west-south-west of Düsseldorf. Unsuccessfully besieged by Charles the Bold of Burgundy in 1474.

PALATINATE (GERMAN PFALZ), p. 94.—A former German State, now belonging to Baden, Bavaria, Hesse, and Prussia, whose territories were originally in the region of the Rhine. In the sixteenth century Heidelberg, the capital of the Electors Palatine, became a great centre of Calvinism.

RHENSE, p. 142.—A hamlet on the left bank of the Rhine, four or five miles above Coblenz. A building called the *Königsstuhl* (king's seat) was erected there in 1376 for the meetings of the electors, in which many imperial elections were made.

SAARBRÜCKEN, p. 250.—A city in the Rhine province, Prussia, twenty-eight miles south-south-east of Trèves. It was the scene of the first action in the Franco-German War of 1870.

SCHMALKALDEN, p. 224.—An ancient town in the province of Hesse-Nassau, Prussia, which gave its name in 1537 to a league of their Protestant princes and free cities, for the common defence of faith and political independence against the Emperor Charles V.

SPIRE (GERMAN SPEYER OR SPEIER), p. 8.—Capital of the Rhine Palatinate, Bavaria, situated at the junction of the Speyerbach and the Rhine, and famous for its cathedral, built in the eleventh century. It became the seat of a bishopric about A.D. 610 and a free imperial city in 1294, and from 1513 to 1689 the seat of the Imperial Chamber. The Diet of Spire in 1529 condemned the Reformation, and the 'Protestation' made at that time by the Reformers gave rise to the name Protestant.

SUDETEN, p. 166.—A mountain system in Moravia, Austrian and Prussian Silesia, Bohemia, and Saxony.

TANNENBERG, p. 164.—A village in East Prussia, fourteen miles south of Osterode. Here, in 1410, the Polish and Lithuanian Army broke the power of the Teutonic Order, and in 1914 the Russian Army was defeated by Hindenburg and Ludendorff.

WEIMAR, p. 3.—The capital of the grand duchy of Saxe-Weimar-Eisenach. It became famous towards the end of the eighteenth century as the German 'Athens,' the centre of German literature, through the residence of Goethe, Schiller, Herder, and Wieland, under the patronage of the Grand Duke Charles Augustus. In February 1919 it was the scene of the National Assembly, which met under the presidency of Ebert, to draw up a Republican Constitution for Germany.

WITTENBERG, p. 203.—A town on the Elbe in the Prussian province of Saxony, famous for its connection with Luther and the early Reformation. Luther nailed his ninety-six theses to the door of the Schloss Kirche in 1517 and burned the Pope's Bull in 1520. The town was bombarded by the Imperialists in 1760; fortified by Napoleon in 1813; and besieged by the Prussians and stormed, January 12–13, 1814.

Appendix

WORMS, p. 7.—A city in the province of Rhine-Hesse, on the left bank of the Rhine. In 1122 it was the scene of the Concordat of Worms, a convention concluded between the Emperor Henry V and Pope Calixtus II, which put an end to the contest regarding investiture between the Emperor and the Pope. (*See also* Appendix IV, 'Diet of Worms.')

IV

NOTES ON PHRASES MENTIONED IN THE TEXT

ARMAGNACS, p. 162.—In mediaeval history, a district in southern France corresponding to the department of Gers. It gave its name to the bands of lawless mercenaries, chiefly natives of that county, who were trained in the civil wars between the Armagnac and Burgundian parties.

BABYLONISH CAPTIVITY, p. 151.—That period in the history of the Church when, in the fourteenth century, the popes, exiled from Italy, lived at Avignon, under French influence. Their stay in France lasted seventy years, corresponding to the period of the Jewish exile in Babylon.

BIEDERMEIER, p. 315.—A good-natured man but Philistine. 'The time of Biedermeier' signifies the period between the War of Liberation and the March Revolution (1816–1848) in which the middle classes, though outwardly comfortable, lived under narrow economic conditions and were suppressed in their political aims. The 'style of Biedermeier' corresponds to the modest but fairly comfortable standard of life of those times, and marks the change of style from that of the First Empire to that of English middle-class culture at the end of the eighteenth century. These features are also evident in the portraits of the period.

BULL, THE GOLDEN, p. 147.—The edict passed by the Emperor Charles IV in 1356. It became the corner-stone of the German Constitution, settling and legalizing the status of the electors and limiting the power of the Crown. It took its name from the bull, or capsule of the seal appended to the document, which was of gold.

CONFEDERATION, THE GERMAN (DEUTSCHER BUND), p. 304.—The Confederation of German States, constituted by the Congress of Vienna in 1816, replacing the ancient Empire, each State remaining independent in internal affairs. The Confederation was dissolved as one result of the war of 1866, and was replaced by the North German Confederation.

CONFEDERATION, NORTH GERMAN (NORD DEUTSCHER BUND), p. 350. —Was formed in 1866 under the presidency of Prussia, and was the model for the German Empire, which took its place in 1871.

Appendix

ELECTORS, COLLEGES OF, p. 142.—In the first centuries of the Middle Ages the German king was elected by the whole body of lords spiritual and temporal. In the thirteenth century the privilege of election was vested in a small body of the princes; the assent of the rest of the nobility being at first assumed, and finally altogether dispensed with.

ENLIGHTENMENT (AUFKLÄRUNG), pp. 279 ff.—A European intellectual movement, lasting from the middle of the seventeenth to the beginning of the nineteenth century. Its leading principle was the encouragement of individual thought, and it took Reason as the final test of truth. The movement began in England with Locke and Hume, and was represented in Germany by Lessing, M. Mendelssohn, Nicolai, and Frederick II.

GÖTTINGEN, THE SEVEN OF, p. 323.—In 1837, seven professors of Göttingen University, Ewald, Gervinus, Albrecht, Weber, Dahlmann, and the brothers Grimm, were expelled by the King of Hanover because they opposed the suspension of the Constitution of 1833.

HAMBACHER FEST, p. 322.—Hambach is a village in the circle of Neustadt, in the Bavarian Palatinate. A political assembly of about 20,000 persons was held at the castle on May 27, 1832, noteworthy as the occasion of the first public appearance of the Republican Party in Germany.

HANSEATIC LEAGUE, OR GERMAN HANSE (OLD GERMAN: HANSE, A BOND), p. 130.—A mediaeval confederation of cities of northern Germany and adjacent countries, called the Hanse Towns, at one time numbering about seventy, with affiliated cities in nearly all parts of Europe, for the promotion of commerce by sea and land, and for its protection against pirates, robbers, and hostile Governments.

HAPAG, p. 337.—Hamburg-Amerika Paket-Fahrt Aktien Gesellschaft (Hamburg-America Steamship Company).

HOLY ALLIANCE, p. 311.—A league formed in 1815 by Russia, Austria, and Prussia to regulate the affairs of Europe 'by the principles of Christian charity,' meaning that each of the contracting parties was to keep all that the league assigned them.

HOLY ROMAN EMPIRE, OR DEUTSCHES REICH, p. 36.—The realm ruled by the Emperor, who claimed to be the representative of the ancient German emperors, and who asserted authority, in theory, over the nations of central and western Europe; it was called Holy from the interdependence of the Empire and the Church. In general, it comprised the German-speaking peoples in central Europe, and had for a long time a close connection with Italy. It began with Otto I, who was crowned emperor in 962, and continued till 1806, when Francis II gave up the crown.

HUMANISM, p. 167.—A name given to the intellectual movement which began in Italy in the thirteenth century, and was first clearly recognizable in the fourteenth. Through Italian poets and orators, it reached the Court of Charles IV, about the time of Petrarch. It is defined by Trench as 'the studies which are considered the most specially adapted for training . . . true Humanity in every man.'

448

Appendix

MERCANTILISM, p. 241.—A system of political economy, which aimed at the regulation of economic matters by the State. It was, in Adam Smith's words, a system 'for enriching the people,' and its essence is that it was to do so by means of commerce, and more particularly by the State regulation of commerce (Clark, *The Seventeenth Century*).

MINNESINGERS, OR MINSTRELS, p. 99.—The earliest lyric poets of Germany were so-called because the subject of their lyrics was 'Minne-sang,' i.e. Love-ditty. They flourished in the twelfth and thirteenth centuries.

PRAEMONSTRATENSIAN, OR NORBERTINE, ORDER OF MONKS, p. 94.— Founded in the twelfth century by St. Norbert, who obtained permission in 1120 to found a cloister at Laon, in France. A spot was pointed out to him in a vision and was called by him 'Pré montré,' or 'Pratum Monstratum,' the meadow pointed out. The Order might be termed 'reformed Augustine.'

PUTSCH, THE KAPP, p. 427.—A revolution attempted in March 1920 by Wolfgang Kapp, a Pan-German politician, against the Republican Government in Berlin.

REUNION, CHAMBERS OF, p. 250.—Special Courts established by Louis XIV in 1680 to decide on the annexation to France of various territories along the eastern frontier, mainly in Alsace.

ROMANESQUE ARCHITECTURE, p. 54.—A general term for all the debased styles of architecture which sprang from attempts to imitate the Roman, and which flourished in Europe from the period of the destruction of the Roman power till the introduction of Gothic architecture. It has been variously termed Saxon, Norman, Lombard, Byzantine, etc., all of which might be considered varieties of the Romanesque. The beautiful Rhenish cathedrals of the twelfth and thirteenth centuries are built in this style.

ROUGH HOUSE (RAUHES HAUS), p. 320.—A reformatory school founded in 1833 at Hamburg by Dr. J. H. Wichern for destitute or vagrant children.

SCHLEMIHL, PETER, p. 329.—Peter Schlemihl's *Wunderbare Geschichte*, a fairy tale remarkable for its realistic character, was published in 1814 and translated into almost every European language. Peter makes a compact with the Devil, giving him the right to take possession of his shadow. The author, Adelbert von Chamisso (1781–1838), came from an old French noble family, which was exiled during the French Revolution. He entered the Prussian military service for some time, and expressed in this tale his feelings, which were divided between his native land and Germany, whose culture he had made his own. He published other important political works, and is also remarkable as a student of natural science.

SCHOLASTIC THEOLOGY, p. 136.—A system founded in the eleventh century by St. Anselm (born in Italy 1033, died at Canterbury 1100). He advocated the subjection of divinity to the test of reason and argument. The Athanasian creed has been cited as a specimen of the attempt to reduce the mysteries of religion to 'right reason.'

Appendix

SMALKALDIC LEAGUE (SCHMALKALDISCHER BUND), p. 224.—An alliance made at Schmalkalden in 1531 by nine Protestant princes and several cities of the Empire, to defend their faith and independence against the Emperor. The leaders of the alliance were the Elector of Saxony and the Landgrave Philip of Hesse.

SPARTACUS UNION, p. 410.—The revolutionary party of the extreme left in the Reichstag, which became active in the winter of 1918 under Liebknecht's leadership. They took their name from Spartacus, a Roman gladiator, who commanded the gladiators in their war against the Romans.

STEELYARD (STALHOF), p. 164.—Originally an office or hall where cloth was marked with a leaden seal as being properly dyed (M. D. Stael, a sample test of dyeing). Later a place in London, comprising great warehouses, called, before the reign of Edward IV, Gildhalla Teutonicorum, or Guildhall of the Germans. Here until expelled in 1597 the merchants of the Hanseatic League had their English headquarters. The name was also given to the company of merchants themselves. They were bound by strict guild rules, under a separate jurisdiction from the rest of London; were exempt from many exactions and restrictions, and controlled for centuries most of the foreign trade of England.

TEUTONIC ORDER, p. 122.—A military order of chivalry, founded at Acre in Palestine in 1190, and confirmed by the Emperor and the Pope. They conquered Prussia between 1230–1280, and afterwards Courland, Livonia, and Esthonia. They were defeated at the Battle of Tannenberg, in 1410, by the united armies of the Empire.

VOSGES, THE GAP IN THE, p. 289.—The Vosges are a range of mountains in eastern France and western Germany, which forms in part the boundary between them. It extends from Belfort northwards, parallel with the Rhine.

'WACHT AM RHEIN' (THE WATCH ON THE RHINE), p. 324.—A German lyric, words by Schneckenburger (1840), music by Karl Wilhelm (1854). It became a national song during the war of 1870–1871.

WARTBURG, FESTIVAL OF, p. 310.—A Commemoration Festival, held under the auspices of German students, at Wartburg, October 18, 1817. Its object was to found a union of German students, in the interests of political liberty and national unity. It was the signal for reactionary measures on the part of the Government throughout Germany.

'WEAVERS' (DIE WEBER), p. 394.—A play written by Gerhard Hauptmann in 1892, in which he describes the miseries of the Silesian weavers during the 'forties of last century.

WORMS, DIET OF, p. 215.—A Diet famous in the history of the Reformation, opened by the Emperor Charles V on January 28, 1521. Luther was summoned before it, refused to recant, and defended his position. His determination was expressed in words which have become famous. Here I stand, I cannot do otherwise. God help me. Amen. (*See also* Appendix III, 'Worms.')

NAME INDEX

Name Index

452

Name Index

Name Index

Name Index

455

Name Index

456

Name Index

Name Index

Name Index

Name Index

460

Name Index

Name Index

Name Index

SUBJECT INDEX

Subject Index

Subject Index

Subject Index

467

Subject Index

Subject Index

Subject Index

Natural sciences—
  in the 16th century, 199
  in the 17th century, 239
  in the 19th century, 337
'New Era' in Prussia, 338, 342
'Nibelungen Faith,' 402
Nobility—
  amongst the Germani, 5 f.
  the reward of service, 10
  intermingling with bondmen, 89
  in the service of the sovereign, 123
  privileged position in the Absolute State, 243 f.
  privileged position in Brandenburg Prussia, 254 f., 259–269 f.
  limitation of privileges, 300 f.
  economic situation after 1815, 313
  see also Princes, Lords of the manor, Orders of knights
North German Confederation, 350 f., 358, 359
North German Lloyd, 337, 383, 436

Occupation of the Rhineland, 426, 427, 431, 432, 439
Officials—
  at the sovereign courts, 10, 13, 34
  princely officials, 110, 143, 144
  in Brandenburg Prussia, 255, 258, 316

Painting—
  wall-painting, 55
  illuminating, 56, 98, 99
  see Romanesque style, etc.
Pan-Germans, 394
Pan-Slavism, 362
Panel painting, 195
Papacy, *see* Empire and Papacy, Church and State
Papal election decree, 63
Parish Act, 380
Parliament—
  English, 173
  demand for a German, 326, 347
  see also National Assembly, Reichstag
Parliamentarism, the danger of present-day politics, 438
Parliamentary government, 359, 368, 410–412
Particularism, 329, 358, 359, 360
Parties—
  Paul's Church, 329
  Prussian House of Deputies, *see* Reichstag
Partitions of Poland, 272, 291
Partitions of the Empire, 9, 11, 16
Peace, endeavours after—
  'The Peace of God,' 44, 45, 77
  Imperial peace, 77, 171

Peace, endeavours after—(*contd.*)
  public peace, 129, 146, 147, 158, 171
  peace conferences at The Hague, 396, 399
  world peace, 396, 399, 417 f., 432 f., 439
  peace settlements, *see* Wars and peace settlements
Peasant life in the 16th and 18th centuries, 244, 259, 269
  liberation of, 299, 312
  ownership of property, 313, 333
Peasant risings, 192
Peasant War, 217 ff.
Peasants—
  rise of, 25, 82
  development of, from the 12th to the 15th century, 83, 121 f., 192
  in the eastern districts, 104
Peoples, Germanic, 5 f.
'Perfidious Albion,' 265
Permutation of consonants, High German, 5
Personality—
  evolution of, in the late Middle Ages, 196 ff.
  importance of, in Classicism, 282 f.
  importance of, in Romanticism, 284, 285
  importance of, for Stein, 299
Philology, *see* Science of language
Philosophy, German idealistic, 278, 282, 285
Pietism, 278, 279
Poetry—
  epic poetry, 14
  religious poetry of the 9th to the 12th century, 14, 46–52, 62, 96
  of chivalry, 99–102, 122 f., 135, 194
  of the citizen, 135 f., 193 f.
  classical, of the Enlightenment and the *Sturm und Drang*, 280–286
  romantic poetry, 283 f., 315 f.
  political poetry of the 'forties, 323 f.
  of Realism, 337
  of Naturalism, 393
Policy of the free hand, 396
Political poetry, 122, 301, 323 ff.
Population of Germany—
  from the 11th to the 13th century, 87
  from the 19th to the 20th century, 316, 382, 384
Power of police of the great landowners, 244, 312, 333, 369

Subject Index

Subject Index

Subject Index